Will Power

Will Power
Essays on Shakespearean authority

Richard Wilson

Wayne State University Press   Detroit

U.S. Edition
published by
Wayne State University Press
Detroit, Michigan 48202

Typeset in 10/12pt Perpetua and Times
by Keyboard Services, Luton

Printed and bound in Great Britain by
BPCC Wheatons Ltd, Exeter

Library of Congress
Catalog Card Number 93–60395

ISBN 0–8143–2491–6
ISBN 0–8143–2492–4 (pbk)

1 2 3 4 5   97 96 95 94 93

In memory of my parents
Dorothy Venn (1926—81)
Sidney Wilson (1921–65)

Contents

Preface

WITHOUT economic depression, the ex-editor of *The Times*, William Rees-Mogg, preached on a dark day of the 1992 slump, 'we might have had no *Hamlet*.' So, though 'every depression has victims who have done nothing to deserve their fate,' the unemployed could take heart from John Shakespeare, a bankrupt Midland tradesman who lived long enough to see 'his son's theatrical and business success' with the turn of the wheel of boom and bust. One of the 'Bright lights that shine out from the gloom,' the son's writing was testimony, on this view, to the 'positive results' of the capitalist cycle, whose 'strange repetitions' wrought 'terrible damage to lives and careers' once every fifty years, so that 'energies' like Shakespeare's could be 'released'. His work was a reassurance, the sermon concluded, that 'What has been happening in the Nineties has happened again and again,' as it had in 1592.[1]

With its history as eternal recurrence and art as timeless consolation, Rees-Mogg's article was a flagrant example of the way Shakespeare functions in our culture as the guarantor of social order and economic meaning. In this collection of essays I set out to challenge these ideas of art and history by examining not what makes Shakespeare our contemporary, but what made him an Elizabethan, looking at his writing not for relevance, but difference. If Shakespeare's word endures today, I reason, this has less to do with the cycle of production and consumption – as so-called New Historicist critics argue – than with the local situation it occupies within discourses of material power. In the final essay I find a model for this privilege in the early modern will; but my aim throughout is to return to the author: not as the universal genius, but as a locus of contingent intentions and desires.

The capacity to raise power, historians suggest, was the pre-condition of modernity. Asserting that 'Not marble, nor the gilded monuments / Of princes shall outlive this powerful rhyme' (Sonnet 55), Shakespeare is conscious of his participation in this process. Authority and authorship combine in the words of this glover's son to usurp the breath of kings, yet his language never loses the mark of its production: 'subdued / To what it works in, like the dyer's hand' (Sonnet 111). For promotion from textiles to texts, is not, perhaps, so powerful a rise; and if modern journalists identify a legitimation of Thatcherism in the drama, that may owe something to the Midland milieu from which they both derive. This is the premise of these essays, which assume that even the most power-laden meaning is local in its social logic, since 'Life begins only at the point where utterance and utterance cross.'[2]

Acknowledgements

'A MINGLED yarn: Shakespeare and the cloth workers', first published in *Literature and History*, 12:2 (Autumn 1986), pp. 164–84.
'"Is this a holiday?": Shakespeare's Roman carnival', in *English Literary History (ELH)*, 54:1 (Spring 1987), pp. 31–44.
'Like the old Robin Hood: *As You Like It* and the enclosure riots', in *Shakespeare Quarterly*, 43:1 (Spring 1992), pp. 1–19.
'Against the grain: Representing the market in *Coriolanus*', *The Seventeenth Century*, 6:2 (Autumn, 1991), pp. 111–48.
'The quality of mercy: Discipline and punishment in Shakespearean comedy', *The Seventeenth Century*, 5:1 (Spring 1990), pp. 1–42.
'Observations on English bodies', in *Enclosure Acts*, John Archer and Richard Burt (eds), (Cornell University Press, 1993).

I wish to thank colleagues in English at Lancaster University for creating the environment in which these essays grew, especially Richard Dutton, Keith Hanley and the late Ray Selden. From History, Lee Beier offered scepticism, and Jeffrey Richards enthusiasm; and in Theatre, Keith Sturgess provided an asylum. Without sustenance from Alison and John Milbank, Robin Hood would have expired; and Discipline and Punishment would never be complete without Bill Fuge. My thanks are also due to the Librarians of Lancaster University and Goldsmith's College, University of London, to Susan Brock of the Shakespeare Institute and to Jackie Jones at Harvester Wheatsheaf for her patience. Tom Craik, Tom Healey, Richard Maber, Kate McLuskie, Alan Sinfield and Stanley Wells gave me the chance to air these arguments in papers; and Linda Boose and Richard Burt commented from afar. David Thacker let me sound off in programmes for the Young Vic, and Mark Wheeler and Damien Whitmore kept me balanced between comfort and despair.

Note on texts

THE text used throughout is *The Arden Shakespeare*, and the spelling of other Renaissance texts has accordingly been modernised.

Introduction:

The return of the author

SHAKESPEARE was dead, to begin with. There is no doubt whatever
about that. The register of his burial on 25 April 1616 was entered in
the Stratford parish records when his body was interred near the north
wall in the chancel of Holy Trinity Church. There they 'laid him full
seventeen foot deep, deep enough to secure him', according to an
echoing seventeenth-century account, as if the mourners feared the
dead man might yet rise from the grave to haunt the living.[1]
Archaeologists doubt, however, that such a preternatural interment
would be practicable in soil so close to the river Avon, and presume
that the dramatist's physical remains in fact lie a normal depth below
his slab in the good state of preservation that is usual for bodies
of the period in the Stratford area. Were the Bardolaters who regularly
propose to exhume the corpse to win their argument, the world would
therefore be able to look into the actual face of William Shakespeare
to determine whether the enigmatic frontispiece of the 1623 Folio
is indeed the image of the deceased Stratfordian or, as often
conjectured, someone more illustrious such as (an inverted and
moustachio'd) Queen Elizabeth. But though intruders dislodged
the adjacent Shakespeare monument during the night of 2 October
1973, searching, the police earnestly deduced, for 'valuable manuscripts written by the Bard',[2] grave-robbers are unlikely ever to
disinter the coffin since the legend of its inaccessibility is allied to a
pharaonic curse cut into the gravestone, which seventeenth-century
travellers attributed to the dying playwright as his own epitaph and
valediction:

> Good friend for Jesu's sake forbear
> To dig the dust enclosed here.
> Blessed be the man that spares these stones,
> And cursed be he that moves my bones.[3]

The material body of the historical person, William Shakespeare, must remain, it seems, for all time immured a few feet beneath the tourists who make the journey to his grave, unfathomable yet proximate, a tantalising presence-in-absence. There is a fable here, of course, of the illusions and discontents of old-style historicism; but if the material man has eluded the spades of the antiquarians, a newer historicism can set to work on a different kind of excavation of the space occupied by the body beside the altar at Stratford, and like archaeology, it can start with the desire, if not to speak with the dead, at least to localise a subject in time and place. Just as archaeology has been electrified by techniques to compute the genetic make-up of primaeval ancestors from data encoded in a modern hair, historicist criticism is energised by the prospect of locating the author not as some real presence, but as an absence or difference within the continuum of discourse that is our speech and writing. While we can never physically recover the past, the critical work we have to do will be to decipher its function in the discursive history of the present, and in Shakespeare's case the verse on the Stratford grave registers the transaction which has made the site a cultural counterpart to Foucault's pendulum: 'an ever-fixed mark' of value 'That looks on tempests and is never shaken' (*Sonnet* 116, 5–6). For from the beginning, the rhyme warns, the Shakespearean benediction has been conditional on a renunciation, and whatever magic inheres in this place has been positive only for those who 'forbear to dig' for the material relics of the benefactor. And the logic of this epitaph has an enduring grip on the community of Shakespeare scholars, since the cultural enterprise that originates here does indeed impose an interdiction on whomever would radicalise its power by exposing its roots. Shakespeare's unique authority derives precisely from this peculiar and primitive hermeneutic pact: that the hidden god will manifest himself only to those who do not seek him out.

At the shrine of Shakespeare studies there has always been a curse, it seems, pronounced on those who disclose the mystery. This malediction was meant originally, we can assume, for the parish sexton, whose practice was to remove bones to the charnel house, and was itself a concrete assertion of personal identity. For according to Philippe Ariès, the historian of death, in pre-modern cultures 'It was important to *see*' the dead, and the anonymity and visibility of the medieval ossuary, where skulls and ribs were displayed, expressed a concept of collective destiny that gave way only slowly in the early modern period to an individualist notion of the grave as 'a fine and private' space of privilege for the property-owning elite. The place of honour inside the parish church occupied *pro tempore* by Shakespeare and his dearest kin would not have been available to his class in any previous era, and they monopolised it during the seventeenth century with an audacity that overrode an older sensibility which had doubtless consigned John Shakespeare, the tanner, to the charnel after 'some eight or nine year' in the graveyard (*Hamlet*, v, i, 161).[4] But if the cantrip was intended for the gravedigger, and its spell tested when the vault was broken in 1827, and 'no workman would meddle with it, because of the curse',[5] its charm has extended to Shakespeare criticism, which, as Michel Foucault remarked, establishes as the paradigm of modern authorship the 'paradoxical singularity' of a name that does 'not pass from the interior of a discourse to the real and exterior individual who produced it', but instead 'marks off the edges of the text' from the life of an author whose proprietary existence none the less validates its authenticity.[6] Like the oracles of the classical world, then, rather than the glass reliquaries in Catholic cathedrals, the Bardic presence retains its numen to the degree that it remains invisible, evading material analysis with the very ruse that solicits speculation. When April comes, folk love to go on pilgrimages to the Grave and the Birthplace not to see, but to *wonder*.

Umberto Eco has drawn the parallel between cultural tourism and the great pilgrim migrations of the Middle Ages, and proposes that it is by routing consumerism through an infinitely regressing *hyperreality* of fakes and souvenirs that post-modern mimesis generates awe and compliance. But while its destination is Disneyland, with its holograms of European art, this new medievalism derives from a sense of the sacred as the inscrutable, and marvel at a God who 'hides himself, is ineffable, can be drawn only through negative theology, is the sum of what cannot be said of him', and in whom 'we celebrate our ignorance and name a vortex, abyss, solitude, silence, absence.'[7] So, if the Shakespeare cult does occupy a devotional niche vacated by religious icons, as Donald Horne suggests,[8] and from its earliest days in Elizabethan London has always been the Mecca of international tourism, as Graham Holderness maintains,[9] it is significant that the magic of the Bard shows no sign yet of that exhaustion through mass exposure Walter Benjamin predicted for all art in the age of mechanical reproduction.[10] For rather than suffer any evaporation of aura through the perpetual repetition to which it is subjected in books, films, cassettes and videos, or devaluation through constant recycling in theatres and schools, industrialised Shakespeare accrues ever more symbolic capital. This aura can 'survive a thousand mechanical reproductions', Terry Eagleton argues, through the very legerdemain that renews consumer capitalism, since while the industry is marketing a 'timeless' essence, each year's *Hamlet* is a new model, and the 'ceaseless proliferation of sameness-in-difference proceeds apace.'[11] The Shakespeare trick, according to Eagleton, is thus to identify culture with capitalism and subsume history into an infinite circularity of signs, as if language was nothing but an exchange of equivalences and a system which perpetuates itself. That the author vanishes behind his words is an illusion, by this light, of the process Shakespeare himself initiated when he made the combustion of reality by language the motor of his work:

> How real is the signifier is the question [Shakespeare] constantly poses. Language is something less than reality, but also its very inner form; and it is difficult to distinguish this 'proper' intertwining of signs and things, in which image and symbol are the very enabling grammar of human relations, from that 'improper' commingling of the two which springs from the imperial interventions of the autonomous sign, shaping reality in its self-indulgent whims. Myth and metaphor should service rather than master society; yet they are not purely supplementary to it either, mere disposable ornaments, since they shape from within the history to which they give outward expression. Fiction seems inherent in reality: politics works by rhetoric and mythology, power is histrionic, and since social roles appear arbitrarily interchangeable, society itself is a dramatic artefact, demanding a certain suspension of disbelief.[12]

For Marxist criticism, Shakespeare vanishes as a precondition of his miraculous productivity-effect: a perpetual motion round 'the fact that he never gives us anything we have not had' and then only 'a quintessential commodity, at once ever-new and consolingly recognisable'. It is by evacuating his space that this god of capitalism is able to 'Shakespeareanise everything,' in Eagleton's view;[13] yet the presence-in-absence of a historical author is still required to operate, like Christ's incarnation, as the transcendental signifier of the mass celebrated daily at the Memorial Theatre. Shakespeare's Word remains sacramental by supremely fulfilling this dual author-function; so that, as Simon During notes, 'On one hand, Shakespeare becomes the effect, as against originator, of his texts, a great deal of institutional power being invested in maintaining the distinction; [yet] on the other, strategies are devised for bringing Shakespeare the man back from the dead' in a different zone from criticism, which is caught in the bind that however much it purges biography from the plays to redeem them from obsolescence, it can represent them only because 'they stand in place of things and events of which they are the material trace . . . gesturing to a loss to which they are immune.'[14] This is the 'hole at the centre' which Marjorie Garber believes explains why Shakespeare's authorship became a pressing 'Question' from the mid-nineteenth century moment when copyright delimited the author-function, and 'having waited, shovel in hand, in Shakespeare's tomb', Delia Bacon was 'assailed by doubts about what she was digging for.'[15] For Garber, the Baconian heresy arose purely from an urge to elevate the writer among those 'transcendent men' whom Emerson thought make 'the farthest reach of subtlety compatible with an individual self' by hovering 'only just within the possibility of authorship', and Whitman's certainty that 'the Avon man' could never have penned such 'amazing works' simply prepared the ground for the exorcism pronounced by Henry James (in his story called 'The birthplace'), that 'there is no author. . . . There are all the immortal people – *in* the work; but there's nobody else.'[16]

As Shakespeare evaporated from the scene of his writing during the late nineteenth century, an emergent modernist aesthetic began to revel, then, in the presumption that, as Mark Twain rejoiced, the playwright *'hadn't any history to record*. There is no getting around that deadly fact.'[17] So, in the very period when a positivist literary history was amassing data which, when collated by Sir Sidney Lee and E. K. Chambers, would make the Warwickshire writer among the best documented of all Elizabethans, a collective amnesia insisted that none of this counted, because, as James averred, 'There should really, to clear the matter up, be no such Person. . . . There *is* no such Person.' In James's tale, the curator of 'the Holy of Holies of the Birthplace,' having initially risked the curse by 'giving the Show away', realises that 'if there's no author, if there's nothing to be said but that there isn't anybody', his fantasy is freed from fact;[18] and the same readerly consolation had appealed to Dickens, who decided that 'It is a great comfort, to my way of thinking, that so little is known concerning the poet. The life of Shakespeare is a fine mystery and I tremble every day lest something should turn up.'[19] This was the 'reverse Micawberism', in Garber's phrase, that Matthew Arnold preached in his famous sonnet, where the Bard was revered as one who 'Did'st tread on earth unguess'd at', and who having ascended into heaven, 'Spares but the cloudy border of his base / To the foiled searching of mortality.' Immortal, invisible, God-only-wise, Arnold's William is in fact the prototypical modernist artist, who possesses genius in proportion to the dissolution of his personality, and who shrinks, like Jesus or the Cheshire Cat, from the sordid interrogation of historicism: 'We ask and ask – Thou smilest and art still, / Out-topping knowledge.'[20] As Garber comments, what constituted the author's transcendence in this aesthetic, therefore, was that his historicity remained a Question, and from the time when Keats exempted Shakespeare's 'life of Allegory' from 'any irritable reaching after fact or reason', the investment of criticism was precisely in '*not* finding an answer'.[21]

In a survey of twentieth-century Shakespeare interpretation, Hugh
Grady shows how the shift from biography to criticism or author to reader
was keyed to the modernist paradigm which privileged spatial over
temporal explanation and structure over process.[22] By this account, the
death of the author in modernist Shakespeare study was symptomatic of
the flight from history which characterises late capitalism, and which
Eagleton traces to the mythopoeia of the modernist masters and
Saussurean linguistics.[23] Thus, James's horror at those historicists who
killed 'the spirit' of the Bard, and who, 'dead as He is . . . kill Him every
day',[24] would be repeated by the pre-eminent modernist Shakespearean,
G. Wilson Knight, whose occultism formed a link between the 'empty
space' of Peter Brook, who divines a universal spirit 'behind the words',
and the shadow-play of Gordon Craig, who claimed to be haunted by the
ghost of Irving.[25] For as Grady argues, far from being eccentric, Knight's
spiritualism, which allowed him to commune with Shakespeare via the
mediation of his own dead brother, ritualised a central modernist project
to transfigure history with tradition. The metaphysics of presence
infusing Shakespearean hermeneutics have rarely been displayed so
nakedly as in Knight's profession of 'child-like faith' in access to 'the
poet's vision', but his belief that this 'spirit world' could then be
spatialised in male/female or Dionysian/Apollonian polarities clearly
belonged among the totalitarian myths of modernism. Like Lawrence's
phoenix, Pound's vortex or Yeats's gyre, the 'wheel of fire' Knight
intuited from the plays was a symbol to mystify history into eternal
recurrence, and if one of its avatars was Jung's swastika (the 'sun-wheel'),
its influence was due to the way it froze the social process of Elizabethan
drama into a still point of turning modernity. For it was not his
reactionary politics which finally eroded Knight's standing, but his
penchant for stage nudity, and so long as his worship of 'Solar Man'
remained in the abstract, the academy was happy to agree with Eliot, that
this Nietzschean naturist had 'found the right way' to interpret
Shakespeare.[26]

Like James's naive curator, Knight was disowned by the Shakespeare
corporation when he began to take the mystery of the corpus *too* literally,
and 'gave the Show away' by posing as a reincarnation of the divine Will.
Yet the photographs he published of himself aged eighty, stripped in
archetypal postures as Caliban, Puck or Timon, only literalised the myth
of eternal return which was propagated by his student Northrop Frye,
who assimilated the plays to the schema of *The Golden Bough* and the
rites of spring; whilst the theme of Shakespeare's mystic royalism
trumpeted in the Jungian titles of his books (*The Crown of Life*, *The
Imperial Theme*, *The Sovereign Flower*, etc.) reinforced the Platonised
image of Elizabethan culture propounded by the other leading modernist

Shakespearean, E. M. W. Tillyard. As Grady shows, the impact of *The Elizabethan World Picture*, which mistook state propaganda for the mind-set of an entire nation, can again be explained by the way that Tillyard's nostalgia locked into the organicist ideology of modernism. Coinciding with the 1944 Education Act, the book remained student reading for so long not because the 'Tudor Myth' it described conformed to any article of Elizabethan faith, but because its reduction of Shakespeare to Anglican platitudes legitimated the conservative syllabus of post-war British education. And if Tillyard's synthesis of Tudor clichés belonged with Leavis's Merrie England of wheelwrights and morris dancing, his historiography was like Knight's in circuiting the social process of drama within a 'grand pattern' of providential unity, to demonstrate how Shakespeare shared with 'every section of the community' an assumption that 'Behind the disorder of history . . . order or degree on earth [had] its counterpart in heaven.'[27] Much of this cosmography was extrapolated from the Tudor moralist, Sir Thomas Elyot, whose pieties were also paraphrased by his namesake in the wartime *Four Quartets*; and the poetry explicates what Knight and Tillyard celebrated: that for modernism, the past is the present, so 'Keeping time, / Keeping the rhythm' of Shakespeare affirms that 'history is a pattern / Of timeless moments'.[28]

'On a winter's afternoon, in a secluded chapel / History is now and England': Eliot's Rotarian epiphany reveals how modernism aimed to 'redeem' the 'people' from time with a vision of the past that transcended history;[29] and Tillyard's 'Tudor Myth' was tolerated by formalist New Critics, Grady concludes, because it did abstract Shakespeare from any real historical context. Even when purporting to address 'Shakespeare's historical background', modernist strategy was to turn history back upon itself; and Alan Sinfield has traced this anti-historicist manoeuvre as its valency switched from positive to negative in the Cold War era and issued in the craze for Jan Kott's nihilist primer, *Shakespeare Our Contemporary*.[30] For by reading *King Lear* through Beckett's *Endgame* (or, as Tom Stoppard did, *Hamlet* through *Waiting for Godot*), writers of the 1960s completed the transcription of Renaissance drama into modernist art, offering the nuclear generation a concept of fate as an 'implacable roller [that] crushes everybody and everything' in its juggernaut revolve.[31] Kott was aware that his image of history as a 'Grand Mechanism, like a great staircase' on which 'every act is a repetition' and 'monarchs change, but the steps are always the same', was simply Tillyard's world order inverted into the 'neue Ordnung' of Hitler and Stalin;[32] but Peter Brook explained that this scenario was true to the critic's Poland, where 'the involvement with the social process that made life so horrible . . . to an Elizabethan' was re-enacted daily.[33] Like the

Czech-born Stoppard, then, Kott was part of an exodus of Eastern
European dissidents who projected their disillusion onto Western social
democracy and heralded the New Right; and if *Shakespeare Our
Contemporary* was an allegory of Soviet empire, its subtext, Sinfield
infers, was the 'absurdism' of a society without God.[34] So, despite its
street-wise argot, Kott's Manichean criticism, with its anti-statism,
sexism and sentimentality over young love, might have been written by
his rival as an existentialist actor in underground Warsaw: Karol Wojtila,
later known as John Paul II.

Kott's title was embraced by a school of theatre directors who had 'no
interest in politics', and had lost 'any sense of or interest in history as a
reality'.[35] For such sceptics, Shakespeare was 'a contemporary of Kott',
Brook reasoned, precisely because 'history constantly repeats its cruel
cycle.'[36] So, if Kott showed how a certain historicism might deliberately
set out to render history meaningless, *Shakespeare Our Contemporary*
can be read as part of a post-Marxist recoil from 'the conviction that
history can be made intelligible' into a Slavic 'world of the spirit'.[37] The
interest of its reduction of history to 'a relentless struggle for power'[38] lies
then in its influence on those who, having read Kott as students, went on
to identify his totalitarian Grand Mechanism with market forces. Thus,
for Stephen Greenblatt, Shakespearean 'energy' arises from its priority,
as the entertainment industry's first joint-stock enterprise, in the
'dizzying, seemingly inexhaustible circulation' of reality and fiction by
which capitalism is sustained.[39] But fascinated by the transposition of
Catholic rites into theatre business, Greenblatt also offers another
instance of critical enchantment, when he sermonises that the 'wonder
centred on the masterpiece' is the same ecstasy as that felt by Aquinas's
teacher, Albert the Great, as 'a systole of the heart' before imponderable
mystery.[40] Thus, in its modish refusal to distinguish fact from fantasy,
New Historicism reverts to the metaphysics of *The Name of the Rose*, and
a fit of post-modern vertigo marks another conversion at the Stratford
shrine. The cause of stupefaction is confessed by Greenblatt, however,
when he volunteers that 'art always implies a return' of 'pleasure and
interest' or 'money and prestige',[41] and that if individual art-works are
not 'sources of numinous authority', what remains marvellous are the
'circulatory rhythms of production and consumption' as they rotate
through the 'hidden places of negotiation and exchange'.[42] Howard
Felperin likens such an aesthetic to a 'bazaar teeming with rug-dealers';[43]
and it does seem that for New Historicism the 'wonder' provoked by
Shakespeare is akin to the commodification of the past as 'heritage' for
mass consumption: a naive veneration transferred from one religion to
another, and laid devoutly before the absconding god of capital and the
hidden hand of 'trade and trade-offs'.[44]

With its mystification of the market as the Word of God, American New Historicism merely perpetuated the conflation of language and history which the Shakespearean drama began, and proved what Foucault early recognised: that the post-modern theory that 'There is nothing outside the text' was the apotheosis, rather than the nemesis, of capitalist authorship, and installed 'the religious principle' of indeterminacy even as it proclaimed 'the death of the author'.[45] For by following the axiom of the anthropologist Clifford Geertz, that 'The real is as imagined as the imaginary', a critical school that had promised to restore literature to history paradoxically annexed history to the branch of linguistics Greenblatt called Cultural Poetics.[46] It was hardly surprising that linguistics, with its synchronic axis, had been crowned the queen of disciplines during the consumer boom of the 1960s; and in the 1980s New Historicism articulated a similar consumerism with its aestheticising of history, extending the principles of textual analysis to every social and material reality, from gender to slavery to Cardinal Wolsey's hat. With its belief in 'language as the medium in which the Real is constructed', as Louis Montrose put it,[47] and its Geertzian notion of politics as a mode of spectacle in the 'theatre state',[48] this was criticism to swallow the Shakespearean conceit that 'All the world's a stage' (*As You Like It*, II, vii, 140), and to play along with the gambit when the Stratford author anticipated modernism, and 'using all the contrivances he set up between himself and what he wrote, cancelled out the signs of his particular individuality', thereby reducing 'the mark of the writer to nothing more than the singularity of his own absence', and his role to that 'of the dead man in the game of writing'. For as Foucault had predicted, by dissolving the social into textuality and the material into meaning, what had started as a revolt against formalism ended by obliterating the historical institution of authorship itself along with 'the visible marks of the author's empiricity'.[49]

New Historicism broke the Marxist base/superstructure and text/context dichotomies, by interpreting literary works as events which intervene materially in the world rather than mirroring reality; but by then reaffirming their status as 'great art', as Greenblatt did, it reduced history to spectacle and social struggle to the effect of 'cultural scripts'. The influence here was an ethnographic grain of Cultural History practised by historians such as Robert Darnton and Natalie Zemon Davis, which by looking for 'fiction in the archives', uncovered narrative rules and rituals in the most earthy early modern practices, such as labour disputes and murder trials.[50] In 1968 Roland Barthes had foreseen that the 'linguistic turn' would collapse history into *story* and reorientate the historian's search into a hunt 'not so much for the real as the *intelligible*',[51] but even he might have been surprised at the extent to which the quest for order and meaning behind appearances would lift history out of the mire of class and conflict in the 1980s. And of no period was this more pronounced than the early seventeenth century, where the loss by Cultural Historians of a 'sense of social agency, of men and women struggling with . . . and transforming the worlds they inherit',[52] was matched by the abandonment by so-called Revisionist historians of belief in the English Revolution. Led by Conrad Russell and Kevin Sharpe, the Revisionists replaced the Whig and Marxist narrative of epic religious, economic and social confrontation with a picture of English society in the Shakespearean era as consensual, quiescent and non-political, and announced that, far from any Revolution, there were no deep trends or great issues in what they insisted was an old-style barons' war which flared up accidentally.[53] Though focusing on high politics, therefore, Revisionism constructed a comparable model of stasis as Cultural History and New Historicism, and did so with similar textualism, since, as Lawrence Stone complained, its discovery of a Stuart world order was made in 'manuscript documents no one else had even heard of, much less read'.[54]

The total victory of the Revisionists in the battle over the meaning of English history was declared by Russell in an article published in 1987;[55] which was the year when Davis launched her Cultural History of 'how sixteenth-century people told stories' to win pardon; and Greenblatt proclaimed the new discipline of Cultural Poetics.[56] That these interventions coincided with the notorious 'Faurisson affair' in France, in which another kind of 'revisionism' denied the Holocaust had ever occurred, and with a fashion for the prophet of hyperreality, Jean Baudrillard, pointed to the general sensation of 'the end of history' as it had been understood by Marx. Instead of class war and human agency, a triumphant informational capitalism found its neo-liberal philosophy, formulated by a State Department ideologue, Francis Fukuyama, in a global textuality and the universal market.[57] It was with fine irony, therefore, that the hubris of this post-modern fantasy of 'the end of ideology' and its 'grand narratives' was crushed so soon by a global stock-market crash in October 1987 that was aggravated by overloaded computers. With the ensuing slump, implosion of communism, and disintegration of Europe into ancient nationalisms, little more was heard about an end to history; and the 1980s closed with a sharp swing back to ideology and narrative in early modern historiography, and the emergence of a counter-Revisionism among a fresh generation of scholars, such as Richard Cust and Anne Hughes, who argued that there was indeed a Revolution in Stuart England, and that evidence for struggle over 'the big questions' of law, liberty, property and religion was to be found by 'detailed understanding of what actually happened . . . from week to week . . . in a particular context.' The future of the past would be in regional studies, they proposed, where research could 'elucidate the aims and intentions of particular agents';[57] and for Renaissance literary study this localist focus was of special significance, since one of its first and most extensive applications, by Hughes, was to Shakespearean Warwick-shire.[58]

Things happened, localist history insisted, making Revolution and also Shakespeare possible. This ran counter to New Historicism and Cultural History, which followed Leavis's dictum that in Elizabethan England 'People *spoke*, so making Shakespeare possible';[59] but it was a reaffirmation of a place long held by Renaissance culture in theory as a site of fracture rather than tradition. Marxist historiography had, of course, traditionally viewed the Renaissance as the crucible of capitalism, where feudal relations of production were sundered by the bourgeoisie and a manorial economy was shattered by money and the market. What is striking, however, is that Marx habitually illustrated this process with quotations from Renaissance literature, and when he sought to typify the profit motive, his *Capital* spoke with the voice of Shylock: 'I crave the law, / The penalty and forfeit of my bond' (*The Merchant of Venice*, IV, i, 203–4). The spectre that haunts *Capital*, S. S. Prawer suggests, is that of Shakespeare's Jew, who throughout is the personification of primitive accumulation.[60] Likewise, Marx's most nauseated image of a money economy comes as exegesis on Timon's rant to 'Yellow, glittering, precious gold'; which 'portrays the essence of money', he deduces, as a power to transform 'black, white; foul, fair' (*Timon of Athens*, IV iii, 29), and every 'human and natural quality into its opposite'.[61] Ever a Victorian, Marx bowdlerises the text of its equation of gold with syphilis; but Timon's medieval revulsion from usury provides *Capital* with a moral perspective on Shakespearean England as the hub of the cash nexus, where the 'visible god' of money circulated all values through 'confounding odds' and universal thievery (388; 437–51). If 'Shakespeare was the Bible of our house', as Eleanor Marx recorded, her father's acting of Thersites and excoriation of imperialist 'wars and lechery' (*Troilus and Cressida*, v, ii, 194)[62] must have jarred with Burckhardt's fashionable glorification of Renaissance self- and world-discovery, yet Marx's Renaissance was oddly similar in the primacy it accorded drama.

Garber distinguishes the 'insistent theatrical metaphor' in Marx's writing as a figure not of stasis but of dialectical history, which, as Benjamin observed, 'is not empty time, but time filled by the presence of the now.'[63] The men of 1848 or 1789, therefore, who, as Marx caricatured them, draped revolution in the 'time-honoured disguise and borrowed language' of 'a great historical tragedy', were acting a play derived from *Julius Caesar* as much as ancient Rome. Yet Shakespeare's Romantic after-life, which Jonathan Bate shows allowed critics such as Hazlitt to deride contemporaries in comparison to Shakespeare's heroes, issued in Marx's notion of the present as a *revision* rather than a repetition of the past, and of history as 'not only diachronic, but at the least *dialogic*'.[64] If Revolution was 'the old mole', King Hamlet's ghost, tunnelling the cellarage, as he joked, Renaissance literature became the forcing-pit of modernity: indeed, 'The battle for man', Marx flatly declared, 'began in Chapter 19, Book 1 of *Don Quixote*' (when the Don fights the ghosts of ideology).[65] While the best example in *Capital*, then, of art's supposedly free unalienated labour is the composition of *Paradise Lost* for a mere £5,[66] Marx disallows any idea of the Renaissance as some pre-capitalist golden age. Rather, his contribution to Renaissance studies, these citations suggest, has been an anti-organicist reading of Cervantes or Shakespeare as texts not of self-fashioning and state-formation, but of social fissure and psychic fragmentation. This is a hermeneutic tradition that includes Christopher Hill's diagnosis of Marvell's schizoid 'double heart' and Franco Moretti's analysis of the 'great eclipse' of sovereignty in *King Lear*;[67] and its result has been an image of Shakespearean culture not as some self-enclosed sign system of endlessly circling representations, but as the threshold of a vital ongoing process. It is to this Marxist understanding, then, of dialogue between the contemporary and the historical that theory owes its interpretation of the Renaissance as the proleptic history of the present.

The first post-industrial criticism discovers its own resemblance in literature of the last pre-industrial culture, Jean Howard speculates, because of their shared terror and exhilaration at 'living inside a gap in history, when the paradigms that structured the past seem facile and new paradigms uncertain'; so that, where 'Previous critical emphasis was on continuity. . . . Now the emphasis is on discontinuity, seen most clearly in Jonathan Dollimore's insistence on the early seventeenth century as . . . standing free of the orthodoxies of the Middle Ages and Enlightenment.'[68] Yet the radical reading of Baroque drama as a rite of disintegration and demystification can be traced back through Marxist criticism to Benjamin's commentary on the German *Trauerspiel* (which stages, he claims, the state of emergency caused by the incapacity of absolutist monarchy to impose its rule), and to Lucien Goldmann's account of the tragedies of Racine (which dramatise the disaffection of the court nobility in a state where absolutism succeeded).[69] These classic Marxist studies, which date the pre-modern 'gap in history' exactly to the reign of 'the royal martyr' Charles I (in Benjamin's case), or the period 1637 to 1667 (in Goldmann's), identified a *telos* of entropy, absence and abandonment in seventeenth-century tragedy, respectively sixty and thirty years before the identical thesis was elaborated in Dollimore's

Radical Tragedy. Likewise, Barthes chose the same ground on which to wage a famous duel with old historicism, when his 1963 book *On Racine* sought to explore systematically not what a seventeenth-century writer could, but what he could *not* say and to 'try out on Racine, in virtue of this very silence, all the languages of our century'. The ensuing scandal popularised the notion of the early modern era as an historical hiatus, when a referential language had yet to be naturalised, and drama was 'an empty site open to eternal signification'. Racine's genius, Barthes argued, was precisely a function of this indeterminacy, which made his work available to the most radical of critical theories.[70]

New Historicism, when it irrupted into Anglo-American criticism around 1980, was neither as historicist nor as novel as it pretended. All its tenets were explicit in Barthes's call for a *nouvelle critique* that would interpret the text from *within* so as to attend to the historicity of signifying practices, the specificity of the institution of the author, and the partiality of the critic; and when Barthes declared that 'to write literary history, one must renounce the individual Racine and move to the level of rules, rites and collective mentalities',[71] he might have been promulgating a New Historicist manifesto. It was, therefore, perhaps only a measure of insularity that Eagleton could ironise how it was difficult to read Shakespeare in 1986 'without feeling that he was familiar with the writings of Marx, Nietzsche, Freud and Derrida',[72] since in France the elective affinity between Renaissance texts and contemporary theory had been currency for so long. It was a starting-point for Foucault in 1961, for instance, when he drew a line in *The History of Madness* between an Enlightenment mentality, founded on reason, truth and science, and a Renaissance scepticism, which in works such as *King Lear* and *Don Quixote* anticipated the cult of madness in Artaud and Genet. Foucault lived to regret the misreading of his valorisation of Lear's Fool when the streets of Paris filled with discharged mental patients; for his image of a pre-medical 'carnival of madmen', terminated with 'The Great Confinement' of the sick and delinquent in the General Hospital of 1656, proved to be the most influential picture of the Renaissance since Burckhardt's. As Dollimore showed, it was Foucault's insertion of Shakespeare and Cervantes into Bedlam that provided a perspective to recover the fundamental importance of the sixteenth and seventeenth centuries;[73] and his book came to seem an exemplary toolkit for both history and psychiatry. For the voyage of the Renaissance Ship of Fools, it suggested, had now ended with the return of the repressed, to pass judgement on the reign of reason in the delirium of a Nietzsche.

From Lear's heath, where 'madness still occupies an extreme place, beyond appeal', to Van Gogh's sunflower field,[74] Foucault's work is a sustained attempt to connect post-modernity with the Renaissance across the intervening epoch of law and reason. The project is clearest in *The Order of Things*, which postulates a Renaissance way of knowing grounded in occult similitudes displaced by the Cartesian logic of classification. Once more, then, the frontier between Renaissance and Baroque becomes a threshold of modernity, traced in *Las Meninas* by Velazquez, which for Foucault is a 'representation of representation' at the point of separation (again 1656) when art withdraws into an aesthetic void. What is purged through this elision, on this view, is discourse itself, which only now, with the 'return of language' as linguistics, recovers the opacity and indeterminacy to wash away the figure of universal Man drawn (in Foucault's most celebrated metaphor) by the Enlightenment in sand. Such heady rhetoric offended historians; yet the reading of the Shakespearean moment as a final fling of non-referential figuration, when 'words wander off' like Quixote,[75] accorded with Althusser's proposition of a shift in the early modern state from repression to ideology; and with Baudrillard's of a switch from symbolic to referential value with the capitalist era of the sign.[76] All these varieties of post-structuralism continued to pay Shakespearean culture the tribute of Marx's grand narrative, as the battle-ground of modern meaning, where, in Foucault's terms, the 'dividing practices' were instituted that made us the subjects that we are. 'My subject', Foucault punned, 'is our subjection; how we have made ourselves objects of our prisons, asylums, hospitals and consciences',[77] and his enquiry led back always to the paradigm-shift registered in the anatomisation of the body, normalisation of the mind, mobilisation of armies and crashing of prison gates at the dawn of carceral society. If the break was abrupt and violent, so indeed, on this view, were the instruments with which the great divide was executed.

Foucault, it is said, devised a new Nietzschean way of thinking about history, which estranged the past to relativise the present. Yet the story told by this Gaullist technocrat remained Marx's narrative of the seventeenth-century watershed; and his attraction for Renaissance students is that by returning to this point of difference, his work exposes the persisting relation between pre- and post-modernity. Those who regret his impact, such as David Cressy in a polemic in *English Literary Renaissance*,[78] on the ground that his relevance is to revolutionary France, misconstrue his notion of the Renaissance as a *liminal* phase, when, as Lee Beier and Pieter Spierenburg confirm,[79] modern techniques of discipline and surveillance were indeed tested in the spinhouses and bridewells of Amsterdam and London. Nor was Foucault the prophet of the 'end of history' his opponents portray; for what he wanted to kill, he insisted, was 'the vast mythical continuum of History for philosophers', not the practice of history by 'new historians' such as his mentors Ariès and Braudel. For it was the *Annales* school, with its localised focus on the micro-politics of families, factories and towns, to which he paid his dues, and the English journal *Past and Present*, that first debated the issue of a 'general crisis of the seventeenth century', he most admired.[80] As Peter Burke has noticed, Foucault's 'archival' method owes more to *Annales* contemporaries, such as Emmanuel Le Roy Ladurie, than is usually supposed; and his final contribution to Renaissance studies may be the ironic one, for a supposed anti-historian, of acting as courier between France and America for that 'history of mentalities' which Anglo-Saxon scholarship for long despised.[81] Foucault repudiated Marxism but deepened Marx's insight that today's struggles begin with the signifying practices of the day before yesterday. If Shakespeare is indeed now 'the testing-ground for Foucault',[82] as Cressy fears, this is because the plays remain, in areas that he exposed, the uncompleted business of the Renaissance.

Foucault resented his reputation as a 'negator of history,' objecting that he did 'nothing *but* history,'[83] and it was in fact his dissatisfaction with 'the linguistic turn' of structuralist thinking, according to his translator, Alan Sheridan, which forced him to 'go back to a time beyond the mid-seventeenth century . . . to find his way forward.' His 'return to history'[84] led him to the proposition that if societies are indeed made by and in language, this takes the material form of *discourse*, which is 'not simply that which translates struggles or systems of domination, but is the thing for which and by which struggle takes place'.[85] Language, that is to say, is always the locus of resistance as well as domination; and it is this Foucauldian concept of discourse as a site of contest that lies behind the development in Britain, during an oppressive period of one-party, right-wing rule, of a school of criticism which asserts that if language does mediate reality, the meanings it assigns may still be challenged, seized or altered. Cultural Materialism is the name adopted by this movement, to underline its conviction that culture is never a closed, self-generating or all-enveloping sign system – as Cultural History and New Historicism tend to assume – but that because it is a material determinant of reality it is ceaselessly in process and contention. So, while Cultural Materialists concede the linguistic argument for the textuality of history, they equally insist on the historicity of texts, and counter what Catherine Belsey calls the deconstructive '*Looking Glass* reasoning' which elides history as a fiction with Foucault's insight that history is always 'fictioned from a political reality that renders it true.'[86] For criticism, this means addressing texts as inextricably social in their logic, and imbricated in specific material contexts, such as buildings, regions, customs, professions and laws. As Gabrielle Siegel writes in a cogent résumé of this position, 'Just as we reject the reduction of literature to a reflection of the world, so also must we reject the absorption of history by the text':

We can begin by remembering that texts represent situated uses of language. Such sites of linguistic usage are essentially local in origin and therefore possess a determinate social logic [which] permits us to examine language with the tools of the social historian, to see it within a local or regional context of human relations, systems of communication, and networks of power that can account for its particular semantic inflections. All texts occupy determinate social spaces, both as products of the social world of authors and as textual agents at work in that world. . . . In that sense, texts both mirror *and* generate social realities, are constituted by *and* constitute the social formations which they sustain, resist, contest or transform.[87]

Like Foucault, with his intensive research in the archives of medicine, penology or psychiatry, the Cultural Materialist critic must work, according to this reasoning, from a premise that *everything is historical* (including history) and as such localised in time and place. Thus, in place of the transcendent Bard of modernist and even New Historicist criticism, Leah Marcus persuasively argues for a 'new topicality' in Shakespeare studies, which will restore history to the plays through meticulous 'local reading' of their discursive contexts, allied to an 'awareness that our activity has local coordinates of its own.' Such localism would 'have affinities with more radical varieties of regionalism' in European politics, and would counteract the anthropological drift towards universal myths and timeless rhythms, by opening the Shakespearean texts up to their historical contingency and even provinciality.[88] Thus, in a demonstration-piece that draws on work by historian David Underdown on the political geography of seventeenth-century English games and customs, Marcus shows that the carnivalesque structure of a comedy such as *The Merry Wives of Windsor* can only be understood within a small-town milieu and strictly topical meanings, a locale that is represented with a different ideological engagement in the variant texts. Topography and topicality converge, therefore, to make us 'less able to talk of archetypes and ritual patterns, more about historical particularity and local difference'.[89] The same high definition has been brought to Renaissance festivity by Le Roy Ladurie in a study of the bloody 1580 Carnival at Romans, which also reveals how cultural forms are traversed by struggle to reinscribe their meaning;[90] and the effect of such micro-histories has been to put the political meat back into carnival and make folkloric readings of Shakespeare, such as that by François Laroque, seem naively essentialist. For as Marcus claims, 'topicality cuts across static explanatory systems and closed cultural forms, opening them to the vagaries of historical process.'[91]

A *newer* historicism will respond to Foucault's partition of universal history into local *histories*, without being seduced by the post-modern fashion of ultra-relativism; and it will do so by heeding his injunction to 'conduct the first-hand historical analysis' necessary to explode every 'sacred, intangible, all-explanatory' narrative.[92] A prime instance of such meta-history is the myth, dating from the First World War, of the Shakespearean playhouse as the cradle of Anglo-Saxon democracy, which my essay on *2 Henry vi* controverted by locating the play within a context of labour conflict in Elizabethan Southwark. Contemporary documents suggested that, far from being an arena of popular protest, as critics assumed, the Rose had closed its doors on local craftsmen and travestied their festive culture; but what was at stake in this topical reading was evinced by Annabel Patterson, whose book *Shakespeare and the Popular Voice* was predicated on her vision of the Bard as a Jeffersonian democrat. Citing a discrepant dating of the crucial episode by a Canadian historian, Roger Manning (not the British historian *Brian* Manning, with whom she confuses him throughout), Patterson vouched for Shakespeare's politics with the riposte that 'Those who have excavated the records disagree, not only in their interpretation, but even as to the facts', a divergence that typified the 'problems facing historicist criticism', and threw into doubt the very existence of the urban crisis on which my argument rested.[93] 'Shakespeare Our Contemporary' was alive and well and a good liberal, it seemed, because Tudor history was so opaque; but this bland textualism was undermined by Manning's misdating of the events in question *by an entire year*. As Christopher Norris objected, apropos Baudrillard's contemptible article, 'The Gulf War has not taken place', those who query the veridical status of all empirical evidence are complicit with a Pax Americana that has most to gain by such a confusion of fact with fiction.[94] For though we only approach history via texts, historicist criticism can still distinguish those which approximate closest to a real world that once existed: in this case, holographs accessible in the Manuscript Room of the British Library.

Local readings of particular texts threaten the essentialist enterprise which recruits Shakespeare to its 'own revised notions of truth and virtue,' Marcus holds, 'by turning us away from a Shakespeare perceived as self-cohesive and universal'.[95] Such is Belsey's aim when she calls for a 'modest historicity' of 'little stories' to expose 'the precariousness of power, capital, patriarchy and racism'. This is historicism with a veritable difference, for it assumes that 'There are many histories to be made, meanings to be differentiated, dissensions to be emphasised' in texts such as Shakespeare's.[96] After reading Foucault, then, the big story of the universal genius gives way to studies of specific plays in local places, and modernism's *folie de grandeur* subsides into a more mundane agenda that returns English to the historical disciplines from which it departed on its

metaphysical crusade at the end of the last century. For Cultural
Materialist criticism has more in common with social history as it appears
in *History Workshop* than with articles in journals such as *New Literary
History*; and if it is aware that the discursive character of society dissolves
the social totality on which such history depends, it operates from
Foucault's precept that 'localizing problems is indispensable for theoretical and political reasons, but does not mean that there are not general
problems.'[97] As feminists have found, Foucault's particularism can be
'disciplined' to accentuate his idea of a continuity of struggle.[98] It was
obtuse of Stone, therefore, to lump all forms of post-modernism together
in his repeated anathema on 'Foucault and his epigones' as the enemies of
history,[99] since critics like Belsey, Sinfield and Francis Barker have done
much to untie the textual knot and sustain the Marxist project of
explaining the relations between language, ideology and the extra-
textual. Above all, these critics have worked to theorise what New
Historicism has effaced with the circulating energies of Cultural Poetics:
the century of English Revolution and Shakespeare's location within it.

Where New Historicism aestheticises history (to adapt Benjamin's
famous aphorism), Cultural Materialism historicises the aesthetic; and
the most radical consequence of this 'historical turn' in criticism has been
the scaling of the highest wall erected by modernism to defend the canon:
the *doxa* of the 'Death of the Author' and the Intentional Fallacy. For the
logical end of historicism is the return of the author, not indeed as the
origin and owner of meaning beloved by nineteenth-century literary
biography, but as a cultural construct determined by the representational
practices of a particular historical era. Likewise, the implication of
cultural materialism is the revival of authorial intention, not as the
sovereign desire of humanism, but as the socially and legally sanctioned
effect of a specific discursive formation. As During notes, it was Foucault
who signalled this development with his repudiation of the ideology of the
aesthetic that had prevailed since 'Schiller's separation of Shakespeare
the man from Shakespeare the works'; and the corollary of his historicis-
ing of authorship is that 'Biography is no longer separable from
textuality: the life is ordered by the work, as the work is ordered by the
life. There is no longer a need to accept criticism's refusal to admit
transactions between lives and texts as proper knowledge. . . . After
Foucault, it is impossible to remain satisfied with knowledge produced by
those techniques of "close reading" that rest on a series of professionally
motivated assumptions about textual autonomy and value.'[100] Nor is it
accidental, by this account, that the cult of the verbal icon should have
originated with Romantic critics of the Bard, since Shakespeare's
executors had devised one of the earliest schemes to protect a set of
transcendent Works from the murky contingency of an authorial life,

when they advertised the Folio as being 'not of an age, but for all time'.
For it is Shakespeare's own evasion of both the privileges and obligations
of humanist authorship which make him so historically significant, as
Marcus explains:

> So far as we know, he took no particular interest in 'authoring' his
> plays; he did not collect and publish them himself. But there are other
> places where we encounter a Shakespeare every bit as captivated by
> the humanist enterprise as contemporaries like Ben Jonson. I am
> thinking in particular of the Shakespeare of the sonnets. . . . The
> extent to which the claims and strategies of authorship impinge on
> Shakespeare's drama is more variable and nearly impossible to
> generalize about . . . [but] if Shakespeare avoided the appearance of
> intentionality, it was at least part of the time by design. We must try to
> distinguish between a lack of intentionality and the avoidance of
> intentionality, which may be a radically different thing.[101]

The question a post-modern Shakespeare criticism must ask itself,
Marcus advises, is 'why we have suppressed that particular cultural
construct of intentionality while at the same time insisting upon
others.'[102] For it is surely one of the strangest aspects of criticism that the
popular misconception of Shakespeare's transcendental anonymity has
been perpetuated in defiance of such massive documentation, and that
this suppression should be repeated by such unlikely collaborators as
Eagleton, who insists on how 'precious little we ever knew' about the
Swan of Avon. For Eagleton recognises that the elision of 'the historical
individual Shakespeare' has been a function of modernity, which has left
the author and his intention 'buried more or less completely out of
sight';[103] yet even he is reluctant to challenge this amnesiac conspiracy.
The reason, of course, is that we actually know *too much* about the
Stratford man for a modernist aesthetic, and even a post-modernist one
cannot yet tolerate so much reality. The problem with this embarrassment of riches is that it comprises such bureaucratic data; but as
Greenblatt contends in one of his more materialist pieces, instead of
expressing frustration that the man Shakespeare left evidence of his
existence only in the form of birth, marriage and death registrations, real-
estate transactions and legal depositions, we should accept that it is our
humanist craving for an inner core of being which is problematic, since in
Elizabethan culture, with its probate courts and parish chests, it was
precisely such private ownership and public *deeds* which formalised a
sense of self.[104] So, if we are to 'bring back, among other methodological
tools of old historicism, an idea called the Author's Intent', as Marcus
urges,[105] it will need to be complemented by a theory of the historicity of

the subject and desire. But above all, it must be informed by a recognition that if we cannot unlock Shakespeare's soul, this may be because, having lived and written just prior to 'the archival empire of print',[106] he had no secret self to share.

If modernist Shakespeareans obeyed Henry James's dictum to 'Dramatise! Dramatise!' a timeless contemporaneity, post-modernist critics take as their watchword Fredric Jameson's imperative to 'Always historicise'.[107] From James to Jameson, the historical turn in Shakespeare studies is a shift, then, of global to local, order to process, speech to writing, and *langue* (language as a system) to *parole* (specific utterance). Instead of celebrating plays as poems, or the canon as some holistic cycle, hermeticised from reality, this involves analysing their situation at the intersection of discourses which, having impacted in the text, ricochet into history, with reverberations long after they are juxtaposed by Shakespeare. It means alertness to the topicality of even the most familiar speeches, on the assumption that, as Mikhail Bakhtin declared, 'Every word gives off a scent of a profession, milieu, faction, man, generation, day, and hour. Every word smells of the contexts in which it has lived its intense social life, for all words are inhabited by intentions.'[108] It is only by attending to this material discursivity that Shakespearean language can be demystified of its irrational mystique and restored to its true scenario, which is the author's society. For if critics such as Eagleton experience nausea at Shakespeare's egotistical volubility,[109] this is surely because the plays have become so detached from circumambient discourses. Whereas what is striking about Tudor parliamentary debates or business correspondence is not how prosaic they seem in comparison, but how Shakespearean. A letter detailing investments from the author's trading agent, Abraham Sturley, to their associate, Richard Quiney, will be impressively like a soliloquy from the plays, for instance, in its richness of metaphor, complexity of syntax, and density of allusion.[110] In Warwickshire, it seems, people *wrote*, so making Shakespeare possible by activating a discourse within which the author could arrogate his place as the most powerful of wills.

'Not marble nor the gilded monuments / Of princes shall outlive this powerful rhyme' (*Sonnet 55*): the authority which the writer steals from death in this myth of Shakespearean authorship is a transcendence of history with which post-structuralism connives through its axiom that 'representations of the social world are themselves the constituents of social reality.'[111] This elision of the extra-linguistic has been licensed, moreover, by a misreading of Foucault, who, far from being such a textualist, declared himself a 'contented positivist', seeing in the 'linguistic turn' in criticism only a mystification of 'the aesthetic principle . . . of the work's enigmatic *excess* beyond the author's death'.[112] He recognised that what is at stake in the 'the death of the author' is agency itself and resistance to the discourses of power. If Shakespeare's is indeed the most puissant word in English, therefore, a Foucauldian critique will look to the ways in which it annexes its urgency from other discourses, such as those of commerce, medicine and law. For Eagleton is right to suspect that Shakespeare's conflation of authority with authorship has much 'to do with the confidence and productive energy of an emergent social class.'[113] The local determination that prescribed the semantics of this author's name at a conflux of phallocentric violence and textual desire was also the field of force from which Shakespearean fiction drew a transcendent charge. Today, however, high theory and low archives converge to render visible what Foucault terms 'the author's empiricity' in the case of Shakespeare, whose writing emerges in a continuum with an imperialist epic, bourgeois narrative and family romance. So, though the author cursed those who expose his transcendental solitude to light, and barred even his own widow a place beside him in the grave,[114] the essays in this collection are constructed on a double rejection of this interdict: refusing either to separate the stories of the subject from the history of society, or to collapse them together. For it is only by such a refusal that criticism can defy will power.

Chapter One

A mingled yarn:

Shakespeare and the cloth workers

'The web of our life is of a mingled yarn, good and ill together.'
(*All's Well That Ends Well*, IV, iii, 68–9)

SHAKESPEARE continues to serve as the poet of 'consensus'. Thus, when the Young Vic Theatre began a series of radical interpretations of his plays in the mid-1980s, the critics savaged the approach as 'Spartish tosh', protesting that this was to tie the texts in 'a political straitjacket', which 'in effect tells Shakespeare what he was writing about'. The productions were 'well-staged, but wrong-headed', and it was 'an atrocity' to expose the young to such 'unashamedly political', 'comic-strip simplifications'. Repelled by drama that was 'A delight to the Race Relations Board', 'Is the theatre the place', gnashed one critic, 'for political statements?'[1] Yet a hundred yards away, on London's South Bank, the National Theatre's *Coriolanus* was simultaneously hailed by the selfsame critics as 'A Triumph', precisely because its director, Peter Hall, had realised what they called 'Shakespeare's burning political relevance'. What they meant was spelt out in The *Daily Telegraph*, where Hall was lauded for a staging that 'transcends logic to underline the political topicality' of a play which was 'about the threat to democracy when workers are misled by troublemakers'. *Coriolanus* was 'a piece for the British 1980s', the critics were agreed, and Hall was to be thanked for 'a totally political reading of the play' in which 'the affairs of the nation were aired with maximum fairness to all sides.' As Michael Billington enthused in The *Guardian*, 'what makes this a great production is that it connects directly with modern Britain to show conviction government and popular anarchy in headlong, nightmare collision.' So, in the year of the Miners' Strike, it seemed that 'the message' of *Coriolanus* was that 'Good government depends on compromise.' And there was a manifest equation between this revelation and the 'greatness' of Hall's interpretation: 'This is the best Shakespeare production to emerge from the National in its 21

22

years', enthused Billington, 'and the reason is not far to seek. Abandoning the academic approach, Hall champions "the radical middle". This *Coriolanus* belongs as much to the SDP [Social Democratic Party] as the SPQR [Senate and People of Rome].' So it was that mere 'academic' considerations, and even dramatic 'logic', were discarded in the interests of the correct political persuasion. Nor was there any question now of presuming to tell Shakespeare what he was writing about. 'A really magnificent production of this great play' was quite literally one that endorsed the politics of the SDP and Dr David Owen.[2]

The charm of newspaper criticism is that it betrays its ideological bias so blatantly. As Shakespeare's plays are packaged in this way, they typify the process by which the classic text is reproduced in our society to authorise the moral claims of market capitalism. Here the confusion of 'maximum fairness to all sides' with the aims of the managerial elite is comically naive; but when one of the most influential of all Shakespeare interpreters, G. Wilson Knight, can crown his career by citing Cranmer's prophecy from *Henry VIII* as vindication of Mrs Thatcher's Falklands' campaign,[3] it would be wrong to look to academic criticism for more sophistication. In fact, the identification of 'the affairs of the nation' with the priorities of its dominant classes has been the hallmark, and arguably the function, of British Shakespeare criticism since the First World War. Central to this criticism has been the image of Shakespeare's theatre itself as a democratic forum, where the citizens of England's supposedly organic pre-industrial community met in a classless mutuality which remains a glowing example to the world. A product of the great panic following the European revolutions of 1917–20, this myth of the democratic Globe was crucial to those, like F. R. Leavis, who idealised Elizabethan England as a lost Eden, a socially homogeneous agrarian culture, whose 'people talked, so making Shakespeare possible'. It was a legend which took definitive shape during the Second World War, when Alfred Harbage identified the Globe as a cradle of Anglo-Saxon democracy, the 'theatre of a nation' for which the only price of admission was 'the possession by each spectator of some spiritual vitality',[4] and Laurence Olivier imaged it as a cockney picture palace in *Henry V*, the trailer for D-Day. With its lords and groundlings, this was the concept of the Elizabethan playhouse that became glued in schools in a thousand papier mâché replicas, and though Andrew Gurr remarks that it ignores 'the non-play-going 80 per cent of London's population', and Ann Jennalie Cook maintains that it distorts the middle-class bias of the Globe's privileged playgoers, it is a fantasy essential to the stature of the National Poet, who, because he appealed equally to all classes, wrote for 'democracy', and 'Not for an age, but for all time'.[5]

It is the idea of Shakespeare's playhouse as the site of 'the world we have lost', an organic community where writing was still inspired by talk, and a more representative arena than Parliament itself, which gives the plays their quasi-legislative force. A popular Globe legitimises the sleight-of-hand by which Shakespeare's historically determined, middle-class drama becomes the modern Magna Carta; an elision further authorised by Derrideans with their anti-historicist mystification of Elizabethan language as a deconstructive feast. And nowhere is this illusion more binding than with respect to the Shakespearean representation of the poor. Of course, it is a well-known embarrassment that the Bard did not love the people as a proper modern democrat should, but it is those commentators who attend to this, such as Shaw and Tolstoy, who have been dismissed as cranks. Academic criticism has responded to their objections that Shakespeare demonised the mob for reasons of social antagonism, by insisting that, on the contrary, what he recorded was merely the eternal empirical facts about lower-class existence. As Philip Brockbank authoritatively reported, the dramatist's depiction of com-moners proves that 'he had an eye for the outrages of the London streets, a nose for the sour breath of the plebeians, and an ear for riotous chop-logic; but at no point in any play do they pervert Shakespeare's objectivity of judgement or his rich human sympathies.' For such critics, there is no inconsistency in Shakespeare's reputation as a popular entertainer and his denigration of the people themselves as (in the words of Coriolanus) 'the rank-scented meinie', and a 'beast with many heads' (III, i, 65; IV, i, 1–2), because 'He is indulgent to the mob as individuals', and besides, 'He has done his duty by the poor when he has reminded us that they are human.'[6]

It is the paternalist dread of popular solidarity that this criticism perpetuates, in a form as offensive as it is unexamined. So, just as Shakespeare's 'rich human sympathies' are evinced in his 'admirable studies of simple people', his 'objectivity' is shown in his 'understanding of the tragic rhythm of political history' whereby 'the populace is transformed into the mob.' As Bradley argued, Shakespeare's 'poor and humble are, almost without exception, sound and sweet at heart, faithful and pitiful', until incited by rabble-rousers: 'He has no respect for the plainer and simpler kind of people as politicians.' Such critics agree that 'Shakespeare hated and despised' popular leaders 'with a bitterness he rarely felt towards any creatures', but maintain that this was because 'He was saying what happens when power falls into the hands of those whose innocence delivers them to any adventurer with enough wit to make the right promises.' Almost unanimously, they endorse as self-evident Shakespeare's analysis – the analysis of the 1571 'Homily of Obedience' – that it is through 'restless ambitious' agitators that the 'ignorant multitude' is converted into an anarchic rabble which is 'beyond all possible defence', because it stands for 'the repudiation of law, learning, society, and natural order'. 'We can only marvel', they concur, 'at the timeliness of Shakespeare's imagination and the certainty of his political judgements. "Big Brother" has thrown a dark enough shadow on our own century for us to be able to acknowledge the accuracy of the diagnosis.' To Shakespeareans like this, organised labour has only one possible purpose, which is to undermine 'the national interest'. Always and everywhere, it is 'the enemy within' the state.[7]

The critics are not, of course, blindly wrong about Shakespeare and the common people; but, influenced themselves by the modernist disgust of the 'unreal city' and its crowd, they universalise a paternalism that belongs to a specific social formation. As they intuit, Shakespeare dramatises the crucial moment when a deferential 'populace degenerates into the uncontrolled and predatory mob'.[8] Put less rhetorically, therefore, his crowd scenes relate to the historical phase that has been documented by historians such as Eric Hobsbawm and George Rudé, when the rulers of the Old Regime were thrown off balance by the mass of urban poor that coalesced into the early modern 'city mob'. This occurred at different times between the sixteenth and eighteenth centuries in the cities of Western Europe, but as Brian Manning has shown, it was London craftsmen and apprentices who first joined together in a mass movement with a coherent set of political demands, and in December 1641 it was this metropolitan mob of 'the lower sort of people' which proved decisive in driving Charles I out of his palace and capital. Later, it was the same corps of 'the common people of London who made up the rank and file of the Parliamentary army', so the mob's ultimate revolutionary role was far from futile. Its origins can be traced back to the gangs and customs of the city's medieval artisanal culture; but the emergent identity of the London mob actually dates from the crisis years at the end of the sixteenth century, when a spate of calamitous harvests and exorbitant wars accelerated the collapse of social consensus in the transition to market capitalism, provoking a rash of urban revolts across Europe which were a forecast of the great revolutionary civil wars to come.[9] Though critics speak of Shakespeare's mutinous crowds, then, as if they represented perennial human traits, it was only around 1590 that conjunctural circumstances produced the point of critical mass that precipitated the popular disorders in London reflected in plays like *Sir Thomas More* and *Julius Caesar*. Until then, urban rioting was extremely rare in England; so much so that a crowd which dared to heckle Mary in 1554 was viewed as an outrage; and when riots began to break out in the capital in the 1590s, memories had to reach back to Evil May Day 1517 – when weavers attacked immigrant competitors – to find a parallel. And it was for this reason that, apart from academic plays like *Gorboduc*, drama of civil discord did not feature on the London stage until after the Armada.[10]

Once welded in economic necessity, the London mob soon displayed the characteristics that made it so different from either the modern crowd observed by Poe, Benjamin and Canetti, or the old-style peasant rout caricatured by Chaucer as a barnyard in *The Nun's Priest's Tale*. What distinguished the mob from either was precisely its sense of purpose, for as Hobsbawm reminds us, the classical mob did not simply riot to order or as a protest, but because it expected to achieve something. So although the new social formation was anathematised by officials as a monstrous Hydra without shape or purpose, it had objectives and organisation which contradicted this governmental canard. It took its leadership from the semi-legal 'yeoman' craft fraternities and its programme from the set of values that E. P. Thompson calls 'the moral economy of the poor': 'a popular consensus as to what were legitimate practices and what were illegitimate' in the community. Thus, according to Hobsbawm, far from being motiveless, the mob had four clearly defined and driving ideas: it believed in cheap, tax-free food; it despised ostentatious wealth and harked back to a 'merry world' of social harmony; it resented entrepreneurs, especially foreign ones; and, most importantly, it assumed that once alerted, the authorities would remedy its grievances. Together, these assumptions made the city mob a formidable corrective both to local profiteering and royal despotism; but the mob possessed one other feature that made it particularly inimical to the nation–state. It legitimated its protests and resistance 'by rite', that is to say, by linking them to the 'wild justice' of traditional folk festivities and calendar games. Thus, as Emmanuel Le Roy Ladurie has recounted in his collective 'psychohistory' of the Carnival uprising in Romans in 1580, the millenialist dream of the Land of Cockaigne could curdle into a cannibal fantasy aimed at the rich, and finally turn to action to 'modify society in the direction of social change'.[11] The mob unwittingly carried the heresy of social justice as a more powerful weapon than its clubs and staves.

Shakespeare's crowd-scenes belong, then, to the period of the emergence of the city mob as a force to be reckoned with in English politics. Though interpreted by modernist critics as if they demonstrated universal imperatives of law and order, no part of Shakespeare's writing is more entangled with the exigencies of his own time and place. That much is clear from his first reaction to the London mob itself, the venomous fourth act of *Henry VI, Part Two*, written during July 1592,[12] when he was suddenly diverted from the palace intrigue that comprises the remainder of the play to fire off an incandescent version of Jack

Cade's 1450 rising. A blueprint for all his later and more famous crowd-scenes, this travesty of evidence is itself a revealing example of Tudor historiography, an instance of the brazen manipulation of documentary records practised to buttress the regime. Its source was Edward Hall's 1548 Chronicle, itself a glorification of the ruling dynasty, but to blacken Cade and his followers still further Shakespeare conflated this account with reports of the Peasants' Revolt of 1381, and Cade with Wat Tyler, producing by this synthesis what critics loftily imagine as a more 'timeless impression of the chaos that occurs whenever the irrational phantoms of desire walk unchecked'. Shakespeare, as Brockbank explained, dispenses with the vulgar 'Positivist view that truth is co-extensive with the facts', to 'emphasise a more significant movement of cause and effect'. So Cade, whom Hall respects as 'a young man of goodly stature and pregnant wit', 'a subtle captain', 'sober in communication' and 'wise in disputing', whose advisers were 'schoolmasters and teachers', is metamorphosed into a cruel, barbaric lout, whose slogan is 'kill and knock down', and whose story as 'the archetype of disorder' is one long orgy of scatological clowning, arson and homicide fuelled by an infantile hatred of literacy and law.

Even the critics are unsettled by the stridency of this cartoon, though they defend it, of course, by maintaining that to libel the workers' leader as a boorish thug is actually to cut 'through the immediate situation' to highlight the 'basic human patttern . . . when any demogogue is successful in persuading the people to act as an uncritical collective.' It does not matter, therefore, that the tax reforms of the Chronicle Cade are described as 'profitable for the commonwealth', for what counts in the eyes of the academy is 'the impious spectacle of the proper order reversed' when workers are driven 'by their leader's vulgar energy and simplifications' into 'taking the law into their own hands'. Hall has Cade 'prohibiting men murder, rape or robbery'; whilst Shakespeare has him inflaming the people's blood lust. In Hall Cade cooperates with 'the king's justices'; whereas in Shakespeare he executes lynch-law. Hall's Cade is 'seen [to be] indifferent' in punishing friend and foe alike; Shakespeare's hangs the gentry for the cut of their clothes. Hall's Cade believes his protest is 'honourable to God and the king'; to seize the throne for himself, Shakespeare's calls the king a usurper. Faced with such systematic misrepresentation of sources, the critics have been in no doubt which of these versions of history is closer to what they see as the essential truth about all social protest. It is Shakespeare, 'with the authority of his moral and artistic insight', who has explored through Cade 'what happens when authority passes to the uninstructed multitude.'[13]

Authority and authorship, this slippage makes clear, are synonymous in Shakespearean politics. In *Julius Caesar*, the worst atrocity by the mob is when they 'tear' the poet Cinna 'for his bad verses' (III, iii, 30); and Cade's most vainglorious crime is when he orders his men to 'burn all the records of the realm' in the flames as the city blazes. To the writer of these scenes, rebellion is the rage of the illiterate against the written word, and the rioters' first act is therefore to lynch the aptly named Clerk of Chartham, 'with his pen and ink-horn about his neck', in fury 'that parchment, being scribbled o'er, should undo a man'. The civil war in this play is between an educated elite who 'write courthand' and sign their names and the illiterate mass who make their mark and communicate only in plain, rude English. So Cade's kangaroo court condemns anyone who 'can write and read', or speak French or Latin, accusing the well-to-do of 'erecting a grammar school', causing 'printing to be us'd', or having 'built a paper-mill'. Christopher Hill remarks that there is some poetic justice in this hatred of education, since a third of those sentenced to death in Shakespearean London 'escaped by pleading benefit of clergy' (including the murderer, Ben Jonson).[14] But here the rebels' grievance that 'because they could not read' the law 'hast hang'd them', is turned by them against 'All scholars, lawyers, courtiers [and] gentlemen' in an indiscriminate bloodbath. And the height of Cade's impudence is when he abolishes all statutes and decrees that henceforth 'the laws shall come out of my mouth . . . my mouth shall be the parliament of England.' There is an animus in these episodes, and in those satirising the people's garbled testimony or laboured puns, which gives the lie to those, like Leavis, who see Shakespeare as rooted firmly in an oral culture. On the contrary, what is advertised here, in a text that was to be one of his earliest publications, is the sneering impatience with the language of peasants and artisans of the literate parvenu. Both in subject matter and in their cavalier distortions, these scenes are a triumph of text over orality. Shakespeare's Cade is a Gargantuan Big Mouth, but nothing could be more unlike the demotic laughter of Rabelais than the young playwright's revulsion from the *vox populi* and the stinking breath he insists goes with it.

Cade's supporters hate 'men that talk of a noun, and a verb'. They are mirror opposites, therefore, of the writer himself, who established a favourite comic practice here of ridiculing all who had not benefited from grammar school. His debunking of bookmen came later; in this very early work he laid bare the cultural prejudices he brought to writing. So, when he parodies popular religion in Cade's sermon lamenting that 'the skin of an innocent lamb should be made parchment', it is an entire rival system of oral authority which the learned writer's script has 'scribbled o'er' to deface it. The writer portrays the poor as philistine vandals, but there is in fact a more subtle vandalism at work when history is rewritten to flatter lawyers and common speech is degraded into crass literalism. Clearly, Shakespeare was wearily familiar with the way in which (as Coriolanus mimics it) the commons 'sighed forth proverbs – / That hunger broke stone walls; that dogs must eat; / That meat was made for mouths, that the gods sent not / Corn for the rich men only' (ı, i, 204–7); and Charles Hobday has itemised his knowledge of the egalitarian tradition that descended by word of mouth in peasant and artisanal communities.[15] But when he gave Cade 'the old seditious argument', as it was known, that 'Adam was a gardener', or had the rioters complain that 'it was never merry world since gentlemen came up', he exploited this familiarity with derision. His stage mobs flaunt the peasants' 'clouted shoon' and craftsmen's 'leather aprons', but these radical emblems are staged to look farcical. Son of a provincial glover whose only testimony is the mark he scratched beside his name in borough records, Shakespeare, who seems to have discriminated between even his own daughters, educating his favourite to write and leaving the other illiterate, used his professional debut to signal scorn for popular culture and identification with an urban elite in whose eyes authority would henceforth belong exclusively to writers.

'There is no document of civilisation which is not at the same time a document of barbarism': Benjamin's sage aphorism was never truer than when the written text held power over life and death in Shakespeare's England.[16] Yet when the stage Cade is butchered by Alexander Iden, a Kentish squire and prototype of the Adamic Kent in *King Lear*, modernist critics applauded what they saw as the victory of 'immaculate authority' over 'the intrusive presence of "Big Brother"', a restoration of 'national sanity' by 'an ornament of the professional classes, perhaps a civil servant or local government officer, a family man with fixed habits and no ideas above his station'. As Benjamin warns, it is through such 'cultural treasures' as the Shakespearean text that 'Whoever has emerged victorious participates to this day in the triumphal procession in which the present rulers step over those they have defeated':[17] but what criticism quaintly salutes in this way as symbolic of the repulse of the labour unions by the commuters of the Home Counties, is, of course, nothing but the obliteration of popular history by Tudor propaganda. Far from securing 'the stability of society', the death of Cade in Shakespeare's play marks an irreparable split in English life, with what Peter Burke has termed 'The Withdrawal of the Upper Classes' from popular culture, a rift that led to the eclipse of folk tradition by the literate world-view.[18] After Cade, there is no commoner who speaks so much in Shakespearean drama, and 'The Triumph of Lent' is the title Burke gives to this silencing of the people's voice in the writers' culture of print and profit. Looked at from this perspective, the playhouses erected in London from 1576 can no

longer be idealised as organic developments from the medieval inn-yard
or street-theatre, the foci of 'a national culture rooted in the soil', as
Leavis taught. In the context of the taming and suppression of customary
culture – the culture, as Burke describes it, of Carnival – Shakespeare's
commercial playhouse, with its joint-stock ownership, must be viewed
as part of the apparatus of the English nation–state: as an institution,
in fact, of separation and enclosure, where bourgeois 'order' was
legitimated by the exclusion of the 'anarchy' and 'sedition' of the
mob. In practice, the ideological function of the 'wooden O' was less to
give voice to the alien, outcast and dispossessed, than to allow their
representatives the rope to hang. Rather than perpetuating a true liberty
of the Bankside, the Globe was an institution where Carnival was
disciplined by Lent.

'The Triumph of Lent' is a phrase with particular relevance to the Cade
interlude, which is often called a saturnalia. A Lord of Misrule, who
capers when wounded 'like a wild Morisco' (or morris dancer), and whose
name connotes a barrel of herrings and an upstart caddie, Cade
personifies the topsy-turvydom of Carnival, with his proclamation of a
Land of Cockaigne, where gutters run wine, bread is dirt cheap, and 'all
the realm shall be in common.' And in his energy and appetite this
Kentish Green Man is the type of 'lusty guts' alleged to lead the
'wildheads of the parish' in the folk games reviled by Puritans like
Stubbes. Shakespeare's researches into the history of Jack Cade's
incursion into London led him to the inglorious story of Sir John Falstaff's
cowardice before the peasants when he fled his Southwark property, and
there is an affinity between the two anti-heroes, since Cade is a draft for
the carnivalesque grotesque body to be comprehensively repudiated in
the fat knight. But here Silenus has a precise artisanal habitat.
Rampaging through Southwark, over London Bridge, and 'Up Fish
Street! Down Saint Magnus' Corner!' Cade and his 'rabblement' follow
the exact route into the heart of civilisation as so many Elizabethan
apprentices in their Shrovetide and May Day tumults, when they forayed
out of the festering suburb into the financial quarter of the City. Their
pillaging then was targeted on the brothels frequented by their
employers, but Shakespeare recycles the old smear that the workers need
only an excuse to fornicate, as the rebels run to the Cheapside prostitutes
or rape the aldermen's daughters and wives as Cade urges. Similarly, he
reproduces one of the deepest establishment myths about the populace
when its festive images of meat and gluttony are literalised as
cannibalism. For like Gargantua, Cade starts his career with a cattle-
slaughtering feast, but in this dystopia the carcasses he hews belong to the
rich, hacked down 'like sheep and oxen', their 'throats cut like calves' and
skin 'flayed to make dog's leather'. 'Thou hast behav'st thyself as if thou

had'st been in thine own slaughter-house', he tells his henchman, Dick, the Butcher of Ashford, rewarding him with a 'licence to kill' in Lent. Butchers, Michael Bristol notes, fought fishmongers in the rite of spring that schematised the medieval economy; but that key Shakespearean metaphor of 'appetite' as a 'universal wolf' (*Troilus and Cressida*, I, iii, 121) has its origin in a class nightmare of Carnival as carnage. So, though Bakhtinians correctly detect the carnivalesque elements in Shakespeare, they underestimate the extent to which these are contained and contradicted.[19] For when the writer has Cade's head impaled, his text arrogates to itself Lent's finality, bringing down the curtain on both comedy and communism.

Cade's bleeding head might be taken as symbolic of the silenced 'World of Carnival' – traditional popular culture – doomed from Shakespeare's time to speak only through the 'distorting viewpoints and intermediaries' of the dominant written culture.[20] Instead, these scenes have been interpreted as a permanently topical warning against the dangers of 'excessive concern for social justice'. Reinforcing the bourgeois myth that workers have no history of their own, but are for ever exploited by troublemakers, critics regularly treat Cade as the 'timeless embodiment of lawlessness', and ignore the signs that the motive for this character assassination stem from Shakespeare's own involvement in social process.[21] In fact, his defamation of Jack Cade was prompted by a crisis in London's culture which, perhaps more than other incidents, explodes the legend of a democratic Bankside. The clue to this local motivation lies in the characterisation of the rebels. The 1450 rising had been an agrarian *jacquerie*, like that of 1381, but Shakespeare changed the occupations of the rioters, who appear not as medieval peasants but Renaissance artisans. Specifically, he made Cade a shearman – a clothing worker involved in the garment-finishing process – and his lieutenants mostly weavers or other 'handicraftsmen' in allied clothing industries. Hill relates how, when the Civil War began, it was reckoned that 'the clothiers through the whole kingdom were rebels by their trade', because of the long-standing radicalism of the textile industry – technically and economically the most advanced sector of artisanal capitalism – and how it was from the clothing workers that the Levellers and other revolutionary groups drew their strength.[22] So, when 'Jack Cade the clothier' erupts into Shakespeare's play, unaccountably railing against the 'silken-coated' army, and condemning the 'serge' and 'buck'ram' lords for clothing their horses in velvet, 'when honester men go in hose and doublet', it is the militant clothing industry of London in the 1590s, rather than, as critics maintain, the 'prejudices of the workers of any age', which forms the context.[23]

'Jack Cade the clothier means to dress the commonwealth, and turn it, and set a new nap on it': the first words of Shakespeare's caricature are a sarcastic résumé of the fiercest Elizabethan industrial dispute, coupled with a gibe at the skills of the shearmen. In 1592 the London clothing workers were fighting a rear-guard action against long-term structural changes in their industry. Their problems arose from the capitalisation of the textile business by dealers determined to break the monopolies and regulations of the gilds and to force open a free market in goods and labour, and their struggle centred on the defence of the city's finishing crafts, undermined by the export of unfinished fabric or cloth dressed in the provinces. Clothing workers were on the sharp end, that is to say, of developments in urban capitalism known to Weber as 'non-legitimate domination', whereby control of production was wrested from producers by free-trading wholesalers or trading companies, in a shift 'from gild-based production to a putting-out or domestic system'.[24] The stresses of this deregulation were most acute in London's suburban parishes, notably St Olave's, Southwark, adjoining the theatre district, where the local shearmen, weavers and feltmakers were unprotected by the City by-laws that held north of the river, and entrepreneurs could breach their apprenticeship walls with impunity. There too the tension was aggravated in the 1570s and 1580s by the influx of war-refugees from Europe, whose competition revived the racism that had long been a virulent factor in London's industrial relations. Yet if these French and Dutch artisans were resented, the middlemen were detested, since their dealing in undressed broadcloth or Midlands hosiery threatened the very survival of the London industries and drove a wedge within the gilds themselves between the craftsmen and the merchants who traded with them. As it happens, Shakespeare would have a financial stake in these capitalist developments, and documents reveal him in the hated role of middleman. They record how in 1598 he invested £30 in a consignment of 'knitted stockings' at Evesham, the main depot for Cotswold woollens, helping to make a shrewd killing in a market where he was assured that 'you may do good, if you can have money.' With his background in the leather industry, Stratford contacts (who tipped him off on this occasion), and London lodging in St Helen's, Bishopsgate, beside Leaden Hall, the largest wool warehouse in Europe, Shakespeare was ideally placed to profit from speculation in Midlands textiles, and his part in this enterprise perfectly illustrates the activities that were driving London craftsmen out of business by diverting trading capital.[25]

Shakespeare's text makes crude humour out of the business of taking 'up commodities', such as 'a kirtle, a petticoat, and a smock'; but historians of the Tudor wool trade describe such broking by letter as a revolutionary technique that would erode the public market by spreading a network of invisible transactions, which an investor such as

Shakespeare could manipulate from a distance. By the end of the seventeenth century the new system had destroyed the London industry and funded cheaper manufacture in West Yorkshire;[26] but Cade's plan to 'dress the whole commonwealth' is Shakespeare's mockery of the Elizabethan finishing workers' utopian solution to the conflict, which was to rig an export monopoly, a scheme that would eventually see its day in Alderman Cockayne's well-named but ill-fated project of 1614 to export only finished material. Similarly, when Cade proposes to the rebels to 'apparel all in one livery', Shakespeare is not anticipating Orwell, as critics like to believe, but sniping satirically at the cloth workers' dream of extending the jurisdiction of the Livery Companies to the unarticled labour in London's extra-mural parishes. These scenes are peppered with slighting allusions to the clothing industries which make Shakespeare's partisanship explicit. It is even sharper in the episode he interpolated earlier in his play, when an armourer's apprentice, Peter Thump, strikes his master dead for disloyalty to the Crown (II, iii, 60–102). In 1592 there were rich pickings for profiteers (such as the Eastlands Company) supplying Essex's 'silken-coated' troops in France,[27] and Shakespeare, who took care to depict his villain as a disaffected veteran returned from Ireland, aligned himself squarely with the empire and the free market in timely opposition to London's small masters.

If it was mercantile money that talked on Shakespeare's earliest stage, however, the industrial metropolis had at least one spokesman in the *petit-bourgeois* press. There, in adventure stories that heroised the 'famous Cloth Workers of England', such as *Jack of Newbury* (1597) – the life of the historical John Winchcomb, a 'poor broad cloth Weaver' who rose to fortune by sticking with his workers – Thomas Deloney voiced the artisanal point of view which Shakespeare attributes to Cade. Nostalgically evoking a world of good fellowship and social mobility that was, in fact, fast coming to an end with the exclusion of journeymen from mastership in the gilds, Deloney canvassed among the literate the creed (which he attributed to an idealised Henry VIII) that 'the trade of Clothing brought benefit to the whole Common Wealth', and that just as the country needed clergy, 'So is the skilful Clothier necessary'. Himself a Norwich weaver, he wrote, he said, for the 'poor people who laboured to get their own bread', so his hero, Jack, embodies a collective fantasy that is not without malice towards those, like the jester Will Summers or foreign merchants, who deserve to be duped. Deloney's Land of Cockaigne is an artisanal paradise where 'city slickers are outwitted by unsophisticated and innocent labourers'; but when the London weavers distributed a bare twenty copies of a pamphlet in 1595, protesting that they were 'greatly decayed and injured' by immigrants and speculators, it was Deloney who was gaoled for it.[28] The fate of the workers' writer differed from that of the dramatist who spoke for his patrons at court and the merchant oligarchy.

The clothing workers' fight was doomed to fail. Their nostalgic corporatism was bound to be swept aside by the market forces Shakespeare heralded. Nor was there a place in the new capitalism for the representation that had united men and masters in the gild, as Shakespeare himself recognised, when he had the commons' petitions against enclosure and abuses spurned in his play by government. Disenfranchised as the merchants rewrote the rules to suit the profit motive, London artisans turned increasingly during the sixteenth century towards unofficial forms of solidarity and action. Typical was the story of the Southwark felt-cap makers whose workshops abutted the playhouses, swindled in the trade by the retail Haberdashers Company and undercut by provincial competition. Their plight was a chronic scandal in the Borough, but when they elected two 'Orators' and appealed for relief in 1579 they were discredited by the classic ploy: they had been duped, the merchants said, by agitators: 'Bradford and Caunton, two of the worst sort of feltmakers, haunters of taverns where they plot devices to live by other men's goods. The best and honestest feltmakers make no such petition.' Throughout Elizabeth's reign the feltmakers were denied an organisation and charter of their own to set them free from such domination by the haberdashers; yet in 1585 they were lectured that if they had only put their complaints about sweatshops and untrimmed goods formally in writing, 'they might have been better considered.'[29] It was at this point, therefore, with the breakdown of social consensus and the blocking of redress, that 'mechanic men' such as these began to organise in the illegal combinations that evolved into the city mob.

The district into which the players intruded with their Rose Theatre in 1587 was home to a complex community whose centre, known as the Maze, was a warren of tenements off the High Street, where 'strangers and other poor people' worked unprotected by legal safeguards in the Liberty of the former Bermondsey Abbey. Like every garment industry, Southwark's production line involved each stage of 'hat manufacture and its branches of hat-block makers, hat-dyers, hat-lining- and leather-cutters, hat shag-makers, hat-tip makers, bonnet-string makers, furriers and trimming-makers'.[30] With such an extended structure, it is not surprising that garment workers have been the advance guard of industrial action, and the flash-point in Southwark came in the sweltering summer of 1592, when conjunctural circumstances similar to those that ignited the explosion in 1517 recurred to exacerbate the long-term confrontation. The price of wool, which had doubled in five years, now stood at its highest level, and the consequence was that the poorest feltmakers were squeezed out of the market. In 1577 a government inquiry had found that soaring prices were hiked by middlemen, but in the manufacturing parishes it was inevitably the neighbouring foreigners who were blamed for outbidding locals. As on Evil May Day, the economic crisis inflamed anti-alien sentiment and the problems of unemployment and immigration became enmeshed. So in May 1592 the Lord Mayor petitioned on behalf of 'the natural born subjects and freemen of the city' who were 'being supplanted by the strangers and their living taken from them', while Dutch manufacturers from Southwark complained in turn to the Privy Council about harassment. Alarmed ministers responded by ordering an urgent census of the extent of the aliens' operations, hoping not to exacerbate hostilities. Evidently their investigators failed in this, because on 6 June officers of the local Marshalsea Prison arrested a feltmaker and his apprentices for offences against aliens, bursting into his house in Bermondsey Street 'with daggers drawn' and 'a most rough and violent manner', in a raid that would spark one of London's worst disorders of the century and end seventy-five years of civic peace.[31]

In their study of England's 'last rising', the 'Captain Swing' riots of 1830 in the South, Hobsbawm and Rudé outline the actions available to workers resisting the onslaught of capitalism in the early modern period, and emphasise that these 'essentially modified traditional collective practices' such as 'annual feasts, processions and waits'. Victims of the decay of customary culture, the poor fell back during times of crisis on the 'World of Carnival' which once defined and guaranteed their roles. So, in 1830 the Sussex 'Bonfire Boys' exploited 5 November by burning farmers' ricks, just as the Yorkshire Luddites went the season's round of 'Ned Ludd's Mummers' at Christmas in 1812, yelling for alms and satisfaction outside the mill-owners' doors with the ludic licence of blackened faces and women's clothes. Those who broke the rules were thereby shamed to 'play the game', as the new machinery which was breaking up the old communities was confronted by the hallowed rituals of dependence and obligation. And in 1592 the Southwark clothing workers similarly turned, for want of an ideology, to a time-honoured cultural script. For as Paul Slack confirms, in the crisis of the 1590s Londoners clung to fragments of what traditions they could, 'whether in streets, in alehouses or in church'.[32] They marched, therefore, as they always had, through the Borough on 11 June, 'Old Midsummer', the Feast of St Barnabas and the longest day, to light a bonfire and perform a play.

Playing with fire had long been part of London's Midsummer Night's revels, a secular version of the solstitial rites of Corpus Christi, and officially it was sponsored by the Merchant Tailors, the powerful 'Gild of Tailors and Linen-Armourers of St John', to celebrate the sheep-shearing that began around this date. Company records itemise regular payments for raising the maypole and costuming wildmen, lions and morrismen in mid-century; and Machyn breathlessly reports that on 11 June 1553 there was 'as goodly a May-game as has been, with giants, games and drums, and devils, and morris dancers, and bagpipes and viols, and many disguised, and the Lord and Lady of May rode gorgeously, with minstrels diverse playing'. Spenser, educated at the grammar school built by the gild in 1561, left a detailed itinerary of the cloth workers' St Barnabas Day festivities in his *Epithalamion* of 1594, which timetables the day's customs as they had been orchestrated in his boyhood, from garland-dressing by the 'merchants' daughters' at dawn, through the 'rough music' of the 'young men of the town', who 'leave [their] wonted labours for the day', and the beating of the city bounds, with wine poured 'without restraint or stay' and sprinkled on 'all the posts and walls', to the bells and bonfires at dusk. Spenser's patrons must have instructed him that 'This day is holy, do ye write it down, / That ye for ever it remember may, / This day the sun is in his chiefest height, / With Barnaby the bright' (263–6); and his poem is a thanks-offering on his wedding-day to a gild culture of schools, almshouses, hospitals and feasts, founded, in the words of the Merchant Tailors' pious prayer, 'that we may in brotherly and true love assemble':[33]

> The whiles the boys run up and down the street,
> Crying aloud with strong confused noise,
> As if it were one voice . . .
> That even to the heavens their shouting shrill
> Doth reach, and all the firmament doth fill,
> To which the people standing all about,
> As in approvance do thereto applaud.
> (*Epithalamion*, 137–44)

'Barnaby bright! The longest day and the shortest night': *Epithalamion* encodes the strategy of incorporation by which the metropolitan patriciate hoped to steal the fire of popular culture; and Stow likewise reports its policy of commensality at Midsummer, when the cloth gilds held feasts and after the sunset 'made bonfires in the streets, every man bestowing wood or labour. The wealthier sort, would set out tables, whereunto they would invite their neighbours to sit and be merry. . . . These were called bonfires of amity amongst neighbours that being before at controversy, were made of bitter enemies loving friends'.[34] Stow was writing, he recognised, at a time when this communality was fraying in a suburb such as Southwark, which was 'in worse case than ever, by means of enclosure for Gardens', but it remained an agenda to inspire the Borough Fair in the week preceding 17 June. There the St

Barnabas Day procession converged on the High Street, where the maypole was erected outside the Marshalsea itself.[35] What unfolded then, if Spenser is correct, was a perennial summer scene, when a stuffed giant would be paraded through a caterwauling crowd and burned to exorcise 'the Puck' and 'evil sprites' (*Epithalamion*, 341), before the young drifted off to spend the shortest night in St George's Fields. But on Midsummer evening in 1592 the rite of solstice came to a premature and unexpected end. For at 'about eight' the celebrations were suddenly stopped when 'the Knight Marshal's men issued forth with their daggers drawn and bastinadoes in their hands, beating the people' indiscriminately and killing 'several innocent persons' among the spectators in the street. In the ensuing 'tumult' the officers lost control and, despite laying about with swords, were only saved from lynching by the arrival on the scene of a hasty posse with the Sheriff and Lord Mayor. As the bodies were laid out in Maypole Lane, and the officers ignominiously withdrew, some 'principal offenders' were picked from the apprentices and carted to Newgate gaol. Midsummer madness had brought the London cloth workers a real carnival of blood.[36]

From revelry to rebellion was a short semantic step in the symbolism of Renaissance culture, and reading between the Carnival signs the Knight Marshal's men had evidently decided that the cloth workers' riotous play had taken it, and that their raucous mêlée was a danger to the prison. But the question for the authorities in getting to what Burghley called 'the bottom of that outrageous fact', was the one that vexes historians in pursuit of the 'elusive quarry' of popular culture, whether, as Burke puts it, 'one is considering songs or rituals: who is saying what, to whom, for what purpose and to what effect?'[37] Interpreting the signs is always problematic in the case of riots and risings, he explains, because what we know about them is filtered through officials who are 'unreliable mediators', interested in interpreting 'as a "blind fury" a movement which the participants saw as a planned defence of specific traditional rights'.[38] What seems to have happened outside the Marshalsea was an instance not of spontaneous combustion but of the early modern sequence depicted by Burke as a 'switching of codes', when festival erupted into political action;[39] but the dilemma for the state was how to determine the point when the ritualised theatre of protest ignited into a political 'theatre of rebellion', in Buchanan Sharp's phrase, especially when the rituals consisted, as they did at Midsummer, of such violent actions as lighting fires, burning effigies and leaping through flames 'with frantic mirth'.[40] 'Actions speak louder than words, and riots may be seen not only as "blind fury", but dramatic expressions of popular attitudes and values';[41] yet deafness to rough music had a long history, and the instinct of magistrates must have been to hear the 'confused noise' of the

bonfire boys with the same bewilderment as Chaucer had listened to the
'shrill shouts' of 'Jack Straw and his men' when they attacked the Flemish
weavers in 1381 on this same ground:

> Of bras thay broghten bemes[1], and of box[2],   [[1]trumpets/[2]wood]
> Of horn, of boon[3], in whiche they blewe and pouped   [[3]bone]
> And therwithal thay shryked and houped:
> It semed as that heven sholde falle.[42]

When he reported to the government next morning the Lord Mayor
was equally convinced that the whole blame lay with the cloth workers,
and that 'the principal actors' were 'certain of the feltmakers out of
Bermondsey Street', who had 'assembled by occasion of a play' only as a
'pretense' to spring their workmates from the gaol. His use of the word
'actors', however, pinpoints the ambiguity of popular theatre at this time.
For if festivity served as a *pretext* for spasmodic protest, throughout
Europe the authorities were also beginning to view the youth societies
which staged traditional parades as standing cells of agitation. Moreover,
the evidence of the sixteenth century's 'rites of violence' suggests that
these suspicions were well founded, and that on Evil May Day in London
or St Bartholemew's Day in Paris, it was sports and drama clubs – the
'Abbeys' or 'Kingdoms' of Misrule – which provided a pre-political
culture with the organisation and occasion to plot concerted coups. In
1514 the people of Islington had levelled fences of nearby enclosures
under the lead of an 'April Fool' in cap-and-bells; and action had been
planned in 1517, according to Hall, in London archery 'fraternities', with
their 'common box', from whence 'a common secret rumour' spread 'that
on May Day next the city would rebel', so that when the cry of 'Prentices
and clubs!' was given, 'out at every door came clubs and weapons [and]
people arose from every quarter'.[43] As Burke comments, evidence of
such confraternities may be more fragmentary in London than in
Florence or Paris (precisely because of the rise of an entertainment
industry), but the feltmakers who 'stirred up the apprentices' in 1696 to
seize the owner of a sweatshop, 'tie him in a wheelbarrow, and in
tumultuous and riotous manner drive him through all the considerable
places in London and in Southwark', were performing a 'riding' which
everyone who belonged to the city's 'green-apron culture' could enjoy.[44]
Initiations in which recruits might be 'rolled in a barrowful of nails', oath-
taking, ballad-reading and elections 'to choose a Grand Captain . . .
whom they crown with great solemnity', formalised such games,
impressing the participants with a solidarity that carried them to the brink
of class consciousness; for whether 'investing a cat' or arranging 'to give
breakfast for all apprentices, they saw themselves as moral agents,

defending the right.'[45] No wonder, then, that their intended victims reacted as they did to the actors who commenced the 'play' outside the Marshalsea in 1592. The officers knew the plot and could see exactly how it had been planned to end.

'The yell was a long one', Charlotte Brontë reported, when she wrote of the 'rough music' of the Luddites, 'and when it ceased, the night was full of the swaying and murmuring of a crowd.'[46] Thus, the cloth workers' ceremonial was perpetuated in the nineteenth century by the Yorkshire mob who carried 'At their head a Straw Man' to be 'solemnly burnt after a great banging of tins.'[47] If folklorists are correct, therefore, to deduce that the shadowy pseudonyms of the champions of popular revolts – Jack Rakestraw, Jack Cade or Ned Ludd – denoted the 'guy' who was both 'a saviour and despised enemy', and that the 'savage cry' during what Caxton called 'the hurling time' was aimed at the foes of customary society through him,[48] it is easy to see how his bonfire sites became locales of symbolic power. The feltmakers knew what they were about when they lit the flame outside the Marshalsea on the exact anniversary of the day in 1381 when it had been set ablaze by Tyler, and of the other Midsummer revolt in 1450 when it had been broken open by Cade (as it is in Shakespeare), to 'let the prisoners out'. If this royal prison stood for the state, the cloth workers' fire signalled the folk justice of the Man of Straw. 'Midnight knocks at the door by disguised men, rough growled demands, and violence against the property of those who refused', were all legitimated in the name of the summer jack, according to this reading;[49] which also explains what next occurred in Southwark, when vigilantes appeared on 18 June at the house in Bermondsey Street of one of the Knight Marshal's henchmen, Robert Levenson, 'intending to drive him out'. Once again, however, the folk scenario was aborted when another officer named Levens 'joined Levenson in resisting the intruders', and shot their leader dead. So, instead of being wheeled backwards around the town, the assailants were carried to Newgate by a squad of jeering apprentices, an infuriated gang of the kind that would provide the muscle of later worker militancy.[50] But it was to prevent these 'renewing their lewd assembly by colour of the time' that the Privy Council now banned all further festivity, imposed a curfew and, taking no risks, closed even the commercial theatres for the summer months. And on St John's Day, 23 June, the City mounted, for the first time in fifty years, an old-fashioned torchlit watch of 'householders and masters of families'. The people's revels were suppressed with a show of street theatre from the propertied class.[51]

The revival of the Midsummer watch was a symptom of the fragmentation of London's consensus, rather than, as critics still believe, a celebration of social harmony.[52] Until 1539 the Midsummer Corpus

Christi procession had indeed expressed corporate solidarity, but after that year the civic festival was postponed from the volatile summer months, to evolve into the November Lord Mayor's Show. Now the restoration of the tattoo for purposes of social control coincided with the refinement of the mayoral feast as propaganda, with the commission for the 1591 inauguration of a masque, *Descensus Astraea* by George Peele. There the incoming Mayor, William Webbe, was flattered with a conceit of England's textile manufacture as a seamless 'web' spun effortlessly by the shepherdess Elizabeth/Astraea from the fleece of her contented flock. London's public was splitting into separate audiences with radically opposing visions of the city's industry and wealth. Even the days on which Londoners enjoyed their pleasures had diverged. Thus, 11 June 1592 had been a Sunday, and ever since the opening of his playhouse in Southwark, Philip Henslowe had obeyed the prohibition on all 'interludes and plays on the Sabbath', barring city workers therefore (as James I complained) on the only afternoon of the week when they did not officially 'apply their labour'. In the Sabbatarian debate dividing England before the Civil War, London's commercial theatre sided with the wealthy masters who saw a strict observance as the means to police their workforce. So, while the poor of Southwark marked the ancient day of the sun, Shakespeare's playhouse had been locked on them, as always, to mark the modern Sunday. As the crowd gathered around 'the Bull Ring' and the maypole in the Borough Street to honour 'Barnaby the bright', the Rose stood silent as the site and symbol of a new phase of metropolitan culture: partitioned, disciplined and hierarchic.[53]

The modernist nostalgia for Elizabethan England as a model of some classless, pre-industrial *Gemeinschaft* cannot withstand the picture that is emerging of London's crystallising class consciousness in the acute social and economic crisis of the 1590s. And with it has also been discredited the unitary conception of power implicit in the received version of 'The Elizabethan World Picture'. As critics such as Jonathan Dollimore and Alan Sinfield remind us, far from constituting a monolithic centralised power system, early modern England was rent by a competitive interplay between numerous blocs and factions, who contested hegemony through a multiplicity of economic, political and cultural practices. Power was splintered and dispersed in this polity, and just as the English state knew a mosaic of distinct and contradictory traditions of law, so authority was legitimated through not one but a plurality of Elizabethan cultures.[54] Nowhere was this fragmentation better demonstrated than in Southwark, with its patchwork of inconsistent jurisdictions, rival courts and capricious liberties. And the events of 1592 exposed the intricacy of the mechanism, for as a Commission of Inquiry sat through the smouldering summer, all parties issued conflicting interpretations of the 'tumult'.

Even the rioters were defended when Webbe scandalised the Privy
Council and wrecked his credit at court by reversing his opinion after
sounding out 'men of best reputation' in the Borough, protesting to
Burghley about the habitual violence of the officers, attesting that the
victims 'were no meddlers but passers by' who 'came to gaze' at the show,
and warning that if 'exemplary punishment' were inflicted on the 'sundry
apprentices' accused of riot, 'it were best the same were done with an
even hand upon the Knight Marshal's men who incited these multitudes
by their violent behaviour.' After 'deeper consideration', Webbe now
concurred with 'the popular sort', moreover, that the roots of the crisis
lay in 'discontentment against strangers such as hinder the trades and
occupations of this City', and predicted 'seditions to kindle the coals of
further disorder' unless the grievances of the cloth workers were
addressed. The feltmakers charivari had at last been heard.[55]

If the Privy Council feared that the 'examinations taken by the Lord
Mayor' were slanted 'very partially and too favourably' towards the
feltmakers, the suspicion would have been confirmed by the tale of
William Longbeard which Webbe later commissioned from the son of a
former Mayor, Thomas Lodge, heroising the leader of a medieval revolt,
who is hanged protesting, 'I did nothing but in mine own defence.' The
occasion was a second riot at Tyburn in October when the mob tried to
halt the execution of its leader, and Webbe was reprimanded for bailing
the offenders. The sense of injustice Lodge publicised was stirred by the
leniency shown Levens and Levenson, who were charged at Croydon
assizes on 3 July with the manslaughter of John Slainsby, a Southwark
butcher. There it emerged that Levenson was himself a former
haberdasher with a grudge against the feltmakers since operating a
sweatshop in 1576; so it was predictable that the accused would jump bail
when Burghley ordered Webbe to release them from Newgate and
disappear by the date fixed for their trial on 19 July. The City, though it
sent counsel to Croydon, had long contested the powers of the Surrey
justices, and seethed at this fiasco. Two days later, it set up a committee to
challenge Southwark's jurisdiction, but this body drifted slowly onto the
legal sands of London's transpontine suburb. As Stephen Mullaney has
argued, the Liberties of the South Bank were too useful to the state as a
liminal zone, 'a borderland whose legal parameters and privileges were
open-ended and equivocally defined', to be roped within the bounds of
civic law. Beyond 'the purview of the sheriffs of London', and so
comprising a 'virtually ungoverned area over which the city had
authority, but no control', Southwark was an inside/outside space,
therefore, where Levenson could infiltrate a sweatshop and Henslowe,
with equal impunity, the Rose. The erection of the Globe on Bankside in
1599 only confirmed what the Mayor had guessed: that the bounds of the

new economic order would be beaten through ideological practices, such as poetry and plays.[56]

It was in the interests of the City Fathers to back their apprentices against the Surrey magistrates and the shocktroops of the royal prison. But Shakespeare's company had no such common cause. With their Sabbatarian alibi, they had every reason instead to seize the opportunity to dissociate themselves from the folk drama of the streets, with its 'whores and zanies' and subversive taint, and to broadcast, as Thomas Nashe now did in *Pierce Penniless*, how their patrons were 'men that are their own masters, as gentlemen of the Court', who crossed to Southwark by river, and that they 'heartily wish they might be troubled with none' of the local 'youth or prentices'. Nashe insulted the City when he defined an upstart as a 'greasy son of a clothier', whose 'weaver's loom framed the web of his honour'; but it was in the plays the actors commissioned that their campaign for respectability was waged fiercest. As the Queen went on progress through the Midlands, to be saluted with masques by John Lyly idealising the wool trade as a country sport of 'shepherds and simplicity, in which nothing is esteemed by whiteness', the professional theatre prepared to impress the censors with a darker product. In the luridly anti-populist *Jack Straw*, Marlowe's frenzied urban horror story, *Massacre at Paris*, and above all the scarifying mêlée appended to *Henry VI*, Shakespeare's company earned exemption from their ban by protesting that, as Nashe swore, far from inciting 'the ruder handicraft servants' to their 'undoing . . . no play they have encourageth any man to tumults or rebellion, but lays before such the halter and the gallows'. Registered with the Stationers on 8 August, when the lives of the clothiers' leaders hung by a thread, this manifesto affiliated the players bluntly with the Crown and its officers against 'any club-fisted usurer, sprung-up by base brokery' who imagined that 'burgomasters might share government and be quarter-masters of our monarchy'. Printed beside a patriotic puff for *1 Henry VI*, which 'ten thousand' had paid to see, Nashe's interference was a reminder not only of the actors' powerful friends, but of the profit lost by the termination of their run. Renaissance drama-clubs were always class-based, Le Roy Ladurie deduces, and festivities frequently ended with the elite raining Lenten blows on the craftsmen's rival league.[57] In 1592 the sweetness of the Rose was likewise to hang before its neighbours the shadow of a noose.

Five years after the Southwark riot, Nashe was still complaining that the 'persecution' of the players by the Lord Mayor and aldermen was like the barbarism of Jack Cade's rebels when 'they hanged up the Lord Chief Justice'.[58] Skilled at hiding behind the Surrey judges from the Recorder of London, the actors knew exactly where they stood in law: outside the old 'moral economy' and in the 'Liberties' of the new market. Their representation of Cade should be interpreted, therefore, within the context of its 'micro-history', as a self-interested aggravation by the Rose managers of an opportune crisis, designed to play off 'the national interest' against the City council. For with his gruesome 'slaughter-house' of victims and plot to rape the burghers' wives, Shakespeare's Cade is a projection of the atavistic terrors of the Renaissance rich. His creator would come to revise his response to popular protest when dearth hit Warwickshire; but it is to his juvenile nightmare of worker revolution that Shakespeareans, with their Freudian sociology and Orwellian imagery, are heirs. If they notice the plebs at all, it is as violators of high culture: like the apprentices who sacked the Cockpit Theatre in Drury Lane on Shrove Tuesday 1617, or the weavers from Ludlow Fair in 1627 who broke into the private performance being given by actors from the Globe and drove them out with flaming brands.[59] The world of Carnival which gave these gestures meaning was suppressed by Puritanism and print, while the literate promoted the writer *The Financial Times* declares to be 'the archetypal bourgeois West Midlander', as the voice of 'the people of Southwark, the people of England of all walks of life, and people of all ages and all countries'. Thus, supporting plans to rebuild the Globe on site in 1985, Southwark's Liberal MP argued that Shakespeare's playhouse 'hadn't been a stuffy theatre putting on plays that none of the locals wanted to see. It was a people's theatre'; and the Labour council of Britain's third most deprived Borough was told that 'The shape of the Globe had united everyone' and would do so again if the 'radical middle' held sway. So, in the fractured inner city the site of Shakespeare's playhouse was treasured as the birthplace of that consensus which was demonstrated by Prince Philip, Lord Olivier, Derno Property Developers and Professor Brockbank, when they joined as patrons to raise the Globe and preserve for ever the foundations of the Rose.[60]

'The British have always enjoyed a little ritual violence', lectured *The Independent*, when poll-tax riots erupted in London in 1990, but though 'the *mobile vulgus*, the fickle crowd, the "mob" of eighteenth century London, was a fearsome sight when it rioted, overturning carriages, setting buildings alight and roaring with drunken pleasure at its own power', no one ever doubted the futility of such 'street theatre', since the 'lusty anarchy' of this 'national game' led inevitably to restoration, and 'the epic of law and order in danger' always ended with rescue from 'the boys in blue'. Thus, the 'dark stereotypes of insurrectionary lawlessness', which the playhouse had staged in Cade's revolt, lived on in the London of the 1990s, along with the belief of Britain's rulers that the scenario of Carnival is one that must proceed, like Shakespeare's, from subversion to containment.[61] It was because of the tenacity of this belief that no one marked the place outside the Marshalsea where the feltmakers had staged their parade. Misdated by editors and then relocated as a 'theatre riot' inside the 'wooden O' itself, even their protest was taken from them to prove that Shakespeare had always spoken for 'the common man'. Yet the illegal combination they began in 1592 would outlast the culture of consensus, for it would be the London weavers, dressed in their uniform green aprons, whose rioting in 1675 carried the mob over the threshold of modern political consciousness (according to Burke); and the feltmakers of 'radical Southwark' whose carnivalesque strike in 1696 was the turning-point from which (the Webbs believed) British Trade Unionism descends.[62] The Midsummer revels of 1592 saw the separation of London's elite theatre from the customs of its neighbourhood; but, patronised by the writer in the antics of Bottom the Weaver, or pilloried in the buffoonery of the Clothier Cade, the cloth worker's festival would have a history of its own.

Chapter Two

'Is this a holiday?':

Shakespeare's Roman carnival

Julius Caesar was the first Shakespearean play we know to have been acted at the Globe, and was perhaps performed for the opening of the new Bankside theatre in 1599. The Swiss tourist Thomas Platter saw it on 21 September, and his impressions help to locate the work within the different cultural practices that went to make the Elizabethan playhouse. To our minds, accustomed to a decorous image of both Shakespeare and ancient Rome, it is just this collision of codes and voices which makes the traveller's report so incongruous and jarring:

> After lunch, at about two o'clock, I and my party crossed the river, and there in the house with the thatched roof we saw an excellent performance of the tragedy of the first emperor, Julius Caesar, with about fifteen characters; and after the play, according to their custom, they did a most elegant and curious dance, two dressed in men's clothes and two in women's.[1]

Along with chimney-pots, feather hats, bound books and chiming clocks in the play itself, we can absorb the cultural shock of the 'house with the thatched roof', but the elegant jig of Caesar and the boy dressed as Caesar's wife is too alienating a mixture for us of what Duke Theseus calls the 'merry and tragical' (*A Midsummer Night's Dream*, v, i, 58). Even the Swiss visitor thought it a curious local custom, and he was lucky to see it, because by 1612 'all Jigs, Rhymes and Dances after Plays' had been 'utterly abolished' to prevent the 'tumults and outrages whereby His Majesty's peace is often broke', alleged to be caused by the 'cut-purses and other lewd and ill-disposed persons' who were attracted by them into the auditorium in droves at the end of each performance.[2] Platter was an observer of a theatre already in the process of expelling gatecrashers and purging itself of the popular customs that had given them entry and legitimated their unwelcome presence. He was

witnessing what Francis Barker has described as the first seeds of
naturalism inside the Elizabethan theatre, and the English inauguration of a new kind of controlled drama, where clowns would learn to
'speak no more than is set down for them,' and laughter, as Hamlet
prescribes, would be made strictly conditional on the 'necessary
question of the play'. Authority in this theatre would come to be
concentrated in what the Prince of Denmark proprietorially tells the
Players are 'my lines' (*Hamlet*, III, ii, 1–45), and the mastery of
the author as producer would be founded on the suppression of just
those popular practices that Platter thought so picturesque: the un-
written scenario of the mummers' dance, the transvestite mockery
of the 'shemale', Dick Tarlton's 'villainous' impromptu gags and,
at the close, the raucous collective belch of disrespect for 'His Majesty's
Peace'. Elite and demotic traditions coexist in embarrassed tension in
Platter's travel diary, where the excellence of the classical tragedy
consorts so oddly with the rumbustiousness of the antic hay. The traveller
did not realise, of course, that the sequence he recorded represented the point of scission between two cultures and for one of them
the literal 'final fling', nor that 'the house with the thatched roof'
was the scene, even as he applauded the performance, of bitter social
separation.[3]

The opening words of *Julius Caesar* seem to know themselves,
nevertheless, as a conscious declaration of company policy towards the
Elizabethan theatre public. They are addressed by the Roman Tribune
Flavius to 'certain commoners' who have entered 'over the stage', and
they are a rebuke to their temerity: 'Hence! home, you idle creatures, get
you home, / Is this a holiday?' Dressed in their Sunday 'best apparel',
these 'mechanical' men have mistaken the occasion for a 'holiday,' and to
the rhetorical question, 'Is this a holiday?' they are now given the firm
answer that for them, at least, it is an ordinary 'labouring day' (I, i, 1–60).
This is an encounter, then, that situates what follows explicitly within the
contemporary debate about the value or 'idleness' of popular culture, a
debate in which, as Christopher Hill has written, 'two modes of life, with
their different needs and standards, are in conflict as England moves out
of the agricultural middle ages into the modern industrial world.'[4] And as
Flavius and his colleague Marullus order the plebeians back to work, it is
a confrontation that confirms Hill's thesis that the Puritan attack on
popular festivity was a strategy to control the emerging manufacturing
workforce. The Tribunes oppose 'holiday' because it blurs the distinctions between labour and reward, and between the deserving poor and
the shiftless work-shy, just as their counterparts among the London
Aldermen complained the playhouses lured 'the prentices and servants of
the City from their works'. In fact, the Tribunes' speeches echo *The*

Anatomy of Abuses (1583) by the Puritan zealot and merchants' censor, Philip Stubbes, and in doing so the actors of the Globe were disarming one of the most powerful, because pragmatic, objections to their trade. As Thomas Nashe protested when the first playhouse was reopened on the South Bank in 1592, professional players were not to be confused with the 'pantaloon' and 'courtezans' of the street. Actors provided a distraction for the courtier or lawyer, who 'if there be never a play for him to go to . . . sits melancholy in his chamber, devising upon felony and treason'; but the citizens could rest assured that 'they heartily wish they might be troubled with none of their youth nor their prentices.' So theatre-owners such as Philip Henslowe were careful to obey the ban on 'interludes and plays on the Sabbath', closing their doors on city workers (as James I complained) on the one afternoon when they were officially free. If working men were present to hear the beginning of *Julius Caesar* and stayed despite it, the implication was clear that they had no business to be there. Theatre, they could infer, was now itself a legitimate business with no room for the 'idle'.[5]

The first words uttered on the stage of the Globe can be interpreted, then, as a manoeuvre in the campaign to legitimise the Shakespearean stage and dissociate it from the subversiveness of London's artisanal subculture. As historians such as Peter Burke have demonstrated, revelry and rebellion were entangled in Renaissance popular entertainments, and it was no coincidence that insurrections such as the Peasants' Revolts of 1381 and 1450, the Evil May Day riot of 1517, or Kett's Rebellion of 1549 should have been sparked off at seasonal plays or have had vivid carnivalesque scenarios. The juridical function of folk drama had been to cement the social ties and obligations of an agrarian community, and when these were threatened in the transition to capitalist economic relations, it was through the 'rough music' of folk customs – charivaris, mummings, mocking rhymes and wakes – that the new masters were called to ritual account. The 'reversible world' of carnival, with its travesty and inversion, was a standing *pretext* for protest; but if, as happened increasingly in early modern Europe, rulers chose to ignore the 'wild justice' of festivity, there could be what Burke calls a sudden 'switching of codes, from the language of ritual to the language of rebellion', when 'the wine barrel blew its top.'[6] This is what happened spectacularly in the bloody Carnival at Romans in 1580, and it was also what occurred less explosively in London during the crisis years of the 1590s, when hunger and unemployment drove 'disorderly people of the common sort' (in the Aldermanic phrase) 'to assemble themselves and make matches for their lewd ungodly pratices' at Shrovetide, May Day or Midsummer: festivals when, like the workers in *Julius Caesar*, they could still 'cull out a holiday' from the industrial working week. Associating all revels with rebellion, the City Fathers were instinctively sure that riotous 'apprentices and servants drew their infection' from the playhouses where people caught the plague; but, as Nashe insisted, this analogy was a kind of category mistake, which miscalculated the new theatre's ideological function. If the playhouse was, as coroners reported, the site of 'frays and bloodshed', it was as the target, rather than the source, of violence, as when apprentices traditionally rampaged on Shrove Tuesday to 'put play houses to the sack and bawdy houses to the spoil' (in 1617 wrecking the Cockpit Theatre, with the loss of several lives). The rough music of charivari was hollered in anger from outside the playhouse walls.[7]

'The disorders of the 1590s were the most serious to menace the metropolis in the decades leading up to the Civil War', writes the urban historian Peter Clark, and what concerns him is how this unprecedented metropolitan crisis was contained.[8] The answer must lie at least partly in the success with which the language of carnival as a discourse of legitimation was requisitioned by the commercial players and then tamed. For as scenes like the opening of *Julius Caesar* remind us, and as history, in Foucault's words, 'constantly teaches us, discourse is not simply that which translates struggles or systems of domination, but *is* the thing for which struggle takes place'.[9] It was no mere evasion of authority, therefore, which led the players to situate their theatres on the southern bank of the Thames, where Platter and his party rowed to unbrace and recreate themselves after lunch. In the complex zoning of the metropolis that dates precisely from this time, Southwark was to occupy the position of a policed and segregated annex to the business and residential quarters on the river's northern side. Within its archaic Liberties, the Bankside was to have the status of a permanent but circumscribed carnival in the city's libidinous economy, a disposal valve in its regulation of productivity and waste. Suspect and sinistral, until the final suppression of Hogarth's Southwark Fair in 1762, the South Bank was to function as the unconscious of the capital of Trade. Nor, in this topography of desire, was it accidental that the Globe was built on ground vacated by the monasteries beside those very institutions that, in Foucault's analysis, shaped the discourses of modern subjectivity. Ringed not only by brothels, but by reconstructed prisons such as the Marshalsea and the Clink, and flanked by newly refounded hospitals such as St Thomas's, the playhouse meshed with a chain of buildings charged with those dividing practices whereby the productive subject was defined by separation from its negative in the sick, the mad, the aged, the criminal, the bankrupt, the sexually delinquent, the indigent and the unemployed: isolated, as Flavius urges and the 1569 Charter of St Thomas's decreed, from 'all Idle, Begging people'.[10] The wooden operating theatre of St. Thomas's survives today as the celebrated arena where the early modern body was cut into its diseased and healthy parts. The 'wooden O' of the Globe next door, which must have resembled it in design so much, operated in analogous ways on the body politic to divide and section the visceral language of carnival, severing productive revelry (or art) from the idleness and infection of rebellion.

'Run to your houses, fall upon your knees, / Pray to the gods to intermit the plague . . .. Draw them to Tiber banks, and weep your tears / Into the channel' (I, i, 53–9): the command of the City Fathers to the commons to pray for deliverance from plague is too close to the rhetoric of the Aldermen and the topography of the Bankside to be accidental, and is clearly a signal at the inauguration of the house of the earnestness with which the management takes the anxieties of its opponents. For if Thomas Platter was a naive theatre critic, as a sociologist he was shrewder when he reported that 'England is the servants' prison, because their masters and mistresses are so severe.' The foreign observer could see what has been confirmed in detail by Lee Beier in his study of masterless men and the vagrancy problem in Shakespearean society, that the public order system which Foucault dated from the foundation of the Paris General Hospital in 1656, was in fact already established in London by 1599.[11] It was a system based, however, less on the crude severity and interdiction of the Tribunes than on the strategy of self-regimentation and surveillance which Brutus proposes as a model for his politics, when he argues for a controlled and strictly rational rebellion:

And let our hearts, as subtle masters do,
Stir up their servants to an act of rage,
And after seem to chide 'em. This shall make
Our purpose necessary, and not envious.
(II, i, 175–8)

The Shakespearean text belongs to a historical moment when a revolutionary bourgeois politics has not yet naturalised its own repressive procedures, and Brutus's Machiavellian *realpolitik* is a complete statement of the technique of the modern state whereby subversion is produced in both consciousness and society to legitimise the order that subjects it. Unruly passions and apprentices are both checked by a regime that contrives to 'Stir up the . . . youth to merriments' the better to invigilate it (*A Midsummer Night's Dream*, I, i, 12); as Hal also demonstrates in his career as *agent provocateur* in Eastcheap. This is a system of discipline whose subtlety, as Brutus recognises, depends not on how it obstructs, but on how it generates desire, so that sexual transgression, for example, will no longer be so much the forbidden, as the very ground through which power manipulates the individual and the community. And it is just this 'subtle, calculated technology of subjection', as analysed by Foucault, operating through the new factories, schools, almshouses and hospitals of Elizabethan London, which surely explains why Bakhtin says so little in his work about either Shakespearean drama or English culture. His theories were most strenuously applied to Elizabethan theatre by Michael Bristol in his attempt to trace the 'carnivalisation' of Shakespearean literature from 'below'; but the argument was not convincing because, as Umberto Eco has remarked, what Bakhtinians crucially forget in their idealisation of the people's carnival is not just the suffering of the Jews and other scapegoats pelted by the revellers, but the revenge of Lent: the confinement, that is to say, of desire within the dialectic of subversion and containment. If carnival were always so emancipatory, Eco adds, 'it would be impossible to explain why power uses circuses.' For, as Nashe boasted, 'any politician' understood the truth of what the actor told the emperor: 'It is good for thee, O Caesar, that the people's heads are troubled about us and our light matters; for otherwise they would look into thee and thy matters.'[12]

When the Privy Council had endorsed the Aldermen's petition in 1597 for the 'final suppression of stage plays', the actors had lodged their 'only suit' – for royal incorporation – through the mouth of Jacques: 'I must have liberty, / Withal, as large a charter as the wind, / To blow on whom I please, for so fools have.' The satirist is 'ambitious for a motley coat' to license him to 'Cleanse the foul body' of the 'infected' City with laughter; but the appeal for a royal livery exposes the ambivalence of Elizabethan theatre, a 'medicine' for contagion, as the Duke retorts, which might prove worse than the disease (*As You Like It*, II, vii, 43–69). This is, of course, the dualism on which all Western culture pivots, in Derrida's thesis, where opposites are locked in a double-bind such as Plato's analogous prescription for social ills of the *pharmakon*: the poison that cures. And the awareness that theatre occupies the marginal position in the social body of the *pharmakos* or scapegoat, in a place where, as the Friar warns the delinquent Romeo, 'Poison hath residence, and medicine power', because 'Two opposed kings encamp them' there (*Romeo and Juliet*, II, iii, 10–14), explains the ambiguity of its status in Western morality since ancient Greece, teetering, the watch committees charge, between liberty and libertinism, or licentiousness and licence. For, as Stephen Mullaney observes of Shakespeare's Bankside, the contradictions of a licensed liberty are not merely semantic:

Like the word, licensing is ambidextrous. A license is a token of the agent who grants it, and an emblem of authority. Once issued, however, a license leaves the control as well as the hands of the licensing agent. With a license one can take liberties; issuing a license is an assertion of authority and a declaration of its limits.[13]

It is the irreducible ambiguity of 'liberty' that accounts, then, for critical debate over Renaissance carnival, and which shapes the scenario when Shakespearean characters proclaim 'Freedom, high-day! High-day, freedom!' (*The Tempest*, II, ii, 182). And in *Julius Caesar* it is a dialectic the Romans experience to their cost, when the freedom they release cancels the liberty they license.

In Shakespearean culture it is understood that 'There is no slander in an allowed fool' (*Twelfth Night*, I, v, 88); but the limits of that freedom are quickly tested in *Julius Caesar* when the Tribunes deny the right of Caesar to license the Cobblers' fooling: 'Wherefore rejoice? What conquest brings he home?' (I, i, 32–3). If this shoemaker's obscene 'cobblers' is deconstructive 'language on holiday', as Wittgenstein termed all figurative equivocation,[14] its inversion of civic decorum is subject to sharp correction. An instant lesson of Shakespearean tragedy, then, is that in a metropolis like Rome or London festive laughter is never unbridled or spontaneous. Like the cobbler–hero of the play produced in the same season as *Julius Caesar* by the rival Rose theatre, Thomas Dekker's *The Shoemaker's Holiday*, this 'saucy fellow' (I, i, 18) thinks his belly-laughter is licensed by the powers that be, since 'we make holiday to see Caesar', he explains, 'and to rejoice in his triumph' (30–1). And in Dekker's wishful-thinking comedy the City gentleman is indeed seen off to the shoemakers' chant of 'clubs for prentices!', as Simon Eyre, who has risen by cobbling to be Lord Mayor, has 'procured that upon every Shrove Tuesday, at the sound of the pancake bell, my fine dapper lads shall clap up their shop windows and away' (*The Shoemaker's Holiday*, scene 17, 45–51).[15] Dekker's cockney carnival is one that 'affirms the roots of drama in holiday celebration and brings the community together';[16] and its morris-dancing craftsmen are free to make merry because the king himself indulges Eyre's laboured humour that he is 'nobly born, being the sole son of a shoemaker' (7, 46), and personally ensures that on pancake day His Madness is not 'dashed clean out of countenance' by reality (19, 12). For though Dekker ends his comedy with troops marching off from 'sports and banqueting' to war (21, 193), his vision of Merrie England is never darkened by political analysis. By a contrast that is surely calculated, *Julius Caesar* opens where *The Shoemaker's Holiday* closes, with the return of an army from a hollow victory, to dampen populist enthusiasm, and call in question what Dekker never queries: the motives of the licensing authorities who indulge the plebs with cakes and ale.

The material conditions of modern subjectivity are inscribed within the

Shakespearean text. Thus, when Portia tries to persuade her husband
Brutus to share 'the secrets of [his] heart' by divulging the details of the
conspiracy against Caesar, which she diagnoses as some 'sick offence
within your mind', she confronts him with a sociological map of the
modern psyche: 'Dwell I but in the suburbs / Of your good pleasure? If it
be no more, / Portia is Brutus' harlot' (ii, i, 268–306). 'Let us suppose that
Rome is not a human habitation, but a psychical entity', Freud would
likewise conjecture, adapting the humanist model of the city of the mind
to the 'unreal' conurbations of modernity, which 'love to hide under clean
busy streets and elegant promenades, the subterranean canals in which
the filth of sewers is drained away and where the whole sexual life of the
young is supposed to take place invisibly, hidden from the moralistic
surface of society'.[17] Thus, pleasure, proletariat, prostitution and the pox
are marginalised together through the bourgeois civilising process, which
commences in a city such as London, as Stow's *Survey* begins, precisely at
the moment when the ancient water-course is 'vaulted over with brick,
and paved level with the lanes and streets where through it passed, so that
houses [are] built thereon, and the course is hidden underground and
thereby hardly known'.[18] Body, language and thought are all held in
subjection by this civic order, where, if woman is man's treacherous other
'half', the householder disciplines his body by confining the female within
a *cordon sanitaire* of guilty secrecy.[19] Brutus's decision to confide in
Portia may conform to the Puritan institution of companionate marriage
as it was developing in Elizabethan London, then, but by succumbing to
blackmail and allowing her indiscretion he destroys them both, as surely
as if he had infected his wife with syphilis, by failing to quarantine desire
in the 'suburbs' of the self, where it should have been confined, like the
brothels (and theatres) of the Bankside.

   In *Julius Caesar*, carnival, the symbolic economy of desire and the
flesh, is a discourse that is always mastered by the dominant. Thus, the
opening scenes take place on the Roman 'feast of Lupercal' – when, as
Brutus records, a slave dressed in wolfskin would be licensed to 'revolt'
and afterwards killed – which took place on 14 February, St Valentine's
Day and the approximate date of Mardi Gras. So, Shakespeare's
revelling artisans connect directly with those 'bands of prentices, 3,000 or
4,000 strong, who, on Shrove Tuesday do outrages in all directions,
especially in the suburbs', in contemporary accounts, and whose
'Kingdoms' and 'Abbeys of Misrule' have been researched, in their
European contexts, by Natalie Zemon Davis.[20] In the play their folk
customs have been appropriated, however, by Caesar to legitimate his
intended coronation. Antony therefore runs in the 'holy chase' to 'touch'
Calphurnia for fertility alongside the city's young butchers (i, ii, 7–8),
while Caesar himself performs in the Shroving game by pretending to give

'the rabblement' the freedom that it shouts for. This would be the tactic of King James's *Book of Sports* (1618), of royalist propagandists such as Herrick, and ultimately of the Restoration, when (contrary to Bakhtin) the customs of 'May-poles, Hock-carts, Wassails, Wakes' would be harnessed to a programme of social conservatism. It belongs to the repertoire of what Hill calls synthetic monarchy: the invented tradition of Elizabeth's Accession Day or the Stuart cult of the Royal Touch as a cure for tuberculosis. And by this cooption of seasonal festivity Caesar turns politics into theatre as 'the tag-rag people . . . clap and hiss him, according as he pleas'd and displeas'd them, as they use to do the players' (I, ii, 255). He is their Carnival King, a Lord of Misrule who governs by exploiting his subjects' desires with his 'foolery' (232), manipulating 'fat, / Sleek-headed men' (190), as he indulges Antony in plays and music when he 'revels long a-nights' (II, ii, 116). Provoking them 'to sports, to wildness, and much company' (II, i, 189), Caesar is the master of ceremonies who knows that 'danger' belongs only to the 'lean and hungry' who can discipline the body to their purposes (I, ii, 193). So his Roman carnival becomes a model of authoritarian populism, the true regimen of bread and circuses.[21]

According to Anne Barton, the theatre image in *Julius Caesar* is uniquely positive and 'the actors are no longer shadowy figures: they are the creators of history.'[22] This may be true, but it oversimplifies the Saturnalian process that the play rehearses whereby discourses, which are the means of struggle, are themselves shaped by that struggle as it unfolds. It does so in Shakespearean Rome like carnival itself, as a masquerade in which successive ideologies which had seemed to be authoritative are 'discovered' and discarded as power is displaced. On Mardi Gras the aim is to see without being seen behind the carnival mask; and here too the eye of power strips the mask of rhetoric from its opponent, revealing – as Cassius demonstrates with his satirical pas-quinades 'wherein Caesar's ambition [is] glanced at' – the brutal drives that discursive practices hide. Thus, the plebeians who are masterless men in their holiday guise are exposed as Caesar's 'idle creatures' by the Tribunes' Puritan rhetoric, which is itself abruptly 'put to silence' when they 'pull the scarfs' from Caesar's statues (I, ii, 282). That demystifica-tion will be completed by the knives of the aristocratic faction, whose mask of republicanism – with its common-law reverence for the ancestral constitution and contempt for the absolutist 'yoke' (60; I, iii, 84) – is worn 'as our Roman actors do' (II, i, 226), until Antony seizes the stage in turn and reveals the carnivorous butchery their Lenten obsequies conceal. This is the radical potential of Shakespearean tragedy that Jonathan Dollimore and others would mobilise as a critical weapon: the revelry with which one discourse decodes the other, as Antony deconstructs the

discursivity of the 'honourable men' (III, ii, 120–230). With 'their hats
pluck'd about their ears, / And half their faces buried in their cloaks' (II, i,
73–4), or masked by handkerchiefs (II, i, 315), the plotters who meet in
'Pompey's theatre' (I, iii, 152) assume the anonymity of carnival and
arrogate its dispensation to kill a scapegoat, just as the real conspirators
of the Dutch Revolt had started their putsch against the Spanish governor
at carnival in 1563, dressed in motley and jesters' caps and bells. In the
Renaissance, as Stephen Greenblatt notes, 'theatricality is one of power's
essential modes'; so when their antic disposition is ripped from these
gamesmen, it is fittingly by the theatricality of a champion 'masker and
a reveller' (v, i, 62). 'A masque is treason's licence' in Jacobean drama, but
the logic of this revelry will be to strip away the 'veil'd look' (I, ii, 360) of
'all true rites and ceremonies' (III, i, 241) to expose the naked will to
power.[23]

The bloody Carnival at Romans in 1580 described by Emmanuel Le
Roy Ladurie provides a paradigm of Renaissance festival as a
'psychological drama or ballet' whose players acted out class struggle
through the 'symbolic grammar' of processions and masquerades. There
the events 'began as a popular revolution and ended as an Elizabethan
tragedy in the bright colours of the Renaissance', when the poor, led by
their champion athlete, a 'coarse and clownish' craftsman known as
Paumier ('Handballer'), had mimed a mock funeral of the rich whose
flesh they pretended to eat on Mardi Gras, until the law-and-order party
had plotted a massacre in retaliation, arrayed for the ambush in the hoods
and dominoes of a torchlit harlequinade. Every episode of this coup and
counter-coup corresponded to a stage in the Shrovetide games, and the
victims went to their deaths as if 'stuck like pigs' by fate.[24] The Roman
carnival in *Julius Caesar* follows a similar itinerary through the
cannibalistic feast of Caesar's assassination and the mock trial of the
conspirators at the funeral, to the revanchist repression of Lent. In
Shakespearean Rome, as in the American South of the Ku Klux Klan, or
the Britanny of the counter-Revolutionary Chouans, the regalia of flaming
torch, hooded mask and noose is an ensemble whose social meaning will
be dictated by the strongest. Likewise, poems, plays, letters, music,
names, dreams, prophecies, clouds, stars and flights of birds are all
discredited as 'idle ceremonies' in *Julius Caesar* (II, i, 197), the random
signifiers on which power enforces meaning. This is a deconstructive
carnival that leads ineluctably to the burlesque textuality of Caesar's
bloodstained 'vesture' as interpreted by Antony through its gaps and
'wounded' tears, and finally, when the corpse is divested of even that last
tattered mask, to the revelation of Caesar's 'will': the testament which is
also, by etymological extension with his 'bleeding piece of earth' (III, ii,
130–60), the signifier of all desire.

At its core, *Julius Caesar* is a play about writing and reading, and its climactic scene is a Shakespearean version of that staple of bourgeois fiction, the discovery and announcement of the deceased's last will and testament. The will, historians demonstrate, was the legal mainstay of England's capitalist revolution and the textual means by which Tudor landowners tightened their grip on property and institutions. Shakespeare took the details of Caesar's will from Plutarch, but by transferring the scene of its reading from the Senate House to the Forum, spotlit its significance as the instrument of discursive power. By Elizabethan standards, however, what would be notable about Caesar's testament would be its charitable legacies, since there was a sharp decline in donation to the poor after the 1540 Act of Wills had entrenched family inheritance. Caesar is similar, then, to those heirless magnates who perpetuated pre-Reformation custom in Tudor London with bequests to charity; and Antony emphasises the anachronism with his prediction that if the Citizens heard the document read, 'they would go and kiss dead Caesar's wounds, / And dip their napkins in his sacred blood, / Yea, beg a hair of him for memory': like old-style Catholics (III, ii, 133–5). Even in death this donor is a scandal to the city's Tribunes; but what matters, for Antony, is that his estate is distributed, rather than consolidated. Diffusion of Caesar's inheritance, an ever-widening circle of benefaction as property descends to his adopted heirs, provides a frame for his executor's dispersal of monological truth. Like the play-within-the-play or the mirror in Renaissance art, this will is a meta-textual key to the semantics of *Julius Caesar*: a representation of representation. Thus, Antony envisages Caesar's hairs scattered like some saint's, so everything once proper to the man will be diffracted; and the sacramental image is a metonym for the diaspora of language and intertextuality of writing as it circulates among the legatees, who 'dying,' will 'mention it in their wills, / Bequeathing it as a rich legacy, / Unto their issue' (III, ii, 136–8).

''Tis good you know not that you are his heirs' (147): beyond his authorial intention, (the bald) Caesar will have more heirs than hairs to leave them, and the linguistic legerdemain, which starts from Antony's wilful wordplay on the word 'will' itself (126), is the 'liberty, freedom and enfranchisement' (III, i, 81) from univocal meaning which is textual revolution. Such Derridean dissemination follows from Antony's erotics of writing, which are, as his wanton way with words suggests, literally a matter of *will power*. Caesar will engender the issue denied him in his sterile marriage and abortive reign by posthumously gratifying the Romans with his written testament, and Shakespeare's personal pun and signature releases the phallocentric implications inherent in the Western conception of writing. To make sense, in this authorial tradition, is to *testify* as a virile man; and the scene excites these connotations by repeating the word 'will' twenty-seven times in thirty lines, through all its libidinous referents of desire, intention and compulsion, as Antony stimulates the Crowd to merge its 'will' with Caesar's, until it cries orgasmically: 'The will, the will! We will hear Caesar's will!' (III, ii, 140). Antony's effeminisation of the Romans thus startlingly prefigures the psychoanalytic hypothesis that would read the phallus as a transcendental signifier which invests all its substitutes, beginning with the pen, with meaning. As the incarnation of the *libido dominandi*, Caesar's 'will' represents his usurpation of the West's symbolic order, but being itself only a signifier it can no more be substantiated than his signature can finalise proof of intention. So the pleasure of this text is, quite literally, a kind of hermeneutic striptease, since after the chief mourner has tantalised the Plebeians into compliance that they 'will compel' him 'to read the will', and even promised to lift the final veil and 'show you him that made the will', (158–60), a climax is deferred with yet another text. Caesar's 'vesture', interpreted by Antony as an epic narrative, interposes itself between the people and their satisfaction, as meaning eludes expression and presence is for ever delayed with supplementary writing:

> Antony: If you have tears, prepare to shed them now.
>   You all do know this mantle, I remember
>   The first time ever Caesar put it on;
>   'Twas on a summer's evening in his tent,
>   That day he overcame the Nervii . . .
>   (III, ii, 170–4)

Where there's a will, in the phallogocentric text of William Shakespeare, there is always a way for power to make its own, which it does by feigning that its 'Will will fulfil' desire, 'Ay, fill it full with wills' (*Sonnet 136*). For though the people enter chanting, 'We will be satisfied: let us be satisfied' (III, ii, 1), plenitude – the satisfaction of 'what you will' – is for ever referred, the puns insinuate, to other kinds of 'will', as one textual signifier displaces another. In the Forum, therefore, the story Antony reads from Caesar's toga typifies all writing, in its evasion of the Crowd's desires. It illustrates the Derridean proposition that 'the meaning of meaning is infinite implication, the indefinite referral of signifier to signifier . . . which gives meaning no respite, no rest, but engages in its own economy so that it always signifies again.'[25] As grotesque as a Metaphysical poem on Christ's winding-sheet, Antony's exposition textualises the cloak to open up its rips to his own meaning: 'Look, in this place ran Cassius' dagger through; / See what a rent the envious Casca made; / Through this, the well-beloved Brutus stabb'd . . .'

(175–7). So, if Caesar's robe is the sheet on which his assassins wrote, Antony is a true deconstructionist in unravelling the seams of their rhetorical contradictions: 'For Brutus . . . was Caesar's angel. . . . This was the most unkindest cut of all' (182–4). As he rescripts the part he is given, Antony thereby folds the parliamentarians' rhetoric inside out, throwing history into doubt and plunging meaning into a polysemous riot that is mimicked by the Citizens, to substantiate that at the point where text and body fuse, discourse and power are one. Caesar had offered his murderers wine on the Ides of March. Served up by Antony, his carved flesh becomes, with cannibalistic literalism, the sacrament of a carnival fraternity of blood:

Antony:	Look you here,
	Here he is himself, marred, as you see, with traitors.
First Plebeian:	O piteous spectacle!
Second Plebeian:	O noble Caesar!
Third Plebeian:	O woeful day!
Fourth Plebeian:	O traitors! villains!
First Plebeian:	O most bloody sight!
Second Plebeian:	We will be revenged.
All:	Revenge! About! Seek! Burn! Fire! Kill! Slay!

(197–205)

If the words of the dead are tongued with fire, in Christian hermeneutics, beyond the language of the living, the writing etched in Caesar's flesh is more powerful than any speech, we see, precisely because its meaning exceeds whatever its authors intended. Writing, Antony demonstrates, is language at its most carnivalesque and delinquent, because, in the Derridean phrase, it is orphaned and taken from the supervision of its parent; as the sum of Caesar's codicils, when they are read, is so much greater than their trivial parts:

Antony:	Here is the will, and under Caesar's seal.
	To every Roman citizen he gives,
	To every several man, seventy-five drachmas.
Second Plebeian:	Most noble Caesar! We'll revenge his death.
Third Plebeian:	O royal Caesar!
Antony:	Hear me with patience.
All:	Peace, ho!
Antony:	Moreover, he hath left you all his walks,
	His private arbours, and new-planted orchards,
	On this side Tiber; he hath left them you,

And to your heirs for ever: common pleasures
To walk abroad and recreate yourselves.
(III, ii, 241–52)

Power cuts its own way in Shakespearean tragedy by appropriating the
radical subversiveness of carnival, and *Julius Caesar* seems to meditate
upon its participation in this process. So, Antony's chicanery as he slips
from text (the will), to culture (the mantle), to body (the historical subject,
Caesar), has the vertiginous effect of presenting everything as a
representation. To this extent, a will signed and sealed like Caesar's merely
exemplifies the irresponsibility of all signs, since no matter how it is
drafted, it can always be rewritten, as Antony very rapidly explains in the
next scene: 'Fetch the will hither, and we shall determine / How to cut off
some charge in legacies' (IV, i, 8–9). Thus, the endowments Caesar
intended for the people fund Antony's war; and the redrafting of the will
instances how every text is vulnerable to a stronger reading, regardless of
authorial intention. Whether or not the testator wrote it as such an
incitement, Antony's cooption and cancellation of Caesar's will triumphs
over Brutus's oratory. So, as it marshals the Crowd to serve its counter-
revolution, and lets 'Mischief' take what course it will (III, ii, 261–2),
Caesarism works through a system of provocation and license that exactly
parallels the dividing practices of early modern London. Partitioned in the
suburb on the river's further side, popular desire will henceforth be
instigated and exploited in the interests of the rulers: 'We'll burn the
body. . . . And with the brands fire the traitors' houses. . . . Go fetch fire'
(255–8). By such means the incendiary torches of Shrovetide and
Midsummer would be transformed into the flambeaux of the Lord Mayor's
Show and the bonfires of Hallowe'en stolen to mark Stuart deliverance
from the Gunpowder Plot. Caesar's will offers the British state a blueprint
for the deflection of the *vox populi* towards the institution of monarchy, for
the liberty of the Bankside would indeed provide the conduit through
which power would recreate itself by regulating the 'common pleasures' of
Londoners in the impending age of mass consumption.

On the dais a decomposing corpse lies 'smell(ing) above the earth . . .
groaning for burial' (III, i, 274–5), while the figure of authority
pronounces from 'the public chair' (III, ii, 64) on the meaning of its
lacerations. From the ritual of hieromancy on the day of the assassination, when 'Plucking the entrails of an offering forth', the augurers 'could
not find a heart within the beast' (II, ii, 39–40), to the consignment of the
remains of Brutus to the pyre (v, v, 55), this is a play fixated with meat,
and its affinity with the art of divination is constantly invoked. Prophecy
from entrails may be primitive exegesis, we infer, but its principle extends
to every interpretation: power goes not to those who merely carve the

carcass as 'a dish fit for the gods' (ii, i, 173), but to the one who ascends 'the pulpit' (iii, i, 250) to bid a textual farewell to the flesh: *carne vale*. Carnival, we are reminded, was the season of the anatomy lecture in an age without refrigeration, and the punitive spectacle of a criminal executed and dismembered by officers of the state to objectify a moral lesson is a juridical process that furnishes this *mise-en-scène*.[26] The division of labour between those who knife Caesar's body and the orator who explicates their inscription installs Antony, indeed, in a professorial role. It may be chance that the best preserved Renaissance playhouse is the Anatomy Theatre of 1594 at Padua; but this is a scene that suggests that the Elizabethan stage shared with its rival a fascination with cutting open bodies to observe the hearts or 'spirit of men' within (ii, i, 168). For the corpse exhibited by Antony stands in the same relation to subjectivity as the cadaver in Rembrandt's painting of *The Anatomy Lesson of Dr Tulp*. It is the material 'earth' (iii, i, 254) on which bourgeois ideology will write its meaning, inscribing a discourse of morality and reason on a scene of lust and blood that 'else were a savage spectacle' (223). This is literally how Antony uses the body, when he effaces his presence in the interpellation of the audience as his obedient subjects:

> For I have neither wit, nor words, nor worth,
> Action, nor utterance, nor the power of speech
> To stir men's blood; I only speak right on.
> I tell you that which you yourselves do know,
> Show you sweet Caesar's wounds, poor poor dumb mouths,
> And bid them speak for me.
>
> (iii, ii, 223–8)

Like Tulp's dissection, Antony's anatomy lesson – to be repeated over the body of Brutus – reproduces the spectacular corporeality of carnival in the service of a new disciplinary order, forcing the corpse to signify 'that which you yourselves do know' about what it is to say 'This was a man!' (224; v, v, 75). And as Antony turns desire in the mob to authoritarian ends, this is also the manoeuvre of the Shakespearean text, which reworks the ceremonies of an older ritual – 'to execute, to dismember, to eat' – not simply to erase them but, as Barker observes of Rembrandt's picture, 'to take them over, to appropriate the ancient vengeful motifs and to rearticulate them for its own new purposes.' Text and painting belong to a moment, that is to say, when bourgeois society still has need of the energies of 'the earlier pageant of sacramental violence', and when its 'image fashions an aesthetic which is rationalistic, classical, realistic, but one to which the iconography of a previous mode of representation is not completely alien.' As Barker explains, 'if it continues to evoke the signs of a punitive corporeality', bourgeois representation 'also aims to draw off and reorganise the charge of these potent residues, and to invest them, transformed', in the name of the rational spirit of capitalism, 'which will soon free itself entirely from the old body, even if it trades at first on the mystique and terror of that abandoned materiality.'[27] By syphoning the subversiveness of popular festivity in the representation of a deflected and contained rebellion, the Shakespearean text thus anticipates the counter-revolution of the Cromwellian Commonwealth, and faithfully enacts the tactics of the Roman Lupercalia to 'stir up servants to an act of rage' the better to police them. Located on the threshold of a century of revolutionary upheaval, *Julius Caesar* is the image of bourgeois ascendency as 'necessary, and not envious' (II, i, 178), separated from popular and sectarian movements, and the natural issue of 'a general honest thought' – as Antony orates over the ashes of Brutus – 'and common good to all' (V, v, 71–2).

Julius Caesar is the representation of the seventeenth-century urban world turned upside down to be restored, where citizens' houses are set alight by the mob in order that property values should be upheld. The question it seems to address by this Shroving ritual is the one that would become, according to Christopher Hill, the crucial dilemma of the Commonwealth, posed eventually by a pamphleteer of 1660: 'Can you at once suppress the sectaries and keep out the King?'[28] Because it arises from a historical juncture when the English bourgeoisie was engaged in a reorganisation of the nation-state to effect this end, it is a text that discloses the materiality of power with self-important openness. In particular, this première Globe play reflects candidly on the process whereby hegemony is obtained through the control of discourse, a process in which the inauguration of the playhouse was itself a major intervention. Victory in *Julius Caesar* goes to those who administer and distribute the access to discourse, and the conspirators lose possession of the initiative in the action from the instant they concede Antony permission to 'speak in the order of [the] funeral' (III, i, 230–50). Inserting his demagogy into Brutus's idealistic scenario, Antony disrupts the 'true rites and lawful ceremonies' of the republic to expedite his counter-coup (241), and secures his domination with the populist ploy of Caesar's will. Censorship, Barker notes, was 'a constitutive experience' in the construction of both the bourgeois subject and modern state, and one that predicated the very possibility of bourgeois enunciation.[29] This text proclaims that fact when the Cobbler and Carpenter are banished, the Tribunes silenced, the Soothsayer ignored, Artemidorus spurned and Caesar choked by the breath of the Crowd; and underscores it when Antony 'damns' his enemies 'with a spot' when 'their names are prick'd on his proscription list' (IV, i, 1–10). The murder by the mob of the poet Cinna for his 'bad verses' and mistaken name (III, iii, 30–5) only confirms what Brutus and Cassius learn to their cost: that power goes to those who command the materiality of signs.

'Cicero is dead, / And by that order of proscription' (IV, iii, 178–9): the reign of terror is cruel but decisive in cutting off the cryptic Greek of the great ironist along with his 'silver hairs' (I, ii, 276; II, i, 144). If Caesar falls through being hard of hearing, then Antony's censorship makes him the paragon of a modern prince. As his own spymaster, he sees 'How covert matters may be best discovered' (IV, i, 46), since his intelligence guarantees that whatever his enemies plan, 'I am in their bosoms', he rests assured, 'and I know / Wherefore they do it' (V, i, 7–8). Shakespeare's hermeneutic drama thus conforms to the analysis of European imperialism by the semiotician Tzvetan Todorov, who in his study of *The Conquest of America* finds that the Incas and Aztecs fell victim to the Spanish Conquistadors not because of bullets or disease, but through their inferior system of signification, defeated despite their numbers, by Cortez's capacity to decipher their semiotic conduct whilst baffling them with his own codes.[30] Likewise, the republicans are defeated in *Julius Caesar* when they lose control of signs. Quarrelling over the meaning of their own correspondence and at cross-purposes in their reading of the 'signs of battle' (V, i, 14–24), Brutus and Cassius become deaf even to Homer's textual warning when they hear *The Iliad* read (IV, iii, 129–37), while the words of Caesar that the Romans record when they 'mark him and write his speeches in their books' (I, ii, 125), come back to haunt the assassins at the end in the shape of the Ghost, which appears the instant Brutus finds 'the leaf turn'd down' in his book and opens it to read, presumably, the ultimate avenging text: '*Veni, vidi, vici*' (IV, iii, 251–75). 'Words before blows' (V, i, 27) is the battle-order in this play, which rehearses the English Revolution by enacting the Gramscian doctrine that the iron fist is preceded by the velvet glove, and that power is first enthroned in pulpits, poetry and plays.

Carnival, *Julius Caesar* shows us, was never a single, unitary symbolic system in the Renaissance, but a discourse over which constant struggle was waged by competing social groups. It is the pretence of the Shakespearean text, however, that the masquerade comes to an end in bourgeois realism, as Antony concludes the action when he declares all 'objects, arts, and imitations . . . out of use and stal'd by other men' (IV, i, 37–8), separating the idleness of drama from the productivity of politics. Thus, the rupture forced by holiday in history would be sealed as the English bourgeoisie effaced its revolutionary past. To make this representation of tragic acquiescence possible, however, the playhouse had been made a site of acrid contestation. The triumph of bourgeois

order was achieved only after many interruptions into the Shakespearean
space of festive rout. So to grasp the operation of the new theatre as an
institution of social segregation it is only necessary to recall those
intrusions from outside the building like that which occurred regularly on
Shrove Tuesday, according to reports, when players half-way through an
'excellent tragedy' were 'forc'd to undress and put off their tragic habits'
by the holiday crowd, and made to

> conclude the day with *The Merry Milkmaids*. And unless this were
> done, and the popular humour satisfied (as sometimes it so fortun'd
> that the players were refractory), the benches, tiles, laths, stones,
> oranges, apples, nuts, flew about most liberally; and as there were
> mechanics of all professions there upon these festivals, every one fell
> to his trade and dissolved the house in an instant, and that made the
> ruin of a stately fabric.[31]

The floor of the new playhouse was not yet quite an arena which the
dominant ideology could call its own, and excluded or enclosed, the
Cobbler and the Carpenter still found means on occasion to deconstruct –
or transvalue – the sign system of the imposing 'house with the thatched
roof'.

Chapter Three

Like the old Robin Hood:

As You Like It and the enclosure riots

IN September 1592, while plague and riot gripped London, Queen Elizabeth made a progress into the West Midlands and was welcomed with pageants devised by John Lyly as a prospectus of pastoral England. When she crossed the Thames at Bisham a 'wild man' sprang from the woods to assure 'the Queen of this Island' that in her presence 'my untamed thoughts wax gentle, and I feel in my self civility. . . . Your Majesty on my knees will I followe, bearing this Club, not as a Salvage, but to beat down those that are.'[1] Elizabeth had left London to the rioters' cry of 'Clubs'; now sylvan power was presented as a force of counter-insurgency. Prompted by the civic emergency, Lyly's wodewose brandished a weapon that was a reminder of the violence surrounding Elizabethan pastoralism, and of the urgent need to secure its boundaries. For as the text explained, it was only the Queen's peace that exempted England from the general European crisis: 'By her it is our carts are laden with corn, when in other countries they are filled with harness: our horses are led with a whip, theirs with a lance.'[2] Banished to Oxfordshire as a princess, she had said that nothing would give her greater happiness than to be a milkmaid of Woodstock, and forty years later her itinerary was restorative. 'Your Highness is come into uneven country', she was therefore reassured as she entered the Cotswolds, 'but healthy and harmless, where a black sheep is a perilous beast', and there were 'no monsters'.[3] Yet when its climax came on 28 September at Rycote – the fortified mansion of her erstwhile companion-in-exile, Lady Norris – the progress ended with the precautionary presentation of an arsenal of arms to Gloriana, for as the 'Old Soldier' and Lord Lieutenant, Lord Norris, swore, Midlanders would show loyalty 'by deeds', if necessary, 'and make it good with our lives . . . what words cannot effect, my sword shall.'[4]

The 1592 progress was riven with the anxiety of its occasion, so though the Queen was saluted as one 'by whom shepherds have their

flocks in safety, and their own lives, and all the country quietness', Pan
was made to pledge her that 'During your abode, no theft shall be in
the woods: in the field no noise: in the valleys no spies, my self will
keep all safe.'[5] Ringed by foes, the security of even the Elizabethan
heartland would depend, it seemed, on a net of paid informers. In
Lyly's play, therefore, pastoral discourse is troubled with rumours,
voiced by foresters like Pan, of sylvan outlawry. If Elizabethan
pastoralism was keyed, as Louis Montrose suggests, to the hegemony
of England's sheepfarming gentry,[6] by 1592 its imaginative ecology.
could not ignore the resistance to enclosure of woodland commoners
and squatters. That the forest had become problematic was signalled
that year with John Manwood's treatise *Of the Laws of the Forest*,
which decried the fact that 'the greatest part of them are spoiled and
decayed' from an absolutist perspective, seeing enclosure as a cir-
cumscription of prerogative.[7] A site of sanctuary, the forest was the
frontier between common law and feudal rights such as pasturage; so it
was destined to be a battleground between the regulated and market
economies, with their warring concepts of legality. Though John
Aubrey supposed that because of the decay of 'petty manors', the
'mean people' of the woods 'live lawless, nobody to govern them', they
in fact had an archaic court of 'Justices in Eyre', whose forest law
theoretically safeguarded the rights of both royal hunter and grazing
commoner. But the forest remained symbolically outside capitalist
order, a concrete sign of communal justice and resistance, never more
challenging to the state than at this moment when the English
woodlands of the Middle Ages were ceasing to exist in reality.[8] When
the Queen journeyed into the Midlands, therefore, it was the
allegiance of foresters that her hosts dramatised, but the woods beyond
Rycote towards which they looked with apprehension.

The wariness of Elizabeth's reception was to be justified in the dearth
of 1596, when 'a great company' converged on Rycote at Michaelmas to
petition Lord Norris for relief, threatening that 'if they could not have
remedy, they would seek remedy themselves, and cast down hedges and
ditches, and knock down gentlemen.'[9] Repeatedly pressed to intervene
'for relief for corn, and for putting down of enclosures', the Lord
Lieutenant did nothing, and it was one of his own servants, named
Bartholemew Steer, who incited rebellion. During the autumn, at fairs
across the Midlands, Steer recruited for 'a rising of the people', preaching
'that he hoped before long to see some ditches thrown down, and it would
never be merry till some of the gentlemen were knocked down, but there
be lusty fellows abroad and we shall have a merrier world shortly.'[10]
Lyly's play had depicted shepherds crowning 'Kings and Queens to make
mirth' at their September sheepshearing, and it was festive culture that

gave the rebels a web of contacts and a politics of Cockaigne, when they heard how 'The poor did once rise in Spain and cut down gentlemen and since that time have lived merrily.'[11] The nucleus of the rising consisted of servants, who were reputed to be 'so kept like dogs they were ready to cut their masters' throats', and its targets were houses of enclosing gentry such as Elizabeth's favourite, Sir Henry Lee of Woodstock. Steer planned a people's progress eastwards to Rycote, where the arms would be seized for a march on London, in expectation that 'when the prentices hear that we be up, they will come and join with us.'[12] Sacked in 1549, Rycote had a history of depopulation and emparkment, its owners, according to the imperial ambassador, being 'loathed by the people'. To storm it the rebels would assemble in the woods on Enslow Hill, an ancient 'Speech Hill' and the forest camp of the insurgents who had been 'hanged like dogs' a generation earlier. The date fixed for the rising was 17 November: Elizabeth's accession day. The 'merry world' of popular action would drive out the hard world of the encloser.[13]

In his study of the rising, John Walter describes the establishment's panic as the years of dearth threatened an English version of continental disorders. Burghley's intelligence was that 1596 'will be the hardest year for the poor in man's memory'; his agents foresaw a repetition of Kett's rebellion, and Justices of the Peace amassed warnings that 'before the year went about there would be cutting of throats' as 'Necessity hath no law.' The government responded by attempting to reactivate feudal obligation. On 2 November a royal proclamation condemned 'rich owners of corn who keep their store from markets to increase prices', and commanded 'good householders' to reside on their estates 'in charitable sort to keep hospitality'. At this moment news of a new Spanish Armada raised the stakes incalculably for the regime, which mobilised 'the lieutenants of every shire' for 'the necessary defence of the realm'.[14] Though his wife remained in London, Lord Norris returned to Rycote. And it was in this period of the sharpest social conflict of the Elizabethan era that another West Midlander – routinely familiar with the terrain – dramatised agrarian conflict in *As You Like It*. Since Montrose tied its form to early modern family politics, it has been impossible to read this comedy as, in Helen Gardner's phrase, 'free of time' or place and transhistorical.[15] Its resemblance to *King Lear* has long been noticed; but it is within the context of the subsistence crisis of the 1590s that its violent plot and implausibly romantic ending have their material meaning. No Shakespearean text transmits more urgently the imminence of the social breakdown threatened by the conjuncture of famine and enclosure. Though Shakespeare had alluded to the contemporary crisis in *A Midsummer Night's Dream*, where 'The ploughman lost his sweat, and the green corn / Hath rotted ere his youth attained a beard' (II, i, 94–5), it *is in As You Like It* that the dire implications of the dearth are brought home immediately to Warwickshire and Stratford.

Idealist critics imagine that '*As You Like It* derives classical stability and poise from the fact that its plot barely exists',[16] but the play is powerfully inflected by narratives of popular resistance, whilst its plot, as Montrose points out, is the brutal story of Elizabethan social transformation. This comedy confounds its own title with a setting of 'winter and rough weather' (II, v, 8) to frame the harshness of its social climate. 'I pray thee Rosalind', pleads Celia in her opening line, 'be merry' (I, ii, 1); but the 'holiday humour' (IV, i, 65) of customary culture is disintegrating in *As You Like It* under the stress of social mobility and competition. Rosalind retorts with a significant metaphor of aristocratic insolvency: 'I show more mirth than I am mistress of, and would you yet I were merrier?' (I, ii, 2–3). The only way she can be 'merry', she objects, will be to forget her father's fall from power and the discrepancy between inherited status and material success, 'the lineaments of Nature' and Fortune's 'gifts'. So, the social reality of this fiction is one where, by feudal standards, Fortune's 'benefits are mightily misplaced' (30–45), and Duke Frederick's usurpation typifies a 'working day world' of struggle (I, iii, 12); as the Midland economy was epitomised in the 1590s by a vicious property feud between Lord Norris and his kinsman, the Earl of Lincoln.[17] 'Care not for work', Barthomew Steer had exhorted his 'good fellows', 'for we shall have a merrier world shortly'; and the 'merry gentlemen' who sing in the snow of Shakespeare's yuletide (I, i, 115–17) agree that 'the winter wind / . . . [is] not so unkind / As man's ingratitude,' the 'bitter sky, / . . . dost not bite so nigh / As benefits forgot' (II, vii, 174–93). If this is 'Merrie England', the 'merry note' of these carols is 'ragged' from the start (II, v, 3, 14), like the 'merry note' of the owl that gives *Love's Labour's Lost* its chilling close. Here the proverbial lore that 'it was never merry world in England since gentlemen came up' (*Henry VI, Part 2*, IV, ii, 8–9) is intensified by Elizabethan hunger, enmity and dispossession:

> Who doth ambition shun,
>   And loves to lie i'th'sun,
> Seeking the food he eats,
>   And pleas'd with what he gets,
> Come hither, come hither, come hither,
>   Here shall he see no enemy,
> But winter and rough weather.
>   (II, v, 35–41)

The 1590s were years in which Stratford-upon-Avon endured a series of calamitous fires, plagues and famines, culminating in the dearth of 1596–7, and the resulting social conflict sears the text of Shakespeare's pastoral comedy. 'My brother . . . keeps me rustically . . . or . . . stays me here . . . unkept; for call you that keeping . . . that differs not from the stalling of an ox? His horses are bred better . . . but I, his brother, gain nothing under him but growth, for the which his animals on his dunghills are as much bound to him as I': the first words of the play plunge the action into the bitter contradictions of England's agricultural revolution. Orlando must feed his brother's hogs 'and eat husks with them', or be 'naught' on his land (I, i, 35–6) ; the servant Adam will be thrown out like an 'old dog' (81). The recurring situation of Shakespearean tragedy here has determinants that would be recognisable to Bartholemew Steer, as the language is his own: the break-up of the feudal household and extended family through the capitalisation of English farming. Oliver's farm, with its mixed plough-teams and manure, is typical of the intensive cultivation of the Midland Plain, where Eric Kerridge notes seed yield doubled to a ratio of 20:1 after introduction of convertible husbandry during Shakespeare's lifetime. And Oliver's commercial discourse, which will be heard again in the diatribes of the grain-hoarding Coriolanus, is that of an improving landowner of so-called Chalk, as opposed to Cheese country, where, as David Underdown explains, nucleated villages, a strong squirearchy and the rhythm of sheep-corn agriculture produced an ordered deference society.[18] 'And what wilt thou do?' Oliver jeers, when Orlando claims his 'poor allottery' of a thousand crowns, 'Beg when that is spent? Well, sir, get you in. I will not long be troubled with you' (75–7). Oliver's is the Elizabethan success story of the rise of gentry by engrossing and enclosure at the expense of evicted relatives and tenants. The text locates his power on the cutting-edge of agrarian change, as it exposes the danger to the social order he provokes, with Orlando's savage reaction: 'Wert thou not my brother, I would not take this hand from thy throat till this other had pulled out thy tongue' (59–61). In 1607 the Midland counties would indeed erupt in enclosure riots: Orlando's rhetoric of violence would be realised then by England's earliest Levellers.

From its beginning, then, when Oliver 'bars' Orlando from 'the place of brother' to 'feed [him] with his hinds' (18), and Duke Frederick banishes Rosalind from a zone 'So near our court as twenty miles' (I, iii, 40), *As You Like It* is a drama of enclosure and exclusion. So, when Orlando exclaims that 'The spirit of my father . . . begins to mutiny' (*I*, i, 21–2) at his disinheritance, his appeal to ancestry ties him to seigneurial tradition, and it is customary culture that provides his pretext for revolt, as it gave Steer and his companions theirs. The opening of *As You Like It* follows other comedies in presenting popular games as contests between

rival groups that might be subject to political manipulation, when the new
Duke exploits carnival, like Theseus, to 'Stir up the youth . . . to
merriments' to legitimate his succession (*A Midsummer Night's Dream*, I,
i, 12), and Oliver fixes the Christmas wrestling to break his brother's neck
(145). Yet 'breaking of ribs' in games of ritual violence might have
unexpected results (I, ii, 128). Seasonal sports were a safety-valve for
rural and artisanal violence, but they offered cover for the protests of the
'lusty guts' whom Stubbes said led the 'wildheads of the parish', like the
gang who cut down the pales of Windsor Park to hunt the deer in 1607,
'under colour of playing football'.[19] So here, the champion Orlando
becomes 'a gamester . . . of all sorts enchantingly beloved', a local hero
too much 'in the heart of the world' to be outfaced (*As You Like It*, I, i,
162–6). To complete the agricultural clearance, therefore, Oliver will
burn down the upstart's cottage with him in it, or drive him off the
land. In this way the Shakespearean text is unequivocal about the
realities of enclosure: depopulation, arson and, as Adam says,
'butchery' of those who dare resist (II, iii, 22–7). It knows commercial
farming will thrust the destitute into vagrancy and crime. Orlando will
become the bogeyman of the Elizabethan rich. He will be a 'masterless
man', a vagabond or beggar. Or he will become a highwayman, the
lawless 'wild man' of the woods, perhaps 'a pick-purse' or 'a horse-
stealer' (III, iv, 21):

> What, would you have me go and beg my food,
> Or with a base and boist'rous sword enforce
> A thievish living on the common road?
> This I must do, or know not what to do
>   (II, iii, 31–4)

Interrogating the Oxfordshire rebels, Sir Edward Coke was determined to discover 'what gentlemen you do know that do favour the
Comunality and that would after you had been up have taken your
parts?'[20] Gentry leadership had been a backbone of revolts like Kett's,
and remained crucial in the folklore of resistance. Thus, in *The Two
Gentlemen of Verona* Shakespeare connected outlawry with social
displacement when Valentine, 'A man . . . cross'd with adversity', joins a
'wild faction' of bandits in the woods. Outlaws, he discovers, 'are
gentlemen, / Such as the fury of ungoverned youth / Thrust from the
company of lawful men', and have a hierarchy of their own. There is
honour among such thieves, who swear to 'do no outrages / On silly
women or poor travellers' (*The Two Gentlemen of Verona*, IV, i, 12; 37;
44–6; 71–2). These characteristics conform to Eric Hobsbawm's portrait
of the primitive rebel, and define the role of the 'noble robber' or

'gentleman of the road' as a focus of communal discontent. As Hobsbawm writes:

> His role is that of a champion, the righter of wrongs, the bringer of justice and social equity. His relation with the peasants is one of solidarity and identity. . . . It may be summarised in nine points. First, the noble robber begins his career of outlawry . . . as the victim of injustice . . . Second, he 'rights wrongs'. Third, he 'takes from the rich to give to the poor'. Fourth, he 'never kills unless in self-defence or just revenge'; Fifth, if he survives, he returns to his people with honour. . . . Sixth, he is admired and supported by his people. Seventh, he dies only through treason, since no decent member of the community would help the authorities against him. Eighth, he is . . . invisible and invulnerable. Ninth, he is not the enemy of the king . . . but of the local gentry, clergy or other oppressors.[21]

This is, of course, an identikit picture of Orlando, and explains his combination of rebelliousness and conservatism which ensures he never loses audience appeal. For the social bandit has a vital role to play, according to Hobsbawm, on the frontier between capitalism and peasant society. In modern Sicily, the American West, pre-Revolutionary France or early modern England, the bandit upholds the collective values of the poor against the 'ambition' of the rich. He is one whom 'ambition shun[s]' (*As You Like It*, II, v, 35), a stalwart of the 'merry world' of popular justice in opposition to the official legal institutions; and as he helps the weak, so the weak help him. In *As You Like It*, therefore, Adam gives Orlando his savings, and Orlando protects the old man. Outlaw and peasant stand together for a world where social relations are constant and true, like 'a lusty winter, / Frosty but kindly' (II, iii, 52–3). That is how Adam is honoured in a tribute that has extra weight if, as theatrical hearsay has it, the part of the aged servant was acted on the stage by Shakespeare himself:

> O good old man, how well in thee appears
> The constant service of the antique world,
> When service sweat for duty, not for meed.
> Thou art not for the fashion of these times,
> Where none will sweat but for promotion,
> And having that, do choke their service up
> Even with the having; it is not so with thee.
> (56–62)

In peasant wisdom, 'When Adam delved', there was no 'gentleman';
but in *As You Like It* such radical levellings are absent. 'Why do people
love you?' Adam asks Orlando rhetorically (5), and the answer the text
supplies is that the primitive rebel is no revolutionary; 'service' – the
clientage of master and servant – will be what he restores. So with Adam
beside him, Orlando becomes, as Celia jokes, uncannily like the
protagonist of 'an old tale' (I, ii, 110). In the earlier outlaw play the
renegades acclaimed Valentine king with an oath, 'By the bare scalp of
Robin Hood's fat friar' (*The Two Gentlemen of Verona*, IV, i, 36). Now
Orlando joins the same criminal fraternity as he follows the route taken
by the exiled Duke, who 'They say . . . is already in the Forest of Arden,
and a many merry men with him; and there they live like the old Robin
Hood of England. They say many young gentlemen flock to him every
day, and fleet the time carelessly as they did in the golden world' (*As You
Like It*, I, i, 114–19). Until the 1900s no one doubted the affinity of *As You
Like It* with the Robin Hood legend, nor that Orlando *de Boys* was an
Elizabethan avatar of the folkloric Robin *à Wood*;[22] but modern critics
have effaced this earthy analogue and stressed instead its literary debt to
the perfumed novel *Rosalynde* (1590) by Lyly's euphuistic colleague
Thomas Lodge. In fact, the 'old tale' mentioned by Celia is undoubtedly
the common source: the pseudo-Chaucerian *Tale of Gamelyn*. Yet it is
easy to see why this 'low' inheritance has been suppressed, since Gamelyn
is the most bloodcurdling of all the outlaw tales. It tells how Gamelyn is
disinherited by his brother John, and how he defeats John's wrestler and
kills his servant. With his faithful retainer Adam, Gamelyn flees to the
forest and becomes the outlaw king. When John is made sheriff, a third
brother pleads for Gamelyn but is clapped in chains. So Gamelyn storms
the court, takes the judge's place, and orders the entire courtroom to be
hanged. As Maurice Keen remarks, the *Tale of Gamelyn* thus presents in
stark outline the carnivalesque principle of popular justice that, when
law is topsy-turvy, to turn it upside-down will be the way to set it
right:

> The iustice and the sherreve bothe honged hye,
> To weyven[1] with the ropes in the winde for to drye.   [1 hang]
> And the twelve sissours[2] too (sowre have   [2 jurors/
>   that rekke!)[3]   3 sad to say]
> Alle were honged faste by the nekke.[23]

The outlaw ballads of medieval England legitimated peasant protest,
but *As You Like It* is one of a cluster of plays written in the late 1590s that
exalt the rank of Robin Hood to make him a gentleman or even, as in

Anthony Munday's serial *Earl of Huntington* (1598), an aristocrat. These are texts that adapt the legend to the contemporary crisis by dramatising the divided loyalty of the propertied. So when Orlando crosses from Chalk to Cheese, from an arable to a pastoral economy, he traverses a symbolic boundary that defined the cultural politics of the Shakespearean Midlands, leaving the 'static and subservient' society of the feldon region for the 'free and mobile' one of the woodlands, and entering the world of popular resistance. For as the Elizabethan topographer William Harrison summarised it, the fundamental demarcation in English life was between arable country, with its orderly parishes, and the dairying and cattle-grazing areas, with their less governable settlements: 'Our soil being divided into champaign ground and woodland, the houses of the first lie uniformly builded together, with streets and lanes, whereas in the woodland countries they stand scattered abroad, each one dwelling in the midst of his own occupying.'[24] Beyond the pale of church and manor, Underdown confirms, woodland districts were vulnerable to immigration, price fluctuations, dearth and social instability, and became as a result the strongholds of popular justice. It was wood-pasture communities that most commonly instituted cucking-stools and evolved the most elaborate public shaming rites, since 'lacking the resources of mediation available in arable villages through squire and parson . . . the wood-pasture village enforced its social norms in its own way, by rituals' rather than by litigation.[25]

'Now am I in Arden', shudders Touchstone, when he crosses from the feldon, 'the more fool I' (II, iv, 12). If 'old custom' gives a role to a clown in the forest (II, i, 2), a townsman is less at home among 'removed' hamlets (III, ii, 123; 334) and 'ill-inhabited' crofts (III, iii, 7). With its emphatic 'dispraise of the country',[26] *As You Like It* engages in the discursive revaluation of woodland that coincided with the sale and 'disafforestation' (the legal alienation) of the Crown forests. In 1600 disposal of royal woods realised £150,000 for the Irish war, and this 'asset-stripping' was accompanied by propaganda to depict the forests as unproductive wastes, the abode of 'people of lewd lives and conversation, who leaving their own countries took the place as a cloak to their villainies.'[27] Thus, the Londoner John Norden defamed their inhabitants as 'given to little or no labour, living very hardly with oaten bread, sour whey and goats' milk, dwelling far from church or chapel, and as ignorant of God or any course of civil life as the very savages amongst the infidels.'[28] The author of *Observations on Land Revenue of the Crown* concluded that while 'gentleness is shown to the stealers of wood and hedge-breakers' who inhabited them, the poor would 'dwell in woods like drones devoted to thievery', whereas 'The forests, if enclosed, would be made secure for travellers and beneficial for the Commonwealth.'[29]

So, far from echoing some neo-platonist debate about court and country, the Duke's prospectus of forest life as 'ugly and venomous' but 'sweet' in uses, chimes with actual projects to extract the 'precious jewel' from 'these woods' by coal-mining or marketing of timber. The Duke reads the forest like an improving 'book' (ii, i, 1–17); if, however, the draining of its running brooks and felling of its trees were upheld by James i as 'a religious work', this was because forests were now to be textualised as the 'nurseries and receptacles of thieves, rogues and beggars'.[30] Thus, migration of displaced population to the woods facilitated their enclosure. Under the Treasurership of Robert Cecil and Lionel Cranfield, royal policy would turn from paternalism to exploitation, as the forest was surveyed and parcelled out to developers, but not without the inscription of its trees within a rhetoric of property that is unintentionally but metonymically initiated by the squatter Orlando, 'with carving "Rosalind" on their barks' (iii, ii, 351).

Shakespeare's drama of feuding dukes predicts that the struggle between the regulated and market economies will be decided 'in the skirts of the forest' (v, iv, 158). And as Victor Skipp reminds us, with his work on subsistence crisis in the Warwickshire Forest of Arden, the site of outlawry in *As You Like It* is far from fanciful. The comedy transports its displaced characters to a wood pasture community where population influx had put intense pressure on customary culture. While Shakespeare wrote, Arden was experiencing acute demographic problems, as timber was cleared for mining, industry and convertible farming, and squatters vied with commoners for land.[31] As Underdown concurs, it is no coincidence that the foresters 'were generally believed to be addicted to crime and violence – "all rogues"', nor that 'between 1590 and 1620 the Henley-in-Arden court leet regularly presented people for engaging in violent affrays in numbers out of all proportion to the population'.[32] With such an explosive mix of commoners and vagrants – reflected in the *dramatis personae* of the play – the peril to the magistracy in the Malthusian crisis of 1596–7 was precisely the 'wild justice' that Shakespeare stages in the bloody saga of the three brothers, the wrestling and the outlaw fraternity in the woods. For, as Christopher Hill observes, the actual Forest of Arden was a hotbed of sedition that 'gave shelter to a shifting population of blacksmiths and nailers as well as to Shakespeare's artless countrymen; to Tinker Fox and his partisans as well as to the Coventry Ranters.' And if the Forest was 'the receptacle of schism and rebellion', this was not because the 'scythesmiths and iron-labourers' of this 'continued village' were ignorant, but because among them was 'found more knowledge than among the poor enslaved husbandmen' of the feldon.[33] As the Sabbatarian Nicholas Bownd complained in 1606, the Bible may have been 'as strange to them as any news you can tell them', but they were not ignorant about Robin Hood.[34] And Arden's laureate, Michael Drayton, agreed that the politics of Robin Hood were only too familiar to his countrymen:

> I think there is not one,
> But he hath heard some talk of him and Little John,
> Of Scarlet, George a Green, and Much the Miller's son,
> Of Tuck the merry friar, which many a sermon made,
> In praise of Robin Hood, his outlaws, and their trade . . .
> From wealthy abbot's chests, and churl's abundant store,
> What often times he took, he shar'd amongst the poor.
> Then taking them to rest, his merry men and he
> Slept many a summer's night under the greenwood tree.[35]

'Under the greenwood tree, / Who loves to lie with me . . .' (II, v, 1–2): the 'merry world' of popular politics surfaces in *As You Like It* in fragments of song; but all the elements of the folk scenario are latent in the play. Thus, when Drayton describes Maid Marian, 'Chief Lady of the Game', with 'clothes tuck'd to knee', braids, and 'bow and quiver arm'd', he preserves a cultural key to Rosalind's cross-dressing as Ganymede.[36] In folk games 'the woman's part' was acted by a 'shemale', a man or boy in drag, and since 'wood pasture villagers were especially concerned about female challenges to patriarchal authority',[37] enclosure riots frequently took the form of masked night-time attacks by bearded 'ladies', like the 'troop of lewd women' who obstructed the enclosure of Rockingham Forest by Cecil in 1602, or 'Captain Dorothy' who led Midland enclosure riots in 1607.[38] John Walter suggests that the explanation for this gender inversion lies in the opinion of authorities such as Lambarde that 'if a number of women do flock together, this is none assembly punishable by statutes', a notion professed by female rioters at Maldon in 1629, who insisted 'women were lawless, and not subject to the laws.'[39] But the logic, Martin Ingram deduces in his survey of ridings and rough music, was indeed that of a 'stylised representation of anarchy', as the world was turned back-to-front or inside out to put the moral economy right.[40] As Natalie Zemon Davis records, Maid Marion had queened over May games long before Robin Hood joined her in the fifteenth century, and her rebelliousness would be perpetuated by Marianne in 1789, with bare breasts and worker's cap. Madge Wildfire who directed tax riots in Edinburgh in 1736, the Whiteboys led by Ghostly Sally, who trampled Irish fences in the 1760s dressed in frocks, General Ludd's Wives, who smashed Lancashire looms in 1812, and Rebecca's Daughters who destroyed Welsh tollgates in the 1840s, all invoked an Amazonian licence harking back as far as 1450, when black-faced and white-gowned men claiming to be under orders of the Queen of the Fairies had raided the deer park of the Duke of Buckingham.[41] So when Celia resolves to disguise herself 'in mean attire, / And with a kind of umber smirch my face', and Rosalind to wear a 'curtle-axe upon my thigh, / A boar-spear in my hand' (I, iii, 107–14), the 'shemale' and the 'blackamoor' act out an impudent challenge to the keepers of the game.

For these class, race and gender trespassers, determined to 'walk not in the trodden paths' (I, iii, 14), Arden means 'liberty, not banishment' (134). In an essay on Robin Hood, Peter Stallybrass has described the ballads as a symbolic system transgressing spatial, bodily and linguistic bounds and inverting the hierarchies of gender, class and church, but he also shows how Robin is 'an ideological sign intersected by differently orientated social interests'. In the age of enclosure the outlaw legend became the semantic field where the liberties of the forest were symbolically fought out between gamekeeper and poachers.[42] Tudor authority therefore deplored the 'plays of Robin Hood, Maid Marian and Friar Tuck, wherein besides the lewdness and ribaldry that is opened to the people, disobedience also to officers is taught', for 'the reversible world' of carnival lent protesters quasi-legal status, like that of the Derbyshire rebels who in 1497 donned 'Robin Hood's clothing and in manner of insurrection went into the woods', or the Nottinghamshire rioters of 1502 led by the 'fellow which had renewed Robin Hood's pageants, which named himself Greenleaf.' Since both the Pilgrimage of Grace and Kett's rebellion had been instigated at folk plays, Cecil was shrewd to call the Gunpowder Conspirators 'Robin Hoods'. Spenser likewise correctly detected the festive structure of resistance when he observed that every corner of Ireland contained a 'Robin Hood'.[43] And in Shakespeare's text it is a mocking game or 'rough music' which authorises the forest trespass and felony of poaching, when 'he that kill'd the deer' has its 'horns [set] upon his head,' and the hunters chant their horn-song of blood-brotherhood:

> Take thou no scorn to wear the horn,
> It was a crest ere thou wast born.
>   Thy father's father wore it,
>   And thy father bore it.
> The horn, the horn, the lusty horn,
> Is not a thing to laugh to scorn.
>   (IV, ii, 14–19)

As Justice Shallow states, when he accuses Falstaff of having 'beaten my men, killed my deer, and broken open my lodge', 'blacking-up' or poaching in disguise, was 'a Star Chamber matter', which the Privy

Council would treat as 'a riot', since an Act of 1485 had made 'tumultuous hunting at night by persons with painted faces or otherwise disguised' an offence against the royal prerogative (*The Merry Wives of Windsor*, I, i, 1–104). It did not require a run-in with Sir Thomas Lucy over deer-stealing in Charlecote Park for Shakespeare to know that 'What were perquisites for one group were crimes for another', nor that in the Robin Hood tradition, 'the question of "Who wins the game?" becomes an argument over "Who owns the game?".'[44] For, as E. P. Thompson observes of these so-called 'Blacks', poaching was never simply a casual country pastime, but was 'retributive and concerned less with venison as such than with deer as symbols of an authority which threatened their economy, their crops and their customary agrarian rights.'[45] 'Blacking' was part of the symbolic repertoire of popular politics in early modern England, so when poachers 'entered into the enclosed park of Sir Edward Greville', Stratford's lord of the manor, and took 'sundry bucks and broke their necks', James I viewed it as a 'contemptuous and exceeding presumptuous' offence against himself.[46] According to Thompson, 'There was an ancient enmity between democracy and these gentle creatures', and it should be no surprise that the outbreak of the Civil War was marked by the slaughter of the herd in Windsor Park by squatters who 'defied the keepers with pikes and refused to be expelled', while in 1642–3 huge crowds chased and killed the deer in Waltham Forest.[47] Jaques had addressed the herd as 'fat and greasy citizens'. He rightly saw that 'To fright the animals and to kill them up / In their assign'd and native dwelling-place' would be construed by the law as an act of symbolic treason against 'The body of country, city, court' itself (II, i, 21–63).

As You Like It introduces all the Sherwood outlaws (even Tuck is identifiable as Martext), but it is in this stag-night horn-dance, when the hunted become hunters, that the play edges closest to those rites of misrule, which, as Robert Weimann shows, linked Tudor village green with metropolitan stage. Jaques explains the rough magic of all such 'charivaris', when he rules: ''Tis no matter how it be in tune, so it make noise enough' (IV, ii, 8–9). Climaxing with this riotous assembly in the woods, the action follows the programme of a 'riding' or 'skimmington': a caterwauling ritual of the Cheese country, whereby customary society 'knew by Shame', according to Marvell, 'Better than Law, Domestic Crimes to tame'.[48] Urged on by rebellious women chanting 'the right butter-woman's rank to market', the 'very false gallop' of their rhyme (95–110), sung 'out of tune' (244), to mock husbands with 'horns' (IV, i, 56), 'like the howling of Irish wolves against the moon' (V, ii, 110), the characters form up two-by-two like the classic 'riding' that historians describe: a procession led by a man wearing horns, with a shemale acting as the 'woman on top', and some deviant ritually beaten with a skimming ladle. This was 'A punishment invented first to awe / Masculine wives transgressing nature's law';[49] or to shame an 'old cuckold' married 'out of all reasonable match' (III, ii, 80). But as Touchstone notices, a skimmington could be targeted as much against a 'walled' enclosure as 'the forehead of a married man' in the Shakespearean period, and the estate of 'a man (who) knows not the end of his own goods' could be as much the mock of 'horn-beasts' as 'a man [who] has good horns and knows no end of them' (III, iii, 45–57). 'As horns are odious, they are necessary' (45): customary justice, as the play stages it, was turning from sexual to economic uses. Thus the 'Robin Hoods' who defended common rights in the Forest of Dean in 1612 typified those in wood pasture who turned rough music against enclosure at this time, bequeathing a symbolic action to the popular movements of the Civil War. For as Underdown notes, the conjuncture of a riot, a forest community, the leadership of 'Lady Skimmington', and a seasonal game marks the point at which custom exploded into political action in the early seventeenth century.[50] Oliver is 'shame[d]' out of his 'unnatural' life (IV, iii, 96,125), but his Jacobean counterparts would find their fences burned.

Trespass, poaching, damaging trees, sending letters in fictitious names, blacking and cross-dressing: *As You Like It* parades all the felonies associated with forest rioters. Performed in the season of the silencing of satire in 1599 (I, ii, 83), this is a text apprehensive that it is playing symbolically with fire: that as the banished satirist Jaques realises, the 'motley coat' of carnival is 'as large a charter as the wind' to license protest or revolt (II, vii, 42–61). Yet if the play includes the 'broken music' of a festive rout (I, ii, 131), it does so to defuse this radical potential, since contrary to Jaques's professional plan to 'tax' the rich with mockery (II, vii, 70–87), the textual refrain is expressly that offenders should 'Take no scorn.' Substituting the patriarchy of 'Thy father's father' for rebellion, its project seems instead to incorporate the energies of charivari in a reconstituted order, which it does from the moment Orlando bursts upon the exiled Duke 'with sword drawn' demanding food. This is a confrontation that restages the action of the early modern food riot, with its 'conservative' aim of reasserting the normative economy; but the fact that it is perversely directed at the figurehead of the old order highlights the self-destructiveness of rural insurrection. For the Duke shares Orlando's nostalgia for 'better days', when paupers 'have with holy bell been knoll'd to church, / And sat at good men's feasts' (114–22), even though he responds with the question posed by the 1597 Poor Law: is this beggar one of the 'deserving poor' or some 'sturdy rogue'? Orlando replies that he is 'inland bred' and civil, but driven by 'distress' to violence:

You touch'd my vein at first: the thorny point
Of bare distress hath ta'en from me the show
Of smooth civility. Yet am I inland bred,
And know some nurture. But, forbear, I say,
He dies that touches any of this food,
Till I and my affairs are answered.

(II, vii, 95–100)

Orlando's claim to be 'inland bred', glossed by editors to mean that Orlando is 'not rustic',[51] in fact affiliates him with the Midland rioters, and seems to vindicate their cause. For it had been Caesar, with his 'thrasonical brag of "I came, saw, and overcame"' (v, ii, 30), who reported that 'the Inlanders or Midland inhabitants of this Island had their beginning in the soil where they inhabited', thereby perpetuating, as Sir Thomas Browne complained, the 'vulgar error' that Midlanders were the 'seed of the Autochthon'.[52] Shakespeare's usage reminds us, then, that Arden puns with Eden in popular lore, and that 'an inland man' is civilised (III, ii, 337) because his country is the heart of the English state, where Adam delved long before courtiers came on progress, and where now as 'an old poor man' he awaits relief (II, vii, 129). Moreover, as the *OED*. records, to be 'inland bred' in the Shakespearean era was to stand in complex mutual dependence with the outlanders, whose ports were 'a wall to defend / Our inland' (*Henry v*, I, ii, 142), but whose imposts had often to be weighed against the Midlanders' protests that 'They cannot spare the corn of the inland growth to be carried out, for fear of famine in these parts.'[53] It was precisely because of its unique inland status that Warwickshire would prove the 'most retarded' of all counties in payment of shipmoney.[54] And Orlando's localist appeal, in boasting of his roots, is likewise to the Tudor moral economy, which regulated the transportation of food through inland counties to London and the coast, but which broke down calamitously after 1595, when, as Buchanan Sharp shows, communities on shipment routes in the Midlands and the West were starved to supply the city and the European market.[55] Nothing relates *As You Like It* to Steer's rising more explicitly than Orlando's inland breeding, nor confronts the court more starkly with the dearth of food. Jaques, the London cynic, scoffs that 'I have eat none yet', but the Midlander seems unanswerable when he retorts, 'Nor shalt thou till necessity be served' (89–90).

'What can rich men do if poor men rise together?' asked the rioters of the 1590s, and *As You Like It* has no reply. Instead it voices the ambivalence of propertied opinion about the unregulated market, and the governmental resolve that, as the Duke assures Orlando when he gasps he 'almost die[s] for food': 'Your gentleness shall force, / More than your force move us to gentleness' (102–4). In *A Midsummer Night's Dream* of 1595 the 'hungry lion' of revolt had roared and run away, being acted by the terrified city worker, Snug. But by the time of the later comedy and in the stricken country, 'the thorny point / Of bare distress' is far more sharp, so 'Now the hungry lion roars' in earnest, even as the contemporary Irish 'wolf behowls the moon' (*A Midsummer Night's Dream*, v, i, 357–8; *As You Like It*, v, ii, 110). With an average holding of fifteen sheep, a dozen cows and a few goats, 'to get your living by the copulation of cattle' (III, ii, 77) in competition with the deer, was always a hazardous business in Arden, as Skipp's statistics prove. Yet as the impoverished shepherd Corin testifies, the causes of distress lie in the market economy that is encroaching the Forest. Aubrey dated the decay of manorial institutions in the woodlands from 1500, and Corin confirms that in Shakespeare country the manorial economy has succumbed to the engrosser, since 'I am shepherd to another man', he bemoans, 'And do not shear the fleeces that I graze' (II, iv, 76). In *Poly-Olbion* of 1612 Drayton's Arden likewise laments that her 'overthrow' has been caused by engrossing and enclosure: 'For, when the world found out the fitness of my soil, / The gripple wretch began immediately to spoil / My tall and goodly woods, and did my grounds enclose: / By which, in little time my bounds I came to lose.' Overpopulated with cottages that 'dislodg'd the Hart', and overgrazed by 'the sundry kinds of beasts . . . / That men for profit breed', Drayton's Arden is the ravaged site of Britain's economic transformation: 'Her people waxing still, and wanting where to build.'[56] Profit, evidently, is the only law of this Forest, as Corin grieves:

> My master is of churlish disposition,
> And little recks to find the way to heaven
> By doing deeds of hospitality.
> Besides, his cote, his flocks, and bounds of feed
> Are now on sale, and at our sheepcote now
> By reason of his absence there is nothing
> That you will feed on.
>   (II, iv, 76–82)

'Assuredly the thing is to be sold' (94): the Shakespearean text knows the fate of sylvan society will hang on London finance, as in actual Midland forests it was the city's projectors and monopolists who profited from improvement and enclosure. So the forest pasture in Arden is bought up by Celia with 'gold right suddenly', to forestall the engrossing farmer Oliver (II, iv, 89–98). Like Queen Elizabeth and Lady Norris, Rosalind and her friend will play at rustics and solve the agrarian crisis through *noblesse oblige*, assuring the pauperised shepherd 'we will mend thy wages' (92). So too Orlando is disarmed by the Duke to 'sit down and feed . . . in gentleness' at an old-style 'good man's feast' (II, vii, 105–24). In the paternalist spirit of King James's *Declaration of Sports*, it is the nobility who must ameliorate the market through rites of commensality. Rosalind and Celia always intended to 'be merry' and 'devise sports' to 'mock the good hussif Fortune from her wheel, that her gifts may henceforth be bestowed more equally'; and spinning Fortune's wheel through counter-revolution, *As You Like It* foretells the Stuart campaign to reunify agrarian society under aristocratic leadership by 'making sport' with economic change (I, ii, 21–33). In the aftermath of the 1607 rising, the landowners of the West Midlands would indeed recognise in country sports 'a sign / Of harmless mirth and honest neighbourhood, / Where all the parish did in one combine, / To mount the rod of peace, and none withstood.' Re-erecting the maypoles of 'Merry England' to 'feast in our defence', nobility and gentry 'came from 60 miles' around, Anthony à Wood recorded, to Robert Dover's Cotswold games. Where rioters had threatened enclosers' mansions, the 'harmless merriment' of wrestling and racing taught the 'glad country', Ben Jonson enthused, to 'advance true love and neighbourhood, / And do both Church and Commonwealth the good.' Thus on the greensward of Dover's Hill the Robin Hood tradition was sentimentalised during the seventeenth century into the innocuous athletics of Jonson's own courtly pastoral, *The Sad Shepherd*.[59]

'Who durst assemble such a troop as he', the admiring Nicholas Wallington asked in a 1636 encomium to Robert Dover, 'But might of insurrection charged be?'[60] It was a question that laid bare the hegemonic work of Shakespearean culture, by that date virtually complete, in neutralising the rites of collective action, grafting the old rural games (in the words of Dover's editor), 'to classical mythology and Renaissance culture, whilst linking them with throne and Church.'[61] In *As You Like It* this work is effected with the incorporation of Orlando's strength inside the enclosure, established within the licensed 'purlieus of the forest', of Rosalind's 'sheep-cote fenc'd about with olive-trees' (IV, iii, 76–77). For, far from valorising the archaic greenwood as a locale of freedom and asylum, as critics suppose, the play breaks up 'the skirts of this wild wood' (V, iv, 158) to reinscribe it within private ownership. Its action is a discursive rehearsal of the enclosure legislation, invoking the 'royal disposition' of the wilderness (IV, iii, 117) only to authorise its destruction. Rosalind's fence of 'olive trees' circumscribing 'antique' oaks (V, iv, 105) is a fitting symbol for Crown policy, since it is within its bounds that deforestation, clearance and depopulation will occur. Pastoral discourse, which promises the Arden woodlanders 'measure heap'd in joy' and 'rustic revelry' (V, iv, 176–7), will conceal the real revolution in the forest economy, which was invariably towards cereal production. If 'improvers continued to worry about squatters and masterless men in sylvan regions', and 'wished to impose gentry control on the egalitarian societies these spawned', this was because of implacable resistance to their schemes to clear pastoral areas for grain.[62] Subsequent improvers would realise that dairying could support a larger population, but in the Shakespearean era the olive branches of Lord Norris and the sheep-masters, intended to pacify the wood pasture community, served merely to secure the commoners' consent to the extinction of their rights and the intrusion of Oliver's capital and corn.

'Then is there mirth in heaven, / When earthly things made even / Atone together' (v, iv, 107–9): the marriage of the princess Rosalind to the yeoman Orlando at a classicised fête like Dover's 'Olympic games' affirms the alliance of England's nobility and gentry and their appropriation of popular laughter. As Orlando jokes, 'Clubs cannot part' such lovers, who unite against insurgency (v, ii, 40). Contrary to Bakhtin's idealisation of carnival, *As You Like It* thus reveals how discourses work through social change and are never indeterminate. In fact, the discursive function of Shakespearean comedy will be to depoliticise carnival, just as 'in every society discourse is controlled and redistributed', as Foucault sees, 'to avert its dangers and evade its formidable materiality'.[63] Orlando's strength was 'overthrown', therefore, the instant he met Rosalind, and sensed that 'something weaker masters me' (i, ii, 249–50). Throughout the play his violence is subdued by his master-mistress, as the sylvan discourse of *Gamelyn* is occluded by Lodge's pastoral, the real Arden is assimilated to the idealised Ardennes, and 'Robin of the Wood' is dignified with the Elizabethan surname 'de Bois'. The last song takes us into a landscape full of crops, yet so free of fences the poor can roam 'between the acres of the rye' and 'o'er the green cornfield' (v, iii, 14–37), though never to graze them, nor 'To glean the broken ears after the man / That the main harvest reaps' (iii, v, 102–3). Despite Celia's vow to waste her time 'By doing deeds of hospitality' (ii, iv, 94), the text foretells the development of Arden, which in Leland's time had 'plentiful of grass, but no great plenty of corn', yet by 1652 had 'grown as gallant a corn country as any in England'.[64] Arden will be improved from wood pasture to cereal farmland of the kind described by Iris in *The Tempest*, 'Of wheat, rye, barley, vetches, oats and pease' (iv, i, 61). This is the arable landscape of the eighteenth century, where the 'pretty country folks' will sport 'In spring time, the only pretty ring time' (v, iii, 14–37), as picturesquely as Dover's lads. Between the sowing and the harvest, these fields are their playground because English culture will bridle insurrection; as out of Orlando's strength comes sweetness, when he kills the lioness menacing his brother. There is real blood on his napkin, because this lion fights

more ferociously than Snug, but Orlando saves the engrosser, reduced to
beggary himself, from the predatory jungle. Thus the 'middling sort'
strangle protest in *As You Like It*, and desert the dispossessed. The
forester William, deprived of Audrey at the end, is therefore told by
Touchstone to 'Tremble and depart'. William's final words to the new
landowner are historically ironic: 'God rest you merry sir' (v, i, 56–8).

'''Twas never merry world / Since lowly feigning was called compli-
ment' (*Twelfth Night*, iii, i, 100–1): Shakespearean comedy moves from
the merry world of 'service' to a world of servility and intimidation.
Though burial registers record the gravity of the famine – worst in Arden,
where the death-rate was shadowed in the obscure demise of Adam – the
Midland oligarchy emerged from the crisis so secure in its control of
popular culture that it would ride out the 1607 rising. Thus, the Old
Shepherd of *The Winter's Tale*, 'that from very nothing . . . is grown into
an unspeakable estate' (iv, ii, 38–40), legitimates his rise by 'welcom[ing]
all' to his sheepshearing (iv, iv, 57); as Dover devised his 'merriment' to
advertise how well 'Lords, knights, swains, shepherds, churls agree.'
Meanwhile on Enslow Hill Bartholemew Steer waited for his merry world
to rise, hopeful of support from Warwickshire, where 'very many have
enclosed in every place',[65] but on the night just ten men came. Though
Queen Elizabeth was never persuaded to revisit, Rycote was preserved.
Without the lead of gentry, none dared risk their necks to attack it: as
historians deduce, the withdrawal of the propertied from collective
action, figured in *As You Like It*, spelt the effective end of agrarian revolt
in England.[66] Touchstone had warned William 'I will kill thee, make thee
away, translate thy life into death, thy liberty into bondage' (*As You Like
It*, v, i, 53), and his jesting was half earnest. For while Steer was hanged
on Enslow Hill, and Arden foresters starved, the 'Rich men' of the
Midlands, as Thomas Fuller lamented, were busy jostling 'the poor
people out of their commons'. By the early seventeenth century,
enclosers had 'turn'd so much of woodland into tillage' in Arden, it was
noted, 'that they produce corn to furnish other counties', while 'the
ironworks destroyed such prodigious quantities of wood, that they
quickly laid the country open, and by degrees made room for the plough.'
A magnate such as Fulke Greville had 'thrown to the ground the better
oaks for timbering', the foresters protested, 'by what right' was not
known.[67] Had he deigned to reply, Greville would doubtless have
answered as Touchstone does to William, that his entitlement was
possession, since according to the modern English law of property, 'To
have is to have' (v, i, 39).

On May Day in 1515, according to Hall, Henry viii and his court had
ridden to Shooter's Hill, the ancient woodland outside London and a site
for popular games like archery. There they were 'ambushed' by two

hundred 'yeomen, clothed all in green with bows and arrows', whose leader, Robin Hood,

> came to the King, desiring him to see his men shoot. Then he whistled and the archers shot at once, so the noise was strange and great. Then Robin Hood desired the king and queen to come into the greenwood and see how the outlaws lived. The king demanded of the ladies if they durst adventure into the wood with so many outlaws. The queen said she was content. Then horns blew till they came to the wood. The king and queen sat down and were served venison by Robin Hood and his men, to their great content.

Soon after, Hall adds, Henry 'took his progress Westwards and heard complaints of his poor commonality, and ever as he rode he hunted and liberally departed with venison.'[68] This episode from the beginning of the early modern era, with its cooption of violence and deflection of privation into pastoral, can stand as a paradigm of the state's appropriation of English carnival. Likewise, at Christmas 1603, *As You Like It* was performed for James I at Wilton House, after a day's hunting in Gillingham Forest.[69] In 1625 this royal forest would be the first sold for disafforestation, when its enclosure by a Scottish courtier, Sir James Fullerton, ignited the Western Rising. Though William might restage the game of Robin Hood – as the ubiquitous 'Williams *alias* Lady Skimmington' led the Gillingham rioters in 'pulling down and defarming all enclosures of that forest' – the King would learn from the comedy how to 'share the good of [his] returned fortune' with investors 'According to the measure of their states' (v, iv, 174), by reviving forest law for profit.[70] Thus Shakespearean comedy made its contribution to the process detailed by John Walter and Keith Wrightson, whereby a society incapable of eliminating dearth preserved itself by 'interpreting and resisting' the disorder that dearth caused.[71] And if the shemale of Shakespeare's Epilogue shocked the Jacobean courtiers by threatening to 'kiss as many as [have] beards' (v, iv, 215), their descendants would pre-empt such subversiveness with the infamous Black Act, making it a capital offence for 'any persons to appear in any forest, chase, park or grounds enclosed with their faces blacked or being otherwise disguised'.[72]

Chapter Four

Against the grain:

Representing the market in Coriolanus

I

THE famine of the 1590s hit Stratford hardest in the winter of 1597–8. Shortage was so acute that the townsmen petitioned local Justices to impose the Privy Council's *Book of Orders* against hoarding. Their aim was to break a cartel of local farmers, who were withholding corn from the marketplace to inflate prices, and whom Lord Burghley condemned as 'wicked people more like wolves or cormorants than natural men'. Yet the old minister also noted they were 'men of good livelihood and estimation', and what exacerbated Stratford's crisis was the storing of grain for brewing by its maltsters. As Richard Quiney, the spokesman of these 'great corn-buyers', protested to the Privy Council, the maltsters were the victims rather than villains of the market, since brewing was Stratford's mainstay: 'our town hath no other special trade, our houses fitted to no other uses, and many servants hired only for that purpose.' On 24 January he had heard from his partner Abraham Sturley how the town's poor were 'malcontent' with the maltsters, but that its brewers trusted to the influence of 'our countryman, Mr. Shakespeare' to secure their own access to its arable fields, believing it 'a very good pattern to move him to deal in the matter. . . . By the instructions you can give him and by the friends he can make, we think it a fair mark for him to shoot at, and not impossible to hit. It obtained would advance him indeed, and do us much good'. We do not know whether the dramatist did play William Tell with high-placed friends for the 'tithes of corn, grain, blade and hay' he later purchased, but we can guess the extent of his concern because on 4 February the authorities complied with the *Orders* and returned an inventory of cornholders, and at the mansion of New Place in Chapel Street ward one of the largest stores was duly entered under the name of William Shakespeare.[1]

Like his property dealing, Shakespeare's involvement with the

83

maltsters embarrasses critics; but the episode is important because it situates the playwright within the economic and power relations that were transforming his society. It locates him within the process that drives the plot of *Coriolanus*: the epochal shift from collective values based on shared consumption to exchange values and private enterprise. And where a paternalistic regime strove to halt this slide by fixing prices to the use of labour – distributing supply to 'good and able subjects' away from the 'loose and idle' with the Poor Law that was just passing through Parliament – Shakespeare's venture capitalism, with cash and credit for hire, suggests he understood how in a market economy all values fluctuated. He invested in labour, grain or land as commodities that were as saleable as wool at Evesham market. To an entrepreneur of the kind the letters reveal – a London 'paymaster' to his Midland partners, able to transfer money and credit in what Keynes called 'the greatest "bull" movement ever known',[2] the English profit inflation that spiralled from 1570 to 1620 – everything was exchangeable. For, as Keynes saw, Elizabethan commerce resembled modern finance capital in its liquidity, and produced an unprecedented awareness (noted by Marx) that money 'will make/ Black, white; foul, fair; wrong right. . . . This yellow slave will . . . place thieves,/ And give them title, knee and approbation / With senators on the bench' (*Timon of Athens*, iv, iii, 28–42). To mercantile capital it was the upstart god of liquidity that ruled the marketplace and decreed that nothing and no one had permanent value. And it was the liquidity of values that was the revolutionary theme of *Coriolanus*.

The Poor Law put a price on the life of every subject by separating the productive from the idle, and in the opening scene of *Coriolanus* the First Citizen acknowledges that 'We are accounted poor citizens, the patricians good' according to such a scale of value (i, i, 14). But what makes him subversive is that he sees the arbitrariness of this valuation, since he knows it is by hoarding corn until it rots that engrossers push up the price of bread to feed the starving: 'If they would yield us but the superfluity while it were wholesome, we might guess they relieved us humanely; but they think we are too dear: our sufferance is a gain to them' (15–21). What the Citizen grasps, therefore, is the functional relation between poverty and plenty in a system where, as Keynes wrote, 'it was out of the reduced standard of life of the agricultural population that the accumulation of capital derived, due to prices outstripping wages'; and 'Looking into the causes of dearth', the Privy Council confirmed that they grew 'not so much by unfruitfulness, but through the greediness of sundry persons who, preferring private gain to public good, engross all manner of grain and so raise prices, to the great oppression of the poor'. Shakespeare's Citizens have warrant, therefore, for suspecting their rulers 'Suffer us to famish, and their storehouses crammed with grain; repeal daily any wholesome act established against the rich, and provide more piercing statutes daily, to chain up and restrain the poor' (79–84). This excoriation clearly alludes to the Elizabethan vagrancy acts and repeal of laws protecting tillage, which the Citizen exposes as means to ensure that, as Keynes put it, 'the fruits of economic progress accrued to the profiteer rather than to the wage earner. For wages in England – and this is the essence of the story – were not rising comparably to prices.'[3]

'They have assembled in a great number', Sturley notified Quiney, 'and travelled to Sir Thomas Lucy on Friday to complain of our maltsters, and on Sunday to Sir Fulke Greville' at his seat of Beauchamp's Court near Alcester. Evidently the conference with Greville, Warwickshire's senior Member of Parliament, only inflamed the conflict, because the shoemaker Thomas West 'came home so full he said he hoped within a week to lead some of them in a halter; and "I hope", saith John Grannams (a weaver) "to see them hanged on gibbets at their own doors."' Greville would have given them harsh words if he repeated his speech on relief from the 1593 Parliament. As leader of the anti-Spanish war party Sidney's worshipper insisted the defence of the realm demanded subsidy from even the poorest, and he brusquely rehearsed 'the scruples in the House' about 'the poverty of the people' only to sweep them aside:

> The poor are grieved to be overcharged. This must be helped, for otherwise the weak feet will complain of too heavy a body; that is to be feared. If the feet knew their strength as we know their oppression, they would not bear as they do. But to answer them, it sufficeth that the time requireth it. And in a prince power will command. To satisfy them, they cannot think we overcharge them when we charge ourselves with them and above them. But if nothing will satisfy them, our doings are sufficient to bind them.

Greville had sat through five Parliaments in silence, but the truculence of this maiden speech provoked disquiet: 'If my speech hath offended', he closed defiantly, 'I will not often trouble you hereafter.' He would restate the Tudor orthodoxy of the body politic throughout his own *Treatise of Monarchy* – praising the Bourse as the heart of the Dutch economy, 'Whereby they want no bullion nor food,/But with the surplus . . ./ Enrich themselves . . . yet do good/To all their limbs' (416) – and he deployed it in the Commons to urge the imperative of 'outward Forces' over 'inward discontent'.[4]

For Greville war was a means to 'qualify the discontent/In people, who when peace is turn'd to war,/Find subsidies no tax, though revenues are' (571); and in Shakespearean Rome there is the same identification of economic with military ends. This equation is typified by Coriolanus, who from the day he 'mammocks' a butterfly as a boy, is rewarded for egotistic waste (I, iii, 60). Like Greville, who made his name as a tactitian during the siege of Antwerp, Coriolanus besieges the Antiates with pitiless efficiency: 'his sword, death's stamp . . . a thing of blood, whose every motion was tim'd with dying cries . . . as if 'twere a perpetual spoil' (II, ii, 107–20). Greville clinched his military reputation suppressing 'mutinies and revolts' (III, i, 125) with a ruse to renege on pay. Likewise, Coriolanus 'stopp'd the fliers' (II, ii, 103) by vowing to share 'the common distribution' (I, ix, 35) while ensuring 'the spoil got on the Antiates/Was ne'er distributed' (III, iii, 4). As Navy Treasurer, Greville inaugurated a war economy, so he resembled Coriolanus in heralding a new type of military entrepreneur who would organise armies 'like a thing / Made by some other deity . . . / That shapes man better' (IV, vi, 91–3). Both real and fictional commanders foreshadowed a juggernaut such as Wallenstein, who in an age when war was Europe's largest industry, made soldiering a speculative business. Though Greville was frustrated by the state, Wallenstein repeated the career of Coriolanus uncannily, from nobleman to potentate on profits of commercial violence. With estates and mines, artillery 'to pierce a corslet' (v, iv, 20) and intelligence to 'circumvent' the enemy (I, ii, 6), mercenaries of his magnitude were the foremost capitalists of their day, since 'in executing commissions on a heroic scale they pursued self-interest with flamboyant disregard of morality. What worked was all they cared about. A more grandiose merger of private and military enterprise had never been seen – nor since.'[5] In 1634 Wallenstein would be cut to pieces by his own 'men and lads', like Shakespeare's hero, on suspicion of double-crossing his employer (v, vi, 111); but not before his Scottish and Irish ironsides had ravaged Germany like 'boys pursuing summer butterflies, / Or butchers killing flies' (IV, vi, 95). The horror of the Thirty Years' War, with its vortex of starvation, rape and pillage, is the reality of contract warfare unleashed imaginatively in *Coriolanus*.

If Hobbes assumed the natural condition of men to be a state of war, Coriolanus personifies the seventeenth-century correlation of warfare with an unregulated market. A restless Hobbesian 'desire of Power after power'[6] actually defines the rival Volscian state, where workers welcome war because it increases demand for labour: 'Peace is a getter of more bastard children than war's a destroyer of men . . . and it makes men hate one another . . . because they then less need one another. The wars for my money. I hope to see Romans as cheap as Volscians' (IV, v, 230–9). Valuing men as units of production, the Poor Law ordered beggars set in stocks, 'stripped and whipped until bloody, and sent from parish to parish'; in *Coriolanus* war is a corollary of this rationale that the unproductive are expendable: the means 'to vent our musty superfluity' of lives (I, i, 225). Like corn or malt, the people are commodities in this economy, 'things created / To buy and sell with groats' (III, ii, 9) or 'multiplying spawn' that Coriolanus prices 'as they weigh' by labour power (II, ii, 74–8):

> In human action and capacity,
> Of no more soul nor fitness for the world
> Than camels in their war, who have their provand
> Only for bearing burthens, and sore blows
> For sinking under them.
>
> (II, i, 246–50)

For Coriolanus war is a continuation of the market by other means, so 'The Volsces have much corn', he taunts the crowd, 'take these rats thither, / To gnaw their garners' (I, i, 258). If each Roman is worth 'four Volsces', his profit-and-loss calculation that 'brave death outweighs' their lives (I, vi, 71–8) makes Coriolanus like a modern crop farmer, who will make such 'quick work' with sword and ploughshare he can 'march from hence to help [his] fielded friends' (I, iv, 11). It is this harvesting imagery which links the story of the Roman warrior to England's agrarian change and dearth; for Coriolanus is characterised not only as a grain hoarder, whose personal value rises with the price of corn, but by metaphor as the type of improving landlord that was enclosing Midland counties for up-and-down or convertible husbandry. Thus, he will 'mow all down before him, and leave his passage polled' (IV, v, 207), while his troops revel in his tracks 'like conies after rain'. Or he will cull the surplus population, 'As Hercules did shake down mellow fruit' (IV, vi, 100). So when he fights against Rome his friends discover 'He could not stay to pick them in a pile / Of noisome musty chaff . . . / For one poor grain or two, to leave unburnt / And still to nose th'offence' (v, i, 25–8). He must count even his family as an unproductive surplus, like the rotten grain he hoards, because he defines a man exclusively by usefulness to his employer, so when he is 'servanted to others' (v, ii, 80), he becomes 'a kind of nothing' (v, i, 13), whose only meaning is his work. Terry Eagleton calls him 'Shakespeare's most developed bourgeois individualist',[7] but he is both more and less. Reducing all values to use, he repels as 'a thing Made by some other deity' (IV, vi, 91): 'a thing', it is reiterated, that 'moves like an engine [as] the ground shrinks before his tread', and which explodes like a cannon and repeats 'like a knell' (v, iv, 19–22). So he commodifies the bread of life like the instrument of England's agricultural revolution, the threshing machine. He is the motor of the future: an alienated and *reified* man whose only value is the labour he can sell.

Coriolanus is sure the law of supply and demand guarantees he will 'be lov'd when he is lack'd' (IV, i, 15), since he is 'worth six' of any competitor and is 'simply the rarest man i'th'world' (IV, v, 164–9). Self-made and, he imagines, self-employed, 'he pays himself for being proud' (I, i, 32), and stands 'himself alone' (I, iv, 51), 'As if a man were / Author of himself / And knew no other kin' (v, iii, 35). Indeed, so confident is he of his own uniqueness, he denies society exists, breaking all 'bond and privilege' of affective ties and responding to his wife's emotional plea with the unanswerable economic question, 'What is that curtsy worth?' (25–7). Unlike the yarn spun by his 'idle huswife' (I, iii, 70–85), Coriolanus's work is always in demand. So, though the commoners appreciate that he has 'faults enough, with surplus' (I, i, 44), being 'poor in no one fault, but stored with all' (II, i, 16), 'He has no equal' in the labour market (I, i, 251), because by 'topping all others in boasting' (II, i, 19), the 'services he has done for his country' (I, i, 29) make him appear invaluable. If he pretends not to be covetous (41), but looks 'upon things precious as they were / The common muck of the world' (II, ii, 125–6), despising his men as wage labourers 'that do prize their hours / At a crack'd drachma' (I, v, 4), this is because, like the engrosser that he is, he is determined to fix his own price:

> They say there's grain enough?
> . . .I'd make a quarry
> With thousands of these quarter'd slaves, as high
> As I could pick my lance.
> (I, i, 194–99)

Pricing other men like sacks of 'quarter'd' corn, Coriolanus proclaims his absolute value; the Citizens, however, maintain there are no absolutes but only man-made scarcities of dearth and war. They know that 'The city is well stor'd' with surplus grain, so they reason that by killing Coriolanus they can have 'corn at their own rates' (I, i, 188). Stratford's 1598 inventory would indeed establish that though only 44 quarters of mill corn, wheat and rye remained in the town, 696 quarters of malted corn were stored by maltsters, so the townsmen seem justified in their appeal to 'have corn at our own price' (9).[8] It is in the context of this chronic problem of grain distribution in a town such as Stratford that the action of *Coriolanus* unfolds. For as local studies suggest, the economics of the play are specific to the Midlands, which did not share the national recovery from the crisis of the 1590s, but suffered shortage until the 1620s *irrespective of the quality of harvests*. Thus, while grain prices fell in southern England after 1600, in Warwickshire they rose by 20 per cent over six years. As eyewitnesses noted, it was the enclosure of the Midland Plain that created this 'want amidst plentifulness' since conversion from open cultivation put towns at the mercy of profiteers: 'by means whereof Corn doth continue at too dear a rate for the poor Artificer and labouring man in Warwickshire.' The food-producing Midlands starved to feed the London consumer; but in this nexus of cash and corn that indexed lives to prices, brewers were the whipping-boys for soaring prices, as in 1586 when Northampton artisans attacked them. A boycott of the Stratford maltsters' ale seems to have been part of such a protest, while the threat to hang them echoed recent rioters like the weaver who harangued a crowd that 'it would never be well until men cut the throats of rich cornmongers', or the labourers who, told grain was 9 shillings a bushel, declared they would rise since 'they were as good be slain in the market place as starve'.[9] To Sturley it did seem that Stratford corn was 'beyond all other countries, dear and over dear'; so 'There is a meeting expected here tomorrow', he warned Quiney, 'The Lord knoweth to what end it will sort!'

'You are all resolved rather to die than to famish?' (I, i, 3): it is within the scenario of an early modern grain riot, with its ritual encounter between rulers and poor, that the opening of *Coriolanus* takes place. For, contrary to the cliché that what we see in this scene is an inarticulate rabble, the plebeians express themselves according to the rules of what E. P. Thompson has called 'a highly complex form of popular action, disciplined and with clear objectives'. Moreover, according to historians, even threats to kill engrossers that punctuate food riots must be read as formulae to coerce authority into action.[10] In *Coriolanus*, therefore, the Citizens act out a traditional programme when they arm themselves 'with pikes, ere we become rakes' (21), and vote to enforce a communal consensus by selling grain at a 'just' price. Their attack on forestalling conforms to the fact that food rioting was never a simple reflex to dearth, but aimed to prevent the market imperative from draining supply. For far from objecting to the market *per se*, what the Citizens resist is the unregulated 'counter market' of producers and middlemen that was transporting food away from the marketplace. Perhaps nowhere in England was the marketplace more vital than at Stratford, where, though malting and glove-making were important, prosperity depended on the town's location as a centre for corn from Warwickshire's 'feldon region to be sold to the north of the county, with dairy products passing the other way'.[11] Yet, as Quiney and Sturley testified, restrictive dealing by surrounding farmers had siphoned off the supply from the corn exchange, leaving Shakespeare's friends divided in loyalty when their neighbours grew riotous 'with the want they feel through dearness of corn'. So, if 'the

moral economy of the crowd' helps explain the tempered reaction of
England's governors to the people's pikestaffs, it also accounts for the
fact that (compared to the rabble-rousing scenes in *Henry vi, Part 2*) the
Citizens in *Coriolanus* are presented so equivocally. It cannot be
coincidental that the Tribunes, who occupy the roles of Shakespeare's
two associates as magistrates and 'wealsmen', are likened to maltsters
who 'allay' their beer (ii, i, 46–54). The impartiality critics detect in the
play was determined, it emerges, by the ambivalence of Stratford's
corporation of brewers and seedsmen as both agents and victims of the
market.

II

'If the drink you give me touch my palate adversely', Menenius baits the
Tribunes, 'I make a crooked face' (55); and in September 1598 Stratford
council would indeed ban the sale of 'strong drink' and order ale-houses
to stock the maltsters' watered brew. At the same meeting Richard
Quiney was appointed to ride to London to lobby for the town's
exemption from taxes for national defence, on account of poverty and
hunger. The relations of the early modern market are inscribed in the
Shakespearean text, and it is apt that when Aufidius is 'fidiuss'd' (or
taxed) by Coriolanus (ii, i, 130), he retreats from 'the market place' to
'the city mills' (i, v, 26; i, x, 31). Similarly, though in Plutarch the rising
which Menenius forestalls is against 'the sore oppression of usurers',
Shakespeare adjusted the circumstances of the revolt to sharpen its
relevance to the subsistence crisis. So, when Menenius lectures the crowd
he retails the dogma that famine is divine retribution, as sermons
attributed it to sabbath-breaking or drunkenness:

> For the dearth,
> The gods, not the patricians, make it, and
> Your knees to them, not arms, must help.
> (i, i, 71–3)

It is in the light of this scaremongering – refuted by the Citizens,
Coriolanus and the Senate itself when corn is doled – that Menenius's
Fable of the Belly must be interpreted. As he slyly rhymes, it is a tale as stale
as the flour that paupers are sold (91), and in its latest formulation, in
Sidney's *Defence of Poetry*, had been cited as the acme of disingenuous
sophistry: 'for the tale is notorious, and as notorious that it was a tale.'[12]
Just as Greville was to mystify 'Exchange' as 'the heart' from whence
'each limb receives his health' (418), Menenius expropriates the carnival

image of the belly to naturalise the invisible transactions of commodity circulation, where, as Jean-Christophe Agnew writes, 'Carried along on a tide of commercial paper that spoke voicelessly the utterances of the absent, commerce now filled the intervals between fairs and the interstices between markets.'[13] For editors notice that the point of Menenius's story of the patricians' meagre diet of bran is a cynical irrelevance to a situation where it is the people who must eke out chaff. By transposing the metonym of the plebeians' aching belly into a metaphor of capitalist ownership, therefore, Menenius effects a semantic slide that enacts the legerdemain of the market, leaving the workers literally lost for their own words. This is sharp practice, incorporating the productivity of the people – its seed and semiotics – in a new circulation of commodities and meanings governed by what Greville called the merchant's 'Unknown mystery . . . / Whereby he raiseth or lets fall all things, / And though inferior, binds or looseth kings' (417), the market's invisible hand:

> Though that all at once cannot
> See what I do deliver out to each,
> Yet I can make my audit up, that all
> From me do back receive the flour of all,
> And leave me but the bran.
> (I, i, 141–5)

Foucault notes that the old idea of the city as a body metamorphosed in the Shakespearean era, as money became the medium of exchange and mercantilism anticipated Harvey's anatomy to describe the liquidity of wealth. In this way the popular body of the marketplace and Corpus Christi became the body politic of market economics and corporate capital. Hobbes's Leviathan is fed, therefore, from veins of profit redistributed through arteries of investment, as goods are carried, according to Menenius, through 'rivers of blood' for a 'receipt' (111). 'Thus circulation became a fundamental category of analysis', Foucault observes, and the arterial analogy signified that 'just as representation covers itself with representations which represent it, so all kinds of wealth are related in a system of exchange.' As Menenius says, all relations between money, goods and labour are aggregated in the Belly's audit, which the limbs naively 'digest'.[14] Similarly, this 'pretty tale' (89) mystifies commodity circulation to render real relations inscrutable. But Menenius is uninterested in the Fable's truth content. As an auditor for his supplier, he laughs, he has been 'The book of his good acts whence men have read / His fame . . . haply amplified; / For I have ever verified my friends with all the size that verity / Would . . . suffer.' If he cheats for

him it is by sleight of hand, as 'Like to a bowl upon a subtle ground, / I have
tumbled past the throw, and in his praise / Have almost stamp'd the
leasing' (v, ii, 15–22). His use is as 'his liar' (30), to be economical with
truth and 'diet' his 'praises sauc'd with lies' (I, ix, 52), since Coriolanus 'is
ill-school'd in / Bolted language; meal and bran together / He throws'
in 'over-measure' (III, i, 137; 318–20). By inflating reputation like
dough, Menenius thus illustrates how the market invests value in a
commodity regardless of intrinsic worth. His lying epitomises the process
sketched by Baudrillard, whereby the language of money became an
all-encompassing signifying system after the Renaissance, as meaning
was detached from referents and use values were transformed into
exchange values characterised by arbitrariness.[15] So, if Rome has a
Senate of shopkeepers, the Citizens are mere consumers according to
this double book-keeping, their common wealth dissolved in private
profit.

   Coriolanus is a text dominated by imagery of digestion, circulation and
liquefaction, as symbolic value, grounded in the rarity of metals or
inheritance of rank, is diluted into the endless exchange of equivalences,
where everything or anyone can stand for something else. It is Menenius,
the knightly victualler, whose function is to lubricate this slide from the
manor to the market. As his name suggests, Menenius appears amenable.
This wholesaler appeals to his retailers through the Falstaffian language
of carnival, with its festive melange of banquets, bowls and buttocks.
Everything he says harks back to the potlatch of the gift relationship,
whereby each desire was gratified, men were defined by gargantuan
consumption, and as Baudrillard writes, 'The reversibility of gift in
counter-gift, of exchange in sacrifice, of time in the cycle, of production in
destruction, and of each linguistic value term', annulled 'time, language,
economic exchange, accumulation and power'.[16] Despite his commercial
practice of adulterating the wheat he sells as craftily as the maltsters water
drink, his assumed mask is therefore as a lord of misrule, 'a humorous
patrician, and one that loves a cup of hot wine, with not a drop of allaying
Tiber in't' (II, i, 46–7). So though it is the plebeians who have the empty
stomachs, his excuse for his hero's ruthlessness is that 'he had not din'd: /
The veins unfill'd, our blood is cold, and then / We . . . are unapt / To give
or to forgive; but when we have / . . . stuff'd our blood / With wine and
feeding, we have suppler souls / Than in our priest-like fasts. (v, i, 50–6).
Menenius is the last Shakespearean politician to 'Stir up the [city's] youth
to merriment' to distract it (*A Midsummer Night's Dream*, I, i, 12). His
enemies know him 'well enough' to suspect that his gamesmanship is
counterfeit, but even they admire the strategy of this 'perfect giber for the
table' (II, i, 81). It is the ancient Roman ploy of bread and circuses. For as
Bakhtin reminds us, eating and drinking were crucial to the imagination

of traditional societies because they symbolised the collective life of the marketplace:

> The encounter of man with the world which takes place inside the open, biting, rending, chewing mouth, is one of the most ancient and important objects of thought and imagery. Here man tastes the world, introduces it to his body, makes it part of himself. . . . Man's encounter with the world in the act of eating is joyful, triumphant; he triumphs over the world, devours it without being devoured himself. The limits between man and the world are erased, to man's advantage.[17]

Menenius is a prototype of Stuart seigneurialism, who makes his 'very house reel' to salute Coriolanus (II, i, 110), and who trumpets the policy of Midland landowners such as Robert Dover that 'We feast in our defence.'[18] But as his empty hands reveal, the world of the play is no longer that of manorial society, where sowing and harvest are shared and celebrated in rites of commensality. As Menenius knows to his credit, Rome has a complex market economy where food is sold for profit through warehouses and mills owned by wholesalers and retailers. It is a community much like Stratford, not only of farmers and labourers, but of 'faucet sellers' (II, i, 70), 'tradesmen . . . in their shops' (IV, vi, 8), and 'apron men' (97), where 'all trades / And occupations' (IV, i, 12) fight to 'feed on one another' (I, i, 187), and the poor hope the 'wars devour' the engrosser (257), whom they consign 'To th'pot' (I, iv, 49). For as Bakhtin explains, food was changing its symbolic meaning in the Shakespearean period as the world of carnival succumbed to privatisation of production and consumption:

> In the oldest system of images food was related to work. It concluded work and struggle and was their crown. Work triumphed in food. Human labour's struggle with the world ended in food, in the swallowing of that which had been wrested from the world. As the last victorious stage of work the image of food symbolised the entire labour process. There were no dividing lines: labour and food represented two sides of the same struggle and victory. Labour and food were collective; the whole of society took part in them. But when food was separated from work as part of a private way of life, then nothing remained of the old images: of man's encounter with the world and tasting of it, the open mouth, the joyous celebration. Nothing was left but a series of artificial, meaningless metaphors.[19]

Like that plausible 'father of the county', Sir Thomas Lucy, Menenius
appears to be 'one that hath always loved the people . . . honest enough'
in doling 'charitable care' (I, i, 50–64). His opinion of the citizens as 'rats',
reveals him, however, as a charlatan whose 'bale' is really bane (161). His
patrician carnival is undercut by Coriolanus, who spurns the moral
economy: 'They said they were an-hungry, sigh'd forth proverbs – / That
hunger broke stone walls; . . . that gods sent not / Corn for the rich men
only' (I, i, 204–6). Likewise, Quiney and Sturley were rebuffed when they
pressed 'the Knights of the Parliament' for relief through Fulke's cousin,
the rapacious lord of the manor, Sir Edward Greville of Milcote, while the
deputation to Lucy met apparent success. On 28 January he relayed to the
Privy Council 'the great complaint of the poor' of Stratford against
engrossers. Ministers apprised Sheriffs of adjoining counties about
'corn-masters having forsaken their usual markets', but caustically
reminded Lucy that relief was his responsibility. One week later
Parliament was dissolved and the Act became law that prescribed five
'overseers of the poor' in every parish, 'to raise a stock of stuff to set the
poor on work, and money for relief of the lame, old, blind and such not able
to work'. In Shakespeare's Rome also, 'They are dissolv'd', sneers
Coriolanus of 'the other troop' of commoners, as five tribunes are selected
to administer relief and 'a petition granted' that he predicts will 'make bold
power look pale' (209–15). His outrage is stirred less by a landlord's fear
that 'a frank donation' will 'nourish disobedience' – 'Which we ourselves
have plough'd for, sow'd and scatter'd' – as by his business sense that dole
cuts the contract between worker and employer: 'They know the corn /
Was not our recompense . . . They ne'er did service for't . . . [they] / Did
not deserve corn gratis.' So the reason why 'The senate's courtesy' fed / The
ruin of the state' is that it broke the ring the farmers rigged to lock the cost of
corn to wages, revealing Coriolanus's own price for grain and services as
exorbitant (III, i, 70; 115–31). It is at this point in staging 'the great debate
on the poor' that the play is most prophetic, for Coriolanus's fury would be
repeated until the nineteenth century in complaints against the Law
employers called 'the Idle Man's Charter'.[20]

Coriolanus reproduces a battle of discourses that seams the text of the
Elizabethan Poor Law. For no sooner had Bacon tabled bills 'Against
Enclosure and Depopulation' in the Commons on the first day of the 1597
Parliament, quoting Ovid as witness that 'Crops grow where Troy once
stood', than a Puritan lawyer named Finch stood up for the propertied,
blaming 'the miserable estate of the Godly sort' on the 'ill-doing of the
idle'. Throughout the debate these two discourses of property and
paternalism duelled, as one side feared that 'because tillage in their hands
yields more profit than dispersed in the hands of many, gentlemen will

become grinders of the poor', warning that 'no realm can have joy or continuance where there groweth cleanness of teeth through scarcity of bread'; while the other retorted that dearth was an act of God, maintaining that 'Men are not compelled by penalties but allured by profit.' The outcome was a text codifying the regime's ambivalence towards the market, as Parliament carried contradictory measures 'for the punishment of rogues, vagabonds and sturdy beggars', 'relief of the poor' and 'erecting of hospitals and working houses'. 'A feast of charity' the paternalist Bacon called it; while for the Puritan William Perkins it was a Law to ensure the idle would 'as rotten legs and arms drop off the body'; and dissolving Parliament on 9 February, Elizabeth fused both idioms when she reproved Midland JPs for dealing with neither vagabonds nor engrossers, likening them to 'dogs in the Capitol, that being set to bark at rebels, annoy good subjects'.[21] It was out of such discursive contradictions that Shakespeare also made a play of analogies between ancient Rome and contemporary Stratford.

'Bid them . . . keep their teeth clean' (II, iii, 62): for Coriolanus the debate about relief is risible. Likewise, 'My speech is against the body of this bill', joked one opponent of the Law, a Wiltshire Member called Jackman, 'not to tick it on the toe, but to stick at its heart.' The belly laughter of the people might be coopted for the modern market, as Menenius shows when he symbolically amputates the Citizen as 'the great toe of this assembly' (I, i, 154). The play charts a movement of appropriation that yokes popular culture to private enterprise, therefore, when the festive crowd which celebrates relief by throwing caps and 'Shouting emulation' (I, i, 211) is pressed into the army. For behind this episode lies the historic change in the structure of labour when the new class of free wage labourers was recruited for capitalist farming. Under the 1563 Statute of Apprentices craftsmen 'meet for labour' might be compelled to mow at harvest and boys taken from towns to work on farms, a regulation designed to restrict the mobility of labour and preserve class distinctions by harnessing the artisans of market towns to the master–servant relationship. The result was a 'Statute Hiring Fair' at Michaelmas in places such as Stratford, when labourers assembled in the market square, 'clad in their best apparel' and wearing badges denoting skills, to bargain with farmers over hours and wages. When a servant was engaged, he would be given an 'old suit, a pair of breeches, an old hat' or a 'fastpenny' as an earnest of employment. Most 'stattit fairs' would be suppressed for riotousness in Hardy's England, though Stratford's Mop Fair survived as a memorial of its former economic importance.[22] Coriolanus transforms the Roman carnival into a specific kind of English festival, therefore, when he challenges 'they That most are willing' to work under the sign 'wherein you see me smear'd':

> If any such be here . . .
> Let him alone, or so many so minded,
> Wave thus to express his disposition,
> And follow Martius. . . .
>   A certain number
> (Though thanks to all) must I select from all . . .
>   Please you to march
> And I shall quickly draw out . . .
> Which men are best inclin'd.
>
>   (I, vi, 66–85)

As lord of the harvest, Coriolanus would be bound to regale his men for work 'Well ploughed, well soughed, / Well reaped, well mowed', in the refrain of the folk rhyme, 'And never a load overthrowed.' Instead, by cancelling their swag, he typifies the Tudor campaign to yoke the marketplace to mastery. Michael Bristol likens him to a Lenten butcher, licensed to kill all year, an image for his scheme to corner supply and disrupt the cycle of glut and scarcity.[23] If Menenius 'revels long a'nights' like Antony (*Julius Caesar*, II, ii, 116), Coriolanus, whose face 'sours ripe grapes' (v, iv, 18), is aligned with critics of festival like Cassius and Casca. He has no need of ales or harvest home as 'lord o'th'field' (I, vi, 47), which he rigs so none doubt his 'true purchasing' (II, i, 138). War is a horse fair where he wagers his plough-team against all-comers (I, iv, 1–7), because his rival, Aufidius, underwrites him as 'greater . . . than he' (IV, v, 165). Each champion hates the other 'Worse than a promise-breaker' (I, viii, 2), yet 'were I anything but what I am', they pledge, 'I would wish me only he' (I, i, 230), so their mutuality binds them in a ring. 'Let the first budger die the other's slave', they compound (I, viii, 5). Constant 'Only . . . with him' (I, i, 234–8), each breaches 'rotten privilege and custom' (I, x, 23) and 'would pawn his fortunes / To hopeless restitution' to compete (III, i, 15); until Coriolanus's price is hiked so high he rejects pay as 'A bribe to pay my sword' (I, ix, 38), declaring he needs no validation, since 'He rewards his deeds with doing them' (II, ii, 128). This solitary reaper goes through 'the gates' to mow alone, (I, iv, 51), so he can brag 'Alone I did it' (v, vi, 116); as even at sixteen, 'When he might act the woman in the scene, / He prov'd best man i'th'field' (II, ii, 96–7). But if Coriolanus makes hay on the field, his self-inflation is doomed to crash when he returns to 'the market-place' (I, v, 26), for what he seems to embody is the fallacy of the drive to fix identity in use. He is a figure for what Baudrillard terms the capitalist era of the sign, when the concept of man as producer chained meaning to stable referents to hold use and exchange values in line. From this moment, Baudrillard proposes, signifiers and signifieds meshed, as if reality preceded the sign, because value's determinant had been located in utility, a vanishing point where labour and reward were made to coincide. The use value of market capitalism thus corresponded to the signified of the classical sign: as signifiers were gripped by signifieds, use value fixed exchange. Coriolanus is a tyro of this symbolic revolution, when meaning was bolted onto use and man became his work.[24]

'If I should tell thee o'er this thy day's work', his commander grants Coriolanus, 'Thou't not believe thy deeds' (I, ix, 1–2). Cominius pinpoints why Coriolanus refuses fanfares. His rejection of applause stems from a fixation that 'Action is eloquence' (II, ii, 76) and labour its own reward. In a famous essay D. J. Gordon traced the way that 'Name is fame' in this text, yet 'Words are torn from what they signify' and 'The absoluteness of the self, the I, cannot be maintained'.[25] Baudrillard historicises what Gordon intuited, that the play dramatises a crisis in subjectivity and representation. For Coriolanus's work ethic is the key to his hatred of the stage. Like Greville, who condemned 'word-sellers', and whom Jonathan Dollimore reads as one of the forerunners of the English revolution in his realist mimesis, Coriolanus spurns 'acclamations hyperbolical' (I, ix, 50) because he wants language to refer to reality, as Greville preferred pictures to 'manifest the life'.[26] A semantic engrosser, he hoards not only seed but meaning from exchange, sure his usefulness speaks for itself: 'Better it is to die, better to starve, / Than crave the hire which we do deserve' (II, iii, 112). His tragedy, therefore, is that he cannot dominate the marketplace as he monopolises the field. In Rome value is liquefied by transaction, as commodities fluctuate in price. No sooner has he fought than he is given a new name as 'sign of what you are' (I, ix, 25). Like the garlands which 'proved him a man', 'th'addition' of a title helps 'Rome know the value of her own' (I, iii, 14; 20; 69). His backers grasp what the individualist must erase: that far from being essential, identity is created by exchange. For when Coriolanus eventually enters the labour market he learns why men are 'so surnam'd': that even one of 'The noble house of the Martians' (II, iii, 236–41) was 'nothing. . . / Till he had forg'd himself a name' (v, i, 13). His mother had cued him as his 'father's son' (IV, i, 10), as he is 'schoolmaster' to his own (I, iii, 56); but even his patronymic had been earned, because there never was a Martius, it seems, without the name negotiated among maltsters and plumbers by those ancestors 'That our best water brought by conduits', in the most exchangeable and liquid form of public work (II, iii, 240).

III

The public water supply of Shakespearean Rome is metonymic of the liquidity of value through exchange, as glove-making and brewing flowered in Stratford on water reputed to be England's best. The circulation of social energy in this play is highly specific. Thus, in the early modern town to which Coriolanus returns like an Elizabethan from the wars, 'All tongues speak of him' (II, i, 203), as 'the commons make / A thunder with their caps and shouts' (II, ii, 264), since power is theatre and is won 'i'th'marketplace' (I, v, 26; II, i, 231; II, ii, 159; III, i, 29; 329; III, ii, 93; 104; 131; v, vi, 3). The campaign that carries Coriolanus towards office reproduces the machinery of English politics, complete with woolsacks to symbolise enclosers' wealth. In particular, electoral procedure is that employed to choose Members of Parliament in the period, as the historian Mark Kishlansky shows, with a candidate adopted at the assizes by the gentry and presented for acclamation to the freeholders outside. But as Kishlansky reveals, this system of *selection* by unanimity was collapsing as Shakespeare wrote, and the text records a clash of values as the people query whether 'if he do require our voices we ought not to deny him', submit 'We may, Sir, if we will', and move that 'the greater part carries it' (II, iii, 1–2; 38). Latent here is the modern idea of the 'greater poll' (III, i, 133) as 'the voice of them all', and of the 'Representative' as 'An Actor of Many men made One by Plurality of Voices', who has his 'words and actions *Owned*', as Hobbes explained, by those he represents. As election superseded selection, contests would indeed become like hiring fairs, with 'voices' pledged in exchange for being voiced in a carnival of flattery and bribes, a reciprocity inimical to grandees like Coriolanus, who had taken office as their 'own desert' (II, iii, 67). Pre-Civil War society had no means to solve the impasse when 'arithmetic' outvoted 'worth' (III, i, 236–43), so an election would be 'addled' when, as happens in Rome, a candidate 'would miss it rather / Than carry it but by the suit of the gentry to him / And the desire of the nobles' (II, i, 235). This was literally a crisis of representation in the marketplace, which Kishlansky believes 'brought England as close to collapse as Coriolanus's Rome', and that the play portrays so accurately it seems Shakespeare must have 'had first hand experience' himself.[27] Though Kishlansky never refers to it, such experience would have been gained in Stratford, when Shakespeare's townsmen revenged the dearth by blocking the election of Fulke Greville.

An aristocrat, like Coriolanus, obsessed by genealogy (as a Neville his mother had 'a charter' as long as Volumnia's 'to extol her blood' (I, ix, 14)), Greville embodied the paradox of England's Puritan nobility as it straddled the market through monopolies and engrossing. 'A lamb indeed, that bars like a bear' (II, i, 10), Fulke crossed the Greville wool trade with the ursine aggression of the Earls of Warwick in his arms and enclosures. Infamous for disafforesting and mining Cannock Wood, he also amassed a fortune from clearance of his estates in Warwickshire, where, as Joan Rees regrets, nothing could 'exonerate him from the charge of being a grasping landlord'.[28] By 1619 his annual income was a colossal £7,000 from land in eleven counties, allowing him to lavish £20,000 on Warwick Castle. He became an expert on farming techniques, advising Cecil on crops and livestock; yet Aubrey thought greed had 'done him more dishonour than Sir Philip Sidney's friendship hath done him honour';[29] and he alienated his constituents by his argument in the Commons that 'For the poverty of the country, we have no reason to think it poor: the dearth of everything showeth plenty of money.' Even at Westminster he disparaged the 'multitude' of Members, defended monopolies by doubting 'whether everything that was vulgarly complained of were of necessity to be amended', and opposed the Union from fear a 'multiplicity' of Scottish 'voices' would 'dispose of' English land.[30] Just as Coriolanus deplored a system 'where gentry, title, wisdom / Cannot conclude but by the yea and no / Of general ignorance' (III, i, 143–5), Greville asserted that Members of Parliament were answerable to the Crown: 'It is said, our countries are poor and we must respect those who sent us hither. Why, so we must remember who sent for us hither.' Though assiduous in his family interests, his 'arrogance and ineptitude' as a Member disappointed his county. As the town clerk of Warwick explained, he was 'one more remote' than was desired: 'living in London and a long time in that private and obscure manner caused him to be disregarded. . . . He was so extremely covetous and subtly cautious that he would neither by purse or power be seen in the affairs of the corporation.' 'Sir Fulke Greville', Stratford's Chamberlain audited against parliamentary expenses for 1598, 'for nothing: 40s'.[31] Not surprisingly, then, when he stood for the Commons in the aftermath of the famine, it seems the Warwickshire electors reminded him to 'think, if we give you anything, we hope to gain by you' (II, iii, 72), with consequences that prefigured *Coriolanus*.

'The people / Must have their voices; neither will they bate / One jot of ceremony' (II, ii, 139–41): if critics are perplexed by the status of the peoples' 'voices' in *Coriolanus* this is because the text reflects contemporary confusion about representative government and what Kishlansky detects as 'an undercurrent of disharmony that would render traditional practice inadequate'. Representation is in flux in this play as it was in Shakespearean Warwickshire, where notables like the Grevilles warned the gentry that 'You are plebeians / If they be senators; and they are no less / When, both your voices blended, the great'st taste / Most palates theirs . . . when two authorities are up, Neither supreme, how soon confusion / May enter' (III, i, 100–10). The process can be illustrated by the struggle for Warwick, which had been in the pocket of the Grevilles since 1586, when Fulke's father had forced a Puritan nominee on the borough after rallying support at 'a solemn dinner' of 'the meanest inhabitants'.[32] The Greville stranglehold lasted a generation, and could only be ended by similar canvassing of the Commons; but in 1621 the

> Burgesses assembled at the Shire Hall had notice of diverse freeholders in the yard, who being demanded the cause of their assembly answered they came to give their voices in the election for the parliament. Mr Bailiff told them they had no voices else they would have been called for, but they replied: 'If we have any voices we choose Sir Clement Throckmorton and Sir Bartholemew Hales', and so cried altogether.

On this occasion Fulke imposed a friend and a nephew against the popular nominees, who withdrew, persuaded the right of choice lay with the corporation; but in 1625 the thwarted candidate, Sir Thomas Puckering, 'profanely complained it appertained not to the corporation to elect, but that it ought to be popular and that all inhabitants had voices'. When the Committee of Privileges adjudicated, the corporation deposed that Puckering 'was not so commodious by sending corn to the market for the general good nor a man of such noble hospitality' as to deserve election; but in 1628 the Committee ruled that the choice did belong to the commonalty, so the election of Fulke's heir Robert was declared void in favour of Puckering. By the 1620s, therefore, Coriolanus's fears were borne out in the county town, as the voices of 'two authorities' were indeed 'blended', until 'the great'st taste' of power slipped into the mouth of 'the common body' (II, ii, 53), and the Greville monopoly was broken by an alliance of commoners with the local Junius Brutus.[33]

If the greatest dilemma facing the seventeenth-century gentry was the conflict between loyalty to the two 'countries' of nation and county, as localist history teaches,[34] events in Warwickshire suggest this problem was but one aspect of a reorganisation of the whole concept of representation in a market economy. By 1628 ideas about representation had shifted towards the belief that electors should act as individuals according to conscience and the 'Freedom of voice' that the Sheriff of Cheshire told the voters was 'your inheritance and the greatest prerogative of the subject, which ought to be kept inviolate and cannot be taken from you by any command'. Yet as late as 1641 Lord Maynard abhorred the electioneering of the Earl of Warwick at 'popular assemblies where fellows without shirts challenge as good a voice as myself'; and the equilibrium of the system depended on neutralising these attitudes through what Kishlansky terms 'self-correcting mechanisms'.[35] In Warwickshire this meant magistrates 'were wont to advise together about the choice of knights of the shire' prior to the adoption meeting – which they do in *Coriolanus* – but that their nominee went uncontested (as happened repeatedly with Greville's successor in his seat, the younger Sir Thomas Lucy), so long as he never 'turned courtier' but 'stood for the good of his Country'.[36] Descended from king-makers, however, Fulke Greville prided himself that 'he never sought for or obtained any place or preferment' by asking for it, and incarnated the Tudor assumption that 'The heir to so much', in the words of J. E. Neale, 'endowed with exceptional qualities and the favour of his prince, was a person of such eminence that his monopoly of a county seat was a natural right'.[37] Yet it was precisely this assertion of the 'quality' of the candidate that was doomed to be crushed by the mathematics of the market and the weight of numerical superiority, once the 'fellows without shirts' established that 'every one of us has a single honour, in giving him our voices with our own tongues' (II, ii, 45), and elections evolved from massed acclamation to the casting of individual votes.

With five residences, Greville had 'inherited . . . the buildings of [his] fancy', and viewed a parliamentary seat as his desert (II, i, 197). He had, in fact, been returned for Warwickshire unopposed four times when he stood again in September 1601. But what had changed was his relationship with the electorate; for when newsletters carried transcripts of debates back to the 'middling sort', supplemented by verbal reports like those given by the Tribunes in Shakespeare's play, his constituents would have known that 'of late / When corn was given gratis [he] repin'd, / Scandal'd the suppliants for the people, call'd them / Time-pleasers, flatterers, foes to nobleness' (III, i, 41–7). His intervention in the Poor Law debate is unrecorded, but he versified what may have been his speech – and the germ of *Coriolanus* – in *Monarchy*, begun around 1599. Using a discourse of Livian constitutionalism devised by Elizabethan antiquaries to equate the Commons with the Roman Senate,[38] he attributed 'the glory of old Rome' to its rulers' inflexibility, 'and not the people's doom: / Proportion from the great world to the small / Showing, with many limbs, one head rules all' (620). By agitating for agrarian relief the Tribunes struck 'A fiery spark', he declared, 'which lacking foreign stuff, / At home finds fuel to make blaze enough' (638):

> What but the people's mutinous conventions
> Under those factious Tribunes, scattered
> Rome's public patrimony? And with dissensions

Her wise opposing Senate threatened,
By their Agrarian Laws, engines of wrong,
Dispersing lands which to the State belong?
(621)

Monarchy was compiled over several years and reads in part like a
diary of its author's bruising electoral experience. It was 'their
tumultuous election of Caesars', he believed, that had ruined Rome:
'This power of choice making the soldiers know, / Their head above had
yet his head below . . . / By which their Emperors forced were / In public,
and self indigence to strain / Laws by mens' voices' (634–5). 'After
Tarquin', he considered, 'though Rome stood entire, / Yet fell she
into many-headed power, / By which like straws, light people set on
fire'; for 'as / These many heads oft civil war invite: / So against
foreign force they worse unite.' Moreover, 'Where many heads have
power . . . / So the best men must be sent away, / By ostracism, to qualify
their fame . . . / Whence Athens, swaying to Democratie, / For ever
changing her Archontes be' (592–607). 'How can the democratical
content', the Midland landowner fumed, 'Where that blind multitude
chief master is? / And where . . . / The most and worst sort govern all
estates?':

Since, as those persons usually do haunt
The market places, which at home have least:
So here those spirits most intrude and vaunt
To do the business of this common beast,
   That have no other means to vent their ill,
   Than by transforming real things to will.
(610–11)

Though Whig historians would claim him, Greville's constitutionalism
was 'too absolute' for modern electioneering (III, ii, 39), being based on
a conviction, reiterated throughout *Monarchy*, that a representative
system 'must omit / Real necessities, and give way the while / To
unstable slightness' (III, i, 141–7). Because 'parliaments assembled be, /
Not for the end of one state, but of all' (292), a 'supreme synod', he
held, must be 'compos'd of nobleness . . . / Where they that clearest
shine . . . worthily deserve a place' (325–8). In 1598 he had himself
become such a star as Navy Treasurer, and the 1601 election was thus
timed to put these principles to the test, in the week of the Spanish
invasion of Ireland. What ensued in Warwick was a drama like
Shakespeare's, when the candidate arrived from the royal ordnance for
the 'after-meeting' of the Michaelmas assize (II, ii, 38) – which coincided

with the hiring fair – but disdained 'To beg of Hob and Dick their needless vouches' in the yard (115), since 'his blood and quality, his service to the State and estimation in her Majesty's opinion deserved to be preferred'. Conceding that their duty was 'To gratify his service that / Hath thus stood for his country' (II, ii, 38–40), the freeholders shouted that they 'chose this man' (II, iii, 153), but instantly 'almost all Repented in their election' (252), causing the Sheriff, Sir Thomas Lucy, to defer assent and 'give public notice into the whole county for a full assembly'. The Privy Council upbraided Lucy for scheming 'to supplant or divert the choice', alleging he had 'of purpose carried the matter to serve some turn of faction and partiality', and implying it was 'a purpos'd thing [that] grows by plot' (III, i, 37); but though the Sheriff promised to 'have the service better accomplished' with a county poll, the damage had been done, since, as the Lord Keeper tartly observed, 'by deferring it to such a preposterous time, Parliament will be gone before that will be thoroughly performed'.[39]

Like Coriolanus, Greville cited Athens, where 'people had more absolute power' (115), as proof 'Democratie / In her craz'd moulds great empires cannot cast' (639). By contrast, England's 'large times, strength-like, kept elections free, / Sheriffs us'd no self art on their county days' and 'Great men' had no need to sell themselves in 'shrapes of majesty', for 'what can scepters lose by choice, / Where they reserve the royalty of voice?' (297). Evidently he expected another such free run in Warwickshire, with electors bought like 'woollen vassals' and drilled 'to show bare heads in congregations, yawn, be still, and wonder, / When but one of my ordinance stood up / To speak of peace or war' (III, ii, 9–13). But as *Coriolanus* records, the conduct of elections was being transformed as society became more adversarial, and 'A seat in the Commons was now to be won in a struggle of will, beliefs and resources. The identity of interests that once characterized elections was becoming a memory of a vanished age. In its place came strife and competition.'[40] Yet contested elections were rare before 1640 precisely because they fragmented the county, and in a system where his function was to compose accord, Lucy's acquiescence in a poll can only have been compelled by a show-down, like that in the play, involving three candidates for two places (II, ii, 4). The Sheriff claimed his 'evil health' prevented him giving the explanation Cecil demanded, but since Stratford's citizens had 'no hope of favour at his hands', Menenius perhaps hints at his predicament when he swears to Coriolanus's family: 'Before he should thus stoop to th'herd, but that / The violent fit o'th'time craves it . . . I would put mine armour on, / Which I can scarcely bear' (III, ii, 32–4). Like all seventeenth-century contests, this one had been propelled by a candidate's pride in status. According to the Privy

Council, Greville deserved 'to be regarded more in this than himself desireth', but now he was faced with the dire consequence of his haughty refusal to push himself 'before others in the election'.[41]

IV

Ministers advised Lucy that they looked 'to be better satisfied as soon as you may repair unto us.' The story he had to tell was of bitter conflict between the Grevilles and the people of Stratford, which dated from the dearth but took a dangerous turn that year, when Edward Greville enclosed the town commons. On 21 January six Aldermen, led by Quiney, armed themselves with picks and spades, broke down Sir Edward's fences, drove cattle onto the commons, and cut wood 'to the damage of £40'. Next day they tried to toll the encloser's corn in the market, but his agent 'smote' the sergeant and 'swore a great oath that whoso put his hand into his sacks should leave his hand behind him' (III, i, 316). The six were charged with riot, detained in the Marshalsea, and released on bail. In June Quiney rode to London with a declaration of common rights signed by elders such as Shakespeare's father, and manoeuvred with his 'brother Sturley' to 'move the court' out of Lucy's jurisdiction. The case was still undecided on 2 September when Quiney was elected Bailiff. At this moment an agrarian dispute became a political crisis, as it does in *Coriolanus*, when Greville challenged Quiney's magistracy. The lords of the manor had never acknowledged Stratford's Bailiffs, and Greville had vetoed Quiney in 1592, until persuaded by his cousin to be more wily. This time there would be no intervention from a politician who himself disputed the people's officers: 'For Tribunes be the Champions they boast, / An heteroclite Magistrate, devis'd without rule, to have all rules by him lost, / Religion scorn'd, laws, duty tyranniz'd' (638). 'What should the people do with these bald tribunes?' Coriolanus asks, 'On whom depending, their obedience fails / To the greater bench?' (164–6). This was evidently the Grevilles' view, and they seemed determined to 'pluck out / The multidinous tongue', by force if necessary (155). Briefing the council's solicitor, Thomas Greene (Shakespeare's kinsman), Quiney therefore begged him to take seriously 'Sir Edward Greville's words, of which you are not ignorant: "Sir, what I urge dare not go against me".'[42]

'You are at point to lose your liberties' (192): Coriolanus's threat to 'throw their power i'th'dust' (169) precipitates the Tribunes' resolve to 'stand to our authority / Or let us lose it' (206–7). Likewise, on 16 September Stratford council declared that 'concerning the election of our Bailiff, we hold the choice to be in ourselves and cannot, in regard of our oaths, whereby we are bound to maintain our privileges, grant to [Greville] any right in that choice.' Such was the weight of the issue that the corporation retained no less a counsel than the Attorney General, Sir Edward Coke, who opined 'that the office of baily may be exercised, Sir Edward's consent not being had.' To the common lawyer it was 'by the consent of all' that magistrates such as Quiney 'were establish'd the people's magistrates' (198), and he advised him to 'bring your Charter' to Westminster, 'Insisting on the old prerogative / And power i'th'truth o'th'cause' against 'Tyrannical power' (III, iii, 1–17). A skirmish between maltster and encloser to 'turn [the] current in a ditch / And make [the] channel his' (III, i, 95), had escalated into a feud over 'th'right and strength o'th'commons' (III, iii, 14) to 'curb the will of the nobility', and the authority of the 'graver bench' (III, i, 38; 105) to muzzle petty magistrates like dogs (in Elizabeth's image) 'as often beat for Barking / As kept to do' (II, iii, 213). If the assizes were a 'county parliament' they depended on cooperation between the elite and the local magistracy. No wonder Lucy deferred the election when the Grevilles and the burgesses faced each other on 26 September. The cousins had sat together in the 1593 Parliament, but now 'The people [were] incensed' against them both as 'innovator[s]' and 'foe[s] to the public weal' (III, i, 30; 174), as the pair seem conflated in the character of Coriolanus. That the dramatist witnessed these proceedings is likely, since he was in Stratford. For once we can be sure where Shakespeare stood: on 8 September he had walked beside the Bailiff into Holy Trinity for the funeral of his father: 'Magister Johannes Shakespeare'.[43]

'Behold these are the tribunes of the people, / The tongues o'th'common mouth. I do despise them: / For they do prank them in authority against all sufferance' (21–3): Coriolanus's contempt for the 'liberties and charters' inscribed 'I'th'body of the weal' (II, iii, 178), regains specificity when read back into the politics of Stratford, with its contentious 'double worship' as a manorial borough (III, i, 141). In the tragedy the delayed election enrages the nobility, since, as Cominius huffs, a contest is a 'palt'ring' that fouls the candidate with a 'dishonour'd rub, laid falsely in the plain way of his merit' (58). As Kishlansky writes, in the game played by magnates like the Grevilles, 'refusal to assent to an MP was a statement of dishonour. Freely given, a place in Parliament was a distinction', whereas 'a contest diminished the worth of victor and vanquished.'[44] 'What is the matter', Coriolanus therefore demands, 'That being pass'd for consul with full voice, / I am so dishonour'd that the very hour / You take it off again?' (III, iii, 58–61). Like Greville, he had counted on his war record to speak for itself: for the freemen to put 'tongues in those wounds and speak for them' (7); but what he confronts is a hiring fair, where his terms of trade are reversed, he must beg the poor on knees 'like his / That hath receiv'd an alms' (III, ii, 120), and the 'price o'th'consulship . . . is to ask it kindly.' Though he dons the servile 'gown' of hire, Coriolanus's undoing is that he will not 'capitulate . . . with Rome's mechanics' over his employment (v, iii, 82), on the grounds that his words and deeds are his own property. But without offering his word as surety of 'a match' (II, iii, 40; 74–81), and an 'article / Tying him' to 'think upon you for your voices . . . which you might, / As cause had call'd you up, have held him to' (184–95), his contract can be voided by the very men whom he once hired. In this seller's market, the text foretells, an elite standing for nothing but itself is sure to be ejected by electors now 'looking for a representative not in some prominent figure who would do great things, but in some one who would bring home local goods'.[45]

Coriolanus is often interpreted via the high road of court politics;[46] yet read with a mind to the thesis that what counted in England were 'country matters' – to 'see / Our tradesmen singing in their shops and going / About their functions friendly' (IV, vi, 7–9) – the play stands as a signpost of the emerging market, connecting county with capital. It is provincial annals that restore meaning to a text where what is at stake is representation of the locality. Thus, what Shakespeare hears in the diatribes of a Greville is the engrosser's dread that the bottom will fall out of his market 'if they by suffrages elect' and 'worth abandon' (646). 'Exorbitant aspiring merit' lacks 'true estimation', Greville objected, 'Where many heads have power' (594), and throughout *Monarchy* there is disgust at a market where value 'Can neither fix'd nor govern'd be, / But idle busy rulers with a breath, / Give doom of honour . . . life or death' (606). The Dutch capitalism Greville admired was, Simon Schama notes, 'an elaborate system of protection' pre-empting risk or competition;[47] and Coriolanus also loathes a marketplace where he must truck with 'people, to earn a dearer estimation' (II, iii, 95). Like the gentry who wrecked a Lewes poll in 1628 by refusing to number themselves with the meaner sort'; or Sir Thomas Wentworth, who claimed victory in Yorkshire in 1625 because his supporters were men of quality, Coriolanus cannot fathom a system that pits a man who 'in a cheap estimation is worth all [their] predecessors since Deucalion' (II, i, 90) against freeholders at 'A kinder value than / He hath hereto priz'd them at . . . / That's thousand to one good one' (II, ii, 58–87). For though he blusters that 'On fair ground I could beat forty of them', his canvassers gauge that ''tis odds beyond arithmetic' (III, i, 240–3) when the opposition can muster 'five hundred voices' and another 'twice five hundred' in a poll (II, iii, 209). The Tribunes' 'catalogue / Of . . . voices' (III, iii, 8) is accurate: when Warwickshire was eventually polled in a by-election for the Long Parliament, the 40 shillings property qualification meant that 1,750 voted.[48]

'Thinking the marketplace', as Peter Stallybrass and Allon White show, has been problematic ever since the fair was separated from the mart, work from idleness. Nowhere more so than in *Coriolanus*, a text that drives its action towards the market square, at the intersection of public and private bodies, labour, theatre, language and economics. In the Rome of the play the marketplace is a locus of contending ideologies just as much as in Stratford, where the Bailiff's mace splintered on the Greville's sword. So when Coriolanus, who swore that 'Were he to stand . . . never would he / Appear i'th'market-place' (II, i, 230), assures his mother, 'I am going to the market-place' (III, ii, 131), he descends into an arena of deep conceptual confusion entailed by the muddle of collective and exchange values.[49] And, as eyewitnesses reported, of all the transactions that took place in the market space, the hustings brought these values into sharpest contradiction. George Wither satirised the new type of candidate as one 'who trotted up and down / To every inn and alehouse in the town / To gain a voice', ready to 'feast the cobbler and the smith . . . upon the drunken tapster fawn, / And leave his word and promises in pawn';[50] and Coriolanus is scandalised that in exchange for votes he too must 'mountebank their loves, / Cog their hearts from them, and come home belov'd / Of all the trades in Rome' (132–4). He cannot accept the contract that bound a 'parliament man' to be the hireling or delegate of a locality as *quid pro quo* for votes and wages (in reality 2 shillings a day): 'To brag unto them, thus I did, and thus', as if 'for the hire / Of their breath only . . . / Thus we debase / The nature of our seats, and make the rabble / Call our cares fears; which will in time / Break ope the locks o'th'senate' (II, ii, 147–9; III, i, 134–7). In the event, therefore, his candidacy founders on the crucial test that lost Fulke Greville the support of Stratford: his accountability to his constituency. Accused of being a 'traitor' to the municipality, Coriolanus dooms himself by damning the majority to burn in hell:

The fires i'th'lowest hell fold in the people!
Call me their traitor! Thou injurious tribune!
Within thine eyes sat twenty thousand deaths,
In thy hands clutched as many millions, in
Thy lying tongue both numbers, I would say
'Thou liest' unto thee, with a voice as free
As I do pray the gods.
(III, iii, 69–74)

This candidate is called to 'the elect' without need of an election. According to Neale, 'Puritanism furnishes the clue' to the electoral history of Shakespearean Warwickshire, where the radical protestantism of the landowning elite grated on the urban 'middling sort'.[51] Coriolanus's avowal of his godly vocation chimes, indeed, with the doctrine of election expounded by Greville in *A Treatise of Religion*, that God 'by works will witness our / Election . . . call his Labourers every hour / And pay the first and last with heavenly gain . . . / Pray then; and think, faith hath her mediation . . . / But give accompt of that which God hath given' (56–7; 79). For a landowner like Greville, the parable of the labourers is the perfect text of economic mastery, since it presents the God of the hiring fair as an employer who fixes pay on his own terms: 'for many be called, but few chosen' (Matthew, xx, 16). But by focusing on this capitalist gospel of heaven and hell at the crux of the action, the play anticipates Weber's proposition that the Puritan dogma of predestination produced the 'unprecedented inner loneliness of the single individual' who 'in the most important thing in life, his salvation, was forced to follow his path alone to meet the destiny decreed for him.'[52] Inspired by a Calvinistic certitude in his calling, Coriolanus bears out Weber's observation that the tendency of belief in 'election' was 'to tear the individual from the closed ties with which he was bound to this world' because in practice the doctrine 'meant that God helped those who helped themselves'.[53] Coriolanus's inhuman fate to 'go alone, / Like to a lonely dragon that his fen / Makes fear'd and talk'd of more than seen' (iv, i, 29–31), is in this sense determined by his theory of society as an agglomeration of atomised and warring individuals whose only relationship is a contract each makes from self-interest, like his covenant with God. Plutarch's hero had been surrounded by aristocratic thugs, who 'flocked about him and kept him company';[54] but Shakespeare's Coriolanus turns in upon the self-affirming liberty of his own 'free voice'. It is the irony of the play that it was just this Puritan concept of the individuated self as origin and author of its meaning which would generate, within the lifetime of a magnifico like Fulke Greville, the conditions for popular sovereignty based on contractual agreement between equals.

With all the rhetorical violence of Puritanism, Coriolanus would rather be cast into 'Vagabond exile', or 'pent to linger / But with a grain a day', than buy votes 'at the price of one fair word' (iii, iii, 89–91). 'Against the grain' of competition (ii, iii, 231), the engrosser's monopoly is sealed in the vicious circle of an identity that consumes itself, like his mother's: 'Anger's my meat: I sup upon myself / And so shall starve with feeding' (iv, ii, 50). Nothing in the source – where the election proceeds in a single stage *prior* to the corn debate – prepares for this deadlock between power and the market, in which the question posed is the seventeenth-century one of 'the price' of office. In fact, the text follows events in Stratford, where the 'addled election' was the chance for the council to trade votes with the candidate for a pledge 'That, as his worthy deeds did claim no less / Than what he stood for, so his gracious nature / Would think upon you for your voices, and / Translate his malice towards you into love, / Standing your friendly lord' (ɪɪ, iii, 184–8). But entreated by Quiney to cease litigation, Fulke's cousin had stated 'it should cost him £500 first.' Then, in a striking analogue of the drama, the corporation paid Sir Edward's wife £20 to intercede. Lady Greville 'laboured and thought she should effect it'; but when she sought 'to solicit him / For mercy to his country' (v, i, 71), it seems that Greville – himself deeply mortgaged – reacted as Coriolanus does to Virgilia: 'Wife, mother, child, I know not. My affairs / Are servanted to others' (v, ii, 80). 'Ply Sir Edward night and day', Sturley egged his 'Brother Quiney', 'weary him, that he may bethink him how he may be rid of you'; but 'O, how I fear', he admitted, 'when I see what Sir Edward can do'. 'If, as his nature is, he fall in rage', the corporation hazarded, 'observe and answer / The advantage of his anger' (ɪɪ, iii, 256–8); but this tactic had merely stung his lordship into a resolve to 'jump [the] body with a dangerous physic' (ɪɪɪ, i, 153). Tragedy grips Rome when Coriolanus 'draws his sword' against the Tribunes (Stage Direction, 221): the fate of Shakespeare's townsmen was likewise sealed when a Greville plotted, as Sir Edward now did, that 'We should win it by the sword'.[55] For Quiney and Sturley the stakes in the Warwickshire election had been raised incalculably. A vote for the Greville interest was now literally the cost of living.

'We shall not need to say anything in the favour of the gentleman', the Privy Council wrote on 7 October to the gentry of Worcestershire, where a fracas arose over the choice of Sir Thomas Leighton,

> because his quality and services to the State sufficiently recommend him. It is not our meaning to restrain a free election, but because it is suspected some proceeding may be used against him, which would greatly displease Her Majesty, we thought good to admonish you not to do yourself the wrong to be transported with any such passion, for that as any favour which should be conferred on the gentleman would be very agreeable to Her Majesty, so she would be very sensible of any evil measure offered him.

Such browbeating ensured the 1601 election returned the largest courtier bloc of any Tudor Parliament. And the Worcestershire result sheds light on the outcome in the neighbouring county, because Leighton's case ran parallel to Greville's. In both seats the government overrode 'opposition of faction' and 'animosity of religion', to impose a Puritan courtier in the national interest. For Sir Thomas, the battle-scarred Governor of Guernsey, was an indispensable defence expert, and if he declined to appeal for his 'wounds' sake to give [him] suffrage' (ɪɪ, ii, 135), his drum beat loudly in this election, as Sheriffs mustered levies for 'the very speedy increase of Her Majesty's forces'. On 20 October sixty Warwick-shire men accordingly embarked at Bristol: a Spanish armada, launched on news that 'The dearth is great, / The people mutinous' (i, ii, 10), would be repulsed by England's well-oiled war machine. And in Stratford, with its 'musty superfluity' of 700 on poor relief (i, i, 224), the pressgang was welcome to Sir Edward, charged with raising cavalry.[56] Like the victory of Corioles, the battle for Cork commenced in the marketplace, with the blackmail that 'if any fear / Lesser his person than an ill report', he should weigh 'his country dearer than himself' (i, vi, 69–72), and line up with his masters.

On 15 October William Parsons was absent from Stratford council, *quia non audet venire*. Twice, in 1598 and 1599, this draper's election as Bailiff had been vetoed by Greville without a fight; now he was afraid to attend meetings chaired by Quiney. The people's party was fragmenting before the lords of the county, as it does at a comparable point in *Coriolanus*, when Menenius castigates the Romans in his role of Sheriff: 'You have made fair hands, / You and your crafts! . . . / Who did hoot him out o'th'city . . . / As many coxcombs / As you threw caps up will he tumble down, / And pay you for your voices' (iv, vi, 118–37); while the Citizens shift with Alderman Parsons: 'For mine own part, / When I said banish him, I said 'twas pity . . . / That we did we did for the best, and though we willingly consented . . . yet it was against our will' (140–6). If Lucy travelled over to his neighbour at this time in hope of finding 'the very road into his kindness' (v, i, 36; 58), he was spurned as rudely as Coriolanus repulses Menenius, because 'Sir Edward Greville's menaces to the Bailiff, Aldermen and Burgesses of Stratford' became a regular item in the council's minutes. While the Bailiff 'set down by the poll' and drafted 'all our townsmen into companies' (iii, iii, 9), Greville's henchman, one Robin Whitney, waged a campaign of harassment. When Quiney had him bound to keep the peace, Whitney warned that 'I do not greatly respect what any man shall say against me, for my carriage shall try itself. Were it not that I would be loth to offend my Master . . . [my] complainants should find that Whitney would not put up the least wrong offered by them.'[57] The implication was that the Bailiff's life hung on Sir Edward's word, as the Tribunes are made to fear their 'throats are sentenced and stay upon execution' by Coriolanus's letters (v, vi, 7). 'You have holp . . . / To melt the city leads upon your pates . . . / To see . . . / Your franchises, whereon you stood, confin'd / Into an augur's bore' (iv, vi, 82–8): the intimidation the play records is something like that in which Quiney led 'the stream o'th'people' (ii, iii, 259) back to the shire hall on 31 October, to mouth the 'voice of occupation and / The breath of garlic-eaters' (98) from the yard.

Some time in 1598 the government compiled a list of England's political elite, counting just five 'Principal Gentlemen' in Warwickshire, among whom were numbered both Grevilles, while Fulke was also classed in the corps of 'Principal Gentlemen of value and service usually in Court'.[58] This was the calibre of the men whose service Shakespeare's friends had denied, and they were reminded of this when Edward Greville said his case 'must be tried before his uncle Fortescue, with whom he could more prevail'. Sir John Fortescue, Chancellor of the Exchequer, would himself be a protagonist in a famous election controversy of 1604, when the Privy Council's attempt to install him as Member for Buckinghamshire was thwarted by the county gentry and country gentlemen in Parliament. Since Gardiner, this debacle has been regarded as decisive for the representative status of the Commons, but recent studies place the court and country conflict within contexts of local economics and the ousting of the Elizabethan old guard. Under James, courtiers could no longer manipulate the hustings if they were embroiled in local property disputes, like Fortescue;[59] but in 1601 the Greville family network was still powerful enough to mobilise a regime 'whose course [would] on / The way it [took], cracking ten thousand curbs / Of more strong link asunder' than Warwickshire's (I, i, 68–70). On 7 October, therefore, a Chancery writ was issued for a new election, overriding Lucy's 'wilful transgression' in ordering a poll. Fulke Greville was never required to 'Appear i'th'market-place. . . . / Nor showing . . . his wounds / To th'people, beg their stinking breaths' (II, i, 231–4), since Lucy was instructed to 'prove [himself] free from factious purpose' by bringing a unanimous return. Cowed into deference, the freemen of Stratford gave their voices for a Greville one more time. It is unimaginable that in return there was not some understanding that the enclosure scheme would be dropped. In any event, at Christmas the Bailiff and burgesses were invited to Beauchamp's Court to thank them for support. 'Bring the good company that accompanied you to Warwick', Fulke's secretary wrote, 'that they may see for whom they travailed, and my Master understand who hath deserved his love'. Quiney's memorandum records his own priority for satisfaction as 'What we were best to do to Sir Edward Greville'.[60]

The politician who would not 'entreat them for [his] wound's sake to give their suffrage' (II, ii, 137) had 'wounds to show . . . in private' (II, iii, 77) to 'his good friends'; yet, like the feasting in the play, this hospitality rang false, for after his Pyrrhic victory Fulke would never stand for Parliament again. His exile from Warwickshire puzzles biographers, but indicates a recoil from the world of contract and exchange that his peers feared as a kind of theatre; where, as Hobbes thought, 'a person is the same that an *actor* is' since commerce made each '*represent* another' and sell his voice and acts like goods.[61] 'Man in business is but a Theatrical person', warned the poet John Hall, because his words and deeds are not inalienably his own; 'but in his retired actions, he pulls off his disguise'.[62] Greville shared this urge to change 'the gown of humility' and 'knowing himself again, / Repair' to his own ground (II, iii, 41; 146). In the rearguard of militant protestantism, he cut an isolated figure in Jacobean politics, whose own dramas were 'no plays for the stage'. He resembles Coriolanus in many ways, but in none more than this anti-theatricalism. A man's 'true stage', he held, was 'that whereon himself is an actor, even the state';[63] and Coriolanus has the same proprietorial notion of Acts of Parliament. Thus, pushed into the marketplace to play 'a part' which, he says, 'I shall blush in acting' (II, ii, 144) – 'a part which never I shall discharge to th'life' (III, ii, 105) – Shakespeare's man of action finds he is useless to 'perform a part [he] hast not done before' (109), which emasculates him like the transvestism he rejected as a boy: 'Some harlot's spirit!' or 'an eunuch' shedding 'schoolboys' tears' (III, ii, 112–16). 'You might have been more the man you are', Volumnia scolds, 'With striving the less to be so' (19); but like Greville's *nonpareil* in Spenser's epitaph, who 'only like himself, was second unto none',[64] Coriolanus will stand for no one but himself: 'I will not do it, / Lest I surcease to honour mine own truth' (120). 'Every man', Stephen Gosson decreed, 'must show himself outwardly to be such as in deed he is.'[65] In refusing to represent others or transfer ownership of his acts as a hireling of his constituents, Coriolanus upholds this Puritan ideal of a private and possessive identity: 'Rather say I play / The man I am. . . . Think me for the man I am' (III, ii, 15; IV, v, 57).

V

Looking back to Elizabethan Parliaments, Greville claimed the Queen 'was never troubled by brick-walls from them', because 'her necessarily expended treasure' was voted from 'common desire', which 'forced every man to believe his fishpond could not be safe while the kingdom stood in danger. Her wars upheld her wealth, and wealth supplied her war.' Taxes were never 'balanced by the self-pitying abilities' of subjects to pay, he fancied, but 'being drawn above their selfness, the audit was taken after, and summed up with a little smart to themselves, wherein they gloried'.[66] 'When he did love his country, / It honour'd him' (III, i, 302), but if the Member for Warwickshire became as deaf to his constituents as his memoir suggests, it was inevitable he would be 'disregarded' once they had decided they would stomach no taxation without representation. Coriolanus, who 'prized' the voters 'As dead carcasses' (III, iii, 121), and who wanted them to 'forget' him once he was elected, 'like the virtues / Which our divines lose' on parishioners (II, iii, 58), similarly finds that instead of a dumb Tudor congregation, he is 'Whoop'd out of Rome' (IV, v, 79) by an uproarious Stuart theatre riot. Like Richard II's catcalled performance (*Richard II*, v, ii, 23); or Caesar's corpsing on the stage (*Julius Caesar*, I, ii, 250), Coriolanus's inability to act is a metonym for the crisis of representation at the onset of market society. For it is theatre which is the mirror of production and consumption in early modern England, and the yard where voices are exchanged a forum where, as Agnew sees, 'the vast question of political, social, religious, and economic representation' is posed in its most compelling form.[67] So the play-within-the-play in *Coriolanus* ends with the actor hooted off by 'the beast with many heads' (IV, i, 1), whose 'monstrous members' (II, iii, 14) are driven by the market to gratify their appetite. His Herculean labours cannot fix this 'Hydra' of exchange (III, i, 93), because when the market has 'devour'd' his 'service . . . Only (his) name remains' as the husk of his expended value (IV, v, 74).

'They think we are too dear' (I, i, 18): the question echoing through this play is the one posed by a market in which men are 'things created / To buy and sell' (III, ii, 10): How much is a man worth? By the turn of the seventeenth century, Agnew notes, wages had fallen to their lowest for three centuries while geographic mobility surged as a result of capitalist farming. Marx's thesis that by breaking bonds of barter, commodity exchange propels labour into a complex of social relations 'beyond the control of the actors', is for none more accurate, Agnew reminds us, than itinerant labourers in Shakespearean England, 'liminaries poised forever on the threshold of their own exchange'.[68] This is the fact that Coriolanus confronts, when, with the pitiless logic he impelled, the discourse of mastery rebounds on him, and 'The service of the foot, / Being once gangren'd, is not . . . respected / For what it was.' Amputated from the body politic like 'a disease that must be cut away', as the Poor Law excised the idle (III, i, 292–308), his banishment enacts the statutory article 'That every person which is by this Act declared to be a vagabond or beggar shall be sent to the parish through which he last passed . . . there to be employed in work until he shall be placed in service'.[69] Thus, 'There is a world elsewhere' for Coriolanus, as he sets out on the highway of the masterless (III, iii, 135), but his manumission merely releases him to sell his labour to a new master, to 'do his country service' (IV, iv, 26): 'so use it / That my . . . services may prove / As benefits to thee . . . / Since I cannot live but to my shame, unless / It be to do thee service' (IV, v, 89–102). All the elements of modern representation inhere in this sale, for as Baudrillard remarks, if 'The modern sign desires, in reference to the real, a binding obligation', yet 'produces only neutral values, that exchange amongst each other in an objective world', it finds an exemplum in the service of the free labourer, who 'is free only to produce equivalences' and whose emancipation is in work.[70] So Coriolanus secures his value as the hireling of Aufidius.

Puritan discourse cemented social order in its discourse of mastery and doctrine of the calling, and Coriolanus's 'sovereignty of nature' – 'Not to be other than one thing, not moving / From the casque to th'cushion, but commanding peace / Even with the same austerity and garb / As he controll'd the war' (IV, vii, 42) – is faithful to the preaching of Perkins in his *Treatise of Vocations*, that 'Even as a soldier must not change his place, wherein he is placed by the General, so must the Christian continue and abide in his calling, without change or alteration.'[71] As Michael Walzer argues, such self-consistency opened the way to a 'new world of discipline and work' based on impersonal commitments,[72] which Coriolanus enters when he is engaged as a day labourer, 'Like to a harvest man that's task'd to mow / Or all, or lose his hire' (I, iii, 36). Every category of Puritan ideology now tells against him, as his contract casts him in the despised boy's role of 'a mistress', the 'Bessy' or shemale in the harvest play Aufidius masters (IV, v, 118; 200), and he 'subsists' (V, vi, 73) as a wage labourer in a market society that seems to have completed its agricultural revolution. For in Antium the customary culture of 'wives with spits, and boys with stones' (IV, iv, 5) has been annexed by authority, and the calendar of feasts is in honour of 'the nobles of the state' (9). In this disciplined order – so prophetic of Hanoverian England – the master is content to allow his agent to 'reap the fame' and pretend that it his, whilst he 'wages' him 'with his countenance, as if / [He] had been mercenary' (V, vi, 36–41), because a labourer's employment is seasonal and confined to the letter of his articles. Aufidius is confident, therefore, that 'Although it seems . . . he bears all things fairly / And shows good husbandry . . . yet he hath left undone / That which shall break his neck . . . Whene'er we come to our account' (IV, vii, 18–26). So, contracted to 'Plough Rome and harrow Italy' (V, iii, 34), Coriolanus discovers as he lets his own mother 'prate / Like one i'th'stocks' (159), that no one is author of himself, but each is an actor in a scene society scripts. His 'revengeful services' to his master (IV, v, 90) end with his subcontract to the woman who has made him what he is, as he undersells 'the blood and labour / Of [his] great action' for a satisfaction of tears 'As cheap as lies' (V, vi, 47). The individualist, it transpires, is nothing outside his text:

> Like a dull actor now
> I have forgot my part and I am out,
> Even to a full disgrace . . .
>   O mother, mother!
> What have you done? Behold, the heavens do ope

The gods look down, and this unnatural scene
They laugh at.
                        (v, iii, 40–2; 182–5)

'Heaven the judicious sharp spectator is', in the Puritan doctrine of election, 'That sits and marks who still doth act amiss';[73] and at his audit the hired hand is called before his master for just such a reckoning, to be paid for betraying his 'business' and 'Breaking his oath and resolution, like / A twist of rotten silk' (v, vi, 95). An agreement between servant and master, *Coriolanus* records, was one text in which the value of a man was indelibly inscribed. So, at the end, the play will 'repair to th'market-place' where the monopolist once dictated his worth (v, vi, 3), to bring him 'to his account' at a 'just' price (IV, vii, 17). As Romans 'are rising' through his subvention (IV, v, 240) – when the market 'for ten thousand' would 'not have given a doit' (v, iv, 57) – Coriolanus's value, 'rais'd' and 'heightened' when Aufidius 'pawn'd [his] honour for his truth', and 'never known before / But to be unswayable and free', is abruptly 'bow'd' (v, vi, 21–5), as his underwriter vows to 'renew me in his fall' (49). Coriolanus, who soared above others 'As far as doth the Capitol exceed the meanest house' (IV, ii, 39), still rates himself at 'Six Aufidiuses, or more' (v, vi, 128), but in terms of the Statute, he is a mere 'boy', who has botched his part and must be 'cut off' like a gangrened limb (138). The 'spoils' he brings 'home . . . more than counterpoise a full third part / The charges of the action' (77), but having thrown 'away / The benefit' of the harvest (66) for the legal figment of 'certain drops of salt' (93), he is just a 'boy of tears' to his employer (100): an actor or apprentice who must be cashiered because his contract has been breached.

'As with a man by his own alms empoison'd, / And with his charity slain' (11), a capitalist master such as Aufidius will end the doling custom, and demand his legal satisfaction. *Coriolanus* spans the transformation of English rural society, the process foretold at Stratford. There, if the ritual calendar took its course, the season that had last seen an enclosure riot, came round with a procession to the lord of the manor on Plough Monday. 'On this day', throughout the Midlands, according to contemporary reports, 'young men yoke themselves and draw a plough about with music, and one or two persons in antic dresses go from house to house to gather money. If you refuse them, they plough up your dunghill'.[74] The response at Milcote to this festive assertion of *communitas* can be imagined, and there is perhaps a reminiscence of 7 January 1602 in the final entrance of Coriolanus, 'Splitting the air with noise' of 'Drums and trumpets', and escorted with 'great shouts of the people' and the capering of 'fools' (49–54). In the Shakespearean text, however, where a former landlord plays the female 'scold' (106), the action has the ironic justice of another Warwickshire farming custom, the 'booting' of 'Boys, who had mischief in the harvest done, / As load o'erturn'd, and foul on posts had run.' In the symbolic repertoire of rural culture, Coriolanus is a farm boy 'booted' for his blunders, not with 'easy fines' (65), but 'blows administered with the master's boots'.[75] This is the local context of his outrage at Aufidius's insult: '"'Boy"! O slave!' (103). Coriolanus is liquidated by the system of mastery to which he subscribed, as he calls to be 'Cut . . . to pieces' by his 'men and lads', like the corn doll staining the 'edges' of the reapers' scythes (111). Thus, as Foucault writes, in the seventeenth century

> the whole creation of values is referred back to the primitive exchange between the landowner and nature. . . . If these men have gone to the trouble to sow and harvest the corn . . . it is because the value of things is founded on utility. . . . Exchange is therefore that which increases value . . . but it is equally that which diminishes value: it gives each one a price, and it lowers the price of each one in doing so.[76]

A generation, wrote Adam Smith, 'is time sufficient to reduce any commodity to its natural price';[77] and by 1620 the wheat–wage ratio had swung against the engrosser. In the end, Shakespearean drama predicts, it will be a Greville who will be 'a butterfly' under the harvest wheel (v, iv, 11): 'for men, like butterflies, / Show not their mealy wings but to the summer, / And not a man, for being simply man, / Hath any honour' (*Troilus and Cressida*, III, iii, 78–81). *Coriolanus* ends in cries of 'Kill, kill, kill, kill, kill him!' (v, vi, 130). In Stratford, too, the market would be murderous, for Richard Quiney, who saved the commons from enclosure and whose right to toll corn in the marketplace was confirmed on 8 January, was stabbed to death in a Greville ambush on 3 May as he patrolled the horse fair, 'the Bailiff being late abroad to see the town'. Like Coriolanus, Edward Greville had contrived 'in mere spite / To be full quit' with his 'country' (IV, v, 83), and 'neither himself punished' his henchmen, 'nor would suffer [them] to be punished, but with a show to turn them away and entertained again'.[78] The Grevilles, it might seem, held a freehold in the killing fields of Stratford, since Edward's father had been executed for murdering two servants to falsify an inheritance, while he had shot his older brother with a bow. Yet acquisitiveness would prove the family's downfall. Edward, bankrupted by a scheme to manufacture starch from bran, died 'a whining and impoverished dependent' of the most implacable of Jacobean capitalists, Lionel Cranfield, who thus succeeded him as lord of Stratford. And Fulke, who seethed like a 'vessel of wrath' in his banishment from Westminster, and who was elbowed out of office under James, was to be murdered himself in 1628 as he 'came from stool' by a servant he had refused an annuity of £20. The quarrel over his vast estate split his family and the Warwickshire gentry until the Civil War.[79]

'Spring come to you at the farthest / In the very end of harvest! / Scarcity and want shall shun you' (*The Tempest*, IV, i, 114–16): Shakespeare's wish that 'distribution should undo excess, / And each man have enough' (*King Lear*, IV, i, 69), was made in the teeth of the realities of Warwickshire. *Coriolanus*, which has been tenuously dated to 1608 and the time of the Midlands Revolt, seems to mediate these realities in ways that key it more obviously to an emerging 'Country' mentality and the contest over the representation of the county. For contrary to both Brecht and conservative critics, there is no insurrection in the play, but rather an 'addled election' with lethal repercussions. Shakespeare's tragedy of broken promises is a drama of representation in an evolving market society, where the exchange of voices between rulers and ruled mirrored that 'tacit contract' between the stage and the authorities that censored political subversion.[80] The electoral background suggests the play was written earlier than the 1607 rising, though after the poetic justice of Fulke Greville's fall in 1604, but whatever its date, it is significant that there is no record of publication or performance during Shakespeare's lifetime. *Coriolanus* may register a change of heart towards the populace – the shift of loyalty that cost the Bailiff his life – but Stratford's maltsters had still to make their peace with the assassins of their 'countryman'. In 1607, when Fulke Greville was improving Wedgnock Park, his auditor therefore noted that clearance required negotiation, since 'Mr. Townsend and Shakespeare have the coppice and bushy close.'[81] In Shakespeare country, it seems, the market imperative was mitigated by the 'theatre of concession and regulation which the moral economy demanded',[82] since what is notable about Stratford is that in 1607 the 'dry stubble' of its commons did *not* blaze into flames (II, i, 256). And when the time came to invoke his tithes, with a new enclosure scheme in 1615, the dramatist extracted a covenant of indemnity for 'loss, detriment or hindrance by reason of any enclosure', but told his cousin, the brother of Greene the town attorney, that 'I was not able to bear the enclosing'. The implications of this remark are disputed, but whether he was unable to 'bear' or 'bar' it, Shakespeare's instinct was, it seems, to reconcile his country with the market. Perhaps it was in recognition of this role that Fulke Greville wished to be known not only as servant to a queen, counsellor to a king and friend to Philip Sidney, but also as 'Master to Shakespeare'.[83]

Chapter Five

The quality of mercy:

Discipline and punishment in Shakespearean comedy

I

'They that have pow'r to hurt and will do none . . .'

ON 17 November 1603 Sir Walter Raleigh was found guilty of treason after a day's trial at Winchester, and condemned, in the words of the barbarous formulation,

> to be drawn on a hurdle through the open streets to the place of execution, there to be hanged and cut down alive, and your body opened, your privy members cut off and thrown into the fire before your eyes, and your heart and bowels plucked out. Then your head to be striken from your body and your body to be divided into four quarters, to be disposed of at the King's pleasure.

Two years earlier it was reported that Raleigh had himself joked and smoked tobacco at an open window above the scaffold while his rival Essex was beheaded, and now his own sentence was calculated to inflict upon his body an even worse ritual of terror and degradation. It was intended as a ceremonial of the kind that Michel Foucault has described as paradigmatic of justice under the Old Regime in Europe, where the savage spectacle of public execution operated as a true theatre of cruelty to display by sheer excess of violence the invincible superiority of power over the subject who dared to challenge it. The destruction of Raleigh was planned, like his derisory trial, to demonstrate by its very ruthlessness and inequity the might of the newly succeeded James over the proudest of the Elizabethans. It would manifest, in Foucault's terms, 'the physical strength of the sovereign beating down upon the body of his adversary and mastering it', since in the meticulous monotony of the scaffold it was the prince himself who was symbolically present, and who seized the body of the condemned man through the law, and 'displayed it, marked, beaten, broken'. James had been outfaced by Raleigh's insolence when they had met in April. The execution would restore to sovereignty the dignity that Raleigh injured at that fatal first encounter.[1]

The date for Raleigh's nemesis was fixed for the year's midnight, 13 December, and it was duly noted that 'A fouler day could hardly have been picked out or a fitter for such a tragedy.' There had been a gory curtain-raiser when the priests in the alleged conspiracy had been hanged, castrated and disembowelled alive, according to the sentence, the executioner taking pains to 'handle' them 'very bloodily'. But James had master-minded an even more dramatic coup as climax. Prior to his own execution, Raleigh was 'prepared for his end' by his 'ghostly father', the Bishop of Winchester, then ordered to watch that of the other condemned aristocrats from an overlooking window, as he had observed the death of Essex. Their sentences had been commuted to beheading, but as the first of them laid his head on the block a messenger struggled shouting from the crowd. He was one of James's young Scottish pages, and he brandished a royal warrant for a two hours' stay of execution. Then when the second prisoner was led to the scaffold, he too was given respite. The same sadistic game was played with the third man, before all three were recalled, 'like men beheaded and met again in the other world', as Sir Dudley Carleton reported to John Chamberlain. 'Now all the actors being together on the stage as use is at the end of a play, the sheriff made a speech of their offences . . . to all of which they assented; then, saith the sheriff, see the mercy of your prince who of himself hath sent a countermand, and given you your lives.' As Carleton commented, 'There was no need to beg a plaudite of the audience' after this denouement, 'for it was given with hues and cries.' Nor was this 'example of the difference of justice and mercy' lost on Raleigh. The French ambassador was informed that 'he beheld the comedy played out by his companions with a smiling face', but Carleton was not so sure. 'Raleigh, you must think', he wrote, 'had hammers working in his head to beat out the meaning of this stratagem.'[2] After the travesty of his trial, he had hoped for justice in 'Heaven's bribeless hall', where 'Christ is the King's Attorney, / Who pleads for all without degrees', since 'He hath angels, but no fees.'[3] Now James had transformed the scene into just such a 'tragical comedy', and the condemned man had been made the spectator of the drama of his own rescue in the nick of time and by the hidden hand of mercy. Next day he received the commutation for which he sued and began the imprisonment that would last, with a final trick release, for thirteen years. In the Tower, the cage where Latimer once awaited the stake was refurbished as his laboratory. Though his sentence was not cancelled, but ominously suspended, Raleigh had exchanged the spectacle of the scaffold for a regime of surveillance and confinement.

'No one but my father', observed Prince Henry, 'would keep such a bird in a cage!' Imprisonment, we are reminded by Foucault, was rare before 'The Age of Confinement' which he dates from the eighteenth century. So if the prisoner had to hammer out the meaning of the royal pardon, the quality of King James's mercy has seemed to contemporaries and historians equally mysterious. Its significance can best be gauged in the light of the theatricality of its occasion. For as Foucault also remarks, the scaffold was a stage on which the action had nothing to do with right or wrong, but everything to do with kingship, and the public execution did not re-establish justice, it reactivated power. In the seventeenth century, it was not, therefore, with all its theatre of terror, a hang-over from an earlier age, for 'its ruthlessness, its spectacle, its physical violence, its unbalanced play of forces, its meticulous ceremonial, its entire apparatus were inscribed in the political functioning of the penal system'. And by its remorseless public unveiling, 'The justice of the king was shown to be an armed justice.' Thus, Elizabethan traitors could expect to be despatched with the maximum of customary cruelty, for as Burghley explained, after sentence had been passed on the Babington conspirators in 1586, 'by protracting of the [execution] both to the extremity of the pains of the action, and to the sight of the people to behold it, the manner of the death would be as terrible as any new device could be.' Monarchy displayed its prerogative, in this interpretation of spectacular power, by the atrocious signs of its omnipotence that it inscribed on bodies, but its rites of punishment were thereby made conditional on the audience's reaction. In an age when princes felt themselves, as Elizabeth declared, 'set on stages in sight and view of all the world', the theatre of the axe and gibbet was likewise dependent for its drama on the participation of the crowd, 'the main character, whose real and immediate presence was required for the performance'. Tyburn and Tower Hill were sites of a form of popular legitimation, where the power of the crown was signalled in blood and witnessed in ghoulish acclamation.[4]

The rites of punishment under the Old Regime required that the vengeance of the people merged with the vengeance of the monarch. But, as Foucault infers, the role of the spectators in this festival of slaughter was ambiguous. Like the city mob that rioted on May Day, the gallows crowd could turn its violence against authority, lynching criminals, snatching the condemned from the noose, or even stoning the headsman. Moreover, every public execution was a kind of civic saturnalia, in which the doomed were licensed to curse their judges or revel in their own infamy. Catherine Belsey has described the 'supreme opportunity' afforded to women at the stake, for instance, when in their 'last dying words', but for perhaps the first time in their lives, condemned 'Witches were assured of an audience.'[5] Such executions were carnivalesque events that released a mass of voices, heroising the victim as often as they glorified the prince. And Raleigh had already charmed an abusive mob into hilarity by his verbal fencing at his trial, so that Carleton thought that 'never was a man so hated and so popular in so short a time.' Interpreted, therefore, as political theatre, King James's clemency must be seen as the upstaging of the most histrionic of his opponents, not by the spectacular display of bloodstained pomp the Winchester townsfolk had expected, but by the crafty refusal of such a demonstration, the curtailment of carnival, and the invisible working of a different kind of power, power at a distance. Denied the platform of the scaffold, and compelled for once to be an onlooker rather than the brilliant centre of attention, the man who believed his whole life to be 'a play of passion'[6] thus saved his neck, but lost his public. And disdaining the duel of a public execution, power took back to itself its prerogative – as important evidently to James as his ancient command over the death penalty – of the final laughter.

In Rubens's Whitehall ceiling the apotheosis of King James I is as the British Solomon, dispensing sagacious judgement and refusing victory through violence.[7] Carleton for one agreed that by staging such a 'play' of magnanimity in contrast to the earlier executions, when the crowd had refused to cheer, James contrived 'in the beginning of his reign, to gain the title of *Clemens* as well as *Justus* . . . and no man can rob him of the praise.'[8] Yet mercy was never an attribute of the Renaissance prince, and Machiavelli had specifically preferred the cruelty of Cesare Borgia to the clemency of Scipio, on the grounds not only that it was necessary to be cruel to be kind, but that 'It is much safer for a prince to be feared than loved.' Furthermore, 'The new prince – above all other princes – cannot escape being cruel', Machiavelli believed, citing the words of Virgil's Dido: 'The newness of my sovereignty forces me to be harsh.'[9] This had, in fact, been the dictum of James himself, as offered to Prince Henry in the *Basilikon Doron* of 1598, where he had urged him to inaugurate his reign not like Nero, with a general amnesty, but with 'the full execution of the Law'. 'Fear no uproars', James had reassured his son, for 'when you have by the severity of Justice once settled your countries, and made them know that you can strike, then may you thereafter mix Justice with Mercy all the days of your life.' If he commenced his reign with clemency, James warned the Prince, 'the offences would soon come to such heaps, and the contempt of you grow so great, that when ye would fall to punish, the number of them to be punished, would exceed the innocent.' The King of Scotland had learned, he admitted, from his own mistaken attempt 'to win all men's hearts to a loving and willing obedience'; but evidently he had also accepted the iron logic of *The Prince*.[10] When he succeeded to the English throne, therefore, mercy was an unexpected and novel technique of the self-styled *Rex Pacificus*.

Reprieving Raleigh, James I began his English reign by deliberately reversing the Machiavellian precept 'that since men love through their own choice and fear at the prince's, a wise prince takes care to base himself on what is his own.' And this reversal had a wider significance than that of *realpolitik*. In fact, the remission of Raleigh's sentence at the beginning of the Jacobean era can be construed to mark a turn away from the spectacular punishment of the Tudor century, with its gruesome tortures and *autos-da-fe*, towards the exemplary punishment of the classical age, with its 'equitable' penalties and 'just' measurement of pain. King James's pardon seems a gesture that takes its meaning from a point of difference in English culture, when the 'atrocious' is giving way to the 'humane' in the system of punishment. This is the transition that Foucault locates at the threshold of modernity, and which he attributes not to compassion, but to the rulers' need to contain the disorder of the populace and to penetrate the resistance of the individual. As he recounts it, the aim of authority became 'not to punish less, but to punish better; to punish with attenuated severity, perhaps . . . but in order to insert the power to punish more deeply into the social body.' The old theatre of punishment would continue to be staged, of course, but with the dawn of the Enlightenment, its bloody pageantry would be flanked by a battery of more subtle, far-reaching devices, appropriate to a state whose end was no longer the imposition of its way through death, but the more ambitious one of the assertion of its will through life itself. Increasingly in the Classical era, the new social supervision assumed by power threw the scaffold into shadow. For as Foucault asks, 'How could power exercise its highest prerogative of putting people to death, when its main role was now to ensure, sustain and multiply life, to put this life in order?' This was the question every European ruler had to answer as political techniques swung away from the ritual of death and towards the administration of life during the early modern period, and the outcome, as the policy of James I predicted, was that the threat of the death penalty became a game of cat-and-mouse. The monarch never relinquished his oldest right of death, but to enforce his new power over life he negotiated a strategic retreat. If death marked the horizon at which the subject finally escaped the sovereign power, capital punishment would be the monarch's last and most solemn reserve. The King of Peace withdrew his warlike violence, evading the death sentence not out of humanitarian respect for life, but the better to bring that life within his control and purview.[11]

Electing to break Raleigh's spirit rather than his body, Jacobean justice seems to anticipate experimentally an entire paradigm-shift which, according to Foucault, took place after 1700. But as Pieter Spierenburg argues in *The Spectacle of Suffering*, his study of 'Executions and the evolution of repression', the Foucauldian history of the prison needs to be supplemented with archival evidence from cities such as Amsterdam or London. For where Foucault highlights Revolutionary France, in other countries 'The infliction of pain and the public character of punishment did not disappear overnight. Both elements slowly retreated in a long, drawn-out process', that began 'with the disappearance of public mutilation in the early seventeenth century', when 'a major change in the direction of a decline of physical punishment had already taken place', whilst 'Around the same time, imprisonment was introduced.' In England or the Netherlands, Spierenburg contends, the shift in the system of punishment and the privatisation of repression that facilitated state formation, were already under way in the Shakespearean period, and 'From about 1600 the seeds of the later transformation of repression were manifest. . . . These developments anticipated the fundamental change in sensibilities of the eighteenth century.' So although the theatrical presentation of pain survived as part of political practice in these states, the monopolisation of violence that public execution symbolised was so secure by 1600, that 'the closing of the curtains' on punishment could proceed far earlier than Foucault imagined. 'Originally, psychic controls were confined to the context of elites', Spierenburg allows, but it was with the curtailment of torture, public execution and exposure of corpses in England and the Netherlands that 'privatised repression' began. As publicity and suffering retreated in the penal systems of these countries, modes of repression changed, and in the 'Golden Age' of Shakespeare and Rembrandt a carceral society was already being formed.[12]

It was as early as 1553 that the London Bridewell was chartered to incarcerate vagrants for the purpose of economic rehabilitation. As Lee Beier notes, because it sought to transform human character, this 'prototype of the reformative policy of modern penology' was 'the most revolutionary of all the institutions' developed to police Tudor society, and its existence 'belies Foucault's argument that the prison idea, with its regimentation and its aim of moulding the malefactor's soul, developed only in the eighteenth century.' An Act of 1576 ordered similar bridewells to be established in every English town and county, so that 'youth may be accustomed and brought up in labour, and then not like to grow to be idle rogues.' The bridewell regime terrified its inmates, who begged for traditional retributive punishment, Beier reports; but Raleigh's prosecutor, Sir Edward Coke, thought 'few are committed to the House of Correction or Working-house, but they come out better.'[13] And it was the

London precedent that the councillors of Amsterdam emulated, Simon Schama confirms, when 'mindful of the inappropriateness of death penalties inflicted on young offenders', they instituted the Rasphuis in 1589, as a 'house where all vagabonds, evildoers, rascals and the like' would be imprisoned for 'improvement and correction', and where, to preserve their dignity, the so-called 'patients' would be admitted under cover of darkness. In 1597 this Saw-House was complemented by a Spinhuis for the improvement of 'fallen women', and there the motto above the door eloquently affirmed the meaning of mercy in the new penology. 'Cry not', the vagrants, prostitutes and thieves were commanded as they entered, 'for I exact no vengeance for wrong but force you to be good. My hand is stern but my heart is kind.'[14] From such an inscription it is clear that, though Foucault dated carceral society from French foundations such as the Paris General Hospital of 1656, it was these first houses of correction which had established, a century before, the institutional context in which discipline and punishment would begin to be recast, from a system of public suffering to one of private reformation. In these Dutch and English workhouses, the normalising practices that defined modern subjectivity were laid down as the separation of the productive from the idle, the deserving from the undeserving, and the discursive framework was erected that would make the eventual abandonment of the death penalty a state necessity. Above all, it was in the bridewells and the Rasphuis that a new strategy of ocular domination would be tested: the strategy, that is to say, which reverses the principle of the dungeon, of a power that withdraws from sight, to become an eye that observes without being observed by a subject under continuous surveillance.

II

'Shall there be gallows standing in England when thou art king?'

Entering his new English kingdom through Berwick on 6 April 1603, King James proclaimed a general amnesty, freeing all prisoners except those held for 'murder, treason or Papistry', and dispensing 'great sums of money for the release of many that were imprisoned for debt'. In his springtime triumph, royal liberality was made to seem as unstinting as the conduit at York, which 'all day long ran white and claret wine'; but at Newark on 21 April an incident occurred that exposed the political implications of Jacobean carnival, when a pickpocket was arrested 'in the Court, all Gentleman-like', who 'confessed that he had from *Berwick* played the cut-purse', whereupon 'His Majesty hearing of this nimming gallant, directed a Warrant to have him hanged, which was accordingly executed.'[15] The new king's English courtiers were appalled by this thunderclap of summary justice, but though James never again ignored due processes, the episode, with its sudden darkening of cockaigne, formed a fitting frontispiece to the Stuart century of merry monarch, maying cavaliers and civil war. It was a prelude whose meaning could be related, as Dudley Carleton recognised in Raleigh's case, to the symbolic form of contemporary comedy. For there too authority set itself to 'Stir up the Athenian youth to merriments' (*A Midsummer Night's Dream*, I, i, 12–13), and festival was appropriated to fortify a challenged monarchy. In a 'golden time' of amnesty, Shakespearean comedy tested the tension between terror and toleration, luring the 'nimming gallant' to his downfall and hinting at a modern prince, who would rule by the incitement of desire in his subjects. And in the suspense of its denouement, it underwrote the strategy that James initiated, of the deferral of sentence of death for an immediate dominion over life. Like 'the wisest fool in Christendom', comedy decked the Elizabethan gallows with garlands, but without removing the threat of 'a good hanging' that overshadowed the 'foolery' (*Twelfth Night*, I, v, 4–13).

In his essay, 'The great eclipse', Franco Moretti charts the decline of kingship in Shakespearean tragedy.[16] Foucault's genealogy of subjectivity reminds us that this deconsecration of majesty did not occur without a displacement of power onto institutions of the modern state such as prisons, hospitals and schools. The absconding king of the Baroque, who spies upon his subjects behind a mask of mercy and permission, is the remote architect, in this analysis, of Bentham's Panopticon that holds us all within its unseen gaze. So just as Moretti observes the eclipse of monarchy in the tragedies, where kings and subjects contest a monopoly of violence, it is in the comedies, where kings resign their violence in order to constrain their subjects, that the 'birth of the prison' can be traced. In these seemingly benevolent texts we can detect the discursive formation of a new sensibility that would transform the operation of discipline and punishment in Europe. If the Tudor monopolisation of violence was staged in the theatre of punishment of Shakespearean tragedy, where the bodies of the defeated were placed to view 'high on a stage' (*Hamlet*, v, ii, 376), like heads of Elizabethan traitors on London Bridge, it was Shakespearean comedy that provided a scenario for the corresponding production of obedient subjects of the state. For the comedies of Shakespeare are fascinated by the power that waits on amnesty and pardon, a power behind the scenes of state such as Falstaff dreams for Hal: 'prithee sweet wag, shall there be gallows standing in England when thou art king? . . . Do not when thou art king hang a thief' (*1 Henry IV*, I, ii, 57). Jacobean monarchy, with its melodramatic game of death to promote an insidious compulsion over life, finds an exemplar, however, not in a character like Henry v, who begins his reign suppressing mercy (*Henry v*, ɪɪ, ii, 79–83), but in the Shakespearean Duke, whose project is instead to secure dominion by renunciation, in a practice that renders him all-seeing but unseen. Whereas Elizabethan power depended upon what Stephen Greenblatt rightly terms a privileged visibility, this model seventeenth-century prince will withhold his visibility and postpone his sanctions until the latest hour. James ɪ warned his son that, despite 'the true old saying, That a king is one set on a stage' ('scaffold' in the first edition), monarchs were liable to diminish their mystery in public, 'where all beholders' eyes are attentively bent to look and pry in the least circumstance of their secretest drifts';[17] as Hal was urged by his father to avoid 'the eyes of men . . . By being seldom seen' (*1 Henry ɪv*, ɪɪɪ, ii, 40–5). Likewise the Shakespearean Duke protests: 'I love the people, / But do not like to stage me to their eyes' (*Measure for Measure*, ɪ, i, 67). Instead of ostentatious presence, the hidden king will be nowhere and everywhere at once, his strength the more dangerous for being suspended and concealed:

> We have strict statutes and most biting laws,
> The needful bits and curbs of headstrong jades,
> Which for these fourteen years we have let slip;
> Even like an o'er-grown lion in a cave
> That goes not out to prey.
>
> (ɪ, iii, 19–23)

Measure for Measure, acted at court within a year of Raleigh's trial, provides a conspectus of the Damoclean methods of the disciplinary state, as Jonathan Dollimore has shown.[18] And its image of the modern despot as 'an o'er-grown lion in a cave' aptly expresses the sinister principle of an omniscient but unregarded gaze. For its plot originates directly from the Duke's 'permissive pass' to 'give the people scope' (ɪ, iii, 35–8), his gambit to withdraw from the theatre of punishment, 'as fond fathers, / Having bound up the threatening twigs of birch, / Only to stick it in their children's sight / For terror, not to use' (ɪ, iii, 23–6). From the outset, then, this play presents a power that has learned the lesson of modernity, that subjection is obtained not by oppression, but by self-repression. The state over which Vincentio presides has long ago begun the experiment of abandoning its public violence in return for private discipline of its citizens, and it knows its legitimacy depends upon its incitement of transgression. Authority has no difficulty producing crime through *agents provocateurs* in Vienna; its problem is the Foucauldian one that follows from these tactics: How can it 'unloose this tied-up justice' (I, iii, 33) and put to death, when it is life that is its responsibility? ''Twould be my tyranny', the Duke frankly admits, 'to strike and gall them/ For what I bid them do' (I, iii, 36–7). His solution is the Jacobean one of power at one remove. 'Mortality and mercy' will 'live' with his substitute (I, i, 44), 'Who may in th'ambush of my name strike home' (I, iii, 41), he anticipates. But he 'lends' Angelo 'terror' (I, i, 19), only in a 'mad fantastical trick' (III, ii, 89) of abdication, not to 'Awake . . . the enrolled penalties / Which have, like unscoured armour, hung by th'wall / So long' (I, ii, 155–7), but to drive the impact of his mercy even deeper into society. Angelo, who ironically believes 'We must not make a scarecrow of the law' (II, i, 1), seems the perfect stooge for this chicanery when he duly revives 'the rigour of the statute' (I, iv, 67), and convinces Escalus, who initially intends to 'be keen and cut a little' (II, i, 5), that 'Mercy is not itself, that oft looks so; / Pardon is still the nurse of second woe' (II, i, 280–1). 'It is but heading and hanging' (II, i, 234) in the city, as Angelo 'puts transgression to't' (III, ii, 92), until the deputy himself discovers his master's voice and learns he can exploit the threat of death for sexual power over Isabella. In this drama where the entire action has the febrile anxiety of the condemned cell, and all the suspense is 'In the delaying death' (IV, ii, 163), the plot hinges on the sudden realisation of the unintended force of Isabella's homily to Angelo on mercy:

> No ceremony that to great ones longs,
> Not the king's crown, nor the deputed sword,
> The marshal's truncheon, nor the judge's robe,
> Become them with one half so good a grace
> As mercy does.
> (II, ii, 59–63)

Measure for Measure is a mirror for magistrates, then, in which Angelo, who begins his rule 'Hoping [to] find good cause to whip them all' (II, i, 136), discovers that the quality of mercy is such as to subjugate more completely than the axe or lash; that, in the words of the commonplace, 'the more power he hath to hurt, the more admirable is his praise, that he will not hurt' (Sidney, *The Countess of Pembroke's Arcadia*, II, 15). So, what the play dramatises is the wisdom of the cryptic *Sonnet 94*, that 'They that have power to hurt and will do none', are those installed in regality: 'They rightly do inherit heaven's graces.' 'Mercy', Isabella assures the judge, 'will breathe within your lips, / Like man new made' (II, ii, 78–9); but the 'new man' so made is 'the demi-god, Authority' (I, ii, 112), as omnipotent as 'Merciful Heaven' (115). Thus we glimpse in the text a strategy of power that will 'make mercy . . . play the tyrant' (III, ii,

188) more effectively than any 'pelting petty officer' (ii, ii, 113). Mercy is next to godliness, Angelo confirms; but he disastrously neglects this maxim when he betrays his pact with Isabella by endorsing the death sentence on her brother. From that moment, when he steps back onto the scaffold, he is once again a puppet of the Duke, who is able eventually to insist 'The very mercy of the law cries out . . . / An Angelo for Claudio, death for death!' (v, 405–6). By allowing himself to be manipulated as the 'scarecrow' of the old theatre of punishment, Angelo thus propels the Duke's more modern scheme to manoeuvre his people into self-subjection. For it is the Duke's aim, as Dollimore sees, to position the characters in confessional subjection, which he does by repressive tolerance, not oppression. 'Ignomy in ransom and free pardon / Are of two houses', Isabella naively holds, and 'lawful mercy / Is nothing kin to foul redemption' (ii, iv, 111–13). What she learns, however, is that 'Mercy . . . would prove itself a bawd' (iii, i, 148) to elicit her subjection. 'Ere he would have hanged a man for the getting of a hundred bastards', Lucio jeers of the Duke, 'he would have paid for the nursing of a thousand . . . he knew the service; and that instructed him to mercy' (iii, ii, 113–16). This commonwealth is endowed with foundling hospitals as well as the bridewell where Pompey is sent for 'Correction and instruction' (iii, ii, 31). In its 'charitable preparation' (iii, ii, 203) it is a blueprint of the new disciplinary order, and its 'morality of imprisonment' (i, ii, 126) is Amsterdam's: 'I exact no vengeance but force you to be good.'

'He who the sword of heaven will bear' in this regime, must resign its corporal use in the interest of a 'Craft' that practises on 'what man may within him hide'; so 'Shame to him', the Duke winces, 'whose cruel striking / Kills for faults of his own liking.' What the play demonstrates instead are the means by which the Prince learns to 'draw with idle spiders' wings / Most ponderous and substantial things' (iii, ii, 254–70), exchanging a web of subjectivity for the executioner's blade. Like the spider's deceptively 'idle' net, carceral power operates dialectically, and depends upon the struggle of those that it entraps. Claudio, who is petrified to be instructed to 'Be absolute for death' (iii, i, 5), offers too little fight, and his confession is as facile as his crime. Discipline has more resistance from the murderer Barnardine, 'A man that apprehends death no more dreadfully but as a drunken sleep' (iv, ii, 140–1). Periodically tested by the Provost with the Jacobean ruse of a mock execution, he remains unmoved. 'Unfit to live or die!' (iv, iii, 63) in the estimate of his 'ghostly father' (iv, iii, 47), the disguised Duke, Barnardine appears to call the bluff of an authority that sets itself to administer a life of which he is oblivious. His obstruction recalls Raleigh's confederate, Grey, who spent his time in his cell 'with such careless regard that he was observed neither to eat or sleep the worse or be any ways distracted from his accustomed fashions'.[19] In his contempt for existence he is in the same category as the suicide, who as Foucault notes, affronted modern power by negating its dominion. So the head of Ragozine is requisitioned from the prison hospital as a token of the capital punishment that the state evades. Only when Angelo himself pleads for 'death more willingly than mercy' (v, i, 474) can power be sure coercion is sufficiently internalised for the three condemned to be summoned, as from the grave, to be reprieved. The denouement positions everyone to 'kneel down in mercy' (v, i, 432), but it is Barnardine whose 'stubborn soul' is enmeshed. 'Thou'art condemned', the Duke repeats, 'But, for those earthly faults, I quit them all, / And pray thee take this mercy to provide / For better times to come' (v, i, 480–3). 'Thoughts are no subjects' (451), Isabella had protested; but in shifting punishment from subjects' bodies to their souls – leaving Barnadine to the 'advice' and 'hand' of his confessor (483–4) – the Duke proves otherwise. And there will be one further reprise of the gentle way of punishment. Lucio is sentenced to be whipped and hanged for Raleigh's crime of 'slandering a prince', but the penalty is commuted at the final moment to 'marrying a punk' (520–2). It is 'an apt remission' (496) for a court that takes desire as its jurisdiction. The Duke grasps Isabella's hand to seal the new political contract: power will give up its right of death for an even tighter grip on life.

'Can you cut off a man's head?' Pompey is quizzed at his initiation into the executioner's 'mystery' (ıv, ii, 1). Though he responds with gallows humour that he cannot imagine 'what mystery there should be in hanging' (37), it is a macabre question that echoes through *Measure for Measure*, a play fraught with 'the sense of death . . . in apprehension' (ııı, i, 77), the very title of which problematises the death sentence. For in this comedy where the bawd changes his coxcomb for the black cap of the hangman, and where repression thus reaches symbolically to the very source of society's desires, whether to kill the condemned becomes a far more complex issue for the state than in the old days, when his head stood 'so tickle on [his] shoulders that a milkmaid . . . [might] sigh it off' (ı, ii, 161). As the executioners, Pompey and Abhorson, discover to their professional cost, 'When vice makes mercy' in the era of correction, 'mercy's so extended / That for the fault's love is the offender friended' (ıv, ii, 110–11). Power, that is to say, buys its complicity in lives it would control by so countenancing faults, in the Duke's words, 'that the strong statutes / Stand like forfeits in a barber's shop, / As much in mock as mark' (v, i, 318–19). As his own informer, his 'business in this state' makes him an omniscient 'looker-on' over society, scientifically watching 'corruption boil and bubble / Till it o'errun the stew' (314–15); but what 'the old fantastical duke of dark corners' (ıv, iii, 156) gains by relinquishing 'the stroke and line of his great justice' (IV, ii, 78) for surveillance of the brothel and the bedroom, is what can only be called the 'micro-justice' of marrying Lucio to a prostitute and Angelo to the discarded Mariana. Angelo had himself bargained to release Claudio 'from the manacles of the all-binding law' in return for 'the treasures' of Isabella's 'body' (II, iv, 93–6); but Vincentio knows better than to supplant one form of corporal oppression with another. He has grasped that the power of the modern state will depend not on the tyrannising of its subjects but on the optimising of desire for the increase of its population.[20] As Lucio predicts, 'This may prove worse than hanging', since 'Marrying a punk . . . is pressing to death, whipping, and hanging' (V, i, 357, 519–20).

Substituting a wedding for a hanging, Shakespearean comedy is one of the earliest discourses to measure the state by the sexual fertility of its subjects, reckoning it will no longer be possible 'to geld and splay all the youth of the city', since 'If you head and hang all that offend that way . . . you'll be glad to give out a commission for more heads' (II, i, 227–36). Its rationale – so often universalised – is the seventeenth-century one that in an age of armies, 'the world must be peopled' (*Much Ado About Nothing*, II, iii, 262), and its policy is 'to remit / Their saucy sweetness that do coin heaven's image / In stamps that are forbid' (*Measure for Measure*, II, iv, 45–6). In the Shakespearean city 'hanging' becomes for the first time a function of eugenics. 'He that is well hanged in this world needs to fear no colours', as Feste leers, since its ruler is an enlightened despot, who breaks the stocks to discharge offenders into procreation, in the knowledge that 'Many a good hanging prevents a bad marriage' (*Twelfth Night*, I, v, 5–19). Where the bodies of the condemned once belonged to the sovereign to maim or destroy, a modern ruler releases them to multiply. So, in the empire of his gaze, the Duke vindicates that critical shift in the economy of punishment whereby, 'starting in the seventeenth century' (as Foucault dates it in *The History of Sexuality*), 'the ancient right to take life or let live was replaced by a power to foster life or disallow it to the point of death.' For what the Duke confirms is that henceforth power will have as its target a body which 'obeys, becomes docile, and increases its production', whose chain will be 'that within' which constitutes its 'stubborn soul', and point of fixture sex.[21] 'Every inch' a rational king, the monarch of comedy will assure his subjects that 'Thou shalt not die: die for adultery! No . . . / To't, Luxury, pell-mell! For I lack soldiers' (*King Lear*, IV, vi, 111–17)

' 'Tis Hymen peoples every town' (*As You Like It*, V, iv, 142): the docile bodies that troop into the house of life, male and female, two by two, at the end of a Shakespearean comedy, to start upon the disciplined business of their reproductive lives, are the automata of this modern 'bio-power'. And their docility has been constituted by authorisation of those 'that have power to hurt' in these plays, but 'will do none . . . / Who moving others, are themselves as stone, / Unmoved, cold, and to temptation slow', those managers of birth control and social welfare, who are the 'owners of their faces' because they hide them (*Sonnet 94*); the absentee Dukes and nameless Kings, whose licence decrees what the city shall allow, and whose power, stronger than any sword, derives from the policing of themselves. 'More nor less to others paying / Than by self-offences weighing', the new Prince finds subjectivity's 'Pattern in himself' (*Measure for Measure*, III, ii, 256–9): 'He doth with holy abstinence subdue / That in himself which he spurs on his power / To qualify in others' (IV, ii, 79–81). As the Friar, he boasts that 'The Duke / Dare no more stretch this finger of mine than he / Dare rack his own: his subject am I not' (V, i, 311–13), but this is to equivocate on subjectivity itself, which needs, he knows, no rack or pincers. He is, in fact, 'One that, above all other strifes, contended especially to know himself' (III, ii, 226): the paragon of modernity precisely to the extent that he is the disciplined 'subject' of himself.

III

'There is a devilish mercy in the judge . . .'

The final command of the Duke in *Measure for Measure* is to dispatch the pardoned Lucio 'to prison' to be married. It is a paradoxical order that defines the commutation when 'the old power over death that symbolised the sovereign was supplanted by the calculated administration of bodies' as the state identified its strength with the increase of its subjects. There is a sound of grating bars at the close of this comedy, as well as wedding bells. Death is evaded, but the 'restraint' that comes 'from too much liberty' (I, ii, 117–18) seems a subtle kind of tyranny. Angelo was shrewder than he knew when he maintained that 'Mercy is not itself that oft looks so' (II, i, 280): an 'injurious love', Juliet calls it, 'That respites me a life whose very comfort / Is still a dying horror' (II, iii, 40–2). Like the incarceration of Barnardine or the suspended sentence of Raleigh, it appears to be an innovatory bondage, which keeps the subject in a limbo of indefinite parole: 'a devilish mercy in the judge, / If you'll implore it, that will free you life, / But fetter you till death' (III, i, 64–6). The gibbet and block have been consigned to history, 'like unscoured armour' (I, ii, 156) in this carceral society, but in its benevolent guise as moral agency the state has acceded to an unprecedented interference in its subjects' lives. Noting the turn in such drama, whereby 'If the King's promise had stood uncontradicted and [the condemned] been executed, the play would have ended with Act III', Belsey infers that by this 'conspicuous absence' of a show of power, 'the royalist project is severely undermined.'[22] But as that learned judge, Portia, submits in *The Merchant of Venice*, sovereignty has nothing to lose by renouncing its ancient prerogative of blood. On the contrary, the gentle way of punishment is the Prince's most inventive ploy, since it is the mysterious 'quality of mercy' that it reinforces authority even as it forswears force:

> It is twice blest,
> It blesseth him that gives and him that takes.
> 'Tis mightiest in the mightiest, it becomes
> The thronèd monarch better than his crown.
> His sceptre shows the force of temporal power,
> The attribute to awe and majesty,
> Wherein doth sit the dread and fear of kings;
> But mercy is above this sceptred sway,
> It is enthronèd in the heart . . .
>   (IV, i, 182–90)

'The quality of mercy is not strain'd': Elizabeth I had been portrayed as Astraea with the attribute of a sieve, alluding not only to virginity, but to her magisterial discernment in straining clemency from justice.[23] But in Shakespearean comedy, mercy 'droppeth as the gentle rain from heaven / Upon the place beneath', like God's rain 'on the just and on the unjust' (Matthew, v, 45), regardless of the law. Unsifted and unstinted, it exceeds every 'attribute' of 'temporal power', whether sceptre, sieve or crown; just as Mercilla is depicted by Spenser with her rusted sword of punishment at her feet and the lion of retribution 'With a strong yron chaine and coller bound'.[24] The iconography of Portia's speech therefore places the question of mercy in the context of the contemporary controversy over legal sovereignty itself, and helps to situate its exercise in Shakespearean comedy within a political field. For, as Portia reminds Shylock, the dialectic of mercy works so that it is 'twice blest': it legitimises 'him that gives' as much as it benefits 'him that takes'. And what 'The thronèd monarch' has to gain from the exercise of mercy has vital ramifications for the politico-juridical system of early modern England, as the *The Merchant of Venice* shows. There the court that tries Shylock's case is convened as a court of equity on the lines of Chancery, with its appellate relation to common law. As dispensed by the Lord Chancellor, equity was the discretionary justice of the Crown, intended, Bacon wrote, 'to abate the rigour of the law', but without power to revoke 'an express statute' or 'break its strength'. So Chancery, according to the jurist William Lambarde, was the 'Gate of Mercy', but its justice was restrained by the letter of the common law, which would triumph under the leadership of Coke.[25] This jurisdictional conflict is replicated in the comedy, where the Duke has striven to 'qualify' the 'rigorous course' of law to release Antonio from the bond, but finds he has 'no means' (7–9) to 'Wrest the law', since 'there is no power in Venice / Can alter a decree established.' As Portia concurs, ' 'Twill be recorded for a precedent, / And many an error by the same example / Will rush into the state; it cannot be' (211–18). Any remedy of 'this strict court of Venice' (200) must conform to Chancery's rule that 'Equity follows Law' to enforce, rather than to annul: 'For the intent and purpose of the law / Hath full relation to the penalty' (243–4), and the party 'shall have all justice. . . . / He shall have nothing but the penalty' (317–18), 'He shall have merely justice and his bond' (335).

The moot declined as a forum for legal education in the Inns of Court at the end of the sixteenth century, and Benchers blamed the students' addiction to plays, a suspicion confirmed by the German lawyer Paul Hentzner in 1598.[26] Shakespearean comedy suggests that in this period when law and letters were still imbricated, the new ideological apparatus of the stage did usurp the didactic function of the moot, where (according to the Benchers of Gray's Inn in 1588) 'doubt with argument increased' had been resolved 'in aptest terms', about 'Prerogatives of prince . . . and each man's right'.[27] Jean-Pierre Vernant claims a juridical role for ancient Athenian drama, where plays were judged by the same jury as decided real disputes to which they referred;[28] and in *The Merchant of Venice* it seems in keeping with the heuristic mechanism of the moot that whereas Portia masquerades as an academic civil lawyer, Shylock rests his case on common law. It is Antonio who demystifies that law with the awareness that 'The duke cannot deny the course of law: / For the commodity that strangers have / With us in Venice, if it be denied, / Will much impeach the justice of the state'. Antonio knows the law will be determined by the fact 'that the trade and profit of the city consisteth of all nations' (III, iii, 26–31); but it is precisely the commercial bias of common law that Shylock effaces, as he 'doth impeach the freedom of the state / If they deny him justice' (III, ii, 277–8). His 'plea / Of forfeiture, of justice, and his bond' (282) is grounded in common-law citation of rights supposedly enshrined in texts like the Magna Carta, which he invokes when he warns 'If you deny me . . . / There is no force in the decrees of Venice' (101–2), and 'If you deny it, let danger light / Upon your charter and your city's freedom!' (38–9). Chancery conceded in the 1590s that 'if the common law be broken, the Court of Conscience must leave things to the conscience of the party himself',[29] so Shylock is assured his case is 'in such rule, that the Venetian law / Cannot impugn you as you do proceed' (174–5). As he realises, in equity 'compulsion' (179) could only be

applied to 'The words expressly . . . enacted in the laws' (303, 344); but
his refusal to admit mercy as a compulsion clearly caricatures common
law at a moment when, as historians such as Christopher Hill have shown,
it had become the cutting edge of bourgeois revolution.[30] When equity
instructed 'do as thou wouldst be done to thee', and demanded, 'How
shalt thou hope for mercy rendering none?' (88), common lawyers could
'stand for judgement' like Coke at Raleigh's trial (103), as Shylock does:
'What judgement shall I dread doing no wrong?' (89).

The moot point in *The Merchant of Venice*, then, is whether the quality
of mercy is constrained by law. As a court of conscience, Chancery had
inherited a Christian discourse from the church, but by 1595 this was
ensnared, as the play records, in the intransigence of common law.
Instead Elizabethan Chancery had become the arena for the bourgeoisie's campaign to curtail royal prerogative and confine the law, as
Shylock intends, to the protection of economic liberty. James I would
pack the Chancery bench with civil lawyers such as Portia's Balthazar, on
grounds that 'justice after the French manner was fitter for the people and
his greatness'; but he could not stem the doctrine, expounded by judges
such as Coke, that English law was 'that which hath been perfected by all
the wisest men in former ages', and was founded, as Shylock argues, on
precedent and written text. *The Merchant of Venice* is itself a text that
registers the advent of textuality in sixteenth-century law reporting, and
with his dogma of scriptural authority, Shylock is at one with Bacon in the
conviction that the office of judges 'is to interpret law, not to make or give
law.'[31] So judgement in Shylock's case foretells the great courtroom
victories of common lawyers against the monarchy; but with mirthless
irony. Portia begs Shylock's mercy, she concedes, as a formality, 'To
mitigate the justice of thy plea, / Which if thou follow, this strict court of
Venice ' Must needs give sentence 'gainst the merchant'. Once refused,
'the law, / The penalty and forfeit' (199–203) must take their course, and
'The Jew shall have all justice' (317): 'The court awards it, and the law
doth give it' (296). Contrary to many critics,[32] equity fails before the law
of property in *The Merchant of Venice*, as it would be blunted by the
English bourgeoisie. Shylock wins his case, and 'justice more than' he
desires (312), but with such straitened legalism that to take the forfeit of
'just a pound of flesh' (322), and thereby 'shed / One drop of Christian
blood' (305–6), will cost him his own life. 'Thou may'st have leave to hang
thyself', Gratiano exults (360); and this is indeed the perversity of
common law, since in 'another hold . . . / It is enacted in the laws of
Venice' that for 'indirect attempts' on Antonio's life, his own now 'lies in
the mercy / Of the Duke' (343–52). Thus the mechanism of Shakespearean
comic justice is laid bare in a *grand guignol* allusion to Judas's suicide.
Authority gives its subjects rope to hang themselves by the pulley of these

palindromic plots – where, as Nerissa smirks, it seems that 'Hanging and wiving goes by destiny' (II, ix, 83) – until they are brought, as Shylock is, down to their knees, to 'beg mercy of the duke' (359).

Judgement in Shylock's case figures the mercilessness of a 'mercenary' society, where to 'go to church' is to 'think upon . . . merchandise', and all Christian bonds are exchanged for commercial ones (25–40). So the jurisdictional constraint of equity by law in *The Merchant of Venice* is metonymic of that state of nature that is the problematic of Elizabethan tragedy, where, as Shakespeare's Ulysses predicts, emancipated from feudal order, 'everything includes itself in power, / Power into will, will into appetite; / And appetite, an universal wolf . . . / Must . . . last eat up himself' (*Troilus and Cressida*, I, iii, 119–24). In Shakespearean tragedy the market is just such a cycle of consumption and desire, cannibalising a humanity that 'must perforce prey on itself, / Like monsters of the deep' (*King Lear*, IV, ii, 49–50). The tragedies are 'truly modern', Moretti believes, because they adumbrate what Hooker dreaded: the 'Tyrannicall power' of appetite when sovereignty gives way to individualism. In his interpretation, the 'de-problematizing' comedies reveal, by contrast, absolutism's 'utopian late-medieval attempt to halt this process by concentrating power in the sovereign', a 'beneficent wizard' who harmonises civil society with a feudal polity.[33] This is a persuasive reading, but it oversimplifies the historical compact between the monarchy and the market and it underestimates the modernity of Shakespeare's comic resolutions. For what those endings anticipate is how, as Perry Anderson shows, there was no immediate conflict between capitalism and absolutism, since absolutism was the glittering carapace under which the bourgeoisie evolved.[34] Thus, in Shakespearean Venice bourgeois *laissez-faire* will strangle the very 'trade and profit of the city' if the mercenary 'have leave to hang themselves'. The *reductio ad absurdum* of Portia's ruling therefore proves the need to regulate the private contracts of individuals in the interests of a higher rationality: a reason of state. Inducing the mercenary to kneel for mercy, this merchant comedy sounds the fanfare not, as Moretti claims, for an anachronistic utopia, but for the actual mercantile system operated by a Cromwell or a Colbert. The mercers of Venice beg for the 'mercy' – a state intervention into a market otherwise fatally constrained – that would materialise in the practices of mercantilism.

Mercantilism, Anderson observes, was the doctrine of the era because it represented the conceptions of a ruling class that had adapted to the market, yet preserved its outlook on the unity of what Bacon called 'considerations of plenty' and 'considerations of power': 'Mercantilism was precisely a theory of the intervention of the State into the economy, in the interests of the prosperity of the one and the power of the other.'[35]

This is a definition of equal aptness to the economy of repression and desire in Shakespeare's comedies. To the extent that they also balance considerations of plenty and power, through the merciful intervention of authority into the mercenary relations of individuals, Shakespeare's romantic denouements share an identical social logic with mercantilism. And if, as Hobbes thought, 'the use of Lawes' in a mercantile state, 'is not to bind the People from all voluntary actions; but to direct them in such a motion, as not to hurt themselves by their own desires, rashnesse, or indiscretion, as Hedges are set, not to stop Travellers, but to keep them in the way', the maze of Shakespearean comedy is truly mercantilist in leading the characters through desire, rashness and indiscretion until these are exhausted in a coincidence of opposites. Absolutism in tragedy, Moretti remarks, is unbridled and 'the royal act resonates over the political body'; but in comic form, as in *Leviathan*, sovereignty concedes that 'a good Law is that which is *Needfull*, for the *Good of the People*'. So the mercurial monarch of comedy yields his interdiction in deference to the Hobbesian maxim that 'Unnecessary Lawes are trapps for Mony', only to tax 'the trade and profit of the city' the more for the 'coffer of the state' (350).[36] *Par pro pari*: mercantilism's slogan, which furnished a title for *Measure for Measure*, determines the equation by which, through devices like the substitution-trick, the transactions of individuals are directed to the profit of 'the general state' (367) in these texts, in emulation of the Tudors, who, as Bacon reported, 'could not endure to have the vein obstructed, which disperseth the blood of trade'. Thus, far from reconstituting a feudalism sundered by the market, Shakespearean comedy – which dates from the heyday of the chartered companies – participates in the reformulation of power described by Foucault, when Machiavelli's analysis of the security of the prince was superseded by 'an extremely different type of rationality' centred on 'relationships between prince and people'. 'The aim of this new art of governing is not to reinforce the prince', the comedies confirm, but 'the state itself'.[37]

Dr Johnson objected that Shakespeare 'is so much more careful to please than to instruct', in his comedies, 'that he seems to write without any moral purpose. . . . He makes no just distribution of good and evil (but) carries his persons indifferently through right and wrong, and at the close dismisses them without further care'.[38] This famous demurrer of 1765 is of a piece with the rejection of mercy by the jurist Beccaria, who argued in the same year that uncertainty of punishment was a tyrannical erosion of a citizen's rights. Such codifiers repudiated clemency, but in the seventeenth century the author of *Leviathan* had theorised the pardoning power as a key to sovereignty, and vindicated the arbitrariness of Shakespearean relief. To Hobbes, justice was still the royal road to power, not a crossroads of right and wrong. So if common lawyers such as Coke strove to circumscribe pardon by act of Parliament, 'What power would he have left to the King', he demanded in *A Dialogue of the Common Laws of England*, 'that thus disableth him to practice Mercy?' It was for public benefit that the dispensing power was preserved, and however attenuated, 'the King did not grant away that power, when he thought good to use it for the Common-wealth.' 'Statutes are not laws to the King' in questions of clemency, Hobbes reiterated, for 'I think, if the King think in his conscience it be for the good of the Common-wealth, there is no power in England may resist.' The prerogative of mercy is a mainstay of the Hobbesian state precisely because it exceeds the 'sceptred sway' of law. For sovereign and individual contradict each other in Hobbes's calculus, with the result that capital punishment is deemed an act of war, whereby we 'lead Criminals to execution with armed men' lest they defend their lives. But 'Pardon taketh from them, to whom it is offered', he reasons, 'the plea of self defence'. Thus it is the very arbitrariness of 'Lenity' that is so numinous to Hobbes, because it legitimates the programme of *Leviathan*, which is also the project of Shakespearean comedy: to yoke the energies of the market to the archaic forms of a monarchic state. Weber called such a system *patrimonial*, comparing its mercy to Arabic 'khadi justice', since its 'irrationality' is similarly intended to reflect the ruler's 'grace'. So though Gratiano would grant Shylock 'A halter gratis', to perpetuate a brutish state of nature (374), it is mercy which is the real gratuity in a patrimonial state and has the quality of 'Grace', because it is truly surplus to the law. Gratuitousness is the quality of mercy that is its most calculated strength. As Portia admits, waiving her fee: 'My mind was never yet more mercenary' (415).[39]

IV

' 'Tis mightiest in the mightiest, it becomes
The throned monarch better than his crown.'

'Upon my power I may dismiss this court', the Duke warns the litigants at the impasse of the trial in *The Merchant of Venice* (IV, i, 104). It is a final flourish of the vestigial prerogative of the sovereign to breach the law. As Moretti reads it, Renaissance tragedy ensues from the prince's assertion of such an absolute sovereignty, as the eclipse of Stuart monarchy would follow from Charles I's revival of the dogma. In Shakespearean comedy, however, the problem posed is not the Machiavellian one of the sovereign's freedom of action, but the modern one, which Foucault regards as a milestone for the seventeenth century, namely, the question of the state itself, its strength and composition. And whereas, for Machiavellian policy the individual had either to submit to sovereignty or die, in a mercantile state 'what the individual has to do is live and produce', which is what makes government a cooption, rather than an obstruction of the market.[40] So the Duke resigns his power to the jurist Bellario, 'Whom I have sent for to determine this' (106), and thence to Portia, yielding prerogative to commercial logic, as Antonio expected, until the market's contradictions are revealed as self-cancelling, and Shylock 'hast not the value of a cord' and 'must be hang'd at the state's expense' (362–3). Mercy in *The Merchant of Venice* is consonant with Elizabethan theory, in other words, that what Bacon termed 'a free jurisdiction' enabled the monarch to 'temper and control' the law, mitigating or suspending statute, but only *pro bono publico*. In 1606, *Bate's Case* would determine that 'the absolute power of the king is not that which is executed to private use of any person, but is only that which is applied to general benefit'; and the Shakespearean text likewise reserves the dispensing power until the law is distinguished from 'the common good'. Absolute power, as Portia interjects, can only operate 'for the state, not for Antonio', who must 'render' mercy to Shylock according to his own interests (370–5); a ruling conforming to judgement in Elizabethan cases such as *Regina* v. *Saunders and Archer*, that royal pardon could not interfere with the right of a private person 'to have revenge to death'.[41] The 'difference' of quality in mercy is precisely that it separates 'the general state' from mercenary interest, since in the words of the Senecan maxim: 'To kings belongs government, to subjects property':

> That thou shalt see the difference of our spirit,
> I pardon thee thy life before thou ask.
> For half thy wealth, it is Antonio's,
> The other half comes to the general state,
> Which humbleness may drive into a fine.
> (365–9)

The prerogative of mercy is not distrained, we see, so long as it is exercised for public good. This was the doctrine promulgated by Lambarde at the time of *The Merchant of Venice*, when he wrote that 'in the government of all commonwealths, sundry things do fall out that do require extraordinary help'; and admitted even by John Pym, when he conceded in 1640 that 'the king had a transcendent power in many cases whereby he might prevent sudden accidents.' Yet proceedings in Shakespearean Venice – where, despite the royal veto, it is also 'enacted

in the laws' that Shylock's 'life lies at the mercy of the Duke' (346–52) –
suggest the constraint that hedged a sovereignty conceived to be both
above and below the law. If mercy was a right that rose above the
'sceptred sway' of 'temporal power' – and but for which, thought Bacon,
'the law were as useless as a sundial when the sun shines not' – Chancery
lawyers were as keen to mystify its operation as common lawyers to
delimit it. Prerogative, Bacon considered, was comparable to God's
power to work miracles. Just as God observed the laws of nature, so kings
'ought as rarely to put in use their prerogative, as God does his power of
working miracles'; and James I's Chief Justice, Sir John Davies, agreed
that by generally observing rules of law, the king 'doth imitate divine
majesty which in the government of the world doth suffer things for the
most part to pass according to the course of nature, yet many times doth
shew extraordinary power in working miracles'. This would be the *via
negativa* of James himself, when he insisted that though a king was bound
by law in private matters, his obligation to his subjects meant he might
dispense with 'doubtsome or rigorous' laws upon 'causes only known to
him'. In the Stuart system sovereignty imitated the *deus absconditus*,
ceding to law what James termed the monarch's 'private right', only to
reassert that since 'monarchy is the supremest thing on earth', it was
'presumption and high contempt in a subject to dispute what a king can
do'.[42] Such is the partial eclipse of power foreseen by the Duke, at least,
when he recommends to Shylock mercy over vengeance, and predicts a
melodrama of reversal and suspense such as Portia will produce:

> Shylock, the world thinks, and I think so too,
> That thou but lead'st this fashion of thy malice
> To the last hour of act, and then 'tis thought
> Thou'lt show thy mercy and remorse more strange
> Than is thy strange apparent cruelty.
>
> (17–21)

As James I would show, mercy that reserves itself, like the *deus ex
machina*, 'To the last hour of act', accrues a mystery 'more strange' than
any atrocity of the old theatre of blood. For what the Shakespearean
scenario effects, as Bacon expressly confirms, is the transfer of mystique
from a religious to a secular authority, when the aura attending Christ in
the miracle play is attached to His deputy, and in the gap left by the
collapse of Christian discourse is inserted the new rationality of public
good. The 'strangeness' of a 'royal grace' that looks 'like power divine'
upon the 'passes' of its subjects in order to condone them (*Measure for
Measure*, v, i, 3; 367–8; 379) will be the keynote of all these 'comedies of
forgiveness', where the 'magical narrative' functions as a socially

symbolic act – in Fredric Jameson's terms – to erase the contradiction between private and public interests by investing the transactions of individuals with providential force.[43] The Shakespearean Duke gauges his subjects are 'amazed at the strangeness' of his proceeding (378–9), and 'marvel why I obscur'd myself . . . and would not rather / Make rash remonstrance of my hidden power' to obstruct them (388–90): sovereignty enhances its *arcanum imperii*, he proves, to the extent that it magically facilitates, rather than debars, the private contract. So though Moretti correctly keys Shakespearean drama to the crisis of feudalism, he is wrong to assume that comic form is unrelated to state formation at the time.[44] In fact, its religiosity, so often re-Christianised by critics, is directly pertinent to the accommodation of the English state to contemporary capitalism. Historians trace a rise in prerogative action from the 1580s, and corroborate the parliamentarians' complaint of a 'great Inundation of the Prerogative Royal' in the half century before the Civil War.[45] What the providential form of Shakespearean comedy underlines, however, is that this abrogation of statute by signet or patent was by no means inimical to private interests, but was an urgent executive response to the market's demand for more equitable remedies than statute could provide. Prerogative became 'a flexible instrument for changing economic needs', its use arising 'from particular circumstances and its very success as a means to private ends the reason for its enhanced status'.[46] The contradiction in this use of royal power to expedite the market would become glaring when prerogative was exploited by the Stuarts to monopolistic ends, and confronted the rival dogma of 'the rule of law', but in Shakespearean comic closure it was elided, through a rehearsal of the Hobbesian syllogism that 'The Law is made by the Sovereign and warranted by every one of the people.' The coincidence on which a Shakespeare comedy turns was thus historically specific, for what it embodied was the interdependence of economic and political interests in this era when the accumulation of capital and the accumulation of men were geared together, 'Each made the other possible', and even Coke could rejoice that 'England is an absolute monarchy.'[47]

Revolution swept away the dispensing power of English kings, but before their system crumbled Elizabeth and James applied it liberally to break barriers on trade and manufacture, license corporations or ease conveyance of land. In the form of royal mercy, the right was invoked for economic reasons by Edward vi to excuse French and Flemish Protestants from the act of uniformity, or even, by Elizabeth in 1586, to absolve Catholics from the penalties of the recusancy laws. Such discretionary authority was a prop of absolutism that could not withstand the seventeenth-century shift from family- to contract-centred ideology, but Shakespearean comedy preserves the discursive context in which the

Tudor and Jacobean compromise was stabilised. The patrimonialism that mercy soldered was already firm, for instance, in *The Comedy of Errors*, where the action is framed by the Duke's announcement to Egeon that he is 'not partial to infringe our laws . . . / Therefore by law thou art condemn'd to die' (i, i, 4–25). Considerations of power and plenty conflict directly in this mercantilist farce, performed, it is assumed, for the lawyers of Gray's Inn in 1594, since Egeon has been sentenced according to 'solemn synods' between rival states 'To admit no traffic to our adverse towns' (13–15). If power and commerce clash, we see, society will be deadlocked in 'mortal and intestine jars' (11):

> The enmity and discord which of late
> Sprung from the rancorous outrage of your Duke
> To merchants, our well-dealing countrymen,
> Who, wanting guilders to redeem their lives,
> Have seal'd his rigorous statutes with their bloods,
> Excludes all pity from our threat'ning looks.
>
> (5–10)

In a memorable passage of *Discipline and Punish*, Foucault images the gentle way of punishment that displaced the scaffold as a neo-classical stage. This 'punitive city' might be a scene by Serlio, where 'each criminal will have a punishment: placards, caps, posters, texts, repeat the code. Perspectives magnify the scene, making it more fearful than it is.' For though 'From where the public sits, it is possible to fear certain cruelties', the 'essential point' is not suffering, but the fact that these penalties '*do not take place*'. They do not need to be exacted, since what this new theatre reveals is the poetic justice that vice and virtue are their own rewards. So 'The great terrifying ritual of execution gives way to this serious theatre . . . and around these representations, schoolchildren gather and adults learn what lessons they must teach.'[48] Shakespearean comedy is just such a dramaturgy, magically cleansed of blood, which in *The Comedy of Errors* comes close to *trompe l'œil*. For already in this play the imbroglio takes place in the shadow of the noose, and the chains and rings that entangle the characters in their 'intricate impeach' before the Duke (v, i, 270), are as ominous as the cords with which they rope each other, bondman or free, 'in a dark and dankish vault', to gnaw their 'bonds in sunder' with their teeth (249–50). The climax comes, indeed, with the cortege 'to the melancholy vale, / The place of death and sorry execution / Behind the ditches' (120–2), of the condemned, 'bareheaded, with the Headsman and other Officers' (Stage Direction, 129); and is sharpened in clamour by the Ephesians for 'Justice, most sacred duke' (133), 'Justice, most gracious Duke . . . / Justice, sweet prince' (189–

200). Flanked by a 'guard with halberds' (185), Duke Solinus vows that 'thou shalt find me just' (203); but the news that Doctor Pinch has been tied by his charges, 'Whose beard they have sing'd off with brands of fire . . . while / [Dromio] with scissors nicks him like a fool' (170–5), fuels the expectation of a fatal end. T. W. Baldwin linked this scene to an actual execution in Finsbury Fields,[49] and Marlovian echoes underscore the *galgenhumor* of its suspense:

> Anon I'm sure the Duke himself in person
> Comes this way . . .
> To see a reverend Syracusian merchant,
> Who put unluckily into this bay,
> Against the laws and statutes of this town,
> Beheaded publicly for his offence.
> See where they come; we will behold his death.
>   (119–28)

'Proceed, Solinus, to procure my fall, / And by the doom of death end woes and all': the opening words of *The Comedy of Errors* dispose Egeon's life and the day's action to a sanguinary law: 'Yet this my comfort; when your words are done, / My woes end likewise with the evening sun' (i, i, 26–7). The implications of that law return to the Duke with Antipholus's demand: 'O, grant me justice, Even for the service . . . I did . . . in the wars . . . even for the blood / That I lost . . . now grant me justice' (v, i, 190–4). A penal exaction of blood for blood will motivate Shakespearean drama, but this early text establishes the comic paradigm by its evasion of such spectacular corporeality. Already the metonymic exchange is one in which domination of the body is abandoned as condition of a deeper, discursive subjection. For here the body of the condemned had been the axis of all 'errors', its 'grained face' unrecognised and 'blood froze up' (307–18). 'We may pity, though not pardon' the prisoner, the Duke had declared (97), since punishment was intended to inspire pathos. But what the recognition scene reveals is that sovereignty will relinquish judicial torment of this body, once Egeon is positioned as its subject. Then the cords that lash him will be untied in favour of the affective tourniquet of a modern family: as his wife declares, 'Whoever bound him, I will loose his bonds' (339). Summoning all 'assembled in this place' to 'hear at large discoursed all our fortunes' (395–6), Emilia thus substitutes a discourse of productive labour for the punitive dictate of the Duke. Throughout the comedies, childbirth figures to naturalise capitalist relations; so here the 'heavy burden . . . delivered' by the mother comprises 'satisfaction' for the accumulated 'wrong' (397–8). For like the substitution-trick or mother/daughter duplication of later comedies, the appearance of the 'natural perspective' of twins (*Twelfth Night*, v, i, 215) separates the characters from the consequences of transgression, incorporating these within a social whole. Inserted into a productive unit, the knotted relations of the characters are unravelled: as Dromio of Ephesus exclaims, 'Ourselves we do remember, sir, by you. / For lately we were bound as you are now' (293–4). The 'rigorous statutes' sealed with blood are invalidated by these new bonds, as the Duke allows, when the son fulfils the letter of the law: 'It shall not need, thy father hath his life' (390). 'The political investment of the body', we see, 'is bound up with its economic use; it is as a force of production that the body is invested with relations of power and domination.'[50] For in the disciplinary order, the life of the reprieved is as valuable as the death of the condemned had been to the sovereign of the Old Regime.

The Comedy of Errors begins with a precedent for Shakespearean justice, when the Duke relaxes 'the extremity' of law, to 'limit' the condemned 'one day' to 'quit the penalty and ransom him' (i, i, 22, 150); it ends with an act that auspicates mercy in the comedies, when the 'pawn of ducats' at the nexus of the intrigue is disclaimed (v, i, 389). The Duke had stated that a reprieve would be 'against our laws, / Against my crown, my oath, my dignity, / Which princes, would they, may not disannul', judging that 'sentence may not be recall'd / But to our honour's great disparagement' (i, i, 142–8). But the 'favour' of respite (149) granted the condemned licenses the marketplace, until the characters' private transactions are legitimated as public interests. This will be the pattern throughout Shakespearean comedy, as sovereignty accedes to the desires of its subjects, abandoning the bloody spectacle that symbolises 'crown' and 'oath' and 'dignity', and dispensing with the 'laws and statutes', to instate a commonwealth where power and plenty merge. The Shakespearean Duke abjures the death penalty, yet withholds his mercy until 'the last hour of act', in order to unite the market with the state. Egeon complains this serves 'But to procrastinate his lifeless end' (158); but what the suspense attends is the precariousness of English state formation, and the paradox that, as Anderson notes, 'the strongest medieval monarchy produced the weakest absolutism', so 'The transition from medieval to modern corresponded to a deep reversal of English development'. It was this 'contradictory fusion of traditional and novel forces that defined the rupture in the island during the Renaissance', Anderson proposes;[51] but the valency of Shakespearean comic form is that it obscures this reversal, whilst sealing the fusion by masking the 'great disparagement' of majesty. In the end, the Duke will be saluted as 'great' (v, i, 204), 'most mighty' (283, 330), and 'Renowned' (393), because the mercy that is 'mightiest in the mightiest' ratifies his subjects' desires. Transposing terror into toleration, the Janus-face of

Shakespearean monarchy thus figures the metastasis of the English
Crown, as the compact it composes prefigures the Hobbesian state, 'that
great Leviathan', where subjects will concede their own subjection in
exchange for the equal subjection of 'every man'.[52]

V

'Pardon's the word to all.'

Arraigned at the Old Bailey in October 1598 for the manslaughter of
Gabriel Spencer, Ben Jonson was saved by a procedure as routine as the
reprieve of Raleigh was exceptional. In the words of the court
memorandum, 'He confesses the indictment, asks for the book, reads like
a Clerk, is marked with the letter T, and is delivered according to the
statute'.[53] Benefit of clergy had been the commonest mitigation of capital
punishment in sixteenth-century London, where around 40 per cent of
accused applied for it in the years 1596–1600, 30 per cent successfully.
The numbers declined with distance from the capital, an index of literacy
on which benefit had been conditional since the turn of the century, when
clerics could no longer be identified by habit or tonsure. Justice 'by the
book' thus corresponded to a complex transition in the organisation of
subjectivity, when the assent that had been signified by the symbolic
obeisance of a medieval elite was starting to be discursively produced, but
when subjection was still required to be signalled in bodily submission to
a visible code. The speaking 'I' of modern subjectivity is inchoate in this
formality of reading 'like a Clerk', prompted by textual cues that are not
yet internalised, and necessitating the shameful marker of a scorching
brand. Jonson, it is assumed, concealed his 'Tyburn T', the indelible seal
of Tudor justice, from seventeenth-century eyes, but the hand that bore
the sign of condemnation, which had already scripted 'a new play called,
Every Mans Humour', had held the book before an 'understanding
auditory' then to externalise subjection. The body that would write in the
seventeenth century was still in the sixteenth a body that was written on,
even if the text the condemned was compelled to read mediated between
outward shame and inner reformation. 'Have mercy upon me, O Lord'
began Psalm 51, the so-called 'neck-verse', 'according unto the multitude
of thy mercies wipe out my wickedness. . . . Lo, thou requirest truth in
the inward parts of me: and therefore wilt thou make me learn wisdom
in the secret part of my heart.' 'Thou desirest no sacrifice', affirmed the
Psalm, 'thou delightest not in burnt offering' but in a 'mortified sprite'.
Yet the 'inward part' of subjectivity was not yet sufficiently mortified with
discourses of wisdom for the body to be spared all sacrifices, and the man

who would live to be an 'author' and hide the burn of shame, was marked like Cain, according to the statute.[54]

The Renaissance text is a vivid material inscription, scoring the flesh to impose subjection, and authorised by its place within a repertoire of penal practices. The 'letter T' burned into Jonson's thumb finds textual endorsement, indeed, in the draconian retribution of his own comedies, where a true poetics of punishment demands spectacular and excruciating recompense for transgression. Though Justice Clement reminds the malefactor in *Every Man In His Humour* that 'I must cut off thy legs, and I must cut off thy arms, and I must cut off thy head; but I did not do it' (Q., v, iii, 108–9), outside the masques Jonson's 'problem of how to redeem and transform characters' scarcely meets such a benign solution.[55] At the end of the 1598 *Every Man In His Humour* Clement had invested the comedian Musco with his robes of office, while the poet Matheo's 'commonwealth of paper' (266) was set on fire, signifying what Jonson would proclaim in the Epistle of *Volpone*: that his 'aim being to put the snaffle in their mouths that cry out: We never punish vice in our interludes', he copied 'the ancients, the goings-out of whose comedies are not always joyful . . . it being the office of a comic poet to imitate justice' (118–24). So despite his name, Clement lays down the law for Jonsonian penalty when he orders Bobadilla and Matheo to 'the cage' and stocks in motley and sackcloth (v, iii, 337–9), and foretells the savage sentences that close *Volpone*. According to Anne Barton, the poetic justice of these implies they are meted by 'the dramatist rather than the magistrates';[66] and they confirm the sensational corporeality of Jonsonian comedy, with Corvino paraded around Venice in an ass's cap and set in stocks, to have his 'eyes beat out with stinking fish, / Bruised fruit and rotten eggs' (v, vii, 135–41); Mosca whipped and chained for life in a galley (114); and Volpone fettered and 'crampt with irons' until 'sick and lame indeed' (124). Declaimed by the *avocatore*, the play's last lines nail the logic of this theatre of corporal torment: 'Mischiefs feed / Like beasts, till they be fat, and then they bleed' (150–1). Jonson's Venetian carnival involves a catastrophic infliction of suffering on the flesh of the condemned, and this 'mortifying of a Fox' (125) substantiates the penal schema of his comedies, which is 'to take enormity by the forehead, and brand it' (*Bartholemew Fair*, v, v, 118) with the livid sign of its subjection. Foucault reminds us that 'the body is involved in a political field; power relations have an immediate effect upon it; they mark it, torture it, force it to emit signs.'[57] The Jonsonian text does not hide this fact, but glories in its immediacy as a discourse of searing punishment and pain.

Branding of felons began to be tokenised in the seventeenth century, when a cold iron was often applied to the condemned, and this coincided with a fall in cases of clergy after about 1590. The penal revolution that would cause the abolition of benefit in 1706 commenced in the last Elizabethan years, when judges were already imposing 'equity on the barbarity of Tudor criminal law', by varying rules to assist or handicap the accused, or by initiating plea-bargaining, thus 'bending forms to the rough demands of "natural" or "rational" justice'.[58] Benefit had been an intermediate technique that enacted the shift from public punishment to private repression by equating inward correction with outward stigma. But the text impressed on the bodies of Tudor subjects had been sufficiently internalised in the minds of their Stuart descendants for a new penology to take hold, based not on the exaction of corporal signs of submission but on discursive subjection through discretionary pardon. It was this reversal in the scope of penality that explains the paradoxical statistic that as benefit declined, sentencing became harsher, and 'Assize judges sentenced more people to be executed in the 1630s than in the 1590s.'[59] Severity was the foil that made mercy meaningful, as from around 1600 an entire social order was constructed around the threat and commutation of capital punishment. For what emerges from records, as J. A. Sharpe reports in his study of *Crime in Seventeenth-Century England*, is that 'There was a draconian legal code with ample provision for the death penalty [yet] an overwhelming majority of those theoretically at risk of the noose evaded it.'[60] 'Albion's Fatal Tree' – the eighteenth-century gallows beneath which patronage was dispensed – was firmly rooted in Shakespearean culture, where felons regularly begged the great to intercede for pardon. 'The prerogative of mercy ran throughout the administration of law' in this system, as Douglas Hay concludes, because 'it put the instrument of legal terror directly in the hands of those with power. . . . It allowed the class that passed the bloodiest penal code in Europe to congratulate itself on its humanity', and above all it 'created the spirit of consent and submission, the "mind-forged manacles" which Blake saw bound the English.'[61]

'The wretched thief begging on his knees for forgiveness is not a literary conceit, but a reality in legal depositions' of early modern society;[62] yet he would never have been granted mercy without surrendering to 'mind-forged' subjection in discourses like literature. Natalie Zemon Davis has indeed traced narrative conventions in the pardon plea; and the granting of reprieve would be underwritten by Hobbes when he considered that 'the end of punishing is not revenge but correction', and defined punishment as 'Evill inflicted by Authority to the end that the will of men may thereby be better disposed to obedience'. In *Leviathan* the law is redirected away from the body of the prisoner to his soul, from vengeance to reform, and past to future. 'Men look not at the evill past', in Hobbes's penology, 'but the good to follow. Whereby we are forbidden to inflict punishment with any other designe, than the correction of the offender, or direction of others.'[63] Likewise, the path to reform is clearly signposted by Shakespearean comedy, which pivots on the same recurring tableau, when in sudden, seemingly gratuitous, reversal, reprieve is granted by the prince. So when the Duke of Verona exonerates Valentine, declaring that 'I here forget all former griefs, / Cancel all grudge, repeal thee home again', to 'Plead a new state in thy unrivall'd merit, / To which I thus subscribe' (*The Two Gentlemen of Verona*, v, iv, 140–3), he signs the warrant for the same reason that he pardons the outlaws: 'They are reformed, civil, full of good, / And fit for . . . employment' (154–5). It is 'thy spirit', he tells Valentine, 'I do applaud' (138), echoing the criminal's own commendation of Proteus: 'Who by repentence is not satisfied, / Is nor of heaven, nor earth; for these are pleas'd: / By penitence th'Eternal's wrath's appeas'd' (79–81). What that 'spirit' comprises to 'satisfy' the prince has been exhibited by Proteus himself, when he admits 'My shame and guilt confounds me . . . if hearty sorrow / Be a sufficient ransom for offence, / I tender't here; I do as truly suffer / As e'er I did commit (73–7). The contract that authority offers the 'reformed', 'civil' and employable, stipulates a 'sufficient . . . tender' of private suffering and remorse for public penalty and pain. It is, as the Duke perceives, 'a new state' for the condemned, but in Hobbesian terms, a binding covenant.

Situated at the point when, as Foucault records, representation shrinks from referentiality into the 'fictitious recess' of its own 'essential void',[64] Shakespearean comedy will erase its juridical force as 'No more yielding than a dream' (*A Midsummer Night's Dream*, v, i, 414). 'If we shadows have offended', plead these texts, by trespassing upon the competence of 'gentles' who have it in their power to 'reprehend', it is no *lèse-majesté*. Instead, the play dissolves into an 'airy nothing' (16) by restoring to its audience their justiciary rights: 'If you pardon, we will mend' (416). This is the reverse of the Jonsonian code, which arrogates a magisterial commission, and it provides a paradigm for the transparency of modern discourse. For what is effaced by this elision is the sign of the death penalty that authorised the text. In *A Midsummer Night's Dream*, for instance, the action proceeds from Egeus's claim that 'according to our law', immediate execution must punish Hermia's infraction of 'the ancient privilege of Athens' and her 'father's choice' (i, I, 41–54), and is accelerated by Theseus's ruling that 'the law of Athens yields you up / (Which by no means we may extenuate) / To death, or . . . single life' (119–21). Though the Duke thus mitigates the statute, 'Either to die the death, or to abjure' desire (65–6), is a judgement the Old Regime must make on those who thwart its 'sovereignty' (82), and the plot unfolds within 'Four days' respite granted the condemned to 'Take time to pause' or 'prepare to die' (83–6). It comprises a carnival 'Without the peril of the Athenian law' (iv, i, 152), which ends when the desires of the lovers are sanctioned as the Duke rescinds the patriarchal law: 'Egeus, I will overbear your will' (188). All the anxiety of the condemned is dispelled in this scenario in the 'tragical mirth' of *Pyramus and Thisbe*, acted by the mechanicals with 'the killing out' (III, i, 12), since any violence 'were enough to hang us all' (I, ii, 72). Thus Shakespearean comedy conceals its power by the representation of a fictionality that 'needs no excuse . . . for when the players are all dead, there need none to be blamed', and the author signs his text not as a magisterial inscription, but as a work of imagination with jurisdiction over nothing but itself: 'if he that writ it had played Pyramus and hanged himself . . . it would have been a fine tragedy' (v, i, 345–50). Such comic form is more modern than tragedy because its techniques of subjection pretend that 'All for your delight / We are not here' (114–15).

Shakespearean comedy is a more modern discursive practice than tragedy, since, generating pleasure and relief instead of pity and terror, it secures not simply submission but assent. James I grasped this when he adopted a comedic persona, writing in his warrant to the Sheriff at Winchester that, 'resolved to mix clemency with justice', he would spare the condemned the 'example and terror' of execution, in response 'to our free entry here with so hearty and general an applause', and the fact 'that at the time of their arraignment none did more readily give assent than their kinsmen and allies'. As for Raleigh, an appeal, he insinuated, would meet 'that clemency which we might very easily be persuaded into'.[65] What Raleigh then penned to his judges was craven enough to close a Shakespearean plot, when he rejoiced that 'We have this day beheld a work of so great mercy, as the like hath been seldom known. . . . And although my self have not yet bin brought so near the brink of the grave, yet I trust so great a compassion will extend itself towards me also.' Only the memory of his unworthiness made him despair of 'so great a grace, who otherwise beheld Pity in the face, the voice, the writing, and the life of my Sovereign'.[66] In similar abasement, Angelo will swear his crime sticks in his 'penitent heart' so deep 'I crave death more willingly than mercy. / 'Tis my deserving, and I do entreat it' (*Measure for Measure*, v, i, 473–4); trapped by transgressions, Bertram will confess 'Both, both! O pardon!' (*All's Well That Ends Well*, v, iii, 306); and Iachimo will protest 'my heavy conscience sinks my knee. . . . Take that life, beseech you, / Which I so often owe' (*Cymbeline*, v, v, 414–16). It seems that 'Pardon's the word to all' in response to this abjection, as Cymbeline crows (422); but the ensuing applause does not celebrate release so much as it salutes the 'new state' of subjection. 'We will include all jars / With triumph, mirth, and rare solemnity', trumpets the Duke (*The Two Gentlemen of Verona*, v, iv, 161–2), for when revenge is pacified, 'A solemn combination shall be made of all our souls' *Twelfth Night*, v, i, 379–80).

So what these nuptials solemnise is that 'This is more than Consent, or Concord; it is real Unitie of them all. . . . This is the Generation of that great LEVIATHAN, or rather Mortall God . . . One Person, of whose Acts a great Multitude, by mutuall Covenants one with Another, hade made themselves every one the Author.'[67]

'You must think, if the spectators were glad, the actors were not sorry', wrote Carleton from Winchester, 'for even those best resolved to death were glad of life, Cobham vowed openly, if ever he proved traitor again never so much as to beg his life, and Grey, that since he had his life without begging, he would deserve it.'[68] Comedy will replace the ritual of execution with this 'gossips' feast' (*The Comedy of Errors*, v, i, 406), because so many are to be born again in docile subjection. Thus, 'In christ'ning shalt thou have two godfathers', Gratiano sneers at Shylock, 'Had I been judge, thou shouldst have had ten more, / To bring thee to the gallows' (*The Merchant of Venice*, IV, i, 395–7). Dispossessed, Shylock accurately weighs the quality of this mercy, when he retorts, 'Nay take my life and all! Pardon not that . . . You take my life / When you do take the means / Whereby I live' (371–4); but forced to become a Christian he can only mumble 'I am not well; send the deed after me, / And I will sign it' (393–4). Humanist critics interpret the silences of the reprieved in these plays as denoting the limits of power's manipulation of the supposed 'inner lives' of its subjects, whereas it is precisely in muteness that the Shakespearean state elicits the most malleable assent, since Shylock's signature will mark the point at which the Renaissance infliction of corporal punishment is contracted into a modern discursive subjection. As Foucault shows, the so-called 'soul' is a palimpsest which requires for its legibility the obliteration of prior discourses; and this is exactly what is signalled in the blankness of Shakespearean silence. Shakespeare's carnival is more modern than Jonson's. By abolishing the scales and knife of the archaic festival of blood, his Duke denies the condemned the right to make an *amende honorable* or to rail against authority in a gallows speech, and so seizes in the monopoly of discourse a more epochal victory than the monopoly of violence.[69] As Hobbes saw, mercy stifles resistance into compliance; so 'The power that I have on you, is to spare you', Posthumus will assure Iachimo ambiguously, 'The malice towards you, to forgive you' (*Cymbeline*, v, v, 419–20). That authority is engraved in Iachimo's silence.

'Pardon's the word' which subsumes all other discourses in this system. Thus, 'If I prove a good repast to the spectators', the condemned Posthumus had bragged to the hangman, 'I am merrier to die than thou art to live', but freed by the king from 'the charity of a penny cord' (167), he survives for his surname to become a by-word for authority (v, iv, 156–95; v, 445). Where 'Hanging is the word' of tragic closure (154),

Shakespearean comedy reframes the subjection of the condemned, from carnivalesque dismemberment to disciplinary discourse, as 'all come under the hangman' to be respited (*The Winter's Tale*, IV, iv, 800). Even Autolycus, who revels in 'tortures will break the back of a man' or deaths 'wit can make heavy and vengeance bitter' (798), and for whom 'beating and hanging are terrors' to be mocked and evaded (IV, iii, 28), is struck dumb by the 'first gentleman-like' pardon of the Shepherd and Clown, granted on promise to 'amend' his life of vagabondage (V, iii, 152). What this comedy extracts, therefore, in the speechlessness of a Barnardine or Autolycus, is as vital as repentence to a state determined, as Foucault puts it, to 'extinguish the dubious glory of the criminal' and 'silence the adventures of the condemned celebrated in almanacs, broadsheets and popular tales'. Reformers would take many decades to reverse the discourse of crime to make it the vehicle of the law, but they commenced by suppressing the song of 'the red blood' that 'reigns in the winter's pale' of outlawry (IV, iii, 4). Thus 'the people was robbed of its old pride in its crimes', silence became the precondition of coercion, and the closing of the curtains on punishment removed the condemned from the theatre of the scaffold to the unsung margin of the workhouse or the bridewell.[70] The villains and vagabonds of these comedies exit towards that confinement which will be the fate of the convicted and certified in the Age of Reason, their very function to be seen without being heard by carceral power. 'Think not on him', the Prince is advised by Benedick, told that Don John is captured, 'I'll devise thee brave punishments for him. Strike up pipers' (*Much Ado About Nothing*, V, iv, 124–5). The old penality had branded its condemnation on the body in letters of fire, but for the Shakespearean text silence and docility replace oaths and wounds as signifiers of the most complete subjection.

'The society that has rediscovered its laws has lost the citizen who violated them';[71] and the Stuart monarchy would follow Benedick's suggestion to put the recidivist out of hearing with martial music. Within six months of his accession James issued an order designating 'The New found Land' the receptacle for 'incorrigible and dangerous rogues', and on 24 January 1615 this was extended in a commission that gave the most prophetic twist to mercy by instituting convict transportation as a *quid pro quo* for pardon. 'Where in it is our desire that Justice be tempered with mercy', James decreed, 'it is our care so to have our Clemency applied as that offenders adjudged by law to die, may live and yield a profitable service in parts abroad.' Henceforth judges would be empowered to 'reprive from execution persons convicted of any felony . . . who for strength of body or other abilities shall be thought fit to be employed beyond the Seas.' In July 1615 the first seventeen convicts were duly saved from the noose, 'to be transported into Virginia, with proviso that they return not again into England'; and on 31 October 1618 the first woman, one Anne Russell, a 'prisoner in Newgate', was reprieved 'to be employed in Virginia', on condition 'that if she return at any time' she would 'be subject to execution'.[72] During the next hundred years shipment to the colonies would supersede benefit of clergy as security for pardon. Jacobean power had devised a Shakespearean contract for the condemned: in return for life, a subjection as total as it was presumed to be productive.

VI

'the rarer action is
In virtue than in vengeance: they being penitent . . .'

With 'all the actors . . . together on the stage', and his enemies stunned 'like men beheaded and met again in the other world . . . nothing acquainted with what had passed no more than the lookers-on with what should follow', the prince can relish his dramatic mastery. In the hiatus he has staged, he can expatiate on the difference between punishment and mercy, and remind the spectators of his command of death, never greater than in this hour of renunciation. So the prince maintains the illusion that he is in control of history, and thus James I convened his courtiers and Privy Councillors at Wilton House, at 'the very hour' when the executions of the condemned were to take place in the neighbouring county. There, pacing the gallery, the King held forth to a spellbound audience on his Solomon-like deliberation. As Carleton enthused, 'he told them how much he had been troubled to resolve this business', and pairing each of the condemned against another, proved reasons both for and against mercy in every case, 'and so went on with Plutarch's comparisons till travelling in contrarieties but holding the conclusion in so different balance that the lords knew not what to look for till the end came out', he triumphantly announced: '"and therefore I have saved them all."' Though it dumfounded Coke, 'The miracle was as great there as at Winchester and it took like effect: for the applause that began about the king went . . . round about the court.' It was a miracle that depended, in a literal sense, on timing. For, as Carleton added, even as James was being cheered at Wilton, a 'cross adventure' was 'like to have marred the play', when the messenger 'could not get so near to the scaffold that he could speak to the sheriff and was thrust out amongst the boys', and only recognition by another favourite enabled the royal 'angel' to wing his way with mercy, 'else Markham might have lost his neck'.[73]

The reprieve on which sovereignty stakes its legitimacy likewise risks

ever more delay in Shakespearean comedy, as rulers struggle with
contingency to impose authority, and closure arrives, as the King fears in
All's Well That Ends Well, 'Like a remorseful pardon slowly carried . . .
that comes too late' (IV, iii, 57–8). Yet it is this very suspense that makes
mercy most productive, as 'travelling in contrarieties', the denouement
becomes, like that of *Cymbeline*, 'The more delay'd, delighted' (v, iv,
102). A monarchy itching to employ 'bitter torture' to 'Winnow truth
from falsehood' (v, v, 133–4), and adamant the condemned 'must /
Endure our law. . . . The whole world shall not save him' (298–9; 322),
will need to be certain that 'conscience' can be 'fetter'd / More than
shanks and wrists' (v, iv, 8–9), before it issues orders to 'Save those in
bonds' to 'taste our comfort' (v, v, 403–4). It is a process involving a
perilous attenuation of monarchical prestige, as Moretti notices, so that
'Jacobean princes are almost always "dukes"', and 'much like other
characters'. Indeed, what makes this comedy amusing is precisely the gulf
between the absolutist pretensions and actual prospects of the ruler, as it
'exalts the king to reduce him to a justice of the peace'.[74] But where
Moretti sees merely the emptying of kingship, comedic suspense in
fact decants a renewed sovereignty in just this transference from scaffold to courtroom. The King will abdicate his personal rule to a
Hobbesian empire that 'Promises Britain peace and plenty' (459): the
title of *Measure for Measure* proclaims a formula for all these plays,
Shakespearean comedy is preoccupied, as Greenblatt and others show,
with the incitement and containment of subversion, but the strategy it
advances is of a displacement in the economy of punishment. Its task is to
transform a savage spectacle of retribution into a modern theatre of
desire. The right of death that went with kings is to be superseded in its
action by the power over life that goes with workhouses, prisons and
asylums. So 'Mortality and mercy' are transposed, and in the play of
substitutions that comprises the Shakespearean plot, the hangman's
hatchet is supplanted by the clinician's gaze. The 'great eclipse' of the sun
king turns out to be the dawn of modern penology, psychiatry and
eugenics.

The form of Shakespearean comedy is determined by its premise that
'kindness' is 'ever nobler than revenge', the victor's 'nature, stronger
than his just occasion' (*As You Like It*, IV, iii, 129–30); and it turns on
absolutism's 'conversion' from the 'mighty power' levied for putting the
outlaw 'to the sword', to a constitutional settlement evading violence (v,
iv, 151–62). It was *Leviathan* that would provide the best gloss on this
manoeuvre, when its seventh Law of Nature 'commandeth Pardon, upon
security of the Future'. 'Revenge without respect to the Example, and
profit to come', Hobbes saw, 'is a triumph or glorying in the hurt of
another, tending to no end (for the End is alwayes to Come)', and

counter-productive, since 'to hurt without reason, tendeth to the introduction of Warre . . . and is commonly stiled by the name of Cruelty.'[75] *Leviathan* would make explicit the reversal of Machiavellian policy which is already the rationale of Shakespearean mercy. For at the apparent zenith of his might, as confident as any Sforza Duke of Milan that 'mine enemies . . . now are in my power' (*The Tempest*, III, iii, 90–1), the Shakespearean prince is made to understand that to restore his monarchy he must abdicate the sword of justice. Certain, therefore, that 'At this hour / Lies at my mercy all mine enemies' (IV, i, 263–4), Prospero is persuaded by Ariel to forgo his rights over the bodies of traitors and the defeated in favour of the 'nobler reason' of enlightenment. Once more Shakespearean comedy presents the founding drama of modernity as a grand renunciation by the monarch of the 'fury' of the scaffold to clear the stage for the 'virtue' of the penitentiary:

> Though with their high wrongs I am struck to the quick
> Yet with my nobler reason 'gainst my fury
> Do I take part. The rarer action is
> In virtue than in vengeance: they being penitent
> The sole drift of my purpose doth extend
> Not a frown further.
>
> (25–30)

Like earlier Shakespearean dukes, Prospero will break the staff which governs life and death, and return the bodies of the condemned to be useful in society, on condition they subject themselves to correction. But of all the comedies it is *The Tempest* which goes furthest in projecting the disciplinary mechanisms of modernity, and which offers the most visionary prospectus for the new mode of power whose action will no longer be the mere containment of danger, but a positive production of subjection. According to Foucault, the seventeenth-century model of disciplinary society was laied out in the quarantined partition of a plague-stricken town, and there is a close homology between that 'segmented, immobile, frozen space', where 'Each individual is fixed in his place. And if he moves, he does so at the risk of contagion or punishment', and the island where Prospero pioneers surveillance on the pretext of a communal emergency. For the disaster which he instigates and manages rages as an epidemic, symptoms of which may be convulsions, cramps or blisters, but which leaves all its victims 'frantic' (57), as 'they devour their reason' (155), and are 'justled from their senses' (158), their 'brains boiled within [their] skull' (59–60), and so rabid with 'madness' (115–16), that for brother 'to call brother / Would even infect [his] mouth' (130–1). Isolated, divided, classified and inspected, the afflicted undergo a purification by fire and water on Prospero's island, that purges their bodies, property and clothes of 'All the infections that the sun sucks up' (II, ii, 1), yet is 'So safely ordered, that there is . . . not so much perdition as an hair / Betid to any creature' cleansed (I, ii, 29–31), 'On their . . . garments not a blemish' (217–18). Servants are 'clapped under hatches' (v, i, 231) in this regime, but as in actual epidemics, internment and disinfection are not ends so much as means to 'assign each individual his "true" name, body and disease'. Like carnival, storm and plague subvert hierarchy, but they are 'met by order whose function is to sort out every confusion', until decontamination is complete, 'their rising senses / Begin to chase the ignorant fumes' (66–7), and the entire population can be enrolled and fixed in a 'great review of the living and the dead'. As Foucault deduces, though terror of plague and rebellion lies behind this coercion, before it stretches the dream of perfect power and a utopia which was to become reality in the prisons of the Enlightenment.[76]

Prospero's 'cell' marks a new era of penality. When the prisoners are released (10–30), it is to take up places as docile bodies in an altogether novel configuration of subjection, as 'They all enter the circle which Prospero had made, and there stand charm'd' (Stage Direction, 57). For if the infected town afforded a model of disciplinary order, its Enlightenment ideal would be the Panopticon, which would complete the magic circle by arranging every madman or prisoner on a periphery around a central figure of authority. The Panopticon, in Foucault's account, is a machine for dissociating seeing from being, because 'in the periphic ring, one is totally seen, without seeing', whilst 'in the centre, one sees everything without being seen.' As in Bentham's penitentiary, so in Prospero's ring, 'each actor is alone and individualised', 'is seen, but does not see' the supervisor, who 'observing, speaks' of the prisoners to the world (Stage Direction, 57). Here King James's fantasy of godlike omniscience is realised, as Prospero reviews the prisoners he has mustered, like 'sleepers' whose 'graves / Have . . . oped, and let 'em forth' (49), passing from one to another to record their 'inward pinches', sure that 'Not one of them / That yet looks on me, or would know me', as they 'stand . . . spell-stopped' (60–83). His invisibility is the final key to Shakespearean mercy; for though the duke will 'present' himself once more 'As I was sometime Milan', with his 'hat and rapier' of office (84–6), disciplinary power will have no need of this antique theatricality, its essence being not its own but its subjects' visibility. Thus Prospero's circle prefigures Bentham's Panopticon in rendering the actual exercise of power unnecessary. What matters from now on is that power will be, in Foucault's words, 'unverifiable', since the prisoner will 'never know whether he is being looked at, but will be sure that he may always be so.' The marvel of panopticism, Prospero demonstrates, is that it internalises the constraint that was formerly applied to bodies, since 'He who is subject to visibility, assumes responsibility for his own subjection'. Moreover, 'It does not matter who exercises power' in this machine, so 'power may throw off its physical weight'. Once the prisoners are assigned their places, Prospero can 'abjure' the 'rough magic' of his theatre of punishment, bury the staff which has been the instrument of spectacular sovereignty, and drown the book from which he has conjured corporal pain (31–57). He does so certain that his abdication is not the end of power but its perfection in a system which serves 'To work my end upon their senses that this airy charm is for' (53), by liberating rather than torturing the condemned.[77]

Prospero will regain his dukedom, but his relinquishment of corporal power will make his state more modern than Renaissance. Like the Panopticon, or the penal colony envisaged by James I, his island has been a privileged space for experiments on his subjects, where a new physics of domination has been tested through the unceasing observation of the condemned. An enlightened despot such as Catherine the Great would command her police to spy on 'everything' whilst remaining unseen, and such a programme is already projected in Prospero's Piranesi-like machine. For if earlier comedies revert to some dungeon where the prisoner remains unseen, like the 'dark room' in which Malvolio is tormented (*Twelfth Night*, III, iv, 136), Prospero's power operates by means of an 'observation strange' (*The Tempest*, III, iii, 87), which is both omniscient and 'invisible' (v, i, 97): 'a faceless gaze', in Foucault's phrase, like 'thousands of eyes posted everywhere', that brings all society into view. Reformers would yearn for a police so ubiquitous it 'could only be compared to celestial bodies',[78] and in *The Tempest* this agency of surveillance has the prophetic shape of Ariel, whose orders from Prospero are precisely to 'Be subject to no sight but thine and mine, invisible / To every eyeball else' (I, ii, 302–3). Divided and dispersed throughout the social body, however, the very function of this *agent provocateur* and informer is to eliminate himself. Prospero's system improvises the classic techniques of carceral power – from Ferdinand's forced labour to the madness induced in Alonso and his court – but in its use of Ariel it predicts the even stronger compulsion that will derive from the distribution of discipline throughout society. For though Ariel can immobilise with a harpy's stare, his function is so to instill in 'men of sin' a 'heart's sorrow' and the transparency of 'a clear life ensuing' (III, iii, 54– 83), that he can dissolve into the 'elements' of their lives (v, i, 318). It was the multivalency of the panoptic gaze, Foucault writes, that it worked equally in prisons, factories or schools; so Prospero's epilogue transmits his magic 'spell' of subjection to the audience, by enthroning its members in his place as arbiters of 'Mercy itself'. If Ariel vanishes into air, it is because surveillance of our crimes is now to be undertaken by ourselves, the judges of normality who are present everywhere:

> As you from crimes would pardoned be,
> Let your indulgence set me free.

Where the Old Regime sought in bloody spectacle to stage a small number of people to a multitude, wrote Bentham's admirer Julius, modern power aims to bring the multitude into the view of a few, or even of an individual.[79] It is a distinction that underpins the programme of Shakespearean comedy to multiply and police the population of a disciplinary society. So if *The Tempest* opens with screams of 'Mercy on us', its final act is one of universal emancipation, as the mass of prisoners are liberated from the cell and prison-hulk (v, i, 232–5). The authority that longed to hang the Boatswain for treason in the storm, will now 'make the rope of his destiny' a cable, and secure itself by respiting him from the gallows (I, i, 10–55; v, i, 217–20). Likewise, Caliban will be spared the punishment of being 'pinched to death', and reprieved to 'seek for grace' (276–96). Criminality will no longer be extirpated but acknowledged as 'This thing of darkness' against which normality is defined (267–76). 'If I have too austerely punished you', the sovereign assures his subjects, 'Your compensation makes amends', since punishment has been their 'test' (IV, i, 1–31). For though the felons sang that 'Thought is free', the tune Ariel led them in proved otherwise (III, ii, 124), and discipline is now inscribed in the very 'discourse' which Prospero imposes on them as individuals in the exemplary 'story of my life' (v, i, 304–14). If Antonio does not reply to his brother's pardon, his silence confirms his infected status in this master narrative (130–4). Prospero embraces his foes, because the modern prince exerts no corporal dominion, but fabricates each a position in the order of discourse, breaking his staff to signify that 'they shall be themselves' (32). He can devote 'Every third thought' to his extinction now (312), certain his faintness will be offset by the power of his 'project' to enthrall. Thus his role nears its end as the discipline he instituted is disseminated. For historically this duke is what Foucault calls a 'Napoleonic character'; a 'Great Observer', such as Bacon heralded, who stands at the juncture of ritual sovereignty and invisible repression. He is 'the individual who looms over everything with a single gaze', at one and the same time the bearer of the ancient sword and the organiser of the new state, who combines in a single, symbolic figure 'the whole process by which the spectacular manifestations of power were extinguished one by one in the daily exercise of surveillance', the vigilance which would soon render useless both the scaffold and the throne.[80]

'We have the man Shakespeare with us', Lady Pembroke is reputed to have written from Wilton at the time of Raleigh's trial, as she schemed to mollify James I with a performance of *As You Like It*. According to his only explicit reference to the King, 'Peace, plenty, love, truth, terror', were indeed the comedic 'servants' of this monarch with which Shakespeare could identify (*Henry VIII*, v, v, 47). His would be the system of coercive mercy installed finally at the Restoration, when public relaxation by a 'Merry Monarch' would lock into the private self-interrogation of a trembling subject such as Samuel Pepys. The society of Charles II's grandfather had stood at the gateway to that repressed and secretive regime, as the Jacobeans began the dismantling of the public scaffold. In the interim it would serve as the stage on which the iron will of Parliament would be incised into the body of the King himself, though that would prove a Pyrrhic victory. For what Charles I displayed 'Upon that memorable scene', had already been demonstrated when his father lapsed from the strategy of mercy to order Raleigh's beheading. For fifteen years the prisoner had been what lawyers nicely termed 'a dead man in the law, that might at any minute be cut off'; but power threw away checkmate on the day in 1618 when it permitted Raleigh to climb to the block. The king forgot that there is more authority in the amnesties of Shakespearean comedy than in the display of bloody heads that brings tragedy to a close. And Raleigh went laughing to his 'latest rest', cracking Mercutio's joke that he would end 'a grave man'. In the Tower he had been plied with comparisons of King James's mercy to that of David, but drily replied that David left others to execute his enemies. He was no longer deceived by the quality of mercy. For all his revelry, he knew he died 'in earnest', triumphant in his gallows speech over the system that condemned him. So though his execution was timed to coincide with the rival spectacle of the Lord Mayor's Show, he regained his theatre, convincing his audience by his 'Roman resolution' that 'We have not another such a head to cut off!' Commanding the occasion, it was Raleigh himself who urged the executioner to 'Strike man, strike.' So, in the image of his own Baroque conceit, 'at the stroke when [his] veins started and spread', the 'everlasting' sign of resistance was his severed head.[81]

Chapter Six

Observations on English bodies:

Licensing maternity in Shakespeare's late plays

I

Shakespeare's son-in-law, John Hall, was a busy man. Commuting between Acton and Stratford and maintaining a medical practice throughout the Midlands, he left notes on patients that are models of bedside briskness and efficiency: a rapid, diagnostic glance he turned impassively on his own body. He suffered from haemorrhoids, aggravated by riding 'daily to several places to Patients', but applied leeches to them and a paste of 'Emollient Herbs'. Emetics, purges, leeches, suppositories: Hall's prescriptions were the last word in seventeenth-century humoral therapy. He caught 'a burning Fever' that 'killed almost all it did infect', but though 'much maciated and weakened, so I could not move myself in Bed without help', cured it by massive infusions of rhubarb, quaffed until 'the disease was cast out by Urine which flowed very much for four days.' Vitamin C was evidently also the secret of Hall's great panacea, his Scorbutic Beer concocted from watercress and herbs rich in ascorbic acid, which he sugared and spiced as a remedy for scurvy. Pride of place in his collection of 'Cures Historical and Empirical experienced on Eminent Persons' was given to his treatment of the 'pious, beautiful, chaste' Countess of Northampton at Ludlow in March 1622, when gallons of his Beer cured her ladyship of fainting and 'Scorbutic ulcerations, beyond the expectation of her Friends'. A century before lime juice was rationed to sailors, Hall's Beer was 'thought so strange', his editor admitted, 'that it was cast as a reproach upon him by those most famous in the profession', but he 'had the happiness to lead the way to that practice generally used by the most knowing'.[1] Thus, if his theories were a last gasp of magic, his practice was the first glimpse of medicine, and Dr Hall entered the pantheon of the Great Instauration: a country physician who stumbled upon the truth along the lonely road from superstition to science.

His own father had bequeathed Hall his 'books of physicks' but had left 'all his books on alchemy, astronomy and astrology' to a servant, since John would 'have nothing to do with these things'.[2] The graduate of Queen's College, Cambridge was selective about his intellectual inheritance, and grew to be a zealous Puritan whose motto was 'Health is from the Lord.' But if health came, as he wrote on his own file, 'without any Art or Counsel of Man', it was still necessary to guard its mystery, and his casebook was intended, according to its preface, 'not to be published til his decease, when men more willingly part with what they have'. He had, in fact, ordered his papers to be burned, but his wife Susanna flouted his will, and sold his notebooks to raise cash in 1644, pretending she did not recognise his handwriting. By a deliberate misreading, therefore, his text was preserved, and posterity received the prescription he was certain would save his own life: 'a Pigeon cut open alive, and applied to my feet, to draw down the Vapours'. If the record is believed, this was a rare failure, since his cases typically conclude that the patient was 'delivered from all Symptoms'. To our minds Hall's *Select Observations upon English Bodies* are a confection of proverbial lore and threadbare jargon, as plausible as the pills its author compounded from spiders' webs, excrement and windpipes of cockerels. The seventeenth century, which thought fruit juice 'strange', had no qualms about such medications, but what interests us is that Hall's text convinced his editors that his clinical gaze revealed the secrets of the body at the patient's bedside. Hall's *Observations* were published in 1657; Foucault traces the origins of the clinic to the founding of the first teaching hospital in 1658. Book and institution mark that critical reversal in the organisation of knowledge whereby experience supplanted theory, *seeing*, in Foucault's account, punctured the time-worn codes of *saying*, and, in the boast of Hall's editors, 'Observation' became 'the Touchstone of what is not good and what is Current in Physick'.

Neutral, intent, self-effacing, a modern consultant glides through Hall's Renaissance surgery, and what impresses his editors is not the exoticism of his pharmacopoeia but the cold eye with which he observes each body. Thus,

> Mrs Wincol, afflicted with a falling out of the fundament, was cured as follows: Camomile and Sack [were] infused on hot coals. Then with linen cloths the Anus was fomented as hot as could be endured. After the Fundament was put up with one's finger, a Spunge dipt in the said Decoction was applied, on which she sate. Note: the Flowers of Camomile are much better.

As Foucault comments, in the clinician's catalogue, the purity of the gaze is bound up with a silence that enables him to listen when the suggestions of the imagination are reduced: 'The gaze will have access to the truth of things if it rests on them in silence. The clinical gaze has a paradoxical ability to *hear as soon as it perceives a spectacle.*'³ This was the mentality of the Paracelsians, who rejected the authorities in favour of experience, and Hall was at one with them in treating Shakespeare's daughter Susanna with an enema of carnations when she was 'miserably tormented with the cholic. This injected gave her two stools, yet the Pain continued, being but little mitigated.' Confounded in his theory, the doctor 'therefore appointed to inject a Pint of Sack made hot. This brought forth a great deal of Wind, and freed her from all Pain.' Thus, 'Mrs Hall of Stratford, my Wife, was cured'; and the disinterest of the observation is the condition of its truth. This was what made Hall's notes so valuable, according to Dr John Bird's Testimony to the first edition: their pretence of banishing all language anterior to observation; so unlike 'the learned Practitioners whose Works fall short in performing the cures they promise [because] they deliver up as their own what they took from other Men upon Trust, through how many hands we know not; likewise giving us as approved, things that had no other ground than their Imaginations.'⁴

The novelty of Hall's case-notes was not lost on his contemporaries. In fact, the concept of a medical history was an epistemological watershed in Shakespearean England, and is usually dated to 1611 and the arrival in London of the French physician Theodore de Mayerne, whose published notes became the model for English practitioners. Francis Bacon was one of the first to recognise the role of such records in the scientific movement, bemoaning in *The Advancement of Learning* (1605) that 'much iteration but small addition' characterised current medicine, which was attributable to 'the discontinuance of the ancient and serious diligence of Hippocrates, which used to set down a narrative of the special cases of his patients, and how they proceeded, and how they were judged by recovery'.⁵ Hall's notes, which begin in 1616, are an answer to Bacon's dream of a classical renaissance, since their will to truth derives wholly, as Dr Bird discerned, from their assumption of a privileged immediacy with nature. But what was truth in 1616 must have seemed faded even by 1657, and these wide-eyed transcriptions can now be read as instances of the myth of original presence that impels the Cartesian drive for certainty. In Hall's case-book writing has become what Socrates imagines it to be in the *Phaedrus*, a mere supplement to the spontaneous language of the body, which speaks imploringly through its symptoms and excretions of a truth prior to the administration of the *pharmakon*. While the therapeutic text thus effaces itself, the body of the patient is textualised as a narrative full of meaning that leads towards the happy closure of a fairy-tale, with the recovery of that prime of health which originates in God. In Hall's pharmacy, the primal truth of life is restored by the purging of the contingent falsehood of disease, and the folkloric formula that the patient lived happily ever after elides 'The absolute invisibility of the origin of the visible, the good/sun/father, the unattainment of presence or beingness', which, as Derrida reminds us, is the *aporia* of all such phallogocentric stories.[6]

In the theatre of John Hall's infirmary bodies disclosed the secret of their symptoms to his peremptory eye. Thus, 'Wife was troubled with Scurvy, Pain of the Loins, Melancholy, difficulty of Breathing, Laziness, the Mother, binding of the Belly, and torment there. February 9 1630.' An enema brought no relief: 'She could not lie in her Bed, insomuch as when any helped her she cried out miserably. For which I used this Ointment: Oil of Almonds, Dil and Roses. After annointing she was quiet all night, yet in the morning was troubled with Wind.' Comprehensive treatment was required, consisting of pills of 'Gillyflowers, Bugloss and Damask-Roses', a 'long Suppository' of honey and cummin, and Hall's Beer fortified with wine boiled 'for eight days stirring twice a day. Dose is three spoonfuls, which may be increased if there be need. And by these was she cured'. To contemporary readers it was their show of disinterestedness that made these notes 'equal to the best published'.[7] Nobody had been scrutinised, if Dr Bird was believed, with the cool regard Hall fixed on patients, and no case history had been recorded as detailed as that which he wrote for 'Elizabeth Hall, my only Daughter' in her sixteenth year. She suffered neuralgia, which Hall treated in January 1624 with purges and 'Opthalmick Water, dropping two or three drops into her eye'. Then, on 22 April, she 'took cold' travelling from London, 'and fell into distemper on the contrary side of her Face, before it was on the left side, now on the right'. Resourcefully, Hall supplemented purges and eyedrops by massaging spices into his daughter's neck and squeezing oil up her nose: 'She ate Nutmegs often. And thus she was restored.' No emergency flustered Dr Hall, as he showed that May, when Elizabeth 'was afflicted with an Erratick Fever: sometimes she was hot, sometimes cold, all in the space of half an hour, and thus she was vexed oft in a day.' Her father purged her with his Beer and rubbed her spine with linament, and 'An hour after, all the Symptoms remitted. Thus was she delivered from Death and Deadly Disease, and was well for many years.'[8]

John Hall was a master of all 'the signs of death', which his editor explained were so 'uncertain: because God Almighty often pardons whom we give over to death, and takes away whom we acquit'.[9] From the Shakespearean period, this testimonial confirms, medical science was convening around the spectacle of the body stricken in disease or death,

as the anatomy theatre became the locus of a knowledge signified not by
the invisibility of health, but in the 'white visibility of the dead'. By a
'strange misconstruction', Foucault remarks, 'that which hides and
envelops' knowledge for early modern medicine, 'a curtain of night over
truth', is, paradoxically, life. However, this projection of illness onto the
plane of visibility gives medical science an opaque base beyond which it
can no longer go: 'That which is not within the gaze falls outside the
domain of what can be known.'[10]

Thus, science came to be defined by that which could not be seen.
Anatomists such as Nicolaas Tulp, depicted by Rembrandt expounding
the lesson of the cadaver, refused to use the early microscopes, on the
grounds that 'when one looks into darkness everyone sees in their own
way';[11] and if such a science could see only last things and signs of death,
its blindness was complete in the one recess that defied its gaze, the place
of birth. An intricate knowledge of the dead was counterpart to an
obtuseness about birth on the part of a profession still gripped by the
Galenic theory that a woman was an inverted man, with ovaries, uterus
and vagina for testicles, scrotum and penis. It was this androcentric
anatomy which accounts for the perpetuation of the lore that two veins
ran from the womb to the breasts to turn blood into milk; that the sex of
an infant was determined by the testicle from which seed came; that a
mother's imagination imprinted the foetus with characteristics; that the
embryo sucked menstrual blood; and that the child bit its way out of the
womb in hunger.[12] When the good doctor went on his rounds, then, the
birth place was literally his blind spot.

In former times, writes Foucault, doctors communicated with the
mystery of life 'by means of the great myth of immortality. Now these
men who watched over patients' lives communicated with their death, in
the rigour of the gaze'.[13] When healing came to depend on the
pathologist's capacity to 'divest / And strip the creature naked, till he
find / The callow principles within their nest',[14] obstetrics could only
advance, the author of the *Observations in Midwifery*, Percival
Willughby, complained, in countries such as Holland, where 'they have
privileges we cannot obtain. They open dead bodies without mutterings
of their friends. Should one of us desire such a thing, an odium of
inhumane cruelty would be upon us from the vulgar.'[15] Willughby based
his obstetrics on those of the so-called 'Father of British Midwifery',
William Harvey, but in the absence of executed females, even the
discoverer of the circulation of the blood was thwarted in his craving to
cut open a woman's body to probe for life's origin. Though he possessed
some foetal bones and a pickled embryo, Harvey spent his career, from
his first anatomy lecture on 16 April 1616, dissecting animals and
breaking eggs in a manic search to 'determine what the cause of the egg

is', eventually deducing that if it was not demonstrable that 'the cock were the prime efficient' of the chick, semen must fertilise by 'celestial influence' like the sun. Male science demanded a male prime mover, and protested it was kept from sight of this 'vital principle' by being deprived of inseminated corpses. Though it had access to the female body through every orifice, it could not see inside to instantiate its presence. In fact, the hunt for spermatozoa was doomed without a miscroscope, but Harvey persisted in believing he would catch an 'image of the omnipotent Creator' in eggyolks or the wombs of deer, where 'I have still thought much more remained behind, hidden by the dusky night of nature, uninterrogated.'[16] Thus the great adventure of science was posited as the release of an original male power from the abyss of female darkness.

Dreaming of its primacy, the patriarchal text asserts its truth against the benighted opacity of the female body. Conspicuously absent from the circle of neighbours and nurses gathered round the childbed, male science viewed birth as an archaic mystery locked within 'a dark chamber', as Willughby wrote, 'with glimmering candlelight behind the woman and five or six women assisting'.[17] Though Thomas Raynald's midwives' manual *The Birth of Mankind* had been printed in 1545, physicians objected that it was offensive that this woman's world could be read about by 'every boy and knave as openly as the tales of Robin Hood';[18] and when Nicholas Culpepper published his *Directory of Midwives* in 1651 it was scorned by 'Gentlemen and Scholars' as 'truly *Culpaper*: paper fit to wipe one's breech with'. Even Culpepper was disgusted that conception occurred 'between the places ordained to Cast out Excrements, the very sinks of the body';[19] and the biblical taboo about the defilement of birth ensured that no English book on midwifery appeared in the century between these publications. So, when Harvey's contemporary, John Hall, attended the childbed, it was in emergencies caused, by his account, through negligent midwives, since birth was not his business. When Mrs Hopper, aged 24, lapsed into a coma because 'the Afterbirth was retained, whence a dire stink ascended to the Brain so there was great danger of death', Hall strapped a hot poltice 'to the belly' and 'delivered her in twenty four hours'.[20] Or when Mrs Lewes took cold after birth and 'fell into an ague, with torment of the Belly', an enema of milk and a steaming poltice ensured 'she was helped suddenly.'[21] Likewise, 'Mrs Finnes, being delivered of her third child', suffered a fever when her midwife fed her cold chicken, and 'fell into an Hydroptick swelling. I was sent for, and perceived it to be a Scorbutic Dropsy. She implored for my help, being in a desperate condition.' Hall pumped an enema of Scorbutic Beer into her, while 'To restore, she had a Restorative framed of Snails and Earthworms. And so she was returned to her former health.'[22]

The Harveian surgical regime exercises jurisdiction over death, but has no power over generation. To witness a birth, indeed, Willughby confessed he had 'crept into the chamber on my hands and knees, and returned, so that I was not perceived by the lady'.[23] Historically, therefore, the childbed will become the threshold of male science, where a tense struggle will take place between doctor and midwife for authority over delivery. What is at stake in this contest is control of fertility, but before women's bodies can be situated in the operating theatre, their subjection to medical knowledge must be secured in the light of the new secular mystery. Carried out of the dim candlelight of vulgar error and superstition, women will become visible in the sunlit positivity of normality and health that is nothing but the brightness of 'great creating Nature' (*The Winter's Tale*, IV, iv, 88). As Willughby declared, it was better for birth to be left to 'the invisible midwife Dame Nature' than forced by 'the officiousness of conceited midwives, whom I would I could bring to observe Nature's ways, how she ripeneth all vegetables and produceth all creatures, with greater ease and speed than art can do, which is but Nature's servant'.[24] In the seventeenth century a benign Nature is constructed, then, in specific institutional contexts, at the point described by Foucault, when case-studies are collected, and the observations of disease are abstracted into an ideal of health. This is the site of the birth of the clinic, 'that borderline but paramount area', where medicine commences 'to dictate the standards of physical and moral relations of the individual' in the interests of 'the order of the nation and the fertility of its people'.[25] And if Hall's case-book helped to organise the new clinical regime, its foundations were also being laid at this time in the texts of his father-in-law, where in another narrative of wives and daughters the female body was observed behind a mask of comparable impersonality and regulated according to the same idea of a husbanded and licensed Mother Nature.

II

Louis Montrose has reminded us how often Shakespearean drama frets over 'the physical link between a particular man and child . . . whether to validate paternity or call it in question'. Aggravating this anxiety, he discerns, is the fact that what we call

> the 'facts of life' have been established as *facts* only recently. That seminal and menstrual fluids are related to generation, that people have both a father and a mother, are hardly novel notions [but] in Shakespeare's age they remained *merely* notions. Although maternity

was apparent, paternity was a cultural construct for which ocular proof was unattainable.[26]

So if, as Lancelot Gobbo warns, 'it is a wise father that knows his own child' in Shakespearean culture (*The Merchant of Venice*, II, ii, 76–7), patriarchy idealised phallic power as a mystical presence, with semen as a prime 'efficient beginning of the child', its 'form or soul', and the 'corrupt, undigested blood' of the mother as its mere 'material cause'.[27] Tellingly, Shakespeare found a paradigm for this mastery in the proprietorial rights and productive relations of his own industry. Theseus puts it crudely when he tells Hermia her father is a god, 'To whom you are but as a form in wax / By him imprinted' (*A Midsummer Night's Dream*, I, i, 49–50); but the *semantic* metaphor, with its metaphysical craving for an originary truth, prior to the corruption of the *corpus*, recurs in the last plays as punningly. When Leontes assures Florizel that 'Your mother was most true to wedlock, Prince, / For she did print your royal father off, / Conceiving you' (*The Winter's Tale*, V, i, 124–6), this is because royalties have been exacted on the text a father claims as 'a copy out of mine' (I, ii, 122). Authorship will be protected in these plays, despite the dread of cuckoldry that convulses a father when he scrutinises his 'offprints' to decide whether 'we are . . . as alike as eggs' (129–36), by securing copyright as strictly in human as in textual reproduction. Signifying only absence of certainty, the Shakespearean phallus will thus figure as transcendentally as Lacan's.

John Hall arrived in Stratford in 1600, it is thought from Montpellier, the centre of humanist surgery.[28] His training may inform the secularisation of healing that occurs in the Jacobean Shakespeare, where 'the powerful grace that lies / In plants, herbs, stones, and their true qualities' (*Romeo and Juliet*, II, iii, 11–12), which had been a natural magic for religious or demonic figures such as Friar Laurence and Puck, is a resource of practitioners like the doctors in *Macbeth*, *King Lear* and *Cymbeline*. But while their administration of 'baleful weeds and precious-juiced flowers' is therapeutic, the prognostic problem they face remains the one that thwarted the Friar when he prescribed the drug that cast Juliet into the underworld, which is how to calculate the *pharmakon* when 'Within the infant rind of this weak flower / Poison hath residence, and medicine power'. If 'The earth that's nature's mother is her tomb: / What is her burying grave, that is her womb' (II, iii, 4–20), the cavern of the female body is never penetrated by the obstetrician, who must accept, with Lady Macbeth's Doctor, that 'More she needs the divine than the physician' (V, i, 71), or that to 'Cleanse the stuff'd bosom of that perilous stuff / Which weighs upon the heart' the patient must minister to herself (*Macbeth*, V, iii, 45–6). It is this *aporia* in male thought that is figured in the tragi-comic Bed-trick, and if one solution is essayed in *Measure for Measure*, where the Duke's superintendence of Marina's conception allegorises a despotic coercion, the other is offered in *All's Well That Ends Well*, where Helena's management of her own pregnancy gives surety that what can never be witnessed by men is legitimate. The French setting and Helena's physician father, Gerard de Narbon, may defer to Hall's experience, but the importance of this Shakespearean play, then, is that it is the first in which medicine, previously the mumbo-jumbo of a Dr Caius or Pinch, can claim a positivity to ensure that 'All's well', and that in the hands of the most suspect of healers, the wise woman or female empiric.

'I say we must not / So stain our judgement', the King of France tells Helena, 'To prostitute our past-cure malady / To empirics' (ii, i, 119–21). His suspicion of folk healing was shared by the medical establishments of London and Paris, whose view of popular remedies was being shaped, as Natalie Zemon Davis has shown, by authorities like Laurent Joubert, Chancellor of the Montepellier Medical Faculty, and in 1578 the first collector of 'Vulgar Errors'. For Joubert and his imitators, such as Sir Thomas Browne or James Primerose, author of *The Errors of the People in Physick* (1651), 'popular culture was shot through with ignorance, and the village goodwives and midwives – practiced yet illiterate, working only with memorized recipes – were its perfect expression.'[29] What made the sage women of the Languedoc or West Country so vexing to the professionals, however, was not their error but their accuracy, for as the jurist opined in judgement of a suit brought by the Paris Faculty against a countrywoman in 1575, 'how many savants have been outdone by a simple peasant woman, who with a single herb has found the remedy for an illness despaired of by physicians.'[30] A deep rift ran through organised medicine, therefore, when its claim to a monopoly of knowledge was exposed by the 'empirics and old women' whom Bacon admitted were 'more happy many times in their cures', and whose consultation Hobbes rated more highly than that of 'the learnedst but inexperienced physician'.[31] While the Royal College of Physicians hounded them, Paracelsians were willing to learn from herbalists and wise women, whose influential champions included Archbishop Abbot and James i. And since the orthodox doctors were unable, as Robert Burton complained, to 'cure many diseases at all, as epilepsy, stone, gout: a common ague stumbles them all', their will to truth was vulnerable to such competition. As Keith Thomas reveals, in an age of 'helplessness in the face of disease', the fable of the healing of the 'fisher king', which Shakespeare announced in the title of *All's Well That Ends Well*, could not have been more fundamental.[32]

'If the world knew of the ignorance of the physicians', John Aubrey thought, 'the people would throw stones at 'em as they walked in the streets.'[33] It is this irreverence towards the truth-claims of medical science which is the occasion of Shakespeare's comedy, where the 'most learned doctors . . . and / The congregated college have concluded / That labouring art can never ransom nature / From her inaidable estate' (115–18). Here, then, the *senex* wears the pantaloon and academic gown 'Of all the learned and authentic Fellows' of the chartered institutions, 'both of Galen and Paracelsus' (II, iii, 11–12), and is challenged by an equally topical lobby of hitherto unlicensed practitioners. The sorority of widow, daughter and pregnant wife which petitions the Crown in the final scene of this play is one that regroups throughout the late plays, opposing a discredited patriarchy and beguiling 'the truer office' of authority's eyes, as the King says (v, iii, 299), with the blinding conundrum of sexual reproduction. Until the parturient mother is acknowledged by her husband, she riddles, ' 'Tis but the shadow of a wife you see' (301); but the puzzle round which this tragi-comedy revolves, tantalising the father that 'Dead though she be she feels her young one kick . . . one that 's dead is quick' (296–7), is a mystery defying masculine enlightenment. Helena suggestively calls her sovereignty over the quick and the dead 'a triple eye' to be stored 'Safer than mine own two' (II, i, 107–8); and Lafeu concurs that her sexuality is prior to either sight or writing: 'I have seen a medicine / That's able to breathe life into a stone . . . whose simple touch / Is powerful to araise King Pippen, nay, / To give Charlemain a pen in's hand / And write to her a love-line' (71–7). For a science based on the phenomenological desire to speak directly to a world flooded in natural light, the ambivalence of phallogocentrism is here exquisite, for how can men lay claim to an immediacy prior to the act of writing, when it is the female body of which they write, and that is their own biological origin?:

> They say miracles are past; and we have our philosophical persons to make modern and familiar, things supernatural and causeless. Hence is it that we make trifles of terrors, ensconcing ourselves into seeming knowledge when we should submit ourselves to an unknown fear.
>
> (II, iii, 1–6)

The Shakespearean text knows what Nietzsche and Derrida will intuit, that 'our philosophical persons' fear 'truth is a woman who has reasons for not letting us see her reasons [since] her name is *Baubo* [the female genitals].'[34] Patriarchy is emasculated by the female enigma in these plays, as Lafeu reports of Helena that 'I have spoke / With one that in her sex, her years, profession, / Wisdom and constancy, hath amaz'd me more / Than I dare blame my weakness' (II, i, 81–4). It was male futility before the 'miracles' of life and death that accounted for the association of midwifery with witchcraft, and what Shakespeare stages in the collusion of patient wives and wise matrons in these comedies is the nightmare that haunted the witchfinders, of maternal control of generation. The jurist Jean Bodin recorded as fact in 1581 that witches worked as midwives, and superstitions concerning the disposal of the afterbirth and burial of stillborn foetuses reflected a suspicion that midwives were the mistresses of infanticide and abortion.[35] The 'weird sisters' of *Macbeth*, who concoct their brew from 'Finger of birth-strangled babe / Ditch-delivered by a drab' (IV, i, 30–1), are figments of this collective fantasy that unsupervised women might pervert the powers of reproduction by seizing foetal organs for black masses. One scene recurs throughout the last plays, therefore, as an organising tableau. The presentation of pregnant mother or new-born infant by midwife to father paradoxically confronts paternity at its most powerful moment with its deepest fear of impotence. Bertram's bafflement at Helena's pregnancy will be repeated with mounting suspicion in these dramas, until the perplexity finally enrages: 'Out! / A mankind witch! Hence with her, out o'door: / A most intelligencing bawd!' (*The Winter's Tale*, II, iii, 67–9). Leontes's fury at Paulina, as he spurns 'the bastard' daughter born to Hermione, taps the paranoia of Jacobean patriarchy, and he vomits its litany of misogynistic stereotypes in his conflation of witch, scold and unruly woman. The midwife is 'dame Partlet' who has 'unroosted' her husband, a 'crone. . . . A callat of boundless tongue' and 'A gross hag!' (74–6; 90–1; 107). 'I'll ha' thee burnt' he warns (114); and the threat, with its echo of actual prosecutions for delivering 'some changeling' in exchange for 'fairy gold' (III, iii, 117–21),[36] underscores the social urgency of the theme of illegitimacy at the climax of the English witch-craze.

It was the invisibility of the reproductive matrix that had excited the misogyny of *King Lear*, where the patriarch's urge to 'anatomize' a woman's body to 'see what breeds' within (III, vi, 74), and repulsion from the 'darkness' of that 'sulphurous pit' (IV, vi, 125–7), was provoked by the male suspicion that 'The dark and vicious place' where a father begot a bastard must 'Cost him his eyes' (V, iii, 171–2). In tragedy's story of the night, the terror of blindness as a form of castration evinces a psychotic unease with the indeterminacy of the female body. And Janet Adelman has described how this nightmare of feminine power is embodied by the figures of Lady Macbeth and the witches, in a play which resolves the inscrutable problem of the mother 'through a ruthless excision of all female presence, its own satisfaction of the witches' prophecy'.[37] In *Macbeth*, the Caesarian surgery that tears the victor from the womb renders him invulnerable, as the apparition of the 'bloody child' portends (IV, i, 77), since it identifies him as 'he, That was not born of woman' (V, vii, 2–3). Because 'Macduff was from his mother's womb / Untimely ripp'd' (V, viii, 15–16), this male child is violently exempted from the riddling bodies and language of the 'juggling fiends' (18), as, cutting the umbilical knot, he frees the royal line from emasculating equivocation. Shakespeare earlier exploited Sir Thomas More's testimony that Richard III was hurried into the world 'feet first' by Caesarian section (*Richard III*, I, i, 20–21), and he would know that Henry VIII commanded the same Neronian operation on Jane Seymour, 'having the womb cut before she was dead, so the child ready to be born might be taken out'. This was the fatal delivery that led Edward VI to be styled 'He that was never born', and the dynasty to adopt its icon of the self-creating Phoenix. The flaming bird was an appropriate image for delivery of a man 'not of woman born', since the name of the father was never more autonomous than in the incision carved into a mother's flesh, which in pre-modern conditions meant certain death from infection.[38] Caesarian section recurs in the tragedies and histories, then, as a final solution to the female puzzle and fulfilment of the *Lex Caesare*, the Roman inheritance law that decreed the womb to be a place where the infant was merely 'imprisoned', and from which, and by whatever means, an heir was justly 'enfranchised' into 'light' (*Titus Andronicus*, IV, ii, 124–5).

'The midwife and the nurse well made way', Aaron schemes when inserting a changeling into the royal bed, 'Then let the ladies tattle what they please'; and the fate of the 'long-tongu'd babbling gossip', stabbed like 'a pig prepared to the spit' for 'caterwauling' his secret, may stand for the violent remedies offered in the tragedies to stabilise masculine truth and inheritance (IV, ii, 57; 146–51). What marks the last plays as modern artefacts, however, is a shift from corporeal oppression to cultural repression, which is what makes them, as Terry Eagleton notes, truly *ideological*: 'These comedies make much of the child-father relationship as a paradigm of possession. My children are mine by derivation from Nature, yet they are also my inalienable products, stamped with my life and labour. . . . Private property is thus naturalized.'[39] But the question this analysis begs is the one that these plays seek to answer: if patriarchy is natural, what is the status of Mother Nature? They do so by a strategy that is a counterpart of John Hall's pharmacopoeia, when they surrender power over women's bodies in exchange for possession of their language. From the mid-sixteenth century, midwives and empirics were, in fact, brought under tight surveillance throughout Western Europe, and an English Act of 1553 instituted licensing by Bishops. Powerless to intrude into the women's chamber, the legislators wrestled to dictate its discourse, and the midwife's oath therefore swore her to 'use no profane words . . . nor any kind of sorcery, invocations, or prayers', and to conduct baptism only according to the sacrament that made Eve the cause of woe. If Marianism, with its fertility charms and holy girdles, was a target of these prohibitions, the aim was above all to insure paternity, as the oath made clear, when it bound a midwife not to 'permit or suffer that women being in labour shall name any other to be the father of a child, than only he who is the true and right father'.[40] It was an interdiction that would remain statutory until 1786, and provide a discursive foundation for the licensing of maternity in Shakespearean drama.

III

Liberal criticism has long identified an accommodation with motherhood in the romances, but as recent critics have pointed out, 'men do not, through a simple identification, adopt the values of nurturance they learn from women' by this manoeuvre; 'rather, men appropriate these values and translate them into patriarchal institutions that place limits on women, albeit in a harmonious atmosphere.'[41] So, though Leontes will assure Paulina that 'Thou canst not speak too much, I have deserv'd / All tongues to talk their bitt'rest' (III, ii, 215–16), when women speak in these works they will be subordinated to male primacy as strictly as the matrons who swore to 'use no mass, Latin service or prayers, than as appointed by the Church of England' in their deliveries. Confined to the 'apt and accustomed words' of baptism, women's role in the ceremonies of childbirth will be restricted, as Paulina promises, to actions as 'holy as / You hear my spell is lawful' (v, iii, 104–5). By these means the 'gossips' whom she nominates for the birth of Leontes's daughter as the customary witnesses of labour (II, iii, 41), will be drafted into 'a gossips' feast' of sponsors (*The Comedy of Errors*, v, i, 405), their 'babbling gossip' (*Twelfth Night*, I, v, 277) reduced to christening the infant in the name of the Father. 'My noble gossips', Henry VIII dubs them, at the end of the most neurotic of all these psychodramas of paternity, since the 'old duchess' and 'Lady Marquess', godmothers to Anne Boleyn's child, have stilled their rumour-mongering voices (*Henry VIII*, v, ii, 202; iv, 12). In fact, Puritans forbade midwives to baptise at all after 1577, and the demotion of the 'godsiblings' to mere gossips indicates how in the discursive system that produced these works women's language was congealing into tattle, while men's attained the truth of 'observation'. They register the process whereby male sense was sifted from female nonsense, as the sage woman declined from the status of a folk healer to that of Sarah Gamp, or the derided 'Lady Margery, your midwife' (*The Winter's Tale*, II, iii, 159).

The Prologue to *Henry VIII* declares that the aim of this dráma will be 'no more to make you laugh', but to ensure that 'Such as . . . hope they may believe, / May here find truth'. If 'All is True' in this text, this will be, then, because ribaldry has been curtailed, as Puritans struggled to suppress the 'time of freedom' when gossips gathered at a birth to 'talk petty treason'.[42] 'A sad tale's best for winter', we learn; but the seriousness of the story of the 'man . . . / Dwelt by a churchyard', whose suspicion of cuckoldry haunts these plays, runs counter to the mocking 'wisdom' of the ladies Mamillius calls 'crickets' by the hearth (*The Winter's Tale*, II, i, 25–31). In *Henry VIII*, 'our chosen truth' (Prologue, 18) has therefore to be asserted over the 'mirth' of Anne's midwife, whose role is to 'deliver' the 'old story' of a lady 'That would not be queen . . . / For all the mud in Egypt', who yet succumbed, 'for little England', to 'venture an emballing' (II, iii, 46–7; 90–2; 101; 106). A scandal of sexual heresy has to be suppressed before her 'royal infant' can be christened a prince of peace (v, iv, 9–16); and the ploy is one familiar ever since the Nurse instructed Juliet: the representation of women's language as a superstitious 'mumbling . . . o'er a gossip's bowl' (*Romeo and Juliet*, III, v, 174). This is a text which alludes to the indictment of Anne for adultery on the accusations of her midwife, Nan Cobham, when the Old Lady who delivers Elizabeth, palmed off by the King with a groom's payment, vows to 'have more, or unsay' that the infant is as like him 'As cherry is to cherry' (v, i, 168–75); but which stifles this seditious hearsay, in favour of the martyrology that hailed the girl as the Protestant Deborah. 'Truth shall nurse her', Cranmer announces, certain of a veracity that wrests the baby from female slander. Thus the male will to truth is predicated on an inquisitorial censorship of women's language, as Henry affirms, when he jests that the child will herself thank the Archbishop, 'When she has so much English' (v, iv, 14; 28).

Anne Boleyn had been condemned on testimony that she had been delivered of a deformed foetus, which was taken as proof of her sexual relations with five men, alleged to have impregnated her by caresses and 'french' kisses.[43] In *The Winter's Tale*, where Hermione's ordeal recapitulates that of Elizabeth's mother, the same radical uncertainty about the facts of life prompts an identical demand about which acts are sufficient for consummation: 'Is leaning cheek to cheek? is meeting noses? / Kissing with inside lip?' (I, ii, 285–6). Leontes's report on his wife's habit of 'paddling palms, and pinching fingers' with Polixenes reads like a transcript of the Crown case in 1536, which was also reliant on the hypothesis that 'To mingle friendship far, is mingling bloods' (109–15); but with Protestant claims dependent on Anne's exoneration, Shakespeare's brief was surely to discredit such suspicion. If the trials of successive Tudor queens are indeed 'devis'd / And play'd to take spectators' in *Henry VIII* and *The Winter's Tale* (III, ii, 36–7), the romance, by disclaiming actuality, recounts what the history obscures: patriarchy's inability to impose mastery on the female body. Denying the Oracle, as

Henry defied Rome, Leontes dooms a dynasty to extinction; yet the line descends through a princess lost in a northern land, to unite two kingdoms. For James I, who commanded a performance for the wedding of Princess Elizabeth in 1613, *The Winter's Tale* must have suggested that if absolutism can exercise no power over the female mystery, it must coopt it. And smarting at aspersions on Mary Stuart's relations with David Riccio, the royal house would follow the dramatic scenario, by instituting, during its pregnancies, a cult of marital devotion. Shakespearean romance would have no more faithful sequel than the companionate marriage of Charles I and Henrietta Maria, where sexuality would be purified with 'All sanctimonious ceremonies', to make it a neo-platonic idyll of 'plain and holy innocence' (*The Tempest*, IV, i, 16; III, i, 82).

At the instant when the midwife cut the umbilical cord and held up the afterbirth, a Stuart royal baby was carried from its mother to be presented to the physicians and courtiers who thronged the threshold of the chamber. This ceremony contrasted grandly with the secretiveness of Tudor confinements, and symbolised the wary encirclement of maternity by absolutism. Yet if its intention was to oversee not only the facts of birth, but their interpretation, the absolutist *accouchement* was not inviolable, as was demonstrated in 1688, when the entourage attending the birth of the Old Pretender failed, after the midwife vanished with her fee, to smother the rumour that he was a miller's son, smuggled into the chamber in a warming-pan.[44] Thus Stuart history collapsed back into the folklore it had appropriated. For if the late plays, with their cast of changelings, estranged children and wandering heirs, worked to legitimate the Scottish line, they also foretold how its sovereignty would be conditional on stories told by women. According to historians, the moral panic about the unruly woman as 'a common scold, raiser of idle reports and breeder of discord' in paternity disputes, reached fever pitch in the period of the romances,[45] and the campaign to bridle gossip registers in the vigilance of the Shakespearean fathers to guard themselves against sexual defamation. What incenses Leontes is patriarchy's impotence to quell Paulina's assertions, which makes her husband a 'lozel, worthy to be hanged, / That wilt not stay her tongue' (*The Winter's Tale*, II, iii, 108–9). Yet the male narrators of these texts must take up their dynastic story as it emerges from the womblike 'dark backward and abysm of time', where a husband takes it on trust that his wife 'was a piece of virtue', because, as Prospero assures Miranda, 'She said thou wast my daughter' (*The Tempest*, I, ii, 50–7). The tale they 'deliver' (v, i, 113) is as unverifiable as paternity, since, as the choric Gower concedes in *Pericles*, it gestates in a matrix that is beyond the light of masculine observation:

The cat, with eyne of burning coal
Now crouches 'fore the mouse's hole;
And crickets at the oven's mouth
Sing the blither for their drouth.
Hymen hath brought the bride to bed,
Where by the loss of maidenhead
A babe is moulded.
                    (*Pericles*, III, Chorus, 5–11)

Since 'Lychorida, our nurse, is dead', Gower explains after the birth of
Marina: 'The unborn event / I do commend to your content' (IV, Chorus,
42–6). A running metaphor analogises these plays to the supplement by
the doctor of the midwife. Play-making and medicine both depend, we
infer, on female delivery, and drama coopts lore which 'Were it but told
you, should be hooted at / Like an old tale' (V, iii, 116–17). Earlier
comedies had condescended to 'the old and antic song' carolled by 'The
spinsters and knitters in the sun' (*Twelfth Night*, II, iv, 3; 44); but as
Autolycus peddles broadsheets to girls who 'love a ballad in print . . . for
then we are sure they are true' (*The Winter's Tale*, IV, iv, 261–2), drama
cites its oral source from the same anxiety of representation which
Derrida finds in Rousseau's nostalgia for the song of the South and the
savage mind: 'Like an old tale still, which will have matter to rehearse,
though credit be asleep and not an ear open' (V, ii, 62–3). The Grand
Narrative of modern knowledge legitimates itself, as Lyotard observes,
by 'smiling into its beard' at customary storytelling;[46] yet the Jacobean
antiquarian movement anticipated Rousseau's metaphysics of presence
by harkening to the dame who was ordinarily silenced with a ducking
stool or bit. There were, in fact, affinities between the English cult of the
'old wives' tale' and the French fad for fairy stories, which began, as
Natalie Zemon Davis shows, in a similar context of centralising
absolutism. The publication of Charles Perrault's *Contes de ma mère
l'oye* in 1697 was dedicated to Louis XIV, when peasants' tales were retold
in 'Perrault's ironic voice' as human stories that naturalised the
monarchy. Thus, Perrault, an architect of the Louvre, recruited 'the old
countrywomen of the Champagne' to serve the nation–state, com-
plementing the researches of his brother Claude, the organiser of
France's first public dissections.[47] The teenage girl anatomised in the
earliest of these demonstrations, at Versailles in April 1667, may not have
appreciated her grandeur, but for the brothers Perrault she yielded up her
mystery in the interests of *la gloire*. If academicians could not fathom
women, they would at least make them 'speak' for the Sun King.[48]

    The body politics of early modern storytelling are vividly displayed,
Robert Darnton observes, in the frontispiece to the first edition of *Mother*

Goose, which depicts 'three well-dressed children listening raptly to an old crone in the servant's quarters'. This image is a reminder that it was midwives and wet nurses who provided a physical link between elite and popular cultures, 'for the audiences of Racine had imbibed folklore with their milk'.[49] Old Mother Hubbard and Mother Goose (so-called from her cackle) were shadows of those real 'goodwives' and 'busybodies' whose lullabies for upper class children seemed so suspect to seventeenth-century fathers, like the 'Ladies' to whose 'wisdom' the pregnant Hermione disposes Mamillius at a critical moment of her marriage: 'Take the boy to you: he so troubles me, / 'Tis past enduring . . . pray you, sit by us, / And tell's a tale' (ii, i, 1–23). As Leontes discovers, since husbands could not silence this *veillée*, they had to accept that the 'stories grandmother told' were 'words as medicinal as true, / Honest, as either, to purge him of that humour / That presses him from sleep' (ii, iii, 37–9). So, laying 'the old proverb' to his 'charge, / So like you, 'tis the worse', Paulina 'professes' to the King to be an 'obedient counsellor' and 'physician' in delivering his child (96–7; 54); but she warns that to 'remove / The root of his opinion, which is rotten' (88–9), he must 'awake [his] faith' in the efficacy of an 'affliction' that 'has a taste as sweet / As any cordial comfort' (v, iii, 76–7; 94–5). The faith-healing the sage women prescribe in these plays, therefore, is truly a *pharmakon* that poisons to cure, being a purge of men's oldest fear. For the sugared pill they administer, with their aphrodisiacs of 'Hot lavender, mints, savory, marjoram' and 'marigold' (iv, iv, 104–5), contains the bitter cathartic that since it is a mother's body which has the 'ordering' of life, a father can only ever 'print' his 'copy' in the 'colours' she provides:

> Behold, my lords,
> Although the print be little, the whole matter
> And copy of the father: eye, nose, lip;
> The trick of's frown; his forehead; nay, the valley,
> The pretty dimples of his chin and cheek; his smiles;
> The very mould and frame of hand, nail, finger:
> And thou, good goddess Nature, which hast made
> So like to him that got it, if thou hast
> The ordering of his mind too, 'mongst all colours
> No yellow in't, lest she suspect, as he does,
> Her children not her husband's!
> (ii, iii, 97–107)

Medical sociologists report that in Britain in the 1990s 'one in ten fathers is under a false impression that their children are their own, while some studies put the figure at one in three.'[50] What is remarkable, then, is that the fear of cuckoldry which features so obsessively in medieval folktales should be so effaced in modern consciousness. Shakespearean comedy suggests that if English husbands learned to 'Take . . . no scorn to wear the horn' (*As You Like It*, IV, ii, 14), this dates from the licensing of maternity under such orderlies as Paulina. For the 'good goddess Nature' of the romances has become what 'Dame Nature' was for science: an archetypal 'outsider inside' or Jacobean equivalent of the *pharmakos*, the scapegoat/sorcerer whose remedies are a necessary evil to prevent the greater ill. This sage matron enters the Shakespearean *polis* as an indispensable Other who vouches for paternity; and it can be no coincidence that incorporation was the strategy urged by obstetricians at the time. A material context for Paulina's actions may be found, for instance, in the petition for a midwives' charter presented in 1616 to James I. Ostensibly drafted by London midwives, this scheme for 'the most skilful in the profession' to be 'incorporated into a Society', was promoted by Dr Peter Chamberlen, head of a Huguenot family which had invented the obstetric forceps. Though opposed by the Royal College, the Chamberlens lobbied for many years against what they called 'the uncontrolled female arbiters of life and death', and according to the midwives' spokeswomen, a Mrs Hester Shaw and Mrs Whipp, bribed a cohort of their 'dear daughters' to employ their 'instruments by extraordinary violence'. In 1634 sixty midwives protested against 'the molestation of Dr. Chamberlen and his project to have the licensing of them'; but science was with the doctor when he predicted dire 'consequences for the health and strength of the whole nation if ignorant women, whom poverty or the game of Venus hath intruded into midwifery, should be insufficiently instructed'. With projects for public anatomy lectures and baths, medical aid and poor relief, the Chamberlens were among those radical Protestants who would revolutionise the English municipality;[51] but the price exacted through the cooption of their 'daughters' was paternal licensing of fertility itself.

IV

When Perdita disdains to force Nature by cultivating 'carnations and streak'd gillyvors', she is lectured that 'over that art / Which you say adds to Nature is an art / That Nature makes'. In a reprise of her own story, Perdita is assured that Mother Nature legitimates those whom 'some call . . . bastards' (IV, iv, 82–92). Thus, Shakespeare's last plays make the same accommodation with the 'gossip' of 'an old tale' (V, ii, 62), as Hall's book does with folk healing, and it is piquant that their emblem for 'great

creating nature' should be his enematic flower. The doctor married
Susanna on 5 June 1607, and *Pericles*, written during her pregnancy the
following winter, immediately stages the conflict over the early modern
childbed, when Thaisa dies delivering Marina, despite the efforts of her
nurse, Lychorida, and her husband's prayers to 'Lucina, Divinest
patroness, and midwife gentle / To those that cry by night'. If such charms
and incantations for divine aid in labour contravened the midwife's oath,
this one goes 'Unheard in the ears of death' (III, i, 9–12). From the first
Shakespearean scene of this text the discursive function of the romances
is revealed, then, to be the Harveian project of separating childbirth from
those wayward sisters already demonised in tragedy. So, after 'a terrible
childbed' with 'No light, no fire', Thaisa's corpse is sunk 'in the ooze' to
appease the 'superstition' of folk who are as 'strong in custom' as weak in
knowledge (50–7). Demographers estimate that 25 out of every 1,000
women died in childbirth in seventeenth-century England, and in time of
plague and famine, the scenario of *Pericles*, mortality was much higher.[52]
Yet out of this calamity the mother's body is salvaged when it is removed
from the perils of the women's room and transferred to the safety of the
clinic. Cerimon's surgery, where he calculates prescriptions and
prognoses with cool exactitude, is imaged as the still centre of a hysterical
world, and in what reads like a wedding-gift to Hall, its ritual is valorised
as a model of professionalism for the observation of the 'disturbances' of
the female body:

> I hold it ever,
> Virtue and cunning were endowments greater
> Than nobleness and riches: careless heirs
> May the latter two darken and expend,
> But immortality attends the former,
> Making man a god. 'Tis known I ever
> Have studied physic, through which secret art,
> By turning o'er authorities, I have,
> Together with my practice, made familiar
> To me and to my aid the blest infusions
> That dwell in vegetives, in metals, stones;
> And can speak of the disturbances that
> Nature works, and of her cures; which doth give me
> A more content in course of true delight
> Than to be thirsty after tottering honour,
> Or tie my treasure up in silken bags,
> To please the fool and death.
>
> (III, ii, 26–42)

The Shakespearean text foregrounds what Foucault would rediscover: the continuities between the old church and the new science. Cerimon is reminded that by instituting his surgery on the site vacated by moribund religion, he has become a high priest of the modern cult of welfare: 'Your honour has through Ephesus pour'd forth / Your charity, and hundreds call themselves / Your creatures, who by you have been restor'd' (43–5). And this Master's empiricism is confirmation that the war against disease is above all, as the Chamberlens knew, a struggle against the nobility, won by 'turning over authorities'. For like the hospital regents painted by Rembrandt at this time, Cerimon sits at the apex of a system of chartered almshouses, bridewells, madhouses and schools that would make their president or professor, as he brags, an institutional god. And the justification for the rise of the medic to such status will be the miracle of the surgery or operating theatre, performed as the doctor ministers to the body of Thaisa, with all the genuflection formerly attending Mass. Christopher Hill has described the 'spiritualisation of the household' accomplished by Puritans;[53] and Hall was foremost among those 'Physicians of the Soul', his editor declares, who perceived the closeness of the body and the soul and believed 'that Sickness is commonly a punishment for Sin'. So, as Cerimon operates on Thaisa to a sound of 'still and woeful music', this new Ephesian mystery literalises the Foucauldian thesis, that to cure her of disorders of the 'mother', the aim of medicine will be to penetrate not merely a woman's womb but her 'o'erpress'd' soul:

> Make a fire within;
> Fetch hither all my boxes in my closet.
> Death may usurp on nature many hours,
> And yet the fire of life kindle again
> The o'erpress'd spirits . . .
>   the fire and cloths.
> The still and woeful music that we have,
> Cause it to sound, beseech you.
> The viol once more; how thou stirr'st thou block!
> The music there! I pray you, give her air.
> Gentlemen, this queen will live.
> Nature awakes a warm breath out of her.
> She hath not been entranc'd above five hours;
> See, how she 'gins to blow into life's flower again!
>   (82–97)

'When I leave his clinic', Freud would exclaim of Charcot's hypnotism of hysterics, 'my mind is sated as after an evening at the theatre'; and the

Chamberlens likewise promised to illuminate 'Nature's most meandering labyrinths of Procreation'.[54] Modern gynaecology, Shakespearean catharsis predicts, will be a rite of exorcism. And with his histrionic cures, Hall was also typical of the 'godly sort' who approached the body at this time as a 'Temple' to be purified and cleansed. Thus, 'Mrs Jackson', he records,

> aged 24, being not well purged after birth, fell into a grievous Delirium; she was angry with those she formerly loved, yet her talk was very religious. By intervals there was a Frenzy. Yet there was a happy success by the following Prescriptions: To the Forehead was applied Water of Lettice. To the Head was applied a Hen new cut open. To the soles of the Feet, Radishes every third hour. There were also Scarifications to the Shoulders. And thus in seven days she was cured.[55]

Like Cerimon, Hall evidently combined his clinical observations with the archaic belief in the uterine origin of hysteria: the 'climbing sorrow' of the 'mother' that 'swells', in Lear's etiology, 'upward toward [the] heart' whenever the womb wanders or over-heats with humours (*King Lear*, II, iv, 56–7). Whether or not he knew Harvey, whom he twice quotes, Shakespeare's son-in-law was at one with him in the conviction that 'No one of experience can be ignorant what grievous symptoms arise when the uterus either rises or falls, is put out of place or is seized with spasm! Mental aberrations, delirium, melancholy, paroxysms of frenzy follow, as if the person were under the dominion of spells.' In his own lifetime Harvey's study of parturition was as celebrated as his theory of circulation, so Hall's obstetrics could derive authority from the great man's treatment of post-natal 'frenzy' by means of 'musical sounds' to 'dilate the uterine orifice' and 'release the foul vapours'. And whatever operation Cerimon actually performs on Thaisa, with his 'vi[a]l' and 'fire and cloths' to rouse her from her 'trance', Harvey, who treated hysterics with intra-uterine injections of 'hot vitriol' or 'cooling air', would have surely certificated his practice.[56]

Before he brings Thaisa to consciousness Cerimon dedicates himself to Apollo. Since the birth chamber had customs from which men were excluded, its rites of confinement and delivery had to be institutionalised if they were to be authorised as a 'lawful business' (*The Winter's Tale*, v, iii, 96). In *Pericles*, therefore, Thaisa convalesces in 'vestal livery' as Diana's nun (III, iv, 9), her attendants reorganised into an order of 'maiden priests' (v, i, 240). The lying-in – when a mother remained house-bound and sexually abstinent for thirty days after delivery – is thereby appropriated as a Persephone-like poetic myth: the post-natal resurrection of the so-called 'lady in the straw', in a purification ritual that fulfils the ordinance of *Leviticus*, to decontaminate the mother 'of the issue of her blood'. So, 'Standing near the altar . . . a number of virgins on each side' (v, ii), Thaisa removes her 'silver livery' to be reunited with her husband (v, iii, 7), in what seems to be an imitation of the Anglican rite of churching, at which the mother, surrounded with women, was led to church by her midwife and permitted to discard her veil to take communion, thus 'bringing the world of women back into contact with the literate world of men'.[57] With its 'accustomed thank-offerings' for safe deliverance from the 'snares of death' and 'pains of hell', churching was condemned by many as a Jewish or papist superstition, but what is striking, according to social historians, 'is its high observance where it might be least expected: in large, urban, Puritan parishes'. Ninety per cent of mothers were churched after childbirth in early seventeenth-century Southwark.[58] So, if Puritans objected to the mother 'coming forth covered with a veil, as if ashamed of some folly',[59] science and religion had little to fear, it seems, from a *rite de passage* which reinstated the husband's claim to his wife's body; as Leontes 'will kiss her' when 'the curtain' is drawn from the face of Hermione (v, iii, 79).

With its benediction that 'The sun shall not smite thee by day, nor the moon by night', churching, Milton sneered, implied that the wife 'had been travailing not in her bed, but the deserts of Arabia';[60] yet this is the liturgy which the Shakespearean romances take seriously enough 'To lock up honesty and honour from / Th'access of gentle visitors', releasing them, as Paulina says, with 'such ado to make no stain a stain / As passes colouring' (ii, ii, 10–19). The final acts of these plays piously rehearse the service celebrated by Herrick at 'Julia's Churching or Purification': 'To th'Temple with the sober Midwife go. / Attended thus (in a most solemn wise) / By those who serve the Child-bed mysteries. / Burn first the Incense . . . and with reverend curtsies come.'[61] This is dramaturgy that derives from the folklore that the woman who dies in childbirth, like Thaisa, or before she has 'got strength of limit', such as Hermione, (iii, ii, 106), can never rest in Christian burial or peace, and that defers to pagan superstition that 'grass will never grow where they tread before they are churched'.[62] For 'churching' returns the child-bearing women of these texts from an inscrutable darkness to the light promised in the service by a reading of Psalm 121: 'I will lift up mine eyes unto the hills, from whence cometh my help.' Thus, after enclosure 'like one infectious' (98) in a 'removed house', where she has been visited 'twice or thrice a day' by her midwife (v, ii, 105), Hermione's sequestration from her family ends, as custom ordained, in liberation from night and immobility, when she is released from the woman's chamber: ' 'Tis time, descend; be stone no more' (v, iii, 99). As Hermione is 'churched', Paulina allows that some will 'think / (which I protest against) I am assisted / By wicked powers.' This is a matter, as it was in Jacobean Stratford, of conscience: 'those that think it is unlawful business / I am about, let them depart' (89–97); but there was no reason for Puritans to 'say 'tis superstition' when a mother was unveiled (43), since such cleansing of what preachers deemed 'the stain' of sexual intercourse, accorded exactly with their doctrine of the female body.[63] Hermione's isolation in her room, where she has been 'kept / Lonely, apart' (17), is perfect confirmation of the thesis that rites of liminality work to reinforce the order they disrupt. 'Dame Margery' the midwife tells Leontes not to 'shun her', because his wife's body has been purged as thoroughly as those of the patients syringed by Dr Hall:

> O, she's warm!
> If this be magic, let it be an art
> Lawful as eating.
> (109–11)

By long seclusion in the woman's room, the female body is readmitted to society clarified of pollution. Though he sided with the vicar of Stratford against maypoles, there is no evidence that Hall opposed churching. The action of *The Winter's Tale* suggests why a doctor might find it expedient to cooperate with cunning women to invigilate a process he could never witness. For though Leontes rants that since maternity is 'coactive' with 'what's unreal . . . And fellow'st nothing: then 'tis very credent' it may 'conjoin with something . . . beyond commission' (I, ii, 141–4), he learns that there is no means for the 'man [who] holds his wife by the arm' to verify his seed within the 'sluices' of her body: 'Physic for't there's none' (192–200). His story seems, therefore, to warn the doctor to heal himself in the pandemic witch-craze, since 'It is an heretic that makes the fire, / Not she which burns in't' (114). Shakespeare had heralded the alliance of Dame Nature and male science in the first play to record Hall's presence, yet there Helena depended not on oral custom but her father's textual 'notes': 'prescriptions / Of rare and prov'd effects, such as his reading / And manifest experience had collected' (*All's Well That Ends Well*, I, iii, 216–21). The wise woman of later comedies reverses this dependence, curing the 'kingly patient' of his 'distemperature', as Marina uses her 'utmost skill' on Pericles, with a 'sacred physic' that requires only 'That none but I and my companion maid / Be suffer'd to come near him' (*Pericles*, v, i, 27; 74–8). Complicit in their mystery, the father is restored to power when he accepts what these cloistered women have 'deliver'd weeping' – the biological conundrum of she 'That beg'st him that did thee beget' – and pledges that henceforth he will 'never interrupt' them (160–5; 195) nor deny 'The child-bed privilege . . . which 'longs / To women of all fashion' (*The Winter's Tale*, III, ii, 103–4). For by dissociating from wayward women, like the witch Sycorax or the Queen in *Cymbeline*, these matrons and their 'fellow maids' (*Pericles*, v, i, 49) are crucial in manoeuvring the female body into compliance. Delivering their own sex at the altar of a masculine religion, their role is to prepare a body like Thaisa's or Hermione's: immobile, aestheticised, above all, ready for inspection.

V

The theatricality of the operation Paulina stages helps explain why the earliest entrance tickets were sold not for a playhouse but the anatomy theatre at Padua, that 'wooden O' where Harvey first looked down from a darkened gallery to observe a spotlit corpse dissected. In this new spectacular space the body will be reanimated, as Descartes proposed in 1641, as a machine propelled by reflexes. This modern body with pumping heart and automatic eyeblink is not the body promised eternal life, but, in Descartes's image, a watch sprung for motion.[64] And the medical gaze has no need of speech when it anatomises such a mechanism, because 'silence . . . the more shows off [its] wonder'. What it reads, of course, are the 'wrinkled' signs of death; but the question that it asks is Harvey's: 'What was he that did make it?': what master 'deemed it breath'd? . . . that those veins / Did verily bear blood?' that 'The very life seems warm upon her lip', and 'The fixture of her eye has motion in't'? 'No longer shall you gaze on't', Paulina connives, 'lest your fancy / May think anon it moves'; and the power which would have ripped open this womb, if necessary, to deliver a Macduff or Posthumus by Caesarian section, fancies it knows the mover. A 'rare Italian master', the text calls him, punning art and nature (*The Winter's Tale*, v, ii, 21–96); but as Harvey wrote, 'I do not think we are greatly to dispute the name by which the first agent is to be called. . . . As the architect is more worthy than the pile he rears, as the king is more exalted than his minister, as the workman is better than his hands' so 'the Supreme Creator is the father.'[65] True to Harvey, it is the father who receives the child in these plays, as Cranmer carries the heir to the king at the end of *Henry VIII*, and foretells a male inheritor who 'shall star-like rise . . . and so stand fix'd' (v, iv, 44–5). No mother appears in *The Tempest*, since for Shakespeare, as for Harvey, male power is at last self-generating. But the beheading of Anne Boleyn and purging of Susanna Hall remind us how much the fiction of a masculine universe was the result of actual 'observations' carried out on female English bodies.

The patriarchal myth of Pygmalion, who 'could put breath into his work' to 'beguile Nature of her custom' (*The Winter's Tale*, v, ii, 97–8), acquired new potency in an era when scientists such as Descartes hypothesised the origin of life in fermentation of semen. Descartes's mechanistic physiology seemed, indeed, to contemporaries to augur a final conquest by the 'master' (96) of Nature's midwifery, as he pursued the dream of the Renaissance, to fabricate some 'Diana as a man-machine'. 'Here is my library', he was reported to have said of his secret anatomy theatre, 'and this', gesturing to a dissected carcass, 'the study to which I now attend'. It was this preoccupation that must have accounted for 'the strange tale circulated by his enemies' that he had usurped creation, and 'made with much ingenuity an automaton in the form of a girl. Descartes was said to have taken this automaton on a vessel, packed in a box. The sailors had the curiosity, however, to open the box, and as the figure appeared to have life, they took it for the devil and threw it overboard.'[66] With its analogues in Greek romance, this is a legend that provides a bearing on the Hoffmannesque riddle of the late plays, posed by Posthumus when he demands: 'Is there no way for men to be but women / Must be half-workers?' (*Cymbeline*, II, iv, 153). In Shakespeare, however, an answer is given by the mothers and midwives themselves, who suffer the Caesarian law that, as Paulina assents, the 'child was prisoner to the womb, and is / By law and process of great nature, thence / Free'd and enfranchis'd' (*The Winter's Tale*, II, ii, 59–61). The dead mother in *Cymbeline* memorialises, indeed, an entire medical revolution, when obstetric forceps displaced the healing art, as she laments how 'Lucina lent me not her aid, / but took me in my throes, / That from me was Posthumus rip', 'I died whilst in the womb he stay'd, / attending Nature's law' (v, iv, 37–45). Such cries witness how much the politics of early modern science, and of John Hall's family, underwrote the Harveian myth of 'great creating nature' and 'the right to life'.

Attending a birth, the Chamberlens arrived with a giant trunk supposed to contain their miraculous 'delivery machine', and after the mother had been blindfolded and the midwife locked out of the room, those 'listening at the door could hear the ringing of bells and clapping of sticks'. In this way, the secret was kept for over a century that the trunk merely contained forceps whose noise the music drowned.[67] Thus, to take control of birth, the new medicine required acts of faith as great as those of the old midwifery. But in July 1643, when Harvey was writing his book *On Generation*, his own faith faltered, as he recalled how he had cut open a pregnant deer in Windsor Forest, to show 'the uterus to his majesty the king and satisfy him' as to the 'prime efficient' of creation, only to discover in consternation 'that there was nothing in the shape of semen to be found in the organ'. 'And whilst I speak of these matters', Harvey interjected, forgive me, if I vent a sigh. This is the cause of my sorrow: whilst in attendance on his majesty during our late troubles, by command of Parliament rapacious hands stripped from my museum the fruits of years of toil. Whence it has come to pass that many observations have perished, with detriment, I venture to say, to the republic of letters.[68]

At that moment, in the doctor's confusion, the claims of science could not have been more tied to those of monarchy; but banished with the court to Oxford, the 'father of English midwifery' recommenced his dissections undaunted, with 'a Hen to hatch eggs in his chamber, which he daily opened to discern the way of Generation'.[69] All might yet be well, the king restored and the riddle of the chicken and the egg solved, if Henrietta Maria could join her husband with reinforcements. But as Harvey cracked eggs and Charles fretted, the Queen was enjoying unaccustomed power at the crossroads of different histories. She was at New Place in Stratford, the guest of Susanna Hall, a widow with chests full of her husband's casebooks and 'play-writings' by her father,[70] which she was sorting for sale to the soldiers or for burning.

Chapter Seven

A constant will to publish:

Shakespeare's dead hand

I

A month before his death, on 25 March 1616, Shakespeare held a pen for the last time and feebly scrawled his signature to revise his will, first dated 25 January, endorsing its alteration with one final affirmative: 'By me.' Ever since the palaeographer Sir Edward Maunde Thompson observed in 1916 that 'the draft in all its roughness, with corrections and interlineations' and the 'hurried action of the business' indicated that 'something more critical than the traditional fever had fastened on the stricken man', Shakespeare's deathbed change of heart has been attributed to his daughter Judith's marriage on 10 February, and to what E. K. Chambers conjectured was some 'lack of confidence' in the bridegroom Thomas Quiney. These dark suspicions were confirmed in 1972, when parish records revealed that Shakespeare redrafted his will the day before Quiney confessed in the church court to 'carnal copulation' with one Margaret Wheeler, who had died a fortnight earlier giving birth to Quiney's stillborn child. Shakespeare revised his will, it seems, in the shadow of domestic tragedy and on the eve of public ignominy, when his son-in-law was to be sentenced to perform 'open penance' before the Stratford congregation on three successive Sundays in a white sheet of humiliation.[1] So the hand that signed this paper was moved by forces that were all too material, and the ink that sealed the final Shakespearean script was scratched at the bottom of each sheet not only to meet legal form, but the most pressing of exigencies. That the Bard died harried by a sexual scandal that may have hastened his end has yet to percolate beyond the academy, but the implications of his eleventh-hour rewriting have not been lost on scholarship. For as Samuel Schoenbaum noted when he collected the archives that make up his voluminous *Documentary Life*, Shakespeare's will has provoked more discussion than any other paper to which he put his name,[2] and the debate about this last text comprises a paradigm of Shakespearean interpretation.

'The Legacies and Bequests therein are undoubtedly as he intended', the antiquary Joseph Greene reported when he stumbled on the will in 1747, 'but the manner of introducing them appears to me so dull and irregular, so absolutely void of the least particle of that Spirit which Animated Our great Poet, that it must lessen his Character as a Writer to imagine the least Sentence of it his production.'[3] But if scholars were inhibited by the myth of the genius whose intentions supremely transcended the 'foiled searchings' of sordid historicism,[4] there were also those who read the records against the grain of this idealist aesthetic, such as B. Roland Lewis, who in the heyday of New Criticism declared that 'the essential spirit of William Shakespeare is to be found in his will, its preparation constituting virtually the last act of his active life'.[5] Recently the eminent Shakespearean E. A. J. Honigmann lent prestige to this position, asserting in *The New York Review of Books* that 'Shakespeare's failure to observe testamentary conventions makes his [will] a most unusual document.' Contrasting its contents with the wills of other London dramatists and theatre managers, Honigmann argues that far from being 'a characteristic will of a man of property in the reign of James I', as G. E. Bentley automatically supposed,[6] Shakespeare's will is indeed deeply 'irregular', since in practically no article does it obey the cultural traditions of the time. For Honigmann, what is extraordinary about the document are not its insertions but its silences, from which the testator would appear 'totally self-centred and shockingly tight-fisted' in neglecting to endow the church; to leave legacies for godchildren, servants, apprentices or colleagues; to release his debtors or redeem the debts of impecunious relatives; and most notoriously, to make any mention of his friends or wife in the first draft, or his brother-in-law in even the revision. The name of Thomas Quiney is only the most wounding omission, by this reading, of an entire instrument based on cold-hearted suppression and exclusion.[7]

The portrait of Shakespeare that emerges from Honigmann's X-ray of the will's gaps and elisions is not, by his admission, an edifying prospect, but the picture of 'an afflicted testator' going ungently into night, cursing the reprobate with his last breath and pointing 'the dead hand' of accusation at his wife. 'He was not in a forgiving mood', this inspection suggests, 'and he may have been too ill for his advisers to nudge him to do what was customary'. So, where the traditional image of 'friendly . . . easy . . . gentle Shakespeare,' presents him 'as he struck others when in congenial company; the will . . . gives us a glimpse of the solitary inner man, and helps . . . explain the sustained rage of a Hamlet or a Prospero'.[8] Reviewing earlier interpretations,

Schoenbaum had warned that it was 'futile to seek dark conceit or intimate revelation' from the will;[9] but what Honigmann's comparison with testamentary practice exposes is purportedly the very 'spirit of the man'. For this humanist critic, the story the legal document tells between its lines is that of a wilfulness that relates not only to the Quiney affair, but to the sources of Shakespearean art. For if he 'broke most of the rules' of testamentary custom, we are to believe, this impatience was a fitting swansong, since 'in the only other record that equals Shakespeare's will in importance as a personal document [the *Sonnets*] he also went his own way and made up his own rules.' So, where its rediscoverer doubted Shakespeare's part in 'the least sentence' of its text, the latest scholarship comes full circle and actually sees 'the unusual features of the will as evidence that the testator himself was largely responsible for its wording and structure'. That 'the will was a draft, from which a fair copy was to have been made had there been time', only validates its authenticity, by this analysis, as an expression of authorial intention. On close reading, Shakespeare's will turns out to be 'one of the most truly original of original wills', its final lack of generosity an indicator not of miserliness but of the ultimate solitude of the creative soul.

If humanist criticism believes in this way that it can pluck the heart of his mystery from Shakespeare's testament, this may be because there is indeed some parallel between its infringement of custom and the transgressive energy of Shakespearean language, which, as Terry Eagleton remarks, constantly subverts an ideological commitment in the plays to traditional order.[10] But by romancing the dramatist's biography as a Balzacian adventure – from the 'lost years' under the Catholic *ancien régime*, through triumph in the playhouse and the corn exchange, to this bitter deathbed – Honigmann individualises the writer and his work, with the result that the historical Shakespeare shrivels to an impotent Old Goriot. In fact, as Lewis proved in his copious annotations, this will was not nearly as eccentric as Honigmann assumes, and if it took Elizabethan tendencies to excess, its intentions appear less singular when read beside the inheritance strategies of seventeenth-century English landowners as a whole. For what made the will, as Lewis admitted, 'all but unique',[11] was actually its zeal in entrenching the primogeniture that would come to obsess the English gentry, making them unlike the middle class of any other European society. Untypical of theatre culture it may have been, but Shakespeare's coldness to brother- and son-in-law, niggardly charity and, above all, stringent treatment of wife and younger daughter, merely gave an extra twist to that tightening of testamentary practice which has been outlined by historians such as E. P. Thompson; when 'the old customary grid of inheritance', with its *lateral* network of social affiliations and obligations, was abandoned for a new documentary and legal system of transmission, focused on selected *lineal* descendants. Shakespeare's will can to be interpreted, then, not as aberration, but as a blueprint for the transfer of common wealth and benefits into private property and capital: an instance, that is, of a historic movement which preoccupies his plays, when the written will came to 'enshrine the wishes of the individual holder' against the rights of his kindred and community.[12]

If Shakespeare's will is notable, as Honigmann finds, chiefly for its 'abruptness' towards customary pieties, this was to become a feature of wills of English gentry. Though historians dispute the date of its onset,[13] they agree that the Shakespearean period experienced 'a deepening conflict as to the very nature of landed property', as 'a collective or communal psychology' gave way to 'capitalist definitions of ownership',[14] and that it was across this rift that society negotiated new forms of self, kinship and community. Thus, M. K. Ashby confirms that wills of the early seventeenth-century squirearchy acknowledge 'a world of wide family connections and affections, a valuation of persons and also objects: charitable bequests are frequent'; but that 'After 1675 the family is recognised as the immediate group of parents and children, charity is absent and money is prominent.'[15] These findings shore up Lawrence Stone's (much-debated) thesis that during this time there was an evolution among the nobility and upper gentry: from an Open Lineage Family, characterised by loyalties to extended kin, patron and community, to a more closed, restricted formation, which he terms the Patriarchal Nuclear Family, centred on loyalties to Church, state and the father as 'a petty tyrant within the home'.[16] And the research carried out by Richard Vann on wills in Banbury suggests that this trend was advanced in Midland market towns, where the tendency for prestigious families to recognise fewer friends or commitments was imitated by lower social strata, so that by 1640 it was rare for Midlanders of Shakespeare's rank to remember kin other than immediate heirs.[17] All the evidence hints, then, that Shakespeare's testamentary priorities reflect the extent to which recognition of kinship had already lost out to recognition of property in his society. His will illustrates the fact that, as Eric Cheyfitz writes, 'while kinship does not die in the West, and while we all recognise our relatives', the question posed by modern property ownership has been *how far* we recognise them, and how this recognition is represented socially.[18]

II

Shakespeare's priority on 25 March 1616 'was to sort out his financial relationship with his new son-in-law', Honigmann infers: 'nothing else mattered so much to him'. To preserve his estate, therefore, Shakespeare's lawyer drew a line at Thomas Quiney. Since this testator would recognise as heirs only his dearest, the son of his dead friend Richard Quiney was 'to receive none of his money, except under stringent conditions',[19] which meant his second daughter was also partially disinherited. For according to Chambers, the first of the three sheets of the will replaced one requiring so much revision it was discarded, and since sheet 2 begins with a cancelled marriage settlement for Judith, he deduced that the original sheet 1 stipulated the provisions for her dowry. So, if Honigmann is right to emphasise omissions, it is possible to conjecture what the January text would have contained if it had followed the customary objectives. Since all English land was theoretically granted by the Crown and conveyed to tenants subject to services, what passed from one generation to another was not ownership but what Thompson terms 'use-rights of a family-within-the-commune'.[20] To prevent the loss of this usufruct by the alienation (or sale) of land out of the community, freedom of testation was circumscribed by the tradition that when a man died leaving wife and issue, only one-third of his estate was devisable by will, while a third went to his wife as dower and the other to his children. Entitlement of heirs was further safeguarded by canons of descent which ruled that inheritance was patrilinear, an heir could never be disinherited, and where 'a father died leaving no male children, his daughters took equal shares of his estate as co-parceners'.[21] By tenurial custom, therefore, Shakespeare would have divided his land equally between his wife and daughters, and his will would have confirmed what Antigonus says in *The Winter's Tale*, that the grid of inheritance was wider than the interests of either a father or the oldest sister:

> I have three daughters . . .
>   They are co-heirs;
> And I had rather glib myself than they
> Should not produce fair issue.
>   (II, i, 144–50)

Demographers calculate that some 30 per cent of marriages failed to produce male children in the century from 1560, and the proportion of testators, like Shakespeare, with no surviving male heir was still higher.[22] Much attention has been payed, therefore, to the circumscribed yet prominent role of heiresses within the patrilinear system. As Thompson and others explain, female tenure and office-holding were stopgaps for patriarchal society, which valued caste more than family and so inserted women as proxies between male heirs, rather than risk alienation of land through distant male succession.[23] It was to protect collective rights against a disastrous redistribution of property through some exogamous marriage that widows were assured their dower (or freebench) and sisters were made coheiresses; and the effect, as Stone records, was indeed to ramify the caste. Thus:

The three coheiresses of the 10th Earl of Shrewsbury married into the old peerage, the three coheiresses of the 2nd Earl of Exeter into the new, the three coheiresses of the 14th Earl of Derby into one or other. One of the two coheiresses of the 3rd Lord Chandos married into the peerage, as did the two coheiresses of the 3rd Earl of Dorset and the heiresses of the 3rd Earl of Cumberland, the 2nd Lord Hunsdon, and the 2nd Lord St. John.

It was thanks to such parcenary inheritance, in-marriage and the legacies of incest, Stone deduces, that boughs were grafted back to family trees and the 'peerage acquired far more by wives than they lost by daughters';[24] so class endogamy dictated that fathers 'looked for a happy and respectable match for all their daughters, rather than bid for a grand match for the eldest.'[25] Though sentiment might influence a father such as Sir Thomas Brews, who wrote in 1477 to his son-in-law John Paston, that he 'would be loath to bestow so much on one daughter that her sisters should fare the worse',[26] partible female inheritance survived because daughters were the means by which dynasties spread their branches in a system where an open lineage provided immunity for a closed caste.

Inheritance customs and the terms of the marriage market theoretically left a Tudor father as little freedom in dividing his estate as he allowed his daughter in choosing a husband; and theory is rigorously applied in *The Taming of the Shrew* when Petruchio, who has 'come to wive it wealthily in Padua' (I, ii, 74), promises Katherina's father she will receive 'Her widowhood' (dower) of a third 'In all my lands and leases whatsoever' if she weds him, which Baptista matches with a dowry of 20,000 crowns (£5,000), and 'After my death the one half of my lands' (II, i, 121–5). The remainder of the Minola estate is then parcelled with Bianca, as a 'prize' to the suitor who 'can assure my daughter greatest dower' (335–6), in an auction exemplifying the trend charted by Stone, when 'The supply of eligible husbands failed to keep pace with demand', putting the fathers of daughters at a disadvantage in a buyer's market, and forcing them to pledge their dowry for the best dower or even fixed jointure that their girls could fetch.[27] Baptista knows that to marry his daughters to the

highest bidders he needs to 'play a merchant's part, / And venture madly
on a desperate mart' (319–20); but Petruchio's machismo reflects the
reality that historically the odds were stacked in favour of the bridegroom, with the result that the average size of an aristocratic dowry rose
much faster than the price index, doubling to £2,000 in the twenty years
from 1570, and climbing to £5,000 by 1650 and £10,000 by 1700, while that
of a dower or jointure steadily fell as a ratio of income.[28] When Petruchio
informs Kate that 'your father hath consented / That you shall be my wife;
your dowry's 'greed on; / And will you, nill you, I will marry you' (262–4),
therefore, his confidence is based on the fact of economic life, rammed
home by Tranio in his mock suit to Bianca, that in a patrimonial system,
where to die with heiresses but no heir could prove catastrophic,[29] it was
the suitor who was a 'father's heir and only son' (357) whose will was
paramount.

An irony of the customary grid, therefore, was that whilst it installed
males as masters of their patrimony, with women as mere vessels of
transmission, it made their possession conditional on eventual surrender,
and encumbered their entitlement with obligations to their wives and
daughters in the form of brides' dowries and widows' dowers. It was to
restrict the power of overbearing husbands such as Petruchio, indeed,
that the late sixteenth and early seventeenth centuries witnessed an
extraordinary growth in the documentation and complexity of marriage
contracts, according to Stone,[30] for in such a system, as Baptista
cautions Bianca's prospective bridegroom, the object of such 'specialties'
and 'covenants' (II, i, 126–7) was to ensure that ownership was
never transferred to an individual to dispose of as he desired or by
default:

> Baptista: I must confess your offer is the best,
> And let your father make her the assurance,
> She is your own. Else, you must pardon me,
> If you should die before him, where's her dower?
> (379–82)

So, when Tranio shrugs that this condition is 'but a cavil', since his
father 'is old, I young', the greybeard Gremio cuts the pretended heir
down to a father's legal size, when he retorts: 'And may not young men
die as well as old?' (83–4). Shakespeare's early comedies pivot on this
paradox, that property which defines identity for Tudor landowners is
only a temporary possession, subject to rights of kin and destined to be
relinquished. It is the custodial quality of ownership in a patriarchal
society – where 'The fact of death makes possible the acquisition of
property from one's ancestors [yet] necessitates its surrender'[31] – that

accounts for the vulnerability of fathers in these plays, who are consistently overruled in the marital interests of their children, as Theseus disallows the father of delinquent Hermia: 'Egeus, I will overbear your will' (*A Midsummer Night's Dream*, IV, i, 178). Though Baptista shows himself a forward-looking parent, therefore, in hoping Petruchio will wrest from Kate 'the special thing . . . / That is, her love' (II, i, 128–9), the patriarchal family represented in *The Taming of the Shrew* gives a father scant option but to affirm a marriage where the bride is so generously dowered, and where what clinches the deal, as the groom reminds him, is that 'You knew my father well' (116). Baptista will 'Provide the feast' (309), then, as was incumbent on the bride's father, and throw in 'twenty thousand crowns – / Another dowry to another daughter' (v, ii, 112), when Kate submits, as concession to the principle of patriarchy, that as sons become fathers, fathers must make way for sons-in-law or sons. As staged by Shakespeare, that is to say, patriarchy renders fathers disposable, as Tranio shows by having his supposed father impersonated (IV, ii), and Petruchio by extending the title of 'loving father' not only to Baptista (II, i, 130), but to the father-in-law of his sister-in-law (IV, v, 61). If it is *permeability* to the claims of extended kin that characterises the pre-modern family, as Stone proposes, to be a father in Shakespearean Italy is certainly to subject one's will to the most open definition of lineage.

In the customary culture of patriarchal Padua, then, an heiress such as Katherina might expect a dowry of some £5,000 to match her dower of one-third of the estate her husband has inherited and 'bettered rather than decreased' (II, i, 128), and this figure corresponds to dowries tendered by richer merchants in contemporary London. Critics who object that women are mere items of exchange in Shakespearean comedy underestimate the degree to which the dowry system operated to insure a wife's life interest, for Stone calculates that marriage portions could plunge relatives into debt for years, whilst if it followed custom, a family 'could on average expect to be paying widows up to a third of its income for over half the time' between 1560 and 1640. These sums suggest that 'excess devotion', such as Bridget Paston's dowry of £30,000 in 1582, or the portions of £12,000 left by the Earl of Bath to three nieces in 1642, was 'a prime cause' of the decline of the aristocracy;[32] but Alan Macfarlane finds the same ratio of three times a father's annual income standard for the dowries of seventeenth-century gentry and tradesmen. Thus the clergyman Ralph Josselin gave his three daughters 'portions varying between £240 and £500 apiece, the squarson Giles Moore gave his daughter £300, and a northern yeoman states that he had £300 with the girl he married.'[33] Lower down the social scale, Henry Hill, a tanner of Banbury, left his daughters £150 each in his will of 1641;[34] and it is against this index that Shakespeare's dowry for Judith can be assessed. Estimates of his annual income vary from the 'Rate of a £1,000' reported by John Ward, Vicar of Stratford from 1662, to the £200 plus conjectured by Chambers. Sir Sidney Lee's £700 is the best substantiated; but the figures imply that according to custom Shakespeare should have settled at least £700 on Judith, putting her in the same bracket as daughters of London merchants, who could expect on average £860.[35] In fact, she did little better than a tanner's daughter, receiving just £150, with interest on another £150 contingent on an equal dower (never forthcoming) from 'such husband' as she might be 'married unto' after three years. Her start in married life could hardly have been less auspicious.

Compared with the terms of his own will, the marriage settlements in Shakespeare's early dramas belong to a different culture, where custom confines a father's freedom of testation and prescribes the rights of kin and community. The patriarchalism of these plays guarantees that a disinheritance like that of Judith Quiney could never succeed, for, as Katherine Mauss remarks, they depict a world in which the property of the landowning class is enmeshed in a network of entitlements, and the ambitions of the individual testator are checked by his dependence upon an inherited status that must be transferred, through women, to the next generation on the exact conditions as those by which he received it. Thus, in *Love's Labour's Lost* Navarre's egotistical covenant with his courtiers to 'Let fame . . . / Live register'd upon our brazen tombs . . . / And make us heirs of all eternity' (i, i, 1–7), is negated because he asks to be installed forever in a place that he is only allowed to occupy for the time being: 'the imagery of inheritance thus seems ill-suited to the aggressively competitive sentiments he uses that imagery to express. Navarre makes, as it were, an excessive demand upon the very system to which he owes his preeminence.'[36] For to be 'heir of all eternity', the King believes, is to 'buy' with 'Th'endeavour of this present breath' an 'honour' which belongs uniquely to the possessor, to bequeath at will (5–6); but such self-determination contradicts the hereditary principle by which it is empowered, since, as Boyet observes, Navarre is a 'Matchless' catch for a bride purely because he is 'sole inheritor / Of all perfections that a man may owe' to ancestry (ii, i, 5–6). For such a prince, it is as 'vain' to try to entail for 'all eternity' property 'with pain purchas'd', as seek to defeat the descent of what he 'doth inherit' (i, i, 72–3), since the testamentary rights of the self-made man are not available to the nobility, for whom it is 'The death of fathers that makes the transfer of title possible, indeed necessary'.[37]

In the battle between ancients and moderns which underlies the badinage of *Love's Labour's Lost*, the humanist model of self-creation espoused by Navarre and his court and funded by bourgeois acquisition collides with the feudal order of patrimony founded on noble descent, whose proxies are the Princess and her ladies, and it is their family names which decide the match. For in this caste governed by endogamy, where to wed some 'Lord Perigort' is the destiny of every 'beauteous heir of Jacques Falconbridge', what distinguishes a daughter is not that she is 'Her mother's' child but that 'She is an heir of Falconbridge' or 'The heir of Alençon' (ii, i, 41–2; 201–5; 181). Thus, though Navarre would separate the title he wins by 'purchase' and self-promotion from that which he inherits – depriving women of their dower, just as he has emparked his estate to bar the commoners the usufruct – he is unable to deny these noblewomen the place of power in his domain which is theirs as their fathers' heiresses. So, he 'must confront everything he has tried to repress: the involvement of women in the process of title transfer [and] the dependence of the present generation upon . . . its predecessors.'[38] What is won by these 'wise girls', then, in their jocular trespass onto private property, are communal rights, and what is lost by the male 'fools' are the self-possessive labours which would 'purchase' a claim to be 'entitled in the other's heart' by 'fierce endeavour' rather than descent (v, ii, 58–9; 807; 842). It is land, not money, which talks in this patriarchy, and which ensures that marriage will be clinched by a 'plea of no less weight / Than Aquitaine, a dowry for a queen' (ii, i, 7–8). The custom of these comedies, where property is never the possession of a self-created individual but an entitlement of ancestors and heirs, is one, in other words, where Shakespeare's own will would breach the canon that an heir may never be disinherited. In these earliest comedies there is not yet a private space from which an individual may lay down the law to kin and dependants as if from beyond the grave.

III

The landlord's scheme to monopolise a name and title is mocked by the rough music of Shakespearean comedy. For as Leonard Tennenhouse explains, though *The Taming of the Shrew* ends in Kate's encomium to her husband as a 'sovereign' who is owed 'Such duty as the subject oweth the prince' (v, ii, 146; 154), Elizabethan culture still 'entertains no distinction between the formation of the domestic unit and adherence to the dominant rules of kinship'.[39] Defeat of a father's power of testation will therefore prove the turning-point when Egeus's plan to 'estate unto Demetrius' his wealth is voided in favour of Lysander's 'crazèd title' (*A Midsummer Night's Dream*, i, i, 92–8); or when Shylock is compelled to 'record a gift . . . of all he dies possessed / Unto his son Lorenzo and his daughter' (*The Merchant of Venice*, IV, i, 385–7). In these plots the father has the obstructive function of the nay-saying *senex iratus* of classical comedy, but without the sanction of Roman law that did, in fact, allow a father to disinherit his heir. And Tennenhouse has shown how this contradiction of paternalism by old-fashioned patriarchy runs on through Jacobean city comedies, which are designed to demonstrate that these concepts represent 'opposing forms of political organization', a difference they mark by staging the 'incompetence of natural fathers, uncles, and grandfathers. . . . With notable regularity, plays by Marston, Middleton, Jonson and Dekker find paternal characters unable to fill the role of patriarch when they act as head of the household.'[40] Jonson takes the formula to a violent extreme in *Epicoene*, where Morose has refused his 'poor despised kinsman', Sir Dauphine Eugenie, an annuity of a third of his income of £1,500 (v, iv, 148; 165–6),[41] and intends to disinherit him outright when the play begins. Such a flagrant contravention of the rights of kinship provokes the charivari which eventually terrorises the old moneybags into signing a deed to confirm the annuity and 'assure the rest' on his nephew when he dies (167):

> Truewit: 'Slid, I would be the author of more [mockery] to vex him; that purpose deserves it: it gives thee law of plaguing him. I'll tell thee what I would do. I would make a false almanac, get it printed, and then ha'him drawn out on a coronation day to the Tower-wharf, and kill him with the noise of the ordinance. Disinherit thee! He cannot, man. Art not thou next of blood, and his sister's son?
>
> (I, ii, 11–17)

Revolted by its 'forced barbarity', critics have long thought *Epicoene* 'to be without a moral', but the heir's 'annihilating epitaph'[42] on the miser condenses the moral economy of all these festive plots, which prise a concession of patriarchal, patrician and public values out of the maw of privacy, property and paternalism: 'Now you may go in and rest, be as private as you will, sir. I'll not trouble you till you trouble me with your funeral, which I care not how soon it come' (v, iv, 199–201). The severity of this repudiation of testamentary power is certainly no more vindictive than that with which Volpone is penalised for manipulating his will to deceive his heirs. Jonson's legacy-hunting farce can be read, indeed, as a biting satire on the monetary grid of inheritance that was superseding custom, consisting as it does of a deathbed vigil that begins as travesty and ends in deadly truth. Where the Latin sources of *Volpone* envisage young love's nightmare – that the rich testator outlives his heirs, 'while he, from being aged, returns to the prime of youth'[43] – Jonson's twist is to turn the joke back on the schemer, who acts sick to tempt the fortune-hunters only to be racked on his real deathbed at the end. Critics who see the play simply as an exposé of legacy-hunting are affronted therefore by the savagery with which Volpone is condemned to the diseases he has faked and his wealth confiscated for 'the Hospital of the *Incurabili*' (v, xii, 120); but the callousness reflects the geniune early modern suspicion of testamentary power and the fear that the propertied might pervert inheritance for their own ends. Thompson reports mock-executions inflicted as late as the eighteenth century by neighbours on landowners who plotted to evade customary entitlements by will;[44] and Volpone's punishment arises from the same folk game. For what seems to be on trial in this carnivalesque scenario, as successive dupes are gulled that they are 'sole heir' with 'wax warm yet' and 'ink scarce dry / Upon the parchment' (i, iii, 46–7), is will-making and the corrupting potential of the will itself:

> Mosca: The weeping of an heir should be laughter,
>   Under a visor.
> Corvino: Why? Am I his heir?
> Mosca: Sir, I am sworn, I may not show the will,
>   Till he be dead: but, here has been Corbaccio,
>   Here has been Voltore, here were others too,
>   I cannot number'em, they were so many,
>   All gaping here for legacies, but I,
>   Taking the vantage of his naming you,
>   'Signior Corvino, Signior Corvino', took
>   Paper, and pen, and ink, and there I asked him,
>   Whom he would have his heir? 'Corvino'. Who
>   Should be executor? 'Corvino'. And
>   To any question he was silent to,
>   I still interpreted the nods he made,
>   Through weakness, for consent; and sent home th'others,
>   Nothing bequeathed them, but to cry, and curse.
>   (i, v, 22–37)

Laughing or crying their way home, the senile heirs of this plutocracy are infantilised by a paternalism which reverses generation and installs itself in permanent possession. Jonson's Venice is a specific modern hell, where the legend that Pluto makes the 'old, young' and embalms with gold those 'whom the spital-house and ulcerous sores / Would cast the gorge at' (*Timon of Athens*, iv, iii, 30; 40–1), defines a phantasmal empire of the will. All who enter here must abandon hope of satisfaction from the dying hand they clutch; for this *danse macabre*, where every would-be beneficiary disinherits an heir or dishonours a wife to procure succession for himself, figures the endless deferral of title in a system of transmission based not on kinship but individual exchange. 'These possess wealth, as sick men possess feavers, / Which, trulier, may be said to possess them', the Republic's 'grave fathers' sermonise (*Volpone*, v, xii, 101–2); thereby admitting they owe their intervention not to patriarchy, but the temptation of testation to defeat itself. For what fixates these characters and decides their fate are the paper and ink of Volpone's will, with which each insinuates himself to be 'Put in first' (IV, vi, 100), and from which all receive their doom. Even the testator is destroyed by his own instrument, when his executor Mosca seizes the letter of the supposed deed that names him heir and Volpone is reduced to actual silence by his assumed demise: 'I could, almost, wish to be without it, / But that the will o'the dead must be observed' (v, iv, 86–7). If young Bonario is reinstated, therefore, as his father's heir by the denouement of this self-consuming plot, it is out of anxiety at paternal power of testation, rather than respect for their 'fatherhoods' of the court, that poetic justice is served:

> Mosca: Are you not he, that have, today, in court,
>   Professed the disinheriting of your son?
>   Perjured yourself? Go home, and die, and stink.
>
> (v, iii, 72–5)

Volpone climaxes with Mosca garbed as a notary, 'a court-book, pen and ink, / Papers afore . . . taking / An inventory' of the deceased's estate for probate: *per testes* as it was called (v, ii, 81–3). With its gallows humour, charlatanism and resurrection imagery, this play can be read as a literalisation of the eternal life promised the defunct by will. For though Volpone's executory devises are self-cancelling, and he is 'mortified' by the technicality that a corporate life hangs on corporeal decay (v, xii, 125), the breath of the undead is what animates the rictus of this plot. If this Aesopian fable confiscates the grapes he rooks, it is a tribute to the Fox's mimetic potency that his testament should so seduce. Here, as in all his work, Jonson relishes the very textual and contractual self-fashioning he deplores as a cheat, and to which, as apologist for an older collective ideology, he is nominally opposed. But *Volpone* witnesses the degree to which identity was already grounded in property in England; and reality, as Stone remarks, offered precedents enough for the legatee eager to benefit by disclaiming a son, like Corbaccio, prostituting a wife, like Corvino, or selling a daughter, like Signior Lupo; while 'The truth about the scramble to obtain the wealth of the great financier Sir Thomas Sutton is hardly stranger than Jonson's embroidery.'[45] In a society where the will was becoming what etymology implies – a symbolic phallus for the impotent testator – the challenge for customary culture was no longer to defraud a miser, but to escape his pen. While Jonson menaces Bonario, Celia and Signorina Lupo with testamentary power, then, the fantasy he stages of the restoration of custom by the invalidation of a testator's intention was the wish-fulfilment of an entire generation, Stone shows, as 'Attempts to insert provisos cutting off the heir if he alienated part of the estate were struck down by judges between 1595 and 1620.' Though it was hard-fought, the 'running battle between landlords and judges'[46] over freedom of testation had not quite been decided yet in favour of *Volpone*.

Jacobean city comedy provides a symbolic form for a social order in which community takes precedence over individuals; indeed, the circumvention of the wills of Jonson's magnates parallels the tactics to which contemporary executors resorted, such as those used to defeat the will of the international arbitrageur Sir Horatio Palavicino. He died in 1600, having settled his land on his son, Henry, as a ward of the Queen, with a dower reserved for his wife, Anna, provided she did not remarry, and a dowry of £5,000 for his daughter, Baptina, willing the rest of his capital equally to Henry and the younger, Toby. During their minority, administration of this fortune was entrusted to the executors: Lady Anna and two Palavicino agents, Giovanni Giustiniano and Francisco Rizzo; while in the event of their death without issue, the estate was to be sold and all the money was to go to Horatio's family in Genoa. The overseers to the will, however, included the ministerial fox, Robert Cecil, and his scheme to frustrate its provisions and exclude the Palavicini furnishes the perfect context for city comedy. Palavicino was on his deathbed when it was alleged he whispered to bar the Italians from executorship; then, in exchange for the wardship of Henry and control of the land, but in defiance of the will, the widow, now sole executrix of some £100,000, was pressed into marrying Oliver Cromwell of Hinchinbrook, a spendthrift ally of Cecil's. Their wedding, solemnised the very day after the year of mourning, was only one of the nuptials marking the plunder of Horatio's estate, however, for in 1606 Cromwell 'bought off an audacious double marriage: he united his twelve-year-old daughter Catherine to the fourteen-year-old Henry Palavicino, and made success doubly sure by marrying another daughter to twelve-year-old Toby.' And when Oliver's heir Henry then married Baptina, the knot was tied to secure the remaining £5,000 dowry for the Cromwells. As Stone remarks, this four-fold alliance would be hard to match in English history for its 'cool effrontery';[47] yet it is the recurring dream of Jacobean comedy.

When James I rode south to claim his English throne, it was Palavicino money that enabled Oliver Cromwell to entertain the monarch better, he declared, 'than anyone since I left Edinburgh'.[48] The wine that ran free at Hinchinbrook, and the gold cups, horses, and fifty-pound gratuities the courtiers took away, commemorated not only a new reign, but the triumph of native festivity, with its conspicuous consumption, over the prudence and economy of international finance. And as she presided at these feasts, the Italian widow whose remarriage had released the dead man's grip personified the customary duty of heiresses to 'buy their thraldoms', as Middleton's Isabella bemoans, 'and bring great portions / To men to keep 'em in subjection' (*Women Beware Women*, I, ii, 170–2). For by this alliance, Stone recounts, Palavicino's children were 'joined with a family of wastrels, his estates were disentagled and alienated, his money wasted in wanton extravagance', and his 'efforts to lay the foundations of a family that would take a permanent and prominent place in the governing class met with total failure'.[49] To modern capitalist eyes, then, the descent of the Palavicino inheritance was the tragedy of the self-made entrepreneur; but by patriarchal standards, the thwarting of his will was a comedy of come-uppance to a bourgeois who had presumed to rise into the aristocracy. With foreigners barred from their legacies, and wealth syphoned from the city to the shire, the Palavicino treasure would ensure that the knight of Huntingdonshire would be able to continue in reckless hospitality until his own death, aged ninety-three, in 1655. In Jonsonian comedy, the London financier had plotted to bring 'knighthood itself' to beggary: 'it shall not have money to discharge one tavern-reckoning, to invite the old creditors to forbear it knighthood, or the new that should be, to trust it knighthood' (*Epicoene*, II, v, 103–4; 113–16); but by breaking Palavicino's will with opportunistic marriages, Sir Oliver and his caste would stave off for a generation the crisis of the aristocracy.

IV

The most celebrated Elizabethan deathbed was also one that betrayed the tension in Renaissance subjectivity, torn between a relational and an individual sense of identity, or 'propriety' and 'property' as signifiers of selfhood.[50] On 17 October 1586 'the shepherd knight', Sir Philip Sidney, circled by his staff in the room at Arnhem where he had lain wounded for a month, added a codicil to his will, declaring that he gave his 'friends Sir George Digby and Sir Henry Goodyear, either of them a ring of . . .' The sentence was unfinished when the hero expired, 'To his last gasp', his biographer states, 'giving things away.'[51] This was the patrician generosity Jonson extolled in his encomium of the Sidney seat at Penshurst: 'whose liberal board doth flow', he applauded, with 'free provisions' and 'all that hospitality doth know'. In a study of the poem and the place, Don Wayne shows that this 'stately home' became for Jonson an ideological domain where the nostalgia for feudal patronage sanctioned private property, and that 'To Penshurst' functions to negotiate the fact, noted by Raymond Williams, that the Sidneys were land speculators who had acquired the estate through Tudor expropriation.[52] Sir Henry Sidney had bought a counterfeit pedigree in 1568; but his son, unaware of the forgery, left a will that almost sabotaged the dynastic pretensions by taking them so seriously. In this 'splendid document expressing the munificence for which Sidney was so loved',[53] the delirious soldier left his brother Penshurst, his daughter a dowry of £4,000, many cousins £100 each, aunts his jewels, friends his armour, numerous servants between £30 and £500, a secretary £400, eight doctors, including the one 'who came to me yesterday', £20 each, and the Queen a ring worth £100. To the end, Sidney remained the paragon of *noblesse oblige*, whose legatees trailed far behind his magnificent cortège; but his father-in-law spent so much honouring the will that when he died he was buried unceremoniously at night, 'in respect of the greatness of his debt'.[54]

Sir Philip Sidney would be remembered by contemporaries as 'above all a *vir generosus*', a man 'in all ways generous';[55] yet the extravagance of his will exposed the psychic and material instabilities from which his subaltern cadre of bureaucrats compounded their self-possession. With its contradictory obligations both to the extended family and egotistic individual, Sidney's last writing was a perfect coda to a pseudo-medieval literary career, but this final homage to a vanishing gift-culture was financed, like Timon's prodigality, by mortgaging the patrimony, and the profusion of the donor was compromised when it bankrupted the heirs. That the testator was conscious of the contradictions is suggested by his instruction to his lawyer to pay his legacies by selling land, made in ignorance of his father's entail invalidating such alienation. The ironies of Renaissance selfhood, entangled in a web of discursive restrictions at the point of grandest self-expression, were seldom so sharp as in Sidney's bid to project his 'bounty and liberality' beyond death, which even the family advisers felt would need to be 'performed according to his simple, sincere good meaning' to be effective.[56] But if the Lord of Penshurst bequeathed a financial nightmare to his descendants that would jeopardise Jonson's Arcadia, his determination to bind his successors to his intentions was completely characteristic of his generation of landowners, whose challenge to their own patrimony would be staged in Shakespeare's history plays and tragedies with the realism evaded in contemporary comedies. For from the outset, what distinguishes the representation of property and power in these texts is the focus on conflict between the will of the father and the rights of kin, or patriarchy and paternalism. The perils of a rampant paternalism had been at the centre of the chauvinistic *King John*, for example, where Philip, the bastard son of King Richard-Cœur-de-Lion, successfully contests the will of his putative father, Sir

Robert Falconbridge, who has absolutely disinherited him, according to the deposition of the younger son and claimant:

> Robert: Upon his deathbed he by will bequeath'd
> His lands to me, and took it on his death
> That this, my mother's son, was none of his . . .
> Then, good my liege, let me have what is mine,
> My father's land, as was my father's will.
>
> (i, i, 109–15)

King John, which dramatises the usurpation of the crown from Arthur, is a play about how to legitimise the illegitimate, and in that sense provides a crude schema for the Shakespearean comedic strategy to overrule the paternal in the interests of patriarchy. John knows the Bastard's claim to England would be as good as his own if he were recognised as the son of Richard, so his ruling is based on the common law dictum, reiterated by Henry Swinburne in his *Brief Treatise of Testaments* of 1590, that 'He which married the woman shall be said to be the father of the child, not he which did beget the same.' 'Whoever bulls my cow', went the maxim, 'the calf is mine';[57] and this brute subordination of paternalism to community expresses the preference of a society where, in absence of proof of paternity, what counts are not the rights of a father but continuity of patrimony. Thus, it is from feudal culture, where (as Norse law proclaimed) 'No one is a bastard through his mother', that the high-born Bastard derives his legitimacy, as he exploits the archaic rule that 'when a man takes another into his keeping and maintains him to fire and pyre, that man becomes the heir of the other'. Stone reminds us that it was not until the thirteenth century that canon law excluded bastards from inheritance;[58] and the plot of *King John* becomes explicable, therefore, once it is grasped that the action encodes a system, like tanistry in Elizabethan Ireland, where ownership is collective, succession goes 'to the strongest', and custom legitimises both Bastard and King as holders of the titles they have arrogated:

> King John: Tell me, how if my brother,
> Who, as you say, took pains to get this son,
> Had of your father claimed this son for his?
> In sooth, good friend, your father might have kept
> This calf, bred from this cow, from all the world;
> In sooth he might. Then, if he were my brother's,
> My brother might not claim him, nor your father,
> Being none of his, refuse him. This concludes:

> My mother's son did get your father's heir;
> Your father's heir must have your father's land.
>   (I, i, 120–9)

To be an 'heir of Falconbridge' in this extended family is to possess a title regardless of testation, for here it is still the order of patriarchy that prevails over the drive to individualise inheritance. When young Falconbridge demands, 'Shall then my father's will be of no more force / To dispossess that child which is not his?' and the Bastard crows: 'Of no more force to dispossess me, sir, / Than was his will to get me, as I think' (130–4), the trumping of Sir Robert's 'will' by King Richard's foretells all those Shakespearean crises when, as Tennenhouse observes, domestic rule by the *pater familias* is overturned with the monarch's absolutist claim to be, as James I asserted, '*Parens patriae*, the father of his people'.[59] Tudor lawyers defined 'time immemorial', from which customary inheritance was supposed to date, as the succession of Richard in 1189; so by law this Bastard is a symbol of 'the very spirit of Plantagenet', recognised as such by his 'grandam' Queen Eleanor (I, i, 167–8). That he no sooner wins than he renounces name and land to join his royal 'kin' (273) confirms that in this system genealogy will predominate over the ambition of the nuclear family to control the transmission of its own. Though Sir Robert Falconbridge 'took it on his death' to regulate his succession in favour of his chosen heir, therefore, his right to devise his estate by will is invalidated by custom; yet as Phyllis Rackin writes, the 'very absoluteness of patriarchal right provides for its own subversion' in this flouting of paternalism, exposing the 'deep contradiction in patriarchal law' between the claims of kinship and the interests of the father.[60] With its Armada clarion that 'Nought shall make us rue / If England to itself do rest but true' (V, vii, 117–18), *King John* elevates community over 'That smooth-fac'd gentleman, tickling commodity', who would sell 'five provinces' of English land to France (II, i, 573; 527); but by the time it was produced in 1590, its patriarchalism would already have been intolerable to Elizabethan land-owners.

Nothing better demonstrates the collective quality of land in customary society than the fact that under its dispensation bastardy, far from any stigma, traditionally flourishes. So by admitting the Bastard into both royal and gentry families, *King John* valorises the customs of the manor, which fostered adoption; yet it is a sign of their decay that the division of patrimony between heirs – Arthur, John, Philip and Robert – should prove so problematic. In an analysis of Midland inheritance customs, Cicely Howell shows that the real Falconbridges were more successful in negotiating freedom to devise property than

Shakespeare's comic backwoodsmen. Inheritance based on partibility and conjugality was eroded, she relates, when testators made cash provision for wives and younger children, until a landholding pattern was established and regions with unigeniture 'became associated with large farms and large portions; areas of partible inheritance with poor farms and small portions.'[61] Thus the will became the main instrument of gentry power in Tudor culture, and it is surely for this reason that its writ is vetoed in the populist *King John*. In fact, the defeat of the Falconbridges is a pyrrhic victory for custom, the consequences of which would be realised in the ambition of the bastard Edmund in *King Lear*, and may even be deliberately anachronistic, since partibility had been largely demolished in the previous generation, when the 1540 Act of Wills formalised the devising of real property in England. Though free alienation of all land would not be complete until the abolition of vestigial customs in 1856, it was from this statute that individual property rights dated. For by granting the testator 'full and free liberty, power and authority to give, dispose, will and devise . . . all his hereditaments at his free will and pleasure', the Act gave landowners an impregnable right to decide the future of their estates; but it also uprooted the concepts of place and person, making ownership the signifier of selfhood and land itself a kind of commodity. And these traumatic changes were to be the subject not of comedy, but of Shakespearean tragedy.

In the West, writes Cheyfitz (contrasting European and American Indian attitudes to land), we are shadows of property; and if we own nothing, even this obscure visibility is denied to us

> Property, in that tangled space where the physical and the metaphysical mix, is the very mark of identity: what we typically call a 'self' or an 'individual', indicating the boundaries that are predicated of this entity. The *self*, like *property*, has its history . . . and the histories of *self* and *property* are inseparable.[62]

The 1540 statute reminds us, however, how recently identity became legally coterminous with ownership and how contentious this remained in Shakespearean society. For the Act had been forced on the Tudor regime after the Pilgrimage of Grace, when the gentry bitterly petitioned for the liberty to control their inheritance forfeited in 1535 under the Statute of Uses, Henry VIII's strategem to cement his overlordship by abolishing wills. Though denounced by the premier landholder, the Duke of Norfolk, as 'the worst act ever made', this neo-feudal enactment continued to be admired by absolutist theorists such as Bacon, who called it 'the most perfectly conceived of any law'.[63] Thus, the Act which supervened in 1540 installed the capitalist notion of the sovereign individual within a very particular material context, when the necessity to sell off the vast monastic estates compelled the king to satisfy the gentry, and the Crown made the unprecedented concession of the right demanded by Shakespearean landowners such as Navarre: to dispose of land as if they were indeed 'heirs of eternity' and the last of their line. Identity would still be cast within a custodial mould, for testators were forbidden to alienate the property of wives; but it can be no coincidence that from this moment – when the modern land market was created by the greatest transfer of real estate in English history – there was what Stephen Greenblatt perceives to be 'a new stress on the executive power of the will',[64] for this was the power inscribed and signed and sealed in *deed* by legal will.

Property and proper names, Greenblatt alerts us, purse and person, were 'inseparably linked' by the Tudor state through bureaucratic innovations such as the 1522 census for Henry VIII's forced loan, and the 1538 parish chest. It was this official tabulation of 'identity and property: and identity *as* property', which, he suggests, accounts for the documentary production of the self in early modern England; a self that remained closer to 'real estate transactions . . . than we imagine'.[65] And if the power to fabricate one's life was at odds in Tudor culture, as Greenblatt finds, with the power to control the identity of others through family and state, this conflict was institutionalised above all in the laws of inheritance, which in instances such as Dacre's Case of 1535, simultaneously elaborated the idea of intention and made it binding on others as 'that which the testator cannot do when he is dead'.[66] Greenblatt's puzzle, then, that in Tudor England 'power of the will' was accompanied by a 'relentless assault upon the will', can be partly solved by the fact that will power – the discursive template of modern selfhood – was materially confined to those who owned the property in the later sixteenth century. For between 1540 and 1640 (when the strict settlement was invented to fix the portions of future children at the time of the parents' marriage) English landowners exercised unparalleled liberty to dispose of land. Thus, in 1557 the 'perpetual entail' was legalised, empowering testators to determine their line of descent *for all time*, and this device swung the balance between the rights of the landowner and those of his kindred decisively his way. Though docked by the courts and private bills in the 1590s, such entails gave the generation of landholders born in mid-century some fifty years to enjoy the right denied to Falconbridge: to master their estates in future as well as for themselves. Untrammelled by entails from *their* fathers, Shakespeare's generation fashioned their unprecedented self-autonomy on a unique opportunity to restrict the freedom of their heirs.[67]

V

Medieval law so abhorred the idea that a dead hand might reach out to manipulate the rights of the living that it restricted charitable bequests and requisitioned 'the temporal lands which men devout / By testament have given to the Church' (*Henry v*, I, i, 6–7) to salvage them from *mortmain*: the condition of perpetual alienation. In customary culture, therefore, the rites of death were organised so that the dying could surrender themselves and their possessions with what Philip Ariès, in his survey of Western beliefs about death, calls 'a compound of resignation, familiarity, and lack of privacy'.[68] Until the nineteenth century in remote communities the death chamber remained open to any passing stranger, since 'Death was always public',[69] and belonged no more to the individual than the property he was leaving. And the last testament performed by the dying dramatised communal identity: a profession of faith, the confession of sins, pardon of survivors, dispositions for burial, the commendation of the soul to God. In the hour of their death, with bed-curtains drawn back for the vigil of families and friends, the men and women of pre-modern societies were never more at home in the household, by this account, but never less tempted to call a house their own. 'The Tame Death', Ariès terms it, this relinquishment of life; when the dying presided over their passing, begged forgiveness, bade farewell and released their grasp on worldly things without the sense of loss of personal possession: 'As virtuous men pass mildly away, / And whisper to their souls, to go'.[70] If Falstaff made 'a finer end', therefore, when he 'babbled of green fields' (II, iii, 10–16), we may be sure that these were not enclosed. 'In a world subject to change', Ariès reminds us, 'the traditional death is a bulwark of inertia and continuity';[71] and what it enshrines is the collective patrimony, as John of Gaunt demonstrates in his deathbed valediction, when he claims immemorial rights for the families who occupy ancestral land:

> This royal throne of kings, this scept'red isle,
> This earth of majesty, this seat of Mars,
> This other Eden, demi-paradise,
> This fortress built by Nature for herself
> Against infection and the hand of war,
> This happy breed of men, this little world,
> This precious stone set in a silver sea,
> Which serves it in the office of a wall,
> Or as a moat defensive to a house,
> Against the envy of less happier lands.
>   (*Richard II*, II, i, 40–50)

In a feudal system of inheritance there can be no distinction between a man and the property from which he takes his name (as Gaunt takes his from Ghent, and Bolingbroke from his seat in Leicestershire); so Gaunt extols England's land and people as a single heritage of blood and soil, to be bequeathed as an heirloom, which, according to common law, could never be devised by will away from the heirs.[72] The image of the ring thus crystallises the idea of the feudal economy as a family economy that was never the property of even the oldest male. For customary society, indeed, the hour of death affirms the equality of the testator among all souls, living and dead. Facing Jerusalem, the crusader of the Middle Ages recollects his family's achievements to pass them on rather than claim them for his own. And as Gaunt's desire returns to the 'womb' of English soil, we see how for patriarchy land and women are mystified as signifiers not of individual possession but of caste. In this culture identity is bound up with the transmission of inalienable rights, rather than the acquisition of property by purchase. Committing his own dust to English earth, therefore, the Christian knight has a sense of place as the locus of patrimonial identity; he does not possess the land so much as it possesses him. This is the collective concept of property which for Ariès accounts for the migration of the dead from their pagan graves outside town walls to their privileged medieval station in the chantry chapel and bosom of the Church. Extramural interment was forbidden to a feudal society, by this reckoning, because its dynastic property rights required that the dead share space with the living in sites that were 'public and frequented, not impure and solitary'.[73] The earth Gaunt extols, therefore, is an inheritance which custom would never permit to be subject to testation, but which is now, he bemoans, alienated by the King's project 'to farm' the 'royal realm' for revenue (I, iv, 45), as if the country were a private estate to be conveyed at will:

This blessed plot, this earth, this realm, this England,
This nurse, this teeming womb of royal kings,
Feared by their breed, and famous by their birth,
Renowned for their deeds as far from home
For Christian service and true chivalry
As is the sepulchre in stubborn Jewry
Of the world's ransom, blessed Mary's son;
This land of such dear souls, this dear dear land,
Dear for her reputation through the world,
Is now leased out – I die pronouncing it –
Like to a tenement or pelting farm.

(II, i, 50–9)

In Shakespearean tragedy, Franco Moretti observes, the monarch is not opposed to competitive individualism or the modern market, as critics presume; rather, the tragic situation arises from a paradox of absolutism that it is the monarch whose policies instigate exchange and make him the forerunner of modern selfhood; an insight confirmed by Tudor landowners who defended their capitalist inheritance strategies with reference to royal practice. As Gaunt predicts, the crisis of absolutism will come about because its 'sovereignty is a power that, having its origin in itself, is released from all control. The king is the only character free to choose and act in a modern sense. . . . Yet precisely what makes a sovereign – self-determination – also proclaims him a *tyrant.*'[74] In *Richard II*, therefore, it is the king whose alienation of Crown estates and imposition of 'blank charters' to subsidise his Irish war (I, iv, 48), unleashes the dynamic of individual property ownership that unravels his power as the paramount feudal lord, whose status is coextensive with the ground he rules. Nothing damaged English monarchy more, Perry Anderson maintains, than the Tudors' 'improvident sale of lands'; but by coincidence the drama traces these developments to the same era as those historians who see the reign of Richard as a threshold, when swathes of English realty first became vested in individual ownership.[75] For what was subversive about this king, the play reiterates, was his programme to break up the legal entity of the communal grid: to 'take from time / His charters, and his customary rights' (II, i, 195–6), by the capitalisation (or, as Gaunt analyses it, subinfeudation) of the 'blessed plot' of English land. So, the debacle significantly ensues not from Richard's favouritism, but from his violation of Bolingbroke's inheritance rights, when he determines to 'seize into our hands / His plate, his goods, his money and his lands' on the death of Gaunt (209–10). As the elder statesman, York, perceives, by expropriating his cousin's property Richard ruptures the very order of succession which makes him king; and the warning is couched in terminology which the historian J. H. Hexter believes, alludes to the common-law tenet (later confirmed in a 1603 case, *Darcy* v. *Allen*) that an Englishman's home is a castle no prerogative can breach:[76]

Seek you to seize and gripe into your hands
The royalties and rights of banish'd Herford? . . .
If you do wrongfully seize Herford's rights,
Call in the letters patent that he hath
By his attorneys-general to sue
His livery, and deny his off'red homage,
You pluck a thousand dangers on your head.

(II, i, 189–205)

Where Holinshed's Bolingbroke opposes corruption, Shakespeare's, Hexter points out, aims only to retrieve his 'rights and royalties' of tenure (ii, iii, 119). These are not modern ownership rights, moreover, since they depend on the offer of homage, the expensive formality by which Tudor heirs took possession of land held for them by the Crown.[77] The topicality emphasises the fact that it is Richard who thwarts law, and as Bolingbroke repeats, frustrates tenurial custom: 'I am denied to sue my livery here, / And yet my letters patent give me leave . . . / And therefore personally I lay my claim / To my inheritance of free descent' (128–35). Richard's conversion of *seisin* (occupancy) into absolute ownership of the land he contrives to 'seize' (ii, i, 160) puns, then, on the transformation of English real estate, as possession became nine parts of the law between 1400 and 1600. Elizabethan in his commercial attitude to lordship, Richard, as Gaunt foresees, will be reduced to a rentier himself when he sells the estates held in trust for his ward; for such a perversion of feudalism will limit his own right to life tenancy: 'Landlord of England art thou now, not king, / Thy state of law is bondslave to the law' (113–14). The exploitation of wardship that was such a windfall for the Tudors thus epitomises the commodification operating throughout the play: from the moment Richard sunders the unity of 'our state, our subjects, or our land' (i, iii, 190), the action has a market logic, as the 'sweet soil' of 'England's ground' (306) is alienated into the 'declining land' (ii, i, 240) of realty, and the lordship of a 'kingdom's earth' (i, iii, 125) falls 'to the base earth' of possession (ii, iv, 20). The King can hold such 'dear earth' in his hands (iii, ii, 6–24); but he can never redeem his 'famous land' (v, iii, 36) from mortgage; nor restore 'the King's name' once it is divided from 'fair King Richard's land' (iii, ii, 85; iii, 47). A play that expresses the same preoccupation with the inscription of the 'dust of England's ground' (ii, iii, 91) as Elizabethan cartography, culminates, therefore with the earth written over to be stripped of usufruct: a 'fearful land' (iii, ii, 110) of 'cursed earth' (iv, iv, 147) and blood-manured ground (iv, i, 137), whose ownership is individualised but denuded of communal substance:

Let's talk of graves, of worms, and epitaphs,
Make dust our paper, and with rainy eyes
Write sorrow on the bosom of the earth.
Let's choose executors and talk of wills.
And yet not so – for what can we bequeath
Save our deposed bodies to the ground?
Our lands, our lives, and all, are Bolingbroke's,
And nothing can we call our own but death;
And that small model of the barren earth
Which serves as paste and cover to our bones.
                                        (iii, ii, 145–54)

Richard II stages the breach of 'The fundamental principle of medieval inheritance: that land belonged to the whole family; every member had a claim to support from it, and responsibility for its management was one of stewardship, not ownership.'[78] So, Richard discovers that by dint of his own fiscal feudalism he must exchange a 'large kingdom for a little grave, / A little little grave', and be buried not in his ancestral chapel, but 'in the king's highway, / Some way of common trade'; like exiled Mowbray, who gives 'His body to the . . . earth' not of Norfolk, but of Venice (III, iii, 153–6; IV, i, 97–8). Private enterprise wins the free testation which goes with absolute possession in this History, but as Gaunt foresaw, such power degrades the immanent value of the 'dear' ground: 'England, bound in with the triumphant sea . . . is now bound in with shame, / With inky blots and rotten parchment bonds' (II, i, 61–4). So 'talk of wills' in *Richard II* articulates the same hostility to a free land market as in the Comedies; but with tragic awareness of the potential of the commercial owner to 'Write sorrow on the bosom of the earth' in deeds of sole entitlement. For unable 'to ear the land' with corn (III, ii, 212), Richard imposes his ownership like some engrosser, merely 'to make a dearth in this revolting land' (III, iii, 163); and this sensation of a Fall of 'the whole land' from an Edenic 'model' of a 'sea-walled garden' (III, iv, 42–3) to a 'model of barren earth' (III, ii, 153), registers an irreversible shift in Tudor England from the matrix of rights and duties to a legalism 'grav'd in the hollow ground' (140). If Richard can never 'rise up from the ground' once he sits to bequeath his body to the earth (v, ii, 116), his funereal posture suits a proprietary impulse that would leave its monuments in every church. For as 'landlord of England' he is like those 'lords of the soil' condemned as 'caterpillars' by William Harrison in his *Description of England* (1587) for 'driving tenants to lose their tenures' so as 'to bring all the wealth into their own hands'.[79] The irony, of course, is that by allowing the inheritance of his kith and kin to be 'all distrain'd and sold' (II, iii, 130), he puts his own heritage in 'broking pawn' (II, i, 293), and starts the transfer of title that leads to Bolingbroke's possession 'in reversion' (II, ii, 38): 'As were our England in reversion his' (I, iv, 35). By treating his patrimony as so much property, the last medieval monarch breaks the metaphysical bond of blood and soil, releasing English earth into that ceaseless circulation of ownership which was to be the first modern land market.

VI

The years '1575 to 1620 were the palmy days of profit', according to Keynes, when 'any level-headed person in England' disposed to make money could hardly help doing so: 'Shakespeare being eleven in 1575 . . . we were just in a position to afford him at the moment when he presented himself. Whether or not Pope was right that Shakespeare "For gain not glory winged his roving flight", his career chanced to fall at the date of dates.'[80] The evolution of Elizabethan inheritance law suggests that this coincidence was not merely adventitious, but that the 'buoyancy, exhilaration and freedom from economic cares felt by the governing class', in Keynes's bullish prospectus of English Renaissance society, were intimately connected, as Greenblatt divines, to 'the wellsprings of the Shakespearean conception of identity' and of Shakespearean art.[81] For the will to paternal power of Shakespeare's generation was grounded in a legal right to acquire property and determine its transmission which had not existed before and would never be so absolute again until the Wills Act of 1837. It was an authority that the dramatist exploited to the full when he revised his own will, which went to exceptional lengths not merely to break customs of partibility and conjugality, but to control the estate in perpetuity by granting all the donor's land in tail male so as to pre-empt any future division among daughters or wives. 'Few Elizabethan wills', Lewis reported, 'were so specific and insistent about this', and it was 'hard to cite a parallel' with the testator's determination to bind his descendants 'to a far generation', as Shakespeare bequeathed all his 'lands, tenements and hereditaments whatsoever' to his daughter Susanna, and 'to the first son of her body lawfully issuing and to the heirs male of the body of the said first son, and for default of such issue to the second son of her body lawfully issuing and to the heirs male of the said second son, and for default of such heirs to the third son . . .' and so *ad infinitum*.[82]

'Item: I give unto my wife my second best bed': it is in the context of the perpetuity devised by Shakespeare to secure a lineal rather than lateral settlement of his estate that this infamous interpolation can be read. Editors who follow Chambers in presuming that common law guaranteed a widow dower of one-third of her husband's estate have been overtaken by studies which detail the earthquake in inheritance strategy occurring between Shakespeare's courtship and his death, following the enactment of the Act of Wills to make bequest of dower 'a matter of personal volition'.[83] For the effect of the Act had been to shift priority from all customary obligations, which thereafter needed to be spelt out to be honoured, making widows 'dependent for provision on arrangements . . . agreed by male relatives rather than enjoying what had been theirs as

of right.'[84] In her study of the widow's share in Berkshire, Barbara Todd
confirms that freebench disappeared as customary tenure was converted
to freehold, and that even where it persisted as a custom of the manor it
prevailed only when it suited husbands to install wives as heads of families
in the hiatus between generations, and was otherwise 'adjusted or
ignored'.[85] In the Vale of Oxford the change to lineal transmission can be
dated to the 1580s, for after 1590 widows were denied right of dower, or
allowed it on strict condition they did not remarry. As Honigmann
deduces, there is every reason to think the same practice obtained in parts
of the Midlands such as Stratford, where Margaret Spufford reports that
'Wills usually provide for the widow with extreme care', and a testator
who wished to ensure customary rights for his spouse, such as
Shakespeare's own lawyer Francis Collins, expressly willed her entitlement.[86] In London, where custom did grant dower, the author had
already taken pains to debar his wife her interest in his property, suggesting
that his bequest of their bed was a caution that any rights of conjugality
would hinge on Raleigh's axiom: 'If thy wife love again let her not enjoy her
second love in the same bed wherein she loved thee.'[87]

While Chambers deplored the 'sheer nonsense' talked about Shakespeare's widow's lot,[88] research vindicates the belief that the terms of his
will single out the bed as a marker of the limit of his submission to custom.
So watertight are these conditions that their effect can only have been to
make Anne one of those widows 'compelled by circumstance . . . to
accept other or lesser provision' than their third.[89] For it was Susanna,
not, as custom dictated, her mother, who was made executrix of the will,
and who 'for better enabling her to perform' its provisions assumed total
direction of the estate, since 'the properties devised to her were about all
the poet owned in 1616.'[90] Of the three women entitled by custom to
equal divisions of his property, Shakespeare's chosen daughter alone was
willed his Stratford house of New Place (purchased in 1597), the family
home in Henley Street (inherited in 1601), 127 acres of land in Old
Stratford (acquired in 1602), and the Blackfriars Gatehouse in London
(bought in 1613). All this was entailed to Susanna and her heirs; in
defiance of spousal claims she was also to receive 'the rest of my goods,
chattels, leases, plate, jewels and household stuff', including tithes in
outlying Stratford (procured for thirty-one years in 1605 and realising £90
per year by 1626), and whatever shares in the Globe and Blackfriars
theatres her father retained. There was one property, however, which
Shakespeare could not devolve to Susanna absolutely, and the mode of its
settlement offers a key to his entire strategy. Copyhold tenancy remained
subject to custom; title to a quarter-acre purchased in 1602 opposite New
Place would thus descend according to the custom of the manor of
Rowington to which it belonged, allowing Anne freebench and Judith

interest in a third. In the event the widow never applied for her entitlement, and Judith's paltry legacy of £150 was made conditional on surrendering 'All her estate and rights' in the copyhold to her sister.[91] By these means Shakespeare made sure that through his will the customs of Old England were more honoured in the breach than the observance.

Though Bacon complained that Tudor legislation left 'the inheritances of the realm tossed upon a sea of legal uncertainty',[92] by relieving testators from customary obligations the Act of Wills in fact gave them the power of which Shakespeare availed himself, to disinherit kindred at discretion. Objections to entails had been voiced on behalf of younger sons by Thomas Starkey and other moralists from the 1530s; and, as Louis Montrose has recounted in an essay on *As You Like It*, 'the place of brother' in Elizabethan society was one fraught with acrimony because fathers used wills to reinforce primogeniture or discriminate between children; as Orlando is disadvantaged when he is 'left by testament' a 'poor allotery' of £250 (I, i, 1–25; 72–4).[93] Joan Thirsk concludes that it was in the gentry that disinheritance was most feared, since there 'the hardships were most keenly felt';[94] and Macfarlane comments that while disinheritance for misbehaviour was inconceivable in peasant society, where 'there were no written wills', since inheritance 'was a matter of splitting up a communal asset', after 1540 the English middle class took a radically different direction in depriving children of their birthright:

> Swinburne, the leading authority on testamentary law, nowhere mentions childrens' right to the real estate of their parents . . . [and] even the eldest son had nothing except at the wish of his father . . . As Chamberlayne put it in the seventeenth century, 'Fathers may give all their estates un-entailed from their own children, and to any one child'.[95]

Parson Josselin was typical of his peers in his constant threats to disinherit his heirs;[96] and Susan Amussen infers that though actual disinheritance remained rare, wills were effective 'as a method of discipline' in the gentry, because 'freedom of testators was real'.[97] 'Witnesses often described how testators saddened by children's absence finally cut them out of their wills';[98] but above all fathers exerted their new prerogative like Capulet, to intimidate children into marriages arranged for them:

> Hang thee young baggage, disobedient wretch!
> I tell thee what – get thee to church a Thursday
> Or never after look me in the face . . .
> Graze where you will, you shall not house with me.
> Look to't, think on't, I do not use to jest.

Thursday is near. Lay hand on heart. Advise.
And you be mine I'll give you to my friend;
And you be not, hang! Beg! Starve! Die in the streets!
For by my soul I'll ne'er acknowledge thee,
Nor what is mine shall never do thee good.
                    (*Romeo and Juliet*, III, v, 160–94)

All the contradictions within Renaissance subjectivity between paternal freedom and filial obedience, a father's right to create identity and a child's duty to acquiesce in one imposed, collide in the threats of disinheritance which are spring-boards for so many Shakespearean plots. That this confrontation is most acute over the choice of marriage partner for a daughter emphasises how it arises from those contrary drives to possess property and control its fate which are specific to the restricted family between 1560 and 1640, when paternal power had to be asserted in the face of the child's emerging right of veto. If he is driven to make what he admits is 'a desperate tender' of Juliet to Paris, on the assumption that rather than be cut out of his will 'she will be rul'd / In all respects by me' (III, iv, 12–16), Capulet is enough of 'a careful father' (III, v, 107) to admit that his 'will to her consent is but a part' as 'within her scope of choice / Lies my consent and fair according voice' (I, ii, 17–19). His prevarication reflects a phase in the history of English marriage when, as Keith Wrightson observes, 'the key to the situation was less parental arrangement than the seizing of the initiative by . . . testators attaching strings to bequests made to unmarried children'.[99] Threat of disinheritance thus became a means whereby fathers could 'nominate a particular husband' or barter their children 'like cattle';[100] and the warning of the Old Athenian of *Timon of Athens* who swears that if his daughter marries the youth who haunts his house by night, he will choose his 'heir from forth the beggars of the world / And dispossess her all', suggests how much money talked to money in a will. For where Lysander had won the heiress of another Old Athenian, Egeus, with moonlight serenades, like Romeo or Valentine, in the later play Lucilius weds only because Timon offers 'To build his fortune' (I, i, 120–46). A father's 'ancient privilege', the *patria potestas*, to condemn a headstrong child to death,[101] is less potent, we see, than his threat to change his will (*A Midsummer Night's Dream*, I, i, 41).

In her review of the relations between father and bride in Shakespeare, Lynda Boose has stressed that in spite of the paternal preference for Paris over Romeo or Thurio over Valentine, both comedies and tragedies consistently slight the father's choice.[102] Equally notable, however, is the increasing penalty exacted for this reverse in plots that parallel the evolving model of the family as a stronghold of the father.

If the rough justice that exalts community over paternity in the early comedies is incompatible with the Puritan doctrine which sanctified the family as a political unit 'under the government of one', as Tennenhouse maintains,[103] the Jacobean Shakespeare exposes the domestic fault lines elided by Jonson. The break with the jocular customs of Elizabethan comedy can be followed, in fact, from *The Merchant of Venice*, where earnestness about property and patrimony explains the ostracism meted out to Jessica, who 'steals from the wealthy Jew', her father (v, i, 15), only to find, as Carol Leventen notices, that she is shunned by her in-laws not merely as Lorenzo's 'infidel' (iii, ii, 218), but 'every father's nightmare'.[104] For what weighs against Shylock's daughter in the moral economy of this play is her dissipation of his wealth, which tarnishes her most when she sells his ring, her mother's heirloom, 'for a monkey' (iii, i, 109). If Jessica is treated more ominously, then, than earlier escapees from parental domination, such as Silvia, this is because theft and extravagance place her beyond the pale of her father. She is the precursor, indeed, of Desdemona, that other Venetian heiress who breaks a father's heart by marrying an 'extravagant . . . stranger' (*Othello*, i, i, 136), and whom Brabantio bestows on Othello with sour recrimination: 'I here do give thee that, with all my heart, / Which, but thou hast already, With all my heart, / I would keep from thee' (i, iii, 193–5). These daughters never obtain even the bleak 'jointure' of posthumous reconciliation that Juliet receives (*Romeo and Juliet*, v, iii, 296), since elopement severs them for ever from their fathers:

> Poor Desdemona! I am glad thy father's dead.
> Thy match was mortal to him, and pure grief
> Shore his old thread in twain.
>   (*Othello*, v, ii, 205–7)

The test of every inheritance system, Jack Goody comments, comes at the point of family fission, since 'splitting property is also a manner of splitting people', which 'creates a particular constellation of ties and cleavages between parents and children, husband and wife, sibling and sibling'.[105] Yet such scission put the enclosed family of Shakespearean England under intense strain, exposing children to blackmail and leading to anomalies like that which gave a husband's father control of a bride's dowry. A 'divided duty', Desdemona terms her double-bind, when, forced to opt between father and husband, she wounds Brabantio with an avowal that she owes the Moor 'so much duty as my mother show'd / To you, preferring you before her father' (i, iii, 181–9). Lawyers such as Bacon fretted over such illogicality, warning that if landowners devised wills to monopolise children's loyalty, the clash between fathers and heirs would 'engender discord in families and draw the kindred into faction', so the ironic effect of entails would be to make 'children disobedient and parents unnatural'.[106] Yet until the strict settlement of the later seventeenth century, when 'A daughter was at last in a position to defy her parents without depriving herself of her portion',[107] fathers were able to do what Brabantio wishes he had, and 'hang clogs' on their heirs with wills (198). So, for every Jessica in Shakespearean drama, there is a Portia, whose name announces how she is 'richly left' because she accepts that 'I may neither choose who I would, nor refuse who I dislike, so is the will of a living daughter curb'd by the will of a dead father' (*The Merchant of Venice*, I, i, 161; I, ii, 22–5). Sacrificing the volitional to the legal sense of 'will', Portia is a fantasy, in Leventen's words, of an 'ideally compliant daughter',[108] who, rather than follow her desire, is 'scanted', as she tells her Moor, by the ghostly paternalism that speaks through the testamentary riddles in the caskets:

> In terms of choice I am not solely led
> By nice direction of a maiden's eyes:
> Besides, the lott'ry of my destiny
> Bars me the right of voluntary choosing:
> But if my father had not scanted me,
> And hedg'd me by his wit to yield myself
> His wife, who wins me by that means I told you,
> Your self (renowned prince) then stood as fair
> As any comer I have look'd on yet
> For my affection.
>
> (II, i, 13–21)

After about 1640, Stone shows, opinion shifted towards the view held by Evelyn, that fathers should match-make for daughters but 'by no means constrain them to take husbands they cannot love';[109] yet if the 'divided duty' of the English heiress was specific to the heyday of free testation, the distinction between the two types of daughter, Jessica and Portia, had lasting implications. For as debate on the pittance awarded to widows, younger sons and disendowered daughters as a result of primogeniture raged in the 1630s,[110] the beneficiaries were founding the Restoration aristocracy. At this crossroads in family history, then, when those whose rights had been extinguished were 'reduced to a landless proletariat or ejected like lemmings from the community',[111] heiresses like Portia had cause to curtsy to paternalism and avoid the fate of the spinster Mariana in *Measure for Measure*, jilted when she loses 'the portion and sinew of her fortune, her marriage dowry' (III, i, 221). As

Leventen senses, by becoming antecedent to the action it controls, paternal authority acquires a 'power beyond the grave' in later Shakespeare,[112] to which dutiful daughters such as Helena submit, acceding to a dowry 'will'd . . . / In heedfull'st reservation' so as to inherit a 'legacy sanctified / By the luckiest stars' (*All's Well That Ends Well*, i, iii, 219–220; 240–1). In these plays, where there is 'no legacy so rich as honesty' (iii, v, 12), and wise women know that 'chastity's the jewel of our house, / Bequeath'd down from many ancestors' (iv, ii, 46–7), those who obey a father's will without querying its terms reap 'the inheritance of it . . . and a perpetual succession for it perpetually' (iv, iii, 270–2). So while Jessica sells her father's ring, Portia and Helena ensure the transmission of jewels that are 'Conferr'd by testament to th'sequent issue' (v, iii, 196); thereby validating a Shakespearean preference that would, in life, install Susanna and her husband not only as sole inheritors of her father, but also his executors, charged with assigning to Judith her resounding portion of nothing.

VII

On 1 April 1600 the Queen's Master of Harriers and former Warden of the Fleet Prison, Brian Annesley, made his will at his manor of Lee in Lewisham, on the Kent outskirts of London; a place where Elizabethan inheritance law was, perhaps, most contradictory. For alone of English counties, Kent had preserved its customary inheritance grid intact, and in an age when title to property in the capital changed freely, land in the so-called 'garden of England' continued to be subject to the antique custom of gavelkind, which ordained equal division between male and female heirs, widow's dower of half a husband's estate, and communal use-rights. 'This shire', reported William Lambarde in *A Perambulation of Kent* (1576), 'even to this day enjoyeth the custom of give-all-kin descent';[113] and by the Tudor century gavelkind had evolved into what Peter Clark calls 'the Kentish custom *par excellence*': a system Harrison claimed dated from before the Romans, and that John Selden admired in his *English Janus* (1610) as the birthright of the county.[114] For though the Kentish gentry procured exemption with dozens of private Acts of Parliament,[115] partibility remained, as Thirsk and others explain, dominant in a region characterised by abundant common pasture and a prosperous yeomanry.[116] Into this ancient network of entitlement and obligation, however, Annesley had intruded, like the Sidneys at Penshurst, with a career typical of the stealth of City finance under the camouflage of neo-chivalry. With proceeds from the Fleet Wardenship he leased in 1571 from his Tyrrel in-laws, interest on collection of fines, and profit from his monopoly on the import of steel and export of rabbit skins,[117] this son of Henry viii's vintner bought a chain of manors in the hop-producing Weald, which made him, by the turn of the century, one of the richest landowners on the Dover road from London. Two of his daughters married Kent notables, but the youngest, named Cordelia, was unmarried when he willed her almost his entire property.

The Annesley case is well known as a striking analogue of *King Lear*;[118] but its relevance to a play which, as Jonathan Dollimore writes, is 'above all about power, property and inheritance',[119] is the ferocity with which the feud sparked by the old man's will highlights struggle over patriarchy and patrimony. For Annesley, far from being the middle manager depicted in Geoffrey Bullough's *Narrative and Dramatic Sources of Shakespeare*,[120] stood near the apex of England's penal apparatus, and his governorship, notable for 'insurrections, slaughter of servants and setting of prisoners in irons and stocks', epitomised the Tudor commercialisation of office.[121] This Warden was, indeed, an expert on prison economics, who in 1598 sat alongside Bacon and the Lord Chief Justice on a commission that fixed fees for inmates after protests about cruelty and misappropriation: £2 per week for a 'poor man' rising to £25 for a 'Duke or Duchess'. Annesley, who opined that 'prisoners ought to lie two in a bed', knew how to price every human need, and perfected an operation which reputedly raised him £4,000 a year 'thorough extortion'. His deputy had been murdered in a prison riot; but the Warden, who counted the seadog Hawkins a friend, braved even a spell of detention for malpractice in one of his own cells, and retired as a Gentleman Pensioner of the Queen, to hunt and farm his large acres.[122] His will was apparently a strategy to settle this estate pre-mortem, since by 1603, when he became senile, his favourite daughter was firmly in charge of 'the government of him and his affairs'. Such arrangements were traditional, reserving for a father the status of a 'sojourner' in the house, and obliging his inheritors to remain 'serviceable' to him with board and lodging.[123] By making Cordelia his sole executrix, Annesley was thus providing for 'the time of his infirmity';[124] but when he also settled on her four farms in Surrey and Sussex, and numerous manors, houses and woods in Kent, her co-heiresses, Grace and Christian, left one property each, had cause to resent the inequality and breach of custom.

The customary death, the Annesley case demonstrates, was a process that included what Nigel Llewellyn describes as 'an important prepara-tory and liminal phase which sometimes reached well before the moment of death itself';[125] yet it also shows how this rite of passage was circumscribed by will, when with the aid of manuals to assist testators to shape their thoughts, such as Swinburne's *Treatise*, William West's

Symbolaeographia (1590), and Thomas Wentworth's *Office and Duty of Executors* (1641), subjects of the post-Reformation state 'prepared their worldy selves' for the total transmission of ownership demanded by law.[126] Where 'old folks at home', in Spufford's phrase, had rested secure, 'sitting in the chimney corner and grateful for house-room provided by their inheritors',[127] transfer of title now left them vulnerable to disputes, such as that which arose when those declared legally defunct recovered to find themselves barred from property because 'the death process, once started, could not be reversed'.[128] Wills were deemed the terminal acts of civil life, so until 1837 could not, for example, devise realty acquired after they had been signed; and the requirement that testators be of 'perfect health and memory' was added to the Act of Wills in 1543 in recognition that finality made this last performance of Renaissance selfhood the one of greatest moment.[129] The sanity of testators became an issue, therefore, from the day Parliament gave them the right to set custom aside; and so it was that during the four years between the signing of his will and his death in July 1604, Annesley existed in legal limbo, neither medieval sojourner nor modern lunatic, as his daughters fought for the inheritance over his living body and extinguished mind. The crisis came in autumn 1603, when the eldest daughter Grace and her husband Sir John Wildgoose sought to reassert gavelkind by having Annesley declared insane and his will void. Editors surmise that this filial impiety is cryptically reported in *King Lear*,[130] where the Fool warns that 'Winter's not gone yet, if the wild-geese fly that way', since:

> Fathers that wear rags
> Do make their children blind,
> But fathers that bear bags
> Do make their children kind.
> (II, iv, 45–9)

'Thou shalt have as many dolours for thy daughters as thou canst tell in a year', the Fool predicts, when Lear discovers the collusion between Goneril and Regan (52–3); and in the Annesley story it seems that Christian likewise hid behind her sister, and that her silence was due to the ruin of her husband, Lord Sandys, for his part in Essex's rising, rather than scruple.[131] In *King Lear* it is the flight of 'wild-geese' which prompts Lear's hysteria; a cue that enhances Kenneth Muir's supposition that it was in fact the scandal which suggested the King's madness, as this appears in no earlier version of the story.[132] For from the start, it is 'the infirmity of his age' clouding Lear's 'division of the kingdom' which dominates the play, and which locates the action within an age of free

testation, the only era when 'the unruly waywardness that infirm and
choleric years bring with them' would affect devolution of property (i, i,
2; 292–8). Certainly, the episode that occurred in October 1603, when
Wildgoose and his lawyers 'repaired unto the house of Brian Annesley',
offered a salutary illustration of the importance now attaching to the
mentality of the testator; for as the son-in-law relayed to Cecil, the
Secretary of State:

> Finding him fallen into such imperfection and distemperature of mind
> and memory as we thought him altogether unfit to govern himself or
> his estate, we endeavoured to take a perfect inventory of such goods
> and chattels as he possessed. . . . But Mrs. Cordell refuseth to suffer
> any to be taken, until she hath had conference with her friends.[133]

Cordelia's resistance was perhaps stiffened by Sir William Harvey, a
neighbour and overseer of the will, whom she would marry in 1607 after
the death of his wife, the Dowager Countess of Southampton, mother of
Shakespeare's patron. For when Cecil ordered a posse of Kent
dignitaries to Lee to 'seal up chests and trunks of evidence and other
things of value', pending 'determination' of the 'emulation between the
gentlewomen' over custody of the father, Cordelia retorted in the spirit of
her namesake:

> I most humbly thank you for the letters it hath pleased you to direct
> unto gentlemen of worship in these parts, requesting them to take into
> their custodies the person and estate of my poor aged and daily dying
> father. But that course so honourable for all parties, intended by your
> Lordship, will by no means satisfy Sir John Wildgoose, unless he may
> have him begged a Lunatic, whose many years service to our late
> Sovereign Mistress and native country deserved a better agnomina-
> tion, than at his last gasp to be recorded and registered a Lunatic. Yet
> find I no means to avoid so great an infamy and endless blemish to our
> posterity, unless it shall please your Lordship, if he must be accompted
> a Lunatic, to bestow him upon Sir James Croft, who out of the love he
> bare to him in his more happier days, and for the good he wishes to us
> his children, is contented to undergo the care of him and his estate,
> without intendment to make one penny benefit to himself by any goods
> of his, or ought that may descend to us his children, as also to prevent
> any record of Lunacy that may be procured hereafter.[134]

Commentators attribute Cordelia's defence of her father's sanity to
kind concern about 'what might happen to him if he were taken away
from her';[135] but, as her praise of Croft reveals, at stake was the fortune

she stood to gain in spite of gavelkind. *Kindness*, in this *cause célèbre*, was not exclusive to one party, but was an imperative of kin as much as kindliness; and when the old man died his eldest daughter disputed his will precisely on the ground that insanity had led him to omit his obligation to his kindred. The case was heard before the prerogative court of Canterbury, where customary rules notionally prevailed, and where, therefore, as Holdsworth shows, the question whether 'rights of children should fetter a father's rights of testation' had become a jurisdictional test; but it was decided, as Cordelia had guessed, in her favour, because, however mad her father's raving on Blackheath, he was never 'registered a Lunatic'.[136] In contrast to the Palavicino case, the Annesley imbroglio thus ended with total victory for testation over custom, and Cordelia obtained the fortune which enabled her to erect the memorial to her benefactor (and her own munificence) that stood until 1841 in Lee churchyard, on the high road out of London: 'Cordell, the youngest daughter, at her own proper cost and charges, in testimony of her dutiful love unto her father and mother caused this monument to be erected for the perpetual memory of their names against the ingrateful nature of oblivious time.'[137] Cordelia was buried beside her father in 1636, but had three daughters by Harvey, who continued to flout the county law (despite taking his title, Lord Harvey of Kidbrooke, from Annesley land in Kent) by again making the youngest, Elizabeth, sole heiress when he died in 1642. This time, however, there was no contest over the preference of a single daughter above her sisters; for by the 1640s the freedom of a landowner to write his will was crushing partibility even in Kent, the heartland of ancient British kindness.[138]

The Annesley case signalled the early modern attack on the last redoubt of the pre-Conquest property system. What happened on the Dover Road as a result was a reversal, indeed, of a fabled battle won in 1067, according to Lambarde, when 'Duke William marched his army toward Dover . . . which so enraged the common people that each man bare a green bough over his head, in such sort as the Duke, thinking it had been some miraculous wood that moved towards him . . . yielded to their request, and by this means he received Dover Castle, and they only of all England obtained for ever their accustomed privileges.'[139] In the Shakespearean era this identity of community and land was prised apart by market forces which had free testation at their cutting edge; but though gavelkind disintegrated, it 'continued to contribute to the intense corporate feeling of Kentish families, and to their patriarchalism'.[140] It was a Kent squire, Sir Robert Filmer, whose *Patriarcha* (1642) promulgated the doctrine that 'the king, as father over many families, extends his care to feed, clothe, and defend the whole commonwealth'; a notion that made sense, his editor remarks, in a county where 'the family head governed not only wife and children but brothers, sisters, grandchildren, nephews, cousins, servants, and tenants'.[141] For when a Kentish patriarch of the seventeenth century referred to his 'family', he still thought 'not only of his relatives but his servants and labourers', an attitude that came naturally in an area where partibility meant that 'not infrequently servants were their master's kinsmen'.[142] So it is hardly surprising that many of the scholars who formed the Elizabethan Society of Antiquaries hailed from Kent; nor that they founded their con-stitutionalism on the axiom 'that the old law was land law and any change in landholding must bring about a general change in law'.[143] Though 'misliked' by King James,[144] Anglo-Saxonists such as Lambarde and John Spelman took courage from the saw that 'the bodies of Kentishmen be free', so it was 'sufficient, for a man to avoid bondage, to say his father was born in Kent', since, 'Gavelkind prevailing everywhere, everyone is a freeholder'.[145] Thus, William Somner's *Treatise of Gavelkind* (1647) 'touched a vital issue' in Stuart politics, and Coke even printed the Kentish Customal alongside Magna Carta.[146] By the light of such reverence for partibility, when the Warden of the Fleet made his will, he truly bequeathed his countrymen an inheritance of manacles and irons.

VIII

'The yeomanry is nowhere more free and jolly than in this shire', wrote Lambarde, 'for besides that the communality of Kent was never vanquished by the Conqueror, it is agreed by all that there were never any bondmen or villains in Kent.'[147] This was the legend of local exceptionalism that made gavelkind such a precious relic for Elizabethan codifiers of England's 'ancient constitution', such as William Camden, who idealised the custom as an unbroken link with the primitive communism that supposedly preceded the 'Norman yoke'.[148] As late as 1778 the county historian, Edward Hasted, attributed the independent spirit of Kentish society to the equal dispersal of land;[149] and it is a myth which haunts Shakespeare's ancient British tragedy through the blunt 'dialect' of Kent, whose double persona of earl and yeoman voices the egalitarian legacy, but whose vow to drive Goneril's 'silly ducking' goose, Osric, 'cackling home to Camelot', lands him not on old 'Sarum plain' but in the stocks (II, ii, 106, 80, 100). 'Who put my man i'th'stocks? . . . Who stock'd my servant?" (II, iv, 180–5): Lear's question rumbles throughout a scene in which the allusion to the Annesley affair frames his realisation that to 'sojourn' with his children he must 'pension beg / To keep base life afoot' (216–17). The answer, of course, is given by the Kentish man himself, whose first words to the 'patron' he says he has 'Lov'd as my father' (I, i, 140), warn of the dire consequences of an unequal distribution of property. It is Kent's objection that 'Thy youngest daughter does not love thee least' which exposes the 'hideous rashness' of Lear's final division of the kingdom (150–1); but the outrage he expresses had simmered from the very start, when he had remarked the uncertainty whether, of the sons-in-law, 'the King had more affected the Duke of Albany than Cornwall', in 'choice of either's moiety'. For it is Lear's 'darker purpose' to make choice of 'curiosity' between 'equals' (1–6; 36) which will set the man of Kent in 'cruel garters' (II, iv, 7).

Historians have traced the effects of partibility among Kentish yeomen, and they find that since 'all the males of a family owned some land', yet 'none owned enough to provide his sole means of subsistence', agriculture continued to be cooperative in the seventeenth century, with the result that by 1660 incomes of £1,000 were 'not rare' and Fuller could report how 'the yeomen in this county bear away the bell for wealth from all in England.'[150] There was more economic sense to gavelkind than a capitalist rationale would suggest; and in *King Lear* the 'service' Kent pays his old 'master' is indeed to 'deliver a plain message bluntly. . . . Not to love a woman for singing, nor . . . to dote on her for anything' in devolving his estate (I, iv, 23–38). The servant knows the rule that 'if a man die seised of an estate, his sons shall have equal portions, and if he have no sons, then ought it to be divided equally amongst his daughters',[151] is an insurance policy in a system of open kin and collective welfare. And since equal succession was a condition of the communality on which a right to sojourn would depend, Lear seems to accept that his plan 'To shake all cares and business from our age, / Conferring them on younger strengths, while we / Unburthen'd crawl toward death', relies on a fair division of his 'daughters' several dowers, that future strife / May be prevented now' (38–44). So, far from being a subversive tactic, as many critics assume,[152] nor 'the ideal state of affairs, codified in English Land Law,' as Lisa Jardine asserts,[153] Lear's declaration that 'we have divided / In three our kingdom' (I, i, 36–7), is sanctioned by the *Lex Kantiae* that Jacobean lawyers associated with King Canute, who decreed 'his heirs should divide his lands among them' equally.[154] Had he remained true to custom, indeed, and split his 'Interest of territory' exactly into three (49), Lear might have enjoyed the retirement the Saxons called *flaetfoering*: 'spending days with each heir in proportion to the quantity of property received', in a family circle where 'equality of rights meant equality of obligations'.[155]

'Ourself, by monthly course, / With reservation of an hundred knights / By you to be sustain'd, shall our abode / Make with you by due turn' (131–4): Lear's proposed itinerary as a 'sojourner' in the mansions of his daughters (II, i, 102; II, iv, 201), a return of the 'amorous sojourn' in his

court of his four actual and prospective sons-in-law (I, i, 46), is justified by
that custodial sense of property which the translators of the King James
Bible must have had in mind when they used the legal term to convey the
transient occupancy God granted the children of Israel: 'The land shall
not be sold: for ye are strangers and sojourners with me' (Leviticus, xxv,
23); and their concurrence: 'we are strangers and sojourners before thee,
as were all our fathers, our days on earth are as a shadow, and there is
none abiding' (1 Chronicles, xxix, 15). In some villages this corporate
mentality required that even gifts made by the deceased were returned at
his death to the communal 'hotch-pot';[156] and if Lear has no abiding place
after retirement, by custom his pre-mortem settlement should have
guaranteed his heirs would remain 'serviceable' to him; as the gentry of
Kent kept open house for their relatives and 'liveried family of lesser kin,
maids, messengers, cooks and riders' right up to the Civil War. As Clark
comments, the hospitality of the Kentish household, 'thrown open to
tenants, neighbours and relatives to feast and revel', was not for show,
but arose from the recognition of collective title that also explains why a
gentry which was loath to impose the punitive vagrancy acts 'bore a
greater weight of social responsibility than in any other county'. For while
bequests to charity and wider kin were elsewhere declining, in Kent
'benefactions increased steadily during the Elizabethan era', making it
'the most generous of all English counties'.[157] Evidently, the attitude of
give-all-kind ran deep in customary society, and *King Lear* is percipient,
therefore, when it shows that equal inheritance was the precondition of
patriarchalism. So, when Lear declares his will, an entire social order is
called in question:

> We have this hour a constant will to publish
> Our daughters' several dowers, that future strife
> May be prevented now . . .
>   Tell me, my daughters,
> (Since now we will divest us both of rule,
> Interest of territory, cares of state)
> Which of you shall we say doth love us most?
> That we our largest bounty may extend
> Where nature doth with merit challenge.
>   (I, i, 42–52)

With this inducement to his co-heiresses to deny 'equalities' (5), and
tender for 'a third more opulent than your sisters' (85), Lear jolts the
ancient rite of succession abruptly into the capitalist land market, with its
unfettered testation. For like Annesley, Lear has acquired a discretionary power unknown to any Celtic patriarch, to break the parcenary law

and exert 'curiosity' on behalf of his chosen daughter. He behaves, that is to say, not as a feudal monarch, but as a modern landowner, and his strategy in fact recalls that of Henry VIII, who seized the chance of the 1540 Act of Wills to determine his own succession and designate the junior, Suffolk branch of his kin over the senior, Scottish branch as his residual legatees, thereby initiating the notion that sovereignty derived 'not from divine sanction but property ownership, with the king as little more than a particularly privileged landlord'.[158] As Tennenhouse remarks, by treating the crown as property in this way, Henry set paternal power over the corporate rules of genealogy invoked by the Stuarts, whose heiress, Mary, Queen of Scots, thus came to personify the tragedy of the extended family.[159] Lear's folkloric love-test is a game, then, with unique resonance for Shakespeare's generation of testators, the first and last to wield the privilege which the King now flexes. Technically a nun-cupative (or oral) testament, Lear's declaration is as binding as the undertaking made in 1604 by Shakespeare's own landlord, Christopher Mountjoy, to settle £260 on his daughter and her husband, to which the dramatist would testify in court some eight years' later.[160] But if Lear's demand for a 'deed of love' (70) transposes royalty into the bourgeois world of London comedy, his map signals the historic dimensions of such a scheme to reify collective title into private ownership, which Thompson views as a manoeuvre 'to secure for the individual family . . . the claims on the resources of future society':[161] So where city comedy disqualifies the testator, *King Lear* is a tragedy precisely because it credits his determination:

> Of all these bounds, even from this line to this,
> With shadowy forests and with champains rich'd,
> With plenteous rivers and wide-skirted meads,
> We make thee lady: to thine and Albany's issues
> Be this perpetual. . . .
> To thee and thine, hereditary ever,
> Remain this ample third of our fair kingdom,
> No less in space, validity, and pleasure,
> Than that conferr'd on Goneril. Now, our joy,
> Although our last, and least . . .
>   what can you say to draw
> A third more opulent than your sisters?
>   (62–85)

King Lear marks a fatal shift in family relations by staging a scenario from which Elizabethan drama flinched, of an omnipotent father who successfully exerts his will over kindred and community, initially in

favour and then against his favourite. This is a drama, then, which is
indeed mapped precisely in time and place, on the edge of customary
culture, at a point when the liberty won by Tudor testators impacts on
the partibility descending, so common lawyers argued, from time
immemorial. Druidic Britain and Jacobean London converge, as they did
for the Annesleys on Dover Road, in a contest for property and power
juxtaposing antiquarianism with topicality, and opposing Romans,
Saxons, Celts and Normans in the historiographical style of Bacon or
Coke. For like Stuart jurisprudence, *King Lear* is an amalgam of
historical strata, in which the archaic 'association of community with
equality runs against the lineage system of Normandy', and the 'Saxon
laws favouring equal division between sons and daughters' are trampled
by the 'formidable figure, dear to Roman jurists, of a father supreme over
all'.[162] Surveys show that this seismic contradiction fissured Western
Europe;[163] and in the tragedy the legal ground is shifting beneath the
characters, as it was in England, as their culture slides from partibility to
testation. The avalanche is detected first by Edmund, Gloucester's
bastard son and the inheritor with most to gain or lose. His customary
status, Kent assures him, is that of a welcome scion of the family, whom
kin may 'blush to acknowledge', yet 'must love' (I, i, 10; 30); but he
instantly senses that the 'curiosity' of Lear's will shatters such traditions
of consanguinity. Though his father publicly reiterates that his legitimate
brother, Edgar, 'by order of law, some year elder . . . is no dearer' in his
'account', and that partibility will 'be acknowleged' (18–23), Edmund
grasps that in Lear's Albion the native custom of give-all-kind has
become infected by primogeniture and preference, the 'curiosity' of
continental nations:

> Wherefore should I
> Stand in the plague of custom, and permit
> The curiosity of nations to deprive me,
> For that I am some twelve or fourteen moonshines
> Lag of a brother? Why bastard? Wherefore base?
> When my dimensions are as well compact,
> My mind as generous, and my shape as true,
> As honest madam's issue? Why brand they us
> With base? with baseness? bastardy? base, base?
>   (I, ii, 2–10)

It was William Empson who pointed out that in both texts the spelling
of this soliloquy slips as Edmund rails against the decline in his status from
a high-born 'bastard' of the Middle Ages to a common 'basetard' of the
seventeenth century;[164] and this reading is strengthened by studies which

suggest that the harsher stigma attached to illicit sexuality and the 'sharp peak in incidence of bastardy between 1591 and 1610', can be seen as expressions of the legal move to restrict the ownership of land to the legitimate.[165] 'Fine word, "legitimate"!', Edmund considers (18); and the novelty of the classification is startling for a caste habituated, as are Gloucester and Kent, to the open family with its permeable definition of kin. By 1590, however, the seigneurial right of a father to 'make his unlawful issue capable of whatsoever he doth bequeath', was confined, according to Swinburne, to the monarch;[166] and the tradition of partibility with equal shares for bastards which survived until 1704 in Ireland provoked outrage from imperialists like Sir John Davies, who thought the 'customs of tanistry and gavelkind unreasonable and absurd'.[167] By the time of *King Lear*, therefore, entails and primogeniture were bringing to an end 'the golden age' of the European bastard, in J. P. Cooper's phrase, as those now branded illegitimate became casualties 'of the process of restricting the numbers of families and kin'.[168] Far from being a 'New Man' of the Renaissance, Edmund's conservatism becomes clear in the context of Lear's display of parental power. Though Gloucester vows he 'would unstate' himself to promote him (96), and undertakes to 'work the means' to make him 'capable' of inheriting (II, i, 82–4), the publication of Lear's will teaches this bastard that customs of share-alike are done, and that only by legally displacing his brother as sole heir will he obtain his due portion. For though just fifteen years separate this text from *King John*, in that time a family revolution has degraded the figure of the high-born bastard from a folk hero to a landless villain:

> Well, then,
> Legitimate Edgar, I must have your land:
> Our father's love is to the bastard Edmund
> As to th'legitimate.
>
> (I, ii, 16–18)

Shakespeare's tragedy of will power starts from the situation where the Annesley case was brought to a judicial end, with the enforcement of a father's right to choose his heir and diminish the entitlement of the remainder of his family. We do not know whether the chronic penury of Sir John and Lady Wildgoose was relieved by Cordelia Harvey's beneficence, nor if she helped Lord and Lady Sandys pay the fine of £5,000 he incurred in the Essex treason;[169] true to the folktale, when the Jacobean Cinderella married her prince, the ugly sisters sank from the story. But in the sequel that Shakespeare added to the Princess Mouseskin/

Cinderella narrative the unrelenting focus is on the consequences of the lucky sibling's transformation, which begin, as Edmund realises, with disinheritance of the most remote, and end with dispossession of the nearest. For like those treatises on the laws of succession which poured from the presses of London and Paris during the Renaissance, and that consisted of 'a series of questions about primogeniture in practice: who is the eldest son? – who is the eldest twin? – should adopted sons succeed? – should bastards?',[170] Shakespeare's plot follows a pitiless calculus from the moment Lear proposes to favour his youngest child, as one relationship after another is sheared from the contracting family. Lear's frantic bidding with his daughters to spare fifty or twenty-five of his 'hundred knights and squires' calibrates this 'shedding by the elite of outer layers of familial ties', as the new 'inward-looking and private aristocratic family' came to view the feudal household as 'more like a tavern or a brothel', in Goneril's words, 'Than a grac'd palace' (i, iv, 240–3); but in this play the 'narrowing of concern to the interests of the nuclear core' that Stone recounts, does not only sear patriarchal bonds with kindred, cousins, clients and retainers, but cuts to the quick of even the emerging domesticated unit.[171] Once unleashed by the King, the unravelling of patriarchy does not cease until it has exhausted the 'sequent effects' of an entire catalogue of familial and political exclusions:

> Love cools, friendship falls off, brothers divide: in cities, mutinies; in countries, discord; in palaces, treason; and the bond crack'd 'twixt son and father.
>
> (i, ii, 103–6)

Gloucester's prognosis, so often universalised by critics, is in fact a prediction of the impending fragmentation of the late medieval extended family, from the perspective of the Elizabethan patriarch unwittingly responsible. For the action of Shakespeare's play is predicated on an insight that patriarchy and paternalism are so incompatible that the ascendency of the father must be at the expense of open lineage. This is the message Cordelia drives home to Lear when she rehearses the 'divided duty' of the early modern heiress in response to testamentary blackmail. Her averral that 'when I shall wed, / That lord whose hand must take my plight shall carry / Half my love with him, half my care and duty' (i, i, 99–101), reiterates the stance of Desdemona, but with a more acute embarrassment that the monopoly of affective bonds by the head of the household 'frees the nuclear family from interference by kin, especially the wife's kin'. Cordelia's disappointment of her father belongs to a historic phase, then, when 'two overlapping family types coexist among upper and middle ranks of society, one slowly but imperfectly replacing the other';[172] and she perceives that the internal contradictions of patriarchy are such that the more her father asserts his prerogative, the sooner the bond will indeed crack between the generations: 'Sure I shall never marry like my sisters, / To love my father all' (102–3). Realising the fears of Bacon and others, Lear will eject himself from hearth and home when his plan to coerce his children with his testament realigns his family not, as he intends, under his own authority, but in atomised and self-sufficient units, of the type France is happy to establish with Cordelia (255–60). The irony of the King's disinheritance of his daughter, therefore, is that it will be such arbitrariness on the part of the Elizabethan testator, vested with absolute power to prefer or dispossess, that will erase his own claim to see his 'children kind' (ii, iv, 49):

> Here I disclaim all my paternal care,
> Propinquity and property of blood,
> And as a stranger to my heart and me
> Hold thee from this for ever. The barbarous Scythian,
> Or he that makes his generation messes
> To gorge his appetite, shall to my bosom
> Be as well neighbour'd, pitied, and reliev'd,
> As thou my sometime daughter.
>
> (i, i, 112–19)

Lear's delusion, like Brian Annesley's, is to presume that his right to sojourn with his children can be reconciled with his 'darker purpose' to devolve his property at will: that the old patriarchal customs can survive the advent of a tyrannical paternalism. Taking up the family drama from the verdict in favour of Cordell Harvey, what the play instead projects is property transmission as it would actually evolve during the seventeenth century, when, in Stone's analysis, paternal power had to accommodate itself to affective individualism, with its restoration of mutual rights and obligations. For the rigour with which Cordelia asserts that she loves her father 'According to my bond; no more nor less' (92), will resound in the contractual doctrine of utilitarians such as Locke, whose critique of patriarchy and concept of marriage as a companionate bond likewise supposed the 'common interest and property' declared by France: 'Thy dowerless daughter, King, thrown to my chance, / Is Queen of us, of ours, and our fair France' (255–6). Such would be the reciprocity of the strict settlement, which healed the rift between generations by providing that 'the powers of the current owner were again reduced to those of a trustee who willed away his rights before marriage';[173] and in *King Lear* this reconciliation is glimpsed with the reunion of 'the old kind King' (iii, i, 28) and his 'kind and dear Princess' (IV, vii, 29) on the eve of battle. In Cordelia's camp it does seem that 'The Gods reward' an ideal of 'kindness' (III, vi, 5), which has nothing to do with 'what kin thou and thy daughters are' (I, iv, 79), but all to do with the imperative that 'from . . . cold'st neglect . . . love should kindle to inflam'd respect' (I, i, 253–4). Yet though Lear at last discovers 'a daughter kind and comfortable' (I, iv, 303) to use him 'kindly' (I, v, 14), and a place at her fireside, their quarters are too exposed to kindle domesticity, even for 'so kind a father' as he becomes (35). Their ensuing rout suggests, indeed, how hard it was in 1605 to imagine kindling flames of loving care in face of the storm raised by the 'great abatement of kindness' (I, iv, 58) in a society so drastically 'unkinn'd' (I, i, 258).

   'I am a very foolish fond old man, / Fourscore and upward, not an hour more or less' (IV, vii, 60): Lear's self-knowledge, with its echo of Cordelia's bond, reduces the patriarch to the impotence of those 'old men childish' denied the right to make a will by Tudor law, along with 'children, mad folks, idiots, bondslaves, villains, felons, heretics, the oulawed, the deaf and dumb, and the blind'.[174] Thus the categories that defined the modern property-owning subject, eliminating so many of the characters, finally disqualify the King himself; for though Albany makes one vain attempt to restore 'this old Majesty' to 'absolute power', the text cannot envisage the restitution of those 'rights' which Lear's own will had breached (v, iii, 297–9). An 'old kind father', by his own account, 'whose heart gave all' (III, iv, 20), he had used his testamentary power, in the Fool's view, like that cockney Caligula who 'in pure kindness to his horse, butter'd his hay' (II, iv, 122). Lear's lunacy, by this light, was that of a generation of fathers who imposed their will upon their heirs; and there is justice, therefore, that the fall of the King should take him on progress into Kent, down the Dover Road to the site of Britain's refusal of Roman inheritance. The riddle, 'Wherefore to Dover?' that teases three acts (III, vii, 50), is solved when Lear capers before the French army, as the men of Kent had done in these very fields 'near Dover' (Stage Direction IV, iii), 'fantastically dressed' (IV, vi, 80) in their legendary garlands of resistance. Where the Normans had spared the morris dancers, however, and acknowledged gavelkind, Cordelia's troops are powerless to save the King or reinstate the 'dear rights' he gave 'his dog-hearted daughters' (IV, iii, 44). The moving wood which symbolised the archaic identity of blood and soil, and deceived the tyrant in *Macbeth*, is now a 'side-piercing sight' (IV, vi, 85) of one lone pensioner 'Crown'd with rank fumiter and furrow-weeds' (IV, iv, 3). For in *King Lear* the green man brings no miracle, and the fathers who crawl or 'smell [the] way to Dover' (III, vii, 91) for 'welcome and protection' (III, vi, 90), discover when they arrive that they have signed away the land of give-all-kind. Gloucester's suicide contract with the 'beggar' who is his son figures the 'unkindness' of all their schemes to bribe their heirs to be both 'more than kin, and less than kind' (*Hamlet*, I, ii, 65):

> Dost thou know Dover? . . .
> There is a cliff, whose high and bending head
> Looks fearfully in the confined deep;
> Bring me but to the very brim of it,
> And I'll repair the misery thou dost bear
> With something rich.
>
> (IV, i, 70–6)

IX

Shakespeare's will was proved on 22 June 1616, not in Worcester, as was usual for Stratford, but in the same Archbishop's Prerogative Court that settled the Annesley estate, and which by this time had declined from a safeguard of custom to a rubber-stamp in complex probate cases of the presumed 'last, sincere wishes of the deceased'.[175] Unless a will was contested, executors paid a fee to be excused attendance when the Court sat in the council chamber below St Paul's Cathedral, but Shakespeare's was sufficiently unconventional, it seems, for its beneficiaries to appear in person.[176] Twenty years earlier the mangled drafting, cancellation and ambiguity regarding the widow's and younger daughter's bequests might have invalidated the document John and Susanna Hall presented, but in 1594 parliamentary pressure had persuaded Whitgift to relax the rules in favour of testators, and a 1604 code further prevented 'too rigid a definition of what constituted a valid will or of the way it must be written'.[177] Even in canon law the Shakespearean text enjoyed an opportune reception, and the dramatist's last directive received the benefit of doubt which momentarily slanted interpretation towards fathers. The paternal power entrenched in Shakespeare's signature would be demonstrated in the coming years in two contrasting narratives, as the Halls prospered through their inheritance and the Quineys subsided into impecuniosity. While Judith and Thomas eked a living from an inn and tobacco shop aptly called The Cage, Susanna and her physician husband led the community from New Place, entertaining a circle which eventually extended to Queen Henrietta. Susanna fortified the entail with further legal action in 1639, when her sister's 'small expectation' was eclipsed by the death of two young sons; and in 1647, when she blocked the intention of her son-in-law, Thomas Nash, to will the estate to his cousin.[178] She died in 1649, 'Wise' and 'Witty above her sex', according to her epitaph, but above all faithful to the letter of her father.

If the tragic cultural implications of testamentary power were unfolded in *King Lear*, the seventeenth-century success-story of Shakespeare's chosen line of heirs might be said to vindicate the optimistic scenario awarded his romantic heroines. In the last resort, the writer's exercise of Jacobean will power was a generic matter that consigned his daughters to the different destinies of comedy and tragedy. For a critic such as Ann Jennalie Cook, happy to abstract from the plays a pluralistic marriage-guidance manual, regardless of dramatic chronology, it is Shakespeare's 'quicksilver elusiveness' and temperamental aversion to the 'orthodoxies of his time', which explains why 'his only consistency' in treating the subject of family relations 'is his inconsistency' and 'free play'.[179] Such a reading is a neat legitimation, we may infer, of post-modern American marriage customs, which veer from 'a nuptial Eucharist' to 'guru-decreed . . . communes with shared partners',[180] but gains little purchase on the actual social process that drove the drama and determined that dramaturgical decisions were neither random nor without historical significance. For a Cultural Materialist criticism, it is the fact that Shakespearean drama was geared to transformations within English society, and was partly instrumental in organising those changes, which compels attention, not the hypothesis that the plays constitute or illuminate some self-enclosed or arbitrary sign-system. Not all the options of early modern domestic life were equally available to all women and men at the same time, and the fates of Judith and Susanna Shakespeare in seventeenth-century Stratford were specific corollaries to the economy of exclusion which operated on their father's stage. Will power, the plays themselves constantly remind us, was intended to generate effects that would last for centuries, and the intentionality invested in the Renaissance author, and programmed into the drama, was a ghostly interference in the lives of all who would succeed. Far from transcendence, Shakespeare's script was subdued to what it worked in, 'like the dyer's hand' (*Sonnet 111*, 7).

In the event, two generations were required to cleanse the bourgeois stain from Shakespeare's intentions, until both his writing and inheritance were immersed in England's ruling culture. John Hall refused a knighthood in 1626; but the project of *All's Well That Ends Well* – where the King yokes the lordly Bertram with Helena, 'A poor physicians daughter', since 'Virtue and she / Is her own dower' (II, iii, 123; 143–4) – would be concluded by the Doctor's only child Elizabeth, when she took as her second husband a minor aristocrat, John Bernard, created a baronet by Charles II. Though Shakespeare had written that 'property by what it is should go, / Not by the title' (130–1), it was through the 'honour and wealth' he devised for her, like Helena's mentor (144), that his grandchild ended her days as Lady Bernard of Abington Manor, Northamptonshire. Thus, the masterplan of the comedies was completed under the terms of the author's will, and his heiress justified not only the arrivism of a Viola or Helena, but the alliance of money with land, town with country, and middle class with nobility, towards which all his hypergamous plots aspire. Susanna survived to witness the realisation of her father's testamentary fantasies on 5 June 1649, in Billesley Church, near Stratford, when a union with a proper landlord purged the family of the taint of the innkeeper's disgrace. Like a true Shakespearean denouement, all the forces of segregation at work for half a century came to a climax in this solemnisation, when the Halls were finally distanced from the elderly couple who kept the alehouse in the former gaol. In a town that judged those 'given to fornications and to taverns' (*Merry Wives of Windsor*, v, v, 158) with increasing severity, Quiney, who had been prosecuted for disorderly drinking and swearing, had fathered yet another bastard, and been insolvent since 1630,[181] personified the 'uncleanliness' that 'the better sort' thought too heinous for 'such toyish censures as pinning in a sheet'.[182] Instead, the shame he shared with his wife was now a foil to the brilliance of their niece.

Shakespeare's favourite daughter, who had sued for slander in 1613 over rumours that she had contracted gonorrhoea from one Rafe Smith,[183] had followed the Puritan precepts Dr Hall preached,[184] and could rest assured her family had plucked those 'weeds' of incontinence excoriated in her father's late plays (*The Tempest*, iv, i, 21). But it seems less likely that this midsummer marriage was celebrated with 'nightly revels and new jollity' (*Midsummer Night's Dream*, v, i, 363), than that feasting was postponed 'Expecting absent friends' (*All's Well That Ends Well*, ii, iii, 183). For if 'funeral baked meats' did not quite 'furnish forth the marriage tables', as Nash had been dead for two years (*Hamlet* i, ii, 179–80), the match was still untimely: four months after the execution of the King, a month before Susanna died, and in the bride's forty-second year. At journey's end, it was too late for the Bernards to secure those 'eternal lines to time' Shakespeare had begun (*Sonnet 18*, 12), and the promise of 'quiet days, fair issue and long life' (*The Tempest*, iv, i, 24) he had sought to entail was blighted at the moment of fulfilment. The testator had succeeded in his plan 'to establish his family and estate in the descent of the male line of gentry';[185] but by willing all his property to one daughter and neglecting the other he had plotted a sequel in which his first male heir, vainly named Shakespeare Quiney, died in 1617 aged six months, while the last of his line, Lady Bernard, lived on in childless plenty. Lear's gift was sealed with Lear's curse of sterility; and though Her Ladyship still had hopes in 1652, when a new settlement vested the

estate in her 'issue' or nominees, there would be no more heirs of
Shakespeare. When she died in 1670, soon followed by Sir John, Henley
Street reverted to the descendants of Shakespeare's sister, but the rest of
the inheritance was sold for £1,060 by a 'loving kinsman, Edward Bagley'.
Long research has unearthed no relationship between the Bard and this
'citizen of London', who may thus be said to embody the ironic revenge of
kinship on the father.[186]

A Bagley succeeded Shakespeare, and New Place, the property on
which the dramatist had thought to stamp his name for all time slipped
back into the possession of his social models, the Cloptons who had lost
the house and ground in 1563, yet lorded over Stratford since the Middle
Ages. As Thompson comments of all such plotlines, we commence by
examining the inheritance systems of particular families: 'but, over time,
family fortunes rise and fall; what is inherited is property itself . . . and
the beneficiary may be not any descendant of that particular family, but
the historical descendant of the social class to which that family
belonged.'[187] The Shakespeares finally earned acceptance by the
Midlands gentry, on this view, when their inheritance was shorn of
customary entanglement and its custodial female presence, and transmitted unconditionally into the monetary grid of the Restoration
establishment. While the living kin of the poet took the well-trodden
genealogical path 'from clogs to clogs in three generations',[188] the land he
had transposed from a lateral to a lineal system of entitlement, wrenching
it from collective into private ownership, was henceforth inherited not as
part of 'a communal equilibrium but the property of particular men and of
a particular social group'.[189] Riding the crest of the Elizabethan wave of
free testation between 1564 and 1616, Shakespeare's historic function,
according to Thompson's analysis, was thus to authorise the individual
and class possession of rights which had hitherto been transmitted
according to the rules of partibility and conjugality; and the will which
ended up as the prize exhibit of the Public Records Office, may indeed in
that sense be interpreted as a paradigm of Shakespearean poetry, which
likewise works to impress the identity of the single writer onto a nexus of
genres, narratives, symbols, tropes and signs that had formerly been
common heritage. Authority and authorship coincide in this document as
they had not done before Shakespeare's lifetime, and would never do so
possessively again.

To write so as to possess meaning not only in the present but for all
time: the hermeneutics of a will provide a fine instance, Derrida has
observed, of the metaphysics of presence and mystique of speech. Thus,
ostensibly dictated for transcription by a lawyer such as Francis Collins,
the formula prescribed in West's *Symbolaeographia*, that 'I, William
Shakespeare of Stratford-upon-Avon . . . gentleman, in perfect health

and memory, God be praised, do make and ordain this my last will and testament', presupposes a commitment on the part of the dying man to stand by his words and the obligations they entail. But it is the nature of such communications that they hold good in contexts where intention no longer applies, while the signature conferring their authenticity is 'the sign of the simultaneous presence and absence of a living hand', that 'implies by definition the actual or empirical nonpresence of the signer'.[190] Of no act is the illusion of self-presence so factitious, then, as of a will, which even as it records 'a constant will to publish', presumes the death of the author and the fact 'For the written to be written, it must continue to "act" even after what is called the author no longer answers for what he has written.' All writing is 'orphaned and separated at birth from its father' in contemporary theory; but nowhere is the 'kinship between writing and death'[191] more patent than in a will. So it is not surprising that the emancipation of an Englishman's right to alienate his patrimony should coincide with the free hand given authorial intention, nor that devolution of property should furnish a juridical analogy for the transmission of intellectual property. English copywright dates from 1709, but that imposture of presence-in-absence so vital to 'Renaissance self-fashioning', its perjured 'subjectivity effect' or 'ghost-writing', was already grounded in the testator's plan to stretch his rights of ownership in perpetuity.[192] For 'What You Will' in Shakespearean writing is a testamentary afterlife nothing short of 'That Eternity Promised By Our Ever-Living Poet' (*Sonnets*: Dedication):

Make but my name thy love, and love that still,
And then thou lov'st me for my name is *Will*
(*Sonnet 136*, 13–14)

In a repeat of Lear's excessive demand on his patrimony, Shakespeare's italicised signature registers an exclusive right of possession which undermines the very universality asserted. But then, the author who signs his playtext with the 'fair name' William, is the same landowner, 'so so' rich, we infer (*As You Like It*, v, i, 20–6), who is both an inheritor and a disinheritor, entailing as his own the real estate that depends for its transmission on his community. So, if will power is the spur to Shakespeare's claims on posterity, it carries the 'irresolvable contradiction' which disturbs all ideas of literary property, according to Peggy Kamuf, and that arises from the authorial wish to transfer the patrimonial right of ownership of a work and to retain in it the moral right of personality.[193] This is the 'double motion' of every text that 'is stated to be *by* someone', in the analysis of Paul de Man, and that thereby insists 'on the subject, on the proper name, on birth, eros and death', while being 'equally eager to escape the coercions of this system'. For though Milton might doubt whether Shakespeare, with his 'livelong monument', has need of 'such weak witness of thy name' as an epitaph, de Man considers that since 'any book with a title page is, to some extent, autobiographical', the very foundation of modern authorship is the figure of *prosopopoeia*, the fiction of the dead or absent who strike us dumb precisely because they 'speak in *their own* persons'. De Man dates this 'claim for restoration in the face of death', with its concomitant deprivation of the living, to 'before the eighteenth century'; and Kamuf to between 1500 and 1800.[194] In fact, what Thomas Docherty terms 'The incipient totalitarianism of a (vocal) authority model', premised on 'the authorial ownership and control of meaning', can be traced much more exactly, he shows, to the 'struggle for self-determination' in Tudor England, and to a state system which for some hundred years keyed identity to social space and individuation to the ownership or transmission of property:[195]

So thou, being rich in *Will*, add to thy *Will*
One will of mine to make thy large *Will* more.
(*Sonnet 135*, 13–14)

If identity is place in the Renaissance, it is because for this society it is property which makes the person. 'What does it matter who is speaking?': the challenge posed by Beckett on behalf of modernism is answered in the Renaissance text, Foucault points out, with a concreteness that explodes the deconstructionist proposition that criticism is purely 'a question of creating a space into which the writing subject disappears', of reducing 'the mark of the writer to nothing more than the singularity of his absence' and his role to that of 'the dead man in the game of writing'. For it is the specificity of the endowment of literature with a personal name and intention that alerts us to the contingency of the 'author function', and which demands that instead of merely perpetuating the immortality of Literature by the erasure of authorial presence, 'We now ask of each poetic or fictional text: From where does it come, who wrote it, when, under what circumstances, or beginning with what design?' Where deconstructionism would 'transpose the empirical characteristics of an author into transcendental anonymity', Foucault argues, criticism must follow Derrida's own historicist hints and address not simply the modern 'death of the author', but 'the space left empty by the disappearance'.[196] So, whether or not the 'Eternity Promised By Our Ever-Living Poet' in the *Sonnets* was dedicated to the Earl of Southampton, Sir William (and Lady Cordelia) Harvey, or simply 'William Himself', as commentators variously suggest, what matters is the Shakespearean conflation of the

authority of God with the divinity of the author.[197] As Joel Fineman
observed, the signature of 'Will' that authorises the *Sonnets*, or the name
of 'William' that personalises the plays, puts an end to the literary epoch
of patronage and inaugurates an era when the 'puffed-up' poetic person
'dares to speak its love' for itself; and when, therefore, the chiasmus of
propriety and property – the claim on what is proper to the self not only
'for an Age, but for all time' – marks the 'passage of person *into*
language'. By this reading, 'the Shakespearean testament of 'Will'' is the
'linguistic desire' for presence and plenitude which is 'the foundational,
constitutive, but heretofore unspeakable paradox' that rives the heart of
modern selfhood:[198]

> *Will* will fulfill the treasure of thy love,
> I fill it full with wills, and my love one.
>   *(Sonnet 136*, 5–6)

If Shakespeare's signature demonstrates that 'William is become a
good scholar' (*2 Henry IV*, III, ii, 8), this is because he has studied to hold
up his head and 'Answer [his] master' back; like his namesake at grammar
school, the William who is sexually precocious enough to know 'what is a
stone' and who proves 'He is a better scholar' than supposed by
memorising his Latin 'genitive case plural' (*The Merry Wives of Windsor*,
IV, i, 14–72); or like the William who bluntly refuses to take King
Henry's shilling (*Henry V*, IV, viii, 70). These signifiers of personal and
family mobility, which efface the vicissitudes of the Warwickshire
William whose wages were once stopped by his employers, 'about the
sack he lost . . . at Hinckley fair' (*2 Henry IV*, v, i, 22), are pointers to the
process of re-presentation through which the author inserts his personality, as Fineman theorises, into the linguistic system. But that so
many cluster around the time in 1597 when the local prodigal returned to
purchase the largest house in Stratford testifies to the material factors that
conditioned the desire to 'make a name' in early modern culture, and
which Montaigne also had in mind when he compared the prize-winning
student who 'hides all the help he gets, and shows only what he has made
of it', to those speculators 'who show off the buildings they purchase, not
what they inherit from others.'[199] Historians have long understood that
'The idea that an author or artist could claim any property rights in his
works arose only with the wish to be original, an "uomo singolare" or
"unico"', but, as David Quint adds, the pedagogical project to compose
out of inherited literary models a new and autonomous self was the goal
of 'a larger bourgeois individualism', and the humanist writer was an
archetype of the 'self-made man of capitalist venture'.[200] The deconstructionist myth of Shakespearean literature as a linguistic funfair where

'words go on holiday',[201] obscures the reality in which the extravaganza was grounded.

Shakespeare's name was an inheritance that language and his father gave him, yet it was a resource that had to be legitimated to be transmitted to his offspring in a capitalist society. Antony Burgess hears it as an unruly hymn to the male libido;[202] but the documents tell a tale of stabilisation, in which the eighty-three phonetic spellings of the surname are disciplined to the uniformity with which the poet was registered in London in papers drafted by his cousin, the town clerk, Thomas Greene, and in signatures to his will.[203] With or without an 'e', the 'Shakspeare' whose patronymic is replicated on the monuments of his wife, daughter and son-in-law, was sufficiently in command of his name and work to protect them with every means available in the first age of mechanical reproduction. So, when his publisher padded the 1612 reprint of *The Passionate Pilgrim* with two poems by Thomas Heywood, Shakespeare made it known he was 'much offended with Mr. Jaggard that (altogether unknown to him) presumed to make so bold with his name', and the volume was rapidly withdrawn. Shakespeare's defence of authors' rights gives the lie to the Derridean fancy that his text proliferated in a polysemous carnival. For as Foucault objects, the author, far from being a 'genius' from whom meaning surges, is the cultural figure who 'limits, excludes, and, in short, impedes' proliferation.[204] 'A constant will to publish' was a counterpart of will power for the generation who, born into the world of weak fathers and strong kin recorded in Elizabethan comedy, lived to rule the paternal roost projected in the Jacobean Shakespeare. Identity was to be guarded by outlawing every illegitimate representation in this society, and a corrupt text prospered no better than the family bastard. Shakespeare's regard for his will was therefore nothing if not prophylactic; and if Tudor spellings of his name signified the plurality of voices consolidated, according to Foucault, into the author function, its patenting as a Jacobean 'brand name' was the pre-emptive signal of a new era, when authorship would cease to be a function of censorship and become 'the principle of thrift' in a system not of promiscuous dissemination, but of textual exchange and mart.[205] If 'Property was thus appalled', in London and Stratford, that Shakestaff's younger 'self was not the same' (*The Phoenix and the Turtle*, 37–8), it ensured that when he signed his will, Shakespeare had been unified in a 'concordant one' (46):

Let no unkind, no fair beseechers kill;
Think all but one, and me in that one *Will*.
(*Sonnet 135*, 13–14)

'This was, indeed, the death of a self', wrote Ariès of the Renaissance deathbed, 'with its lone biography and lone capital of works and prayers'. The scene of death was analogous to that of authorship, then, because their final hour was one of the few occasions when pre-modern individuals grasped 'the right to make arrangements for one's soul, body and property' that defines a modern subject. Yet such self-assertion was conditional on its negation, and however personalised, its rites of law and writing remained enmeshed in the archaic customs of oral culture.[206] This was the paradox from which Donne wrung pathos, striving in poems like 'The will' to give up the ghost and 'undo / The world by dying' (46–7). For all his histrionics, he insisted his legacies were worthless, and that his intent was to be *undone* and 'end, where I begun'.[207] But if Donne payed lip-service to an older collect, it is 'the living will of the dead' which Greenblatt divines in the textual traces of 'the supremely gifted alumnus of Stratford Grammar School'. For a New Historicist, 'the "life" that Shakespeare's works seem to possess long after the death of the author' emanates from 'the social energy encoded in them'; yet he cannot resist the Romantic vision of 'an originary moment, in which the master hand shapes the social energy into the sublime aesthetic object'.[208] It has been the argument of this essay that this solicitation by a ghostly hand which seems to create *ex nihilo* (the literary appropriation of the noumenal 'I am'), is a mimetic concomitant of the paternalistic order that prevailed in England between 1560 and 1640 and sought to perpetuate itself through a tyrannical testation. History and language conspired to make the name of Will, who left no son and gave so little of himself away, the signifier of signifiers, where all the desire, sexuality, power and volition of a body, family, state and society coincided in one 'Will in overplus' (*Sonnet 135*, 2). Yet his heirs bent his will to theirs, as Antony rewrote Caesar's (*Julius Caesar*, IV, i); and though the author cursed those who move his bones, his successors must likewise dare to exhume the writing subject if they are to escape his interdiction of history. For it is only by breaking the sign of Shakespeare's will that I am free to sign myself a will son.

Notes

Preface

1. W. Rees-Mogg, 'Bright lights shine out from the gloom', *The Independent*, 30 November, 1992, p. 17.
2. V. N. Voloshinov, *Marxism and the Philosophy of Language*, trans. L. Matejka and I. Titunik, (Cambridge, Mass., 1986), p. 41.

Introduction: The return of the author

1. S. Schoenbaum, *William Shakespeare: A documentary life* (Oxford, 1975), p. 250.
2. *Ibid.*, p. 256.
3. *Ibid.*, p. 250.
4. P. Ariès, *The Hour of Our Death*, trans. H. Weaver (Harmondsworth, 1983), p. 61.
5. *The Athenaeum*, 9 July 1881; E. K. Chambers, *William Shakespeare: A study of facts and problems*, 2 vols (Oxford, 1930), Vol. 2, p. 181.
6. M. Foucault, 'What is an author?', trans. J. V. Harrari, in P. Rabinow (ed.), *The Foucault Reader: An introduction to Foucault's thought* (Harmondsworth, 1986), pp. 106–7.
7. U. Eco, *Travels in Hyperreality*, trans. W. Weaver (London, 1987), p. 93 and *passim*.
8. D. Horne, *The Great Museum: The re-presentation of history* (London, 1984), pp. 122–3.
9. G. Holderness, 'Bardolatry: or, The cultural materialist's guide to Stratford-upon-Avon', in G. Holderness (ed.), *The Shakespeare Myth* (Manchester, 1988), pp. 8–9.
10. W. Benjamin, 'The work of art in the age of mechanical reproduction', in *Illuminations*, ed. H. Arendt, trans. H. Zohn (London, 1973), pp. 224–5.
11. T. Eagleton, 'Afterword', in Holderness (ed.), *op. cit.* (1988), p. 205.
12. T. Eagleton, *William Shakespeare* (Oxford, 1986), pp. 12–13.
13. Eagleton, in Holderness (ed.), *op. cit.* (1988), p. 206.
14. S. During, *Foucault and Literature: Towards a genealogy of writing* (London, 1992), pp. 218 and 221.
15. M. Garber, *Shakespeare's Ghost Writers: Literature as uncanny causality* (London, 1987), pp. 6–10.
16. R. W. Emerson, 'Shakespeare, or, The poet', *Representative Men in Ralph Waldo Emerson: Essays and letters* (New York, 1983), p. 720; W.

Whitman, 'November Thoughts', in *Complete Poetry and Prose of Walt Whitman, as Prepared by Him for the Death Bed Edition* (New York, 1948), p. 404; H. James, 'The birthplace', in *The Jolly Corner and other Tales*, ed. R. Gard (Harmondsworth, 1990), p. 138. All quoted in Garber, *op. cit.*, pp. 8–10.

17. M. Twain, 'Is Shakespeare dead?' in *What is Man? And Other Essays* (New York, 1917), p. 372. Quoted in Garber, *op. cit.*, p. 10.
18. James, *op. cit.*, p. 139.
19. C. Dickens, Letter to William Sandys, 13 June 1847, in *Complete Writings of Charles Dickens*, ed. 'by his sister-in-law' (Boston, Mass., 1923), p. 206. Quoted in Garber, *op. cit.*, pp. 10–11.
20. M. Arnold, 'Shakespeare,' in *The Poems of Matthew Arnold*, ed. K. Allott (London, 1965), pp. 48–9.
21. J. Keats, letters to George and Thomas Keats and George and Georgiana Keats, 21 December 1817, and 14 February and 3 May 1819, in *The Selected Letters of John Keats*, ed. L. Trilling (Garden City, N. J. , 1956), pp. 103 and 229. Garber, *op. cit.*, p. 11.
22. H. Grady, *The Modernist Shakespeare: Critical texts in a material world* (Oxford, 1991).
23. T. Eagleton, *Literary Theory: An introduction* (Oxford, 1983), pp. 110 and 141.
24. James, *op. cit.*, p. 139; P. Brook, 'Shakespeare is a piece of coal', in *The Shifting Point: Forty years of theatrical exploration, 1946–1987* (London, 1988): 'History is a way of looking at things that doesn't interest me very much. Shakespeare doesn't belong to the past. It's like coal'; G. Craig, *Henry Irving* (London, 1930), pp. 241–7.
25. G. Wilson Knight, *The Wheel of Fire: Interpretation of Shakespeare's Tragedy* (revised edn, London, 1949), p. 3; *Shakespearean Production* (London, 1964), pp. 288–9.
26. C. G. Jung, *The Spirit in Man, Art and Literature*, trans., R. F. Hall (London, 1966), p. 96; T. S. Eliot, Introduction to Knight, *op. cit.* (1949), pp. xxi.
27. E. M. W. Tillyard, *The Elizabethan World Picture* (London, 1943); *Shakespeare's History Plays* (London, 1944), p. 21. For comments, see Grady, *op. cit.*, pp. 158–89.
28. T. S. Eliot, *Four Quartets* (London, 1944), 'East Coker', 39–40; 'Little Gidding', 234–5.
29. *Ibid.*, 'Little Gidding', 233–7.
30. A. Sinfield, 'Royal Shakespeare: theatre and the making of ideology', in J. Dollimore and A. Sinfield (eds), *Political Shakespeare: New essays in Cultural Materialism* (Manchester, 1985), pp. 161–2. See also J. Dollimore and A. Sinfield, 'History and ideology: The instance of *Henry v*,' in J. Drakakis (ed.), *Alternative Shakespeares* (London, 1985), pp. 208–9.
31. J. Kott, *Shakespeare Our Contemporary*, trans. B. Taborski (London, 1965), p. 39.
32. *Ibid.*, pp. 31 and 59.

33. P. Brook, Introduction, *ibid.*, p. xi.
34. Dollimore and Sinfield, *op. cit.* (1985), p. 208.
35. Terry Hands interviewed in Holderness, *op. cit.* (1988), p. 123; Peter Brook in R. Berry, *On Directing Shakespeare* (London, 1977), p. 129.
36. Kott, *op. cit.*, p. 30; Brook, *ibid.*, p. x.
37. *Ibid.*, pp. x and 30.
38. *Ibid.*, p. 7.
39. S. Greenblatt, 'Towards a poetics of culture', in *Learning to Curse: Essays in early modern culture* (London, 1990), pp. 153–4: originally published in *Southern Review*, 20 (1987), pp. 3–15.
40. Greenblatt, 'Resonance and wonder', *op. cit.* (1990), p. 181.
41. Greenblatt, 'Towards a poetics of culture', *ibid.*, p. 158.
42. Greenblatt, 'The circulation of social energy', in *Shakespearean Negotiations* (Oxford, 1988), pp. 5–7; 'Towards a poetics of culture', *op. cit.* (1990), p. 154.
43. H. Felperin, *The Uses of the Canon: Elizabethan literature and contemporary theory* (Oxford, 1990), p. 152.
44. Greenblatt, 'The circulation of social energy', *op. cit.*, 1988, p. 7.
45. Foucault, *op. cit.*, p. 104.
46. C. Geertz, *Negara: The theatre state in nineteenth-century Bali* (Princeton, N.J., 1980), p. 136.
47. L. Montrose, 'Renaissance studies and the subject of history', *English Literary Renaissance*, 16 (1986), p. 6.
48. Geertz, *op. cit.*, *passim*. For the influence of this anthropological model of society, see Greenblatt's seminal New Historicist essay, 'Invisible bullets: Renaissance authority and its subversion, *Henry iv and Henry v*,' in R. Wilson and R. Dutton (eds), *New Historicism and Renaissance Drama* (London, 1992), p. 98: 'Theatricality is not set over against power but is one of power's essential modes.'
49. Foucault, *op. cit.*, pp. 103–4.
50. For Greenblatt on 'unique, inexhaustible, and supremely powerful works of art', see *op. cit.* (1988), pp. 2 and 4. R. Darnton, *The Great Cat Massacre and Other Episodes in French Cultural History* (Harmondsworth, 1984); N. Z. Davis, *Fiction in the Archives: Pardon tales and their tellers in sixteenth-century France* (Stanford, Calif., 1987). Davis defines her project as the attempt to describe 'how sixteenth-century people told stories . . . and how through narrative they made sense of the unexpected and built coherence into experience' (p. 4). For an important survey of the textualist turn in 1980s historiography, see L. Hunt, 'Introduction: History, culture, and text', in L. Hunt (ed.), *The New Cultural History* (Berkeley, Calif. and London, 1989), pp. 1–22.
51. R. Barthes, 'The discourse of history', trans. R. Howard, in *The Rustle of Language* (Oxford, 1986), p. 140.
52. G. Siegel, 'History, historicism, and the social logic of the text in the Middle Ages', *Speculum: A journal of medieval studies*, 65 (1990), p. 74.
53. For a graphic account of the battle over Revisionism in seventeenth-century historiography, see L. Stone, 'The revolution over the

revolution', *The New York Review of Books*, 11 June 1992, pp. 47–52.
54. *Ibid.*, p. 48.
55. C. Russell, *The Times Literary Supplement*, 9 January 1987, p. 16.
56. Davis, *op. cit.*; Greenblatt, *op. cit.* (1990): see note 39.
57. For a blistering polemical response to this hypertextualist mania, see C. Norris, *Uncritical Theory: Postmodernism, intellectuals and the Gulf War* (London, 1992).
58. R. Cust, 'Revising the high politics of Stuart England', *Journal of British Studies*, 30 (1991), p. 325; A. Hughes, *Politics, Society and Civil War in Warwickshire, 1620–1660* (Cambridge, 1987). See also R. Cust, *The Forced Loan and English Politics, 1626–28* (Oxford, 1987); and R. Cust and A. Hughes (eds), *Conflict in Early Stuart England: Studies in religion and politics, 1603–42* (London, 1989).
59. F. R. Leavis, 'Joyce and the revolution of the word', in *Scrutiny*, 2, 2 (September 1933), p. 200.
60. S. S. Prawer, *Karl Marx and World Literature* (Oxford, 1976), p. 327; see also, pp. 11, 63, 85 and 352.
61. *Ibid.*, pp. 78–9.
62. Eleanor Marx, quoted in *ibid.*, p. 356.
63. Garber, *op. cit.*, pp. 56–8; Benjamin, 'Theses on the philosophy of history,' *op. cit.*, p. 263.
64. J. Bate, *Shakespearean Constitutions: Politics, theatre, criticism, 1730–1830* (Oxford, 1989); Felperin, *op. cit.*, p. 156.
65. Quoted in Prawer, p. 120.
66. *Ibid.*, p. 310.
67. C. Hill, 'Society and Andrew Marvell', in *Puritanism and Revolution: Studies in interpretation of the English revolution of the seventeenth century* (London, 1958), pp. 324–50; F. Moretti, 'The great eclipse: Tragic form as a deconsecration of majesty', in *Signs Taken For Wonders: Essays in the sociology of literary forms*, trans. S. Fischer, D. Forgacs and D. Miller (revised edn, London, 1988).
68. J. Howard, 'The New Historicism in Renaissance studies', in Wilson and Dutton (eds), *op. cit.* (1992), p. 22; J. Dollimore, *Radical Tragedy: Religion, ideology and power in the drama of Shakespeare and his contemporaries* (Brighton, 1984; revised edn, Hemel Hempstead, 1989).
69. W. Benjamin, *The Origin of German Tragic Drama*, trans. J. Osborne (London, 1977), especially, pp. 64–74; L. Goldmann, *The Hidden God: A study of the tragic vision in the 'Pensées' of Pascal and the tragedies of Racine*, trans. P. Thody (London, 1964), especially, pp. 46–9 and 103–112.
70. R. Barthes, *On Racine*, trans. R. Howard (New York, 1964), pp. ix–x.
71. *Ibid.*, p. 172.
72. Eagleton, *op. cit.* (1986), pp. ix–x. Cf. Dollimore, *op. cit.* (1984), p. 154:

It might be thought that to use the writing of Marx, Brecht, Foucault and others to elucidate early seventeenth-century England, far from restoring a correct historical context for its drama, is itself unhistorical. . . . Nevertheless the one has its roots in the other. Brecht develops his dramatic theory in relation to the earlier period, and there are real similarities between Althusser's theory of ideology and Montaigne's account of custom . . . [while] the ancestry of Marxism has been taken to include Machiavelli and Galileo.

73. See, for example, the highly Foucauldian 'Transgression and surveillance in "Measure for Measure"', in Dollimore and Sinfield, *op. cit.* (1985), Chap. 4.
74. M. Foucault, *Madness and Civilisation: A history of insanity in the Age of Reason*, trans. R. Howard (London, 1971), pp. 31 and 286.
75. M. Foucault, *The Order of Things: An archaeology of the human sciences*, trans. anon. (London, 1970), pp. 16, 46–50 and 386–7.
76. L. Althusser, 'Ideology and ideological state apparatuses', in *Lenin and Philosophy and Other Essays*, trans. B. Brewster (London, 1971), pp. 142–5; J. Baudrillard, 'Symbolic exchange and death', trans. C. Levin, in *Jean Baudrillard: Selected writings*, ed. M. Poster (Oxford, 1988), pp. 124–6.
77. Quoted in M. Ignatieff, 'Michel Foucault', *University Publishing*, 13 (Summer 1984) (Berkeley, Calif.), p. 1.
78. D. Cressy, 'Foucault, Stone, Shakespeare and social history', in *English Literary Renaissance*, 21, 2 (Spring 1991), pp. 121–33. The conflation of Foucault with his sworn adversary Lawrence Stone in this article may be compared with the now-notorious misreading of Foucauldian New Historicism as 'a kind of Marxism' in E. Pechter, 'The New Historicism and its discontents: Politicizing Renaissance drama', *PMLA*, 102 (1987), p. 292.
79. L. Beier, *Masterless Men: The vagrancy problem in England, 1560–1640* (London, 1985), pp. 164–9; P. Spierenburg, *The Spectacle of Suffering: Executions and the evolution of repression, from a preindustrial metropolis to the European experience* (Cambridge, 1984), pp. 202–5.
80. Quoted in D. Eribon, *Michel Foucault*, trans. B. Wing (Cambridge, Mass., 1991), pp. 164–5.
81. P. Burke, *The French Historical Revolution: The Annales school, 1929–1989* (London, 1990), p. 102.
82. Cressy, *op. cit.*, p. 124.
83. M. Foucault, *Remarks on Marx: Conversations with Duccio Trombadori*, trans. R. J. Goldstein and J. Cascaito (New York, 1991), p. 129.
84. A. Sheridan, *Michel Foucault: The will to truth* (London, 1980), pp. 6 and 205.
85. M. Foucault, 'The order of discourse', trans. I. McLeod, in R. Young (ed.), *Untying the Text: A post-structuralist reader* (London, 1981), pp. 52–3.
86. C. Belsey, 'Literature, history, politics,' in Wilson and Dutton (eds), *op. cit.*, pp. 37–8.
87. G. Siegel, *op. cit.* (see note 52), p. 77.
88. L. Marcus, *Puzzling Shakespeare: Local reading and its discontents* (Berkeley, Calif., 1988), pp. 36–40.
89. L. Marcus, 'Levelling Shakespeare: Local customs and local texts', in *Shakespeare Quarterly*, 42, 2 (Summer 1991), p. 178.

90. E. Le Roy Ladurie, *Carnival at Romans: A people's uprising at Romans, 1579–1580*, trans. M. Feeney (Harmondsworth, 1981).

91. F. Laroque, *Shakespeare's Festive World: Elizabethan seasonal entertainment and the professional stage* (Cambridge, 1991); Marcus, *op. cit.* (1988), p. 37.

92. Foucault, *op. cit.* (1991), p. 129.

93. A. Patterson, *Shakespeare and the Popular Voice* (Oxford, 1989), pp. 34–7.

94. Norris, *op. cit.* (see note 57).

95. Marcus, *op. cit.* (1988), p. 36.

96. C. Belsey, 'Making histories then and now: Shakespeare from *Richard II* to *Henry V*,' in F. Barker, P. Hulme and M. Iverson (eds), *Uses of History: Marxism, postmodernism and the Renaissance* (Manchester, 1991), pp. 29–31.

97. Foucault, *op. cit.* (1991), p. 152.

98. For a stimulating account of the feminist appropriation of Foucault, see J. Sawicki, *Disciplining Foucault: Feminism, power, and the body* (London, 1991).

99. See, for instance, Stone's denunciation, 'History and post-modernism', *Past and Present*, 131 (May 1991), pp. 217–18, together with the considered replies by P. Joyce and C. Kelly in 133 (January 1992), pp. 204–13.

100. During, *op. cit.*, p. 237.

101. Marcus, *op. cit.* (1988), pp. 40–1.

102. *Ibid.*, p. 42.

103. Eagleton, *op. cit.* (1988), p. 204.

104. S. Greenblatt, 'Psychoanalysis and Renaissance culture,' *op. cit.* (1990), p. 141.

105. Marcus, *op. cit.* (1988), pp. 41–2.

106. During, *op. cit.*, p. 222.

107. H. James, Preface to the New York edition (1909), p. 1; F. Jameson, Preface, *The Political Unconscious: Narrative as a socially symbolic act* (London, 1981), p. 9.

108. M. Bakhtin, 'Discourse in the novel', in *The Dialogic Imagination* (Austin, Tex., 1987), p. 106.

109. Eagleton, *op. cit.* (1988), p. 203.

110. See the correspondence reproduced in E. I. Fripp, *Master Richard Quyny, Bailiff of Stratford-upon-Avon and Friend of William Shakespeare* (Oxford, 1924), *passim*.

111. The *Annales* historian Robert Chartier, in 'Intellectual history or sociocultural history?', in D. LaCapra and S. L. Kaplan (eds), *Modern European Intellectual History: Reappraisals and new perspectives* (Ithaca, N.Y., 1982), p. 30. A statement of the extent of retreat from the materialism of the earlier *Annales* generation of Marc Bloch and Fernand Braudel.

112. 'Contented Positivist: M. Foucault and the death of a man', *Times Literary Supplement*, Thursday 2 July 1970, no. 3566, pp. 697–8.

113. Eagleton, *op. cit.* (1988), p. 203.

114. For the tradition that the curse prevented the opening of the grave for Shakespeare's wife and daughters, see Chambers, *op. cit.*, Vol. 2, p. 181.

A mingled yarn: Shakespeare and the cloth workers

1. Reviews of *Othello* in *The Financial Times* and *The Times*, 12 May 1984, and *The Stage and Television Today*, 24 May 1984; of *Macbeth* in *The Guardian*, 20 October 1984, *The Sunday Times*, 28 October 1984, *The Evening Standard*, 23 October 1984, *The Field*, 10 November 1984; and of *Hamlet* in *The Financial Times*, 6 February 1985.
2. Reviews of *Coriolanus* in *The Guardian*, *The Daily Telegraph*, *The Times* and *The Financial Times* for 17 December 1984.
3. In C. Woolf and J. M. Wilson (eds.), *Authors Take Sides on the Falklands* (London, 1982), p. 67.
4. F. R. Leavis, 'Joyce and the revolution of the word', *Scrutiny*, 2, 2 (September, 1933), p. 200: 'A national culture rooted in the soil'; A. Harbage, *Shakespeare and the Rival Traditions* (New York, 1952), p. 25; see also *Shakespeare's Audience* (New York, 1941), *passim*.
5. A. Gurr, *The Shakespearean Stage, 1574–1642* (Cambridge, 1980), p. 196; A. J. Cook, *The Privileged Playgoers of Shakespeare's London* (Cambridge, 1983), *passim*.
6. J. P. Brockbank, 'The frame of disorder: *Henry VI*,' in J. R. Brown and B. Harris (eds), *Stratford-upon-Avon Studies*, Vol. 3: *Early Shakespeare* (London, 1961), p. 87; M. M. Reese, *The Cease of Majesty: A study of Shakespeare's history plays* (London, 1961), p. 126. For the Renaissance background to this prejudice, see C. Hill, 'The many-headed monster in late Tudor and early Stuart political thinking', in C. H. Carter (ed.), *From the Renaissance to the Counter-Reformation: Essays in honour of Garret Mattingley* (London, 1968), pp. 296–324.
7. Brockbank, *op. cit.*, p. 88; A. C. Bradley, *Shakespearean Tragedy* (London, 1904), p. 326; R. W. Chambers, 'The expression of the ideas – particularly the political ideas – in the three pages of *Sir Thomas More*', in A. W. Pollard (ed.), *Shakespeare's Hand in the Play of Sir Thomas More* (London, 1920), p. 168; Reese, *op. cit.*, p. 126; D. Traversi, *An Approach to Shakespeare: 'Henry VI' to 'Twelfth Night'* (London, 1968), p. 33. 'The homily on obedience' is quoted from *Certain Sermons Appointed by the Queen's Majesty* (London, 1587).
8. Traversi, *op. cit.*, p. 33.
9. E. Hobsbawm, *Primitive Rebels* (Manchester, 1971), p. 111; G. Rudé, *Ideology and Popular Protest* (London, 1980), pp. 87–8, 138–9; B. Manning, *The English People and and the English Revolution* (London, 1976); J. F. C. Harrison, *The Common People: A history from the Norman Conquest to the present* (London, 1984), pp. 193–4. For the European context, see T. Aston (ed.), *Crisis in Europe, 1560–1660* (London, 1965); and D. R. Kelly, *The Beginning of Ideology: Consciousness and society in the French Reformation* (Cambridge, 1981), p. 340.

10. See D. Bevington, *Tudor Drama and Politics* (Cambridge, Mass., 1968), pp. 233–4. For the minor 1554 disturbance, in which the heckling was led by a Protestant clothier, see J. Proctor, *The History of Wyatt's Rebellion* (London, 1554), pp. 54–5. For the passivity of urban society in Tudor England, see P. Zagorin, *Rebels and Rulers, 1500–1660*, Vol. I: *Society, States and Early Modern Revolution* (Cambridge, 1982), p. 235; and P. Clark and P. Slack (eds), *Crisis and Order in English Towns, 1500–1700* (London, 1972), p. 19. The crisis in London in the 1590s is discussed in P. Clark (ed.), *The European Crisis of the 1590s: Essays in comparative history* (London, 1985), Chap. 1; in M. J. Power, 'London and the control of the crisis of the 1590s', *History*, 70 (October, 1985): pp. 371–85; and S. Rappaport, 'Social structure and mobility in sixteenth-century London: part I', *London Journal*, 9 (1983), pp. 128–31.
11. E. P. Thompson, 'The moral economy of the English crowd in the eighteenth century', *Past and Present*, 50 (February, 1971), pp. 76–136; Hobsbawm, *op. cit.*, pp. 110–13; E. Le Roy Ladurie, *Carnival at Romans: A people's uprising at Romans, 1579–1580* (Harmondsworth, 1981), p. 292. For the topos of the mob as a Hydra without aims, leadership or collective consciousness, see the definitive survey, C. A. Patrides, 'The beast with many heads: Renaissance views on the multitude', *Shakespeare Quarterly*, 16 (1965), pp. 241–6.
12. The date of *2 Henry VI*, was conclusively established by H. R. Born in 'The date of *2 Henry VI*', *Shakespeare Quarterly*, 25 (1974), pp. 323–34. Born's conclusion that 'Shakespeare finished the two sequels [to *Henry VI, Part 1*] by late July or early August [1592]' has since been accepted by N. Sanders, *The New Penguin Shakespeare of 2 Henry VI* (Harmondsworth, 1981), p. 42. Though rival theories are sifted by M. Hattaway in the *New Cambridge* edition (Cambridge, 1991), pp. 60–8, Born's dating remains unchallenged.
13. Reese, *op. cit.*, pp. 122–3, 126; Brockbank, *op. cit.*, pp. 87–8; Sanders, *op. cit.*, pp. 35–6; E. M. W. Tillyard, *Shakespeare's History Plays* (London, 1944), pp. 183–5. All quotations from Hall's Chronicle are from G. Bullough, *Narrative and Dramatic Sources of Shakespeare: Earlier English history plays* (London, 1960), pp. 113–18.
14. C. Hill, *op. cit.*, p. 303.
15. C. Hobday, 'Clouted shoon and leather aprons: Shakespeare and the egalitarian tradition', *Renaissance and Modern Studies*, 23 (1979), pp. 63–78.
16. W. Benjamin, 'Theses on the philosophy of history, VII', in *Illuminations*, ed. H. Arendt, trans. H. Zohn (London, 1970), p. 258.
17. *Ibid.*; Reese, *op. cit.*, p. 125; Sanders, *op. cit.*, p. 37.
18. P. Burke, *Popular Culture in Early Modern Europe* (London, 1978), pp. 270–81.
19. M. Bristol, 'Lenten butchery: Legitimation crisis in *Coriolanus*', in J. Howard and M. O'Connor (eds), *Shakespeare Reproduced: The text in history and ideology* (London and New York, 1987), p. 215; M. Bakhtin,

Rabelais and his World, trans. I. Iswolsky (Bloomington, Ind., 1984), p. 275.

20. C. Ginzburg, *The Cheese and the Worms: The cosmos of a sixteenth-century miller*, trans. J. Tedeschi and A. Tedeschi (London, 1980), p. xv.
21. Reese, *op. cit.*, 125–6.
22. C. Hill, *The World Turned Upside Down: Radical ideas during the English Revolution* (Harmondsworth, 1975), pp. 23, 97 and 112.
23. Reese, *op. cit.*, p. 125.
24. See A. L. Beier, 'Engine of manufacture: The trades of London', in A. L. Beier and R. Finlay (eds.), *The Making of the Metropolis, London, 1500–1700* (London, 1986), pp. 160–1.
25. The documents are reproduced in E. Chambers, *William Shakespeare* (London, 1930), pp. 101–3. For the economic background, see G. Unwin, *Industrial Organisation in the Sixteenth and Seventeenth Centuries* (Oxford, 1904), pp. 112–25. Cloth amounted to 80 per cent of England's exports by the mid-sixteenth century and had increased on even this proportion by the mid-seventeenth: see A. G. R. Smith, *The Emergence of a Nation State: The commonwealth of England* (London, 1984), p. 177.
26. P. J. Bowden, *The Wool Trade in Tudor and Stuart England* (London, 1962), pp. 70 and 93. For the importance of Evesham in the distribution of Cotswold wool, see, p. 30.
27. See BL, Lansdowne MS, 70, fos 13–16, 20–2, for the controversy over the irregular sale of ordnance and matériel to the expeditionary force.
28. T. Deloney, *The Novels of Thomas Deloney*, ed. M. E. Lawlis (Bloomington, Ind., 1961), 'Jack of Newbury', pp. 3 and 58; 'Thomas of Reading', p. 267; F. O. Mann (ed.), *The Works of Thomas Deloney* (Oxford, 1912), pp. xxvi–xxx. For the economic background, see F. Consett, *The London Weaver's Company*, Vol. 1 (London, 1933), pp. 146–52.
29. Unwin, *op. cit.*, pp. 130–5.
30. J. Stow, *Survey of the Cities of London and Westminster*, ed. J. Strype (London, 1720), Vol. 2, iv, pp. 74–5; E. Walford, *Old and New London* (London, 1873), pp. 108–9.
31. BL, Lansdowne MS, 71, fo. 15. The minutes from the City records are printed in W. H. Overall (ed.), *Remembrancia: Analytical index to the series of records known as the Remembrancia, preserved among the archives of the City of London, 1579–1664* (London, 1878), p. 474; where, however, they are wrongly dated 30 May, a mistake subsequently followed by Shakespeare scholars. For the feltmakers' petition and the government response, see J. R. Dasent (ed.), *Acts of the Privy Council*, Vol. 22, p. 506, 2 June 1592. See also P. Williams, *The Tudor Regime* (London, 1979), pp. 329–30.
32. E. Hobsbawm and G. Rudé, *Captain Swing* (London, 1969), p. 18; P. Slack, 'Metropolitan government in crisis', in Beier and Finlay, *op. cit.*, p. 75;
33. J. Stow, *The Survey of London*, ed. V. Pearl (London, 1987), pp. 92–3;

R. T. Sayle, *Lord Mayor's Pageants for the Merchant Taylors Company in the Fifteenth, Sixteenth and Seventeenth Centuries* (London, 1931), pp. 15, 102; J. G. Nichols, *The Diary of Henry Machyn* (Chetham Society, London, 1880), pp. 20, 72–3 and 89; J. C. Smith and E. de Selincourt (eds), *The Poetical Works of Edmund Spenser* (Oxford, 1912), pp. 580–4; C. M. Clode, *Memorials of the Guild of Merchant Taylors* (London, 1875), pp. 130–1. For fire symbolism, see Le Roy Ladurie, *op. cit.*, pp. 289–90.

34. Stow, *op. cit.*, pp. 92–3.
35. *Ibid.*, pp. 381–2. For Southwark Fair, see A. R. Wright, *British Calendar Customs* (London, 1940), Vol. 3, p. 3. Hogarth painted the Fair in 1733 when its violence was notorious. An anonymous drawing of 1640 depicts a drummer and dancers weaving their way around the Maypole over the bodies of drunks (reproduced in T. Burke, *The Streets of London* (London, 1940), plate 17). The hangover is recalled by Shallow, when he reminds Falstaff of how they 'lay all night in the Windmill in Saint George's Fields' (*2 Henry IV*, III, ii, 189–90).
36. Details of the riot are in BL, Lansdowne MS, 71, fos 15 and 17, and the minutes of the Privy Council in *APC*, Vol. 22, pp. 549 and 592; Vol. 23, pp. 19, 24, 28, 220, 232 and 242. For Southwark see D. J. Johnson, *Southwark and the City* (Oxford, 1969), pp. 67–72 and 227–29.
37. *APC*, Vol. 23, p. 20, 9 July 1592; P. Burke, 'Popular culture in seventeenth-century London', in B. Reay (ed.), *Popular Culture in Seventeenth-Century England* (London, 1988), p. 32.
38. Burke, *op. cit.* (1978), p. 76.
39. *Ibid.*, p. 203.
40. B. Sharp, 'Popular protest in seventeenth-century England', in Reay, *op. cit.*, pp. 284–5; R. Chambers, *The Book of Days: A miscellany of popular antiquities* (London, 1869), Vol. 1, p. 815. See R. Darnton, *The Great Cat Massacre and Other Episodes in French Cultural History* (Harmondsworth, 1984), p. 83, for continental analogues.
41. Burke, *op. cit.* (1978), p. 75.
42. G. Chaucer, *The Canterbury Tales*, ed. V. A. Kolve and G. Olson (New York, 1989), pp. 229–30, 'The Nun's Priest's Tale', lines 628–35. See N. Simms, 'Nero and Jack Straw in Chaucer's *Nun's Priest's Tale*', *Parergon*, 8 (April, 1978), pp. 2–12.
43. N. Zemon Davis, *Society and Culture in Early Modern France* (London, 1975), Chaps. 4 and 6, 'The reasons of misrule' and 'The rites of violence', see especially, pp. 104–8, 111–14 and 184–5. E. Hall, *Hall's Chronicle or The Union of the Noble and Illustrious Families of Lancaster and York* (London, 1548; repr., London, 1809), pp. 587–9.
44. Burke, *op. cit.* (1988), pp. 37–8.
45. S. R. Smith, 'The London apprentices as seventeenth-century adolescents', *Past and Present*, 60 (1973), pp. 149–61, esp pp. 158–9 and 161. See also B. Capp, 'English youth groups and "The Pinder of Wakefield"', *Past and Present*, 76 (1977), pp. 127–33; and S. Smith, 'The apprentices' parliament of 1647', *History Today*, 22 (1972), pp. 576–82.

46. C. Brontë(Currer Bell), *Shirley* (London, 1899; Haworth edn), p. 352.
47. N. Simms, 'Ned Ludd's nummers play', *Folklore*, 89, 16 (1978) p. 174.
48. Caxton quoted *ibid.*, p. 173. For Jack Straw's name, see also F. W. D. Brie, 'Wat Tyler and Jack Straw', *English Historical Review*, 21 (1906), pp. 106–11; and T. Pettitt, ' "Here comes I, Jack Straw": English folk drama and social revolt', *Folklore*, 95, 1 (1984), pp. 320, esp. pp. 7–9.
49. Simms, *op. cit.*, p. 175. See also A. W. Smith, 'Some folklore elements in movements of social protest', *Folklore*, 77, 1 (1967), pp. 241–50.
50. *Surrey County Sessions* (London, 1886), ed. H. Jenkinson and D. L. Powell, 2324: Croydon Assizes, 3 July 1592; *APC*, Vol. 23, p. 24, 9 July 1592. For the ritual violence of apprentice gangs, see Darnton, 'Workers revolt', *op. cit.*, pp. 79–104.
51. *APC*, Vol. 22, p. 549, dated (possibly wrongly) 23 June. Editors persist in confusing this prohibition on performance with the subsequent one imposed as a result of plague, a mistake traceable to Chambers (e.g. Hattaway in the *New Cambridge* edition, *op. cit.*, p. 64). The management of the Rose were successful in lifting the ban six weeks early, on 13 August (see note 57 below). See also Stow, *op. cit.* (1720), Vol. 2, iv, pp. 19–20.
52. M. Bristol, *Carnival and Theatre* (London, 1985), pp. 4–5, 201.
53. D. H. Horne (ed.), *The Life and Minor Works of George Peele* (New Haven, Conn., 1952), 'Descensus Astraea', pp. 214–19. *APC*, Vol. 21, p. 324, minute of 25 July 1591. The Rose Theatre reopened in February 1592, and Chambers concludes that by that time the controversy over Sunday playing had been won by the Sabbatarians as far as the commercial theatres were concerned (E. Chambers, *The Elizabethan Stage* (Oxford, 1923), Vol. 1, p. 315; Vol. 4, p. 307). See also Burke, *op. cit.* (1988), p. 39; W. B. Whittaker, *Sunday in Tudor and Stuart Times* (London, 1933), pp. 45–6. For King James's comments, see L. A. Govett (ed), *The King's Book of Sports* (London, 1890), p. 30. See also C. Hill, 'The uses of Sabbatarianism', *Society and Puritanism in Pre-Revolutionary England* (London, 1964), pp. 145–218. For the increasing segregation of metropolitan culture as the traditional festivals made way for 'professionalised entertainment' with its 'passive audience', see Burke, *op. cit.* (1988), pp. 38–41; and R. Ashton, 'Popular culture in seventeenth-century London', *London Journal* 9 (1983), pp. 3–19.
54. See especially, A. Sinfield, 'Power and ideology: An outline theory and Sidney's "Arcadia" ', *English Literary History*, 52 (1985), pp. 261–5.
55. BL, Lansdowne MS, 71, fo. 17. The cloth workers delivered a further petition against the foreign weavers on 2 July: *HMC*, 9(d), Salisbury MSS, 4, p. 216. For the longstanding tug-of-war over jurisdiction in Southwark between the Surrey magistrates and Knight Marshal on one side, and the City of London and the Recorder of London on the other, see Johnson, *op. cit.*, pp. 226–9 and 286–7. Technically the Marshalsea also had its own Court with jurisdiction within the 'verge': a radius of twelve miles of wherever the Queen happened to be.
56. Burghley's irritation with Webbe's defence of the cloth workers is

recorded in *APC*, Vol. 23, pp. 19–20 and his order for the release of Levenson and Levens from Newgate, Vol. 23, p. 24: minutes of 9 July 1592. T. Lodge, *The Complete Works* (New York, 1963), Vol. 2, 'The life and death of William Longbeard', p. 32; *Surrey County Sessions* (London, 1886), 852: Kingston Assizes, 23 July 1576; 2324: Croydon Assizes, 3 July 1592; 2366: Southwark Assizes, 19 July 1592. The inquest which returned a verdict of manslaughter against the Knight Marshal's officers had been held at Southwark on 20 June. S. Mullaney, *The Place of the Stage: License, play, and power in Renaissance England* (Chicago, 1988), p. 21.

57. T. Nashe, *The Unfortunate Traveller and Other Works*, ed. J. B. Steane (Harmondsworth, 1972), 'The defence of plays', in 'Pierce Penniless', pp. 64 and 112–15 (and see *Lenten Stuff*, pp. 405–6, for mockery of Deloney's claim that the cloth workers were indispensable to the English economy); R. Warwick Bond (ed.), *The Complete Works of John Lyly* (Oxford, 1902), Vol. 1, p. 477, 'Speeches delivered to Her Majesty this last progress' (Oxford, 1592); Le Roy Ladurie, *op. cit.*, p. 279. The documents submitted to persuade the Privy Council to exempt the Rose from the ban on assemblies, together with the warrant for the reopening of the theatre dated 13 August 1592 (subsequently rescinded due to plague) are printed in Chambers, *The Elizabethan Stage* (Oxford, 1923), Vol. 1, pp. 311–12.

58. *Ibid.*, Vol. 4, p. 319. Nashe was protesting about the arrest of Ben Jonson and the actors after the performance of *The Isle of Dogs*.

59. See Chambers, *ibid.*, Vol. 1, p. 265 for the Shrove Tuesday apprentice riots, and M. C. Bradbrook, *The Rise of the Common Player* (London, 1963), p. 115 for the Ludlow episode. Bradbrook assumes that the rioters arrived at the private performance, which was in Shrewsbury, drunk; but for the actual motives and economic background – a bitter struggle to protect local finishing crafts from the entrepreneurial operations of the Midland dealers – see Unwin, *op. cit.*, pp. 186–90.

60. *The Financial Times*, 12 May 1984, review of Young Vic *Othello*; D. Devlin, 'Drama behind the scenes', *Southwark Globe*, publicity brochure of the International Shakespeare Globe Centre distributed throughout south London in March 1985; S. Hughes, 'Simon Hughes MP writes . . .', *ibid.*

61. *The Independent*, editorial, 10 March 1990.

62. Burke, 'Popular culture in seventeenth-century London', in Reay, *op. cit.*, pp. 46–7; see also R. M. Dunn, 'The London weavers' riot of 1675', *Guildhall Studies in London History*, 1 (1974). For the 'factious people' of 'radical Southwark', see Hill, *The World Turned Upside Down: Radical ideas during the English Revolution* (Harmondsworth, 1975), pp. 112 and 354; and for the feltmakers' strike of 1696, see S. Webb and B. Webb, *A History of Trade Unionism* (London, 1894), p. 46; and Unwin, *op. cit.*, pp. 213–27. The riot was misdated by Overall (see note 31); and the account offered in B. Manning, *Village Revolts: Social protest and popular disturbances in England, 1509–1640* (Oxford, 1988), muddies the

waters still more by displacing the events by a year and a month and by echoing the account in *A PC* without reference to BL Lansdowne MSS, which provide the City and cloth workers' sides of the conflict. The upshot of these mistakes and the reliance on Chambers by literary critics is that the context of *2 Henry VI* continues to be buried beneath the anachronistic myth of Shakespeare as a 'democrat'. Thus, M. C. Bradbrook automatically assumed that the feltmakers' protest was a 'theatre riot' inside the Rose and evidence of Shakespeare's 'common audience': *op. cit.*, p. 114; and by perpetuating this error C. Rutter suppresses any connection with popular festivity (*Documents of the Rose Playhouse* (Manchester, 1984), p. 62). Meanwhile, as Penry Williams writes, 'The true tensions and dissatisfactions underlying these disturbances have yet to be revealed' (*op. cit.*, p. 330).

Is this a holiday?: Shakespeare's Roman carnival

1. Quoted in T. S. Dorsch (ed.), *Julius Caesar* (The Arden Shakespeare) (London, 1955), p. vii.
2. Order of the Middlesex County Sessions, 1 October, 1612; reproduced in E. K. Chambers, *The Elizabethan Stage* (Oxford, 1923), Vol. 4, pp. 340–1.
3. F. Barker, *The Tremulous Private Body: Essays on subjection* (London, 1984), p. 18.
4. C. Hill, 'The uses of Sabbatarianism', *Society and Puritanism in Pre-Revolutionary England* (Harmondsworth, 1972), p. 163.
5. T. Nashe, 'Pierce Penniless', *The Unfortunate Traveller and Other Works*, ed. J. B. Steane (Harmondsworth, 1972), pp. 114–15; Privy Council Minute repr. in Chambers, *op. cit.*, Vol. 4, p. 307; L. A. Govett, *The King's Book of Sports* (repr., London, 1890), p. 30.
6. P. Burke, *Popular Culture in Early Modern Europe* (London, 1978), p. 203. See also B. A. Babcock (ed.), *The Reversible World of Carnival: Symbolic inversion in art and society* (Ithaca, N.Y., 1978).
7. Chambers, *op. cit.*, Vol. 1, pp. 264–5.
8. P. Clark, *The European Crisis of the 1590s: Essays in comparative history* (London, 1985), p. 54.
9. M. Foucault, 'The order of discourse', trans. I. McLeod, in R. Young (ed.), *Untying the Text: A post-structuralist reader* (London, 1981), pp. 52–3.
10. R. E. McGraw, *Encyclopaedia of Medical History* (London, 1985), p. 138.
11. A. L. Beier, *Masterless Men: The vagrancy problem in England, 1560–1640* (London, 1985). For Platter's comment, see, p. 164.
12. M. Foucault, *Discipline and Punish: The birth of the prison*, trans. A. Sheridan (Harmondsworth, 1979), p. 221; M. Bristol, *Carnival and Theatre: Plebeian culture and the structure of authority in Renaissance England* (New York and London, 1989), *passim*; U. Eco, 'The frames of comic freedom', in T. Sebeok (ed.), *Carnival!* (New York, 1984), p. 3.

See also M. Bakhtin, *Rabelais and his World*, trans. H. Iswolsky (Bloomington, Ind., 1984). Nashe, *op. cit.*, p. 115.

13. S. Mullaney, *The Place of the Stage: License, play and power in Renaissance England* (Chicago, 1988), pp. 43–4.
14. Quoted in C. Norris, 'Post-structuralist Shakespeare: text and ideology', in J. Drakakis (ed.), *Alternative Shakespeares* (London, 1985), p. 50.
15. T. Dekker, *The Shoemaker's Holiday*, ed. A. Parr (London, 1990), scene 17: ll. 45–51.
16. *Op. cit.*, p. xv.
17. S. Freud, *Civilisation and its Discontents*, trans. J. Rivere, ed. J. Strachey (London, 1979), p. 7; S. Zweig, quoted in F. Heer, 'Freud, the Viennese Jew', trans. W. A. Littlewood, in J. Miller (ed.), *Freud: The man, his world, his influence* (London, 1972), p. 11.
18. J. Stow, *The Survey of London*, eds H. B. Wheatley and V. Pearl (London, 1987), p. 15.
19. See especially J. Tambling, *Confession: Sexuality, sin, and the subject* (Manchester, 1990), p. 84.
20. N. Zemon Davis, 'The reasons of misrule,' in *Society and Culture in Early Modern France* (Oxford, 1987), pp. 97–123.
21. R. Herrick, *The Poems of Robert Herrick*, ed. L. C. Martin (Oxford, 1965), p. 5; C. Hill, *The World Turned Upside Down: Radical ideas during the English Revolution* (Harmondsworth, 1975), pp. 353–4.
22. A. Barton, *Shakespeare and the Idea of the Play* (Harmondsworth, 1967), p. 141.
23. J. Dollimore, *Radical Tragedy: Religion, ideology and power in the drama of Shakespeare and his contemporaries* (Brighton, 1984); S. Greenblatt, 'Invisible bullets: Renaissance authority and its subversion: *Henry IV* and *Henry V*', in J. Dollimore and A. Sinfield (eds), *Political Shakespeare: New essays in Cultural Materialism* (Manchester, 1985), p. 33; C. Tourneur, *The Revenger's Tragedy*, ed. R. A. Foakes (London, 1966), v, i, 181.
24. E. Le Roy Ladurie, *Carnival at Romans: A people's uprising in Romans, 1579–1580* (Harmondsworth, 1981), pp. 192–215; for cannibalistic symbolism, see, pp. 173 and 198.
25. R. Harland, *Superstructuralism: The philosophy of structuralism and post-structuralism* (London, 1987), p. 135.
26. See especially W. S. Heckscher, *Rembrandt's 'Anatomy of Dr. Nicolaas Tulp': An Iconological Study* (New York, 1958), pp. 97–106. For an authoritative discussion, see also J. Sawday, 'The fate of Marsyas: Dissecting the Renaissance body', in L. Gent and N. Llewellyn (eds), *Renaissance Bodies: The Human Figure in English Culture, c. 1540–1660* (London, 1990), pp. 111–35.
27. Barker, *op. cit.*, p. 76.
28. Hill, *op. cit.* (1975), p. 347.
29. Barker, *op. cit.*, p. 51.
30. T. Todorov, *The Conquest of America: The question of the other* (New York, 1984).

31. E. Gayton, 'Festivous notes upon Don Quixote' (London, 1654), quoted in Chambers, *op. cit.*, Vol. 1, p. 265.

Like the old Robin Hood: *As You Like It* and the enclosure riots

1. All quotations of Lyly from J. Lyly, 'Speeches delivered to Her Majesty this last Progress', in R. Warwick Bond (ed.), *The Complete Works of John Lyly*, (Oxford, 1967), Vol. 1, pp. 471–90; for the passage quoted. here, see, p. 473.
2. *Ibid.*, p. 475.
3. *Ibid.*, p. 477.
4. *Ibid.*, p. 488.
5. *Ibid.*, p. 475.
6. L. A. Montrose, 'Of gentlemen and shepherds: The politics of Elizabethan pastoral form', *English Literary History*, 50 (1983), pp. 415–59.
7. J. Manwood, *A Brief Collection of the Laws of the Forests*, (private edn, London, 1592); *A Treatise and Discourse of the Laws of the Forest* (London, 1615, repr. Amsterdam 1976), dedication to Lord Howard.
8. See R. Marienstras, *New Perspectives on the Shakespearean World* (Cambridge 1985), pp. 11–39; J. Aubrey, *Wiltshire: The topographical collections of John Aubrey*, ed., J. E. Jackson (London, 1862), p. 9; D. Underdown, *Revel, Riot and Rebellion: Popular politics and culture in England, 1603–1660* (Oxford 1985), p. 34.
9. Quoted in J. Walter, 'A "rising of the people"? The Oxfordshire Rising of 1596', *Past and Present*, 107 (May 1985), pp. 90–143, esp. p. 98.
10. *Ibid.*, p. 100.
11. *Ibid.*, p. 108.
12. *Ibid.*, pp. 106–7.
13. For the intended targets of the rising, see pp. 12–14.
14. *Ibid.*, p. 91; P. L. Hughes and J. F. Larkin (eds), *Tudor Royal Proclamations* (New Haven, Conn., 1969), pp. 165–72.
15. L. A. Montrose, '"The place of brother": *As You Like It* and social change', *Shakespeare Quarterly*, 32 (1981), pp. 28–54; H. Gardner, '*As You Like It*', in J. Garrett (ed.), *More Talking about Shakespeare* (London, 1959), pp. 17–32. *As You Like It* is 'Shakespeare's most Mozartian comedy, consistently played over by a delighted intelligence', in Gardner's representative evaluation (p. 18).
16. A. Barton, '*As You Like It* and *Twelfth Night*: Shakespeare's sense of an ending', in M. Bradbury and D. Palmer (eds), *Shakespearian Comedy* (Stratford-upon-Avon Studies 14) (London, 1972), pp. 160–80, esp. p. 162.
17. For the bitter and occasionally bloody feud between Lord Norris and the Earl of Lincoln, paralleling the strife between the Dukes in *As You Like It*, see N. J. O'Connor, *God's Peace and the Queen's: Vicissitudes of a House, 1539–1615* (London, 1934).
18. For Stratford-upon-Avon in the crisis of the 1590s, see J. M. Martin 'A

Warwickshire market town in adversity: Stratford-upon-Avon in the sixteenth and seventeenth centuries', *Midland History*, VII (1982), pp. 26–41; E. Kerridge, *The Agricultural Revolution* (London, 1967), pp. 184–95; Underdown, *op. cit.*, pp. 4–8.

19. Quoted in C. Chevenix Trench, *The Poacher and the Squire: A history of poaching and game preservation in England* (London, 1967), p. 100; C. Holmes, 'Drainers and fenmen: The problem of popular political consciousness in the seventeenth century', in A. Fletcher and J. Stevenson, *Order and Disorder in Early Modern England* (Cambridge, 1985), p. 171.

20. Walter, *op. cit.*, p. 127.

21. Hobsbawm, *Bandits* (Harmondsworth, 1985), p. 42.

22. A significant connection between *As You Like It* and the Robin Hood tradition, a commonplace of eighteenth- and nineteenth-century Shakespeare criticism, was last argued seriously by A. H. Thorndike, 'The relation of *As You Like It* to Robin Hood plays', *Journal of English and German Philology*, IV (1902), pp. 59–69. A rare modern endorsement comes from W. G. Zeeveld, *The Temper of Shakespeare's Thought* (New Haven, Conn., 1974), p. 219.

23. *The Tale of Gamelyn, The Complete Works of Geoffrey Chaucer: The Canterbury Tales*, ed. W. W. Skeat (Oxford, 1894), pp. 879–82. M. Keen, *The Outlaws of Medieval England* (London, 1961), p. 92.

24. J. Thirsk, *The Agrarian History of England and Wales* (Cambridge, 1967), Vol. 4, p. 111; W. Harrison, *The Description of England*, ed. G. Edelen (Ithaca, N.Y., 1968), p. 217.

25. Underdown, *op. cit.*, p. 103.

26. See A. Stuart Daley, 'The dispraise of the country in *As You Like It*', *Shakespeare Quarterly*, 36 (1985), pp. 300–14.

27. C. E. Hart, *The Free Miners of the Forest of Dean* (Gloucester, 1953), pp. 174–5.

28. Norden quoted in Thirsk, *op. cit.*, p. 411.

29. P. A. J. Pettit, *The Royal Forests of Northamptonshire: A study in their economy, 1558–1714* (Gateshead, 1968), 64–70.

30. James I quoted in T. G. Barnes, *Somerset, 1625–1640: A county government during the 'personal rule'* (Cambridge, Mass.), p. 151.

31. V. H. T. Skipp, *Crisis and Development: An ecological case study of the Forest of Arden, 1570–1674* (Cambridge, 1978).

32. Underdown, *op. cit.*, p. 34.

33. C. Hill, *The World Turned. Upside Down: Radical ideas during the English Revolution* (Harmondsworth, 1975), pp. 43–7; see also, pp. 50–6 for forest society.

34. N. Bownd, quoted in K. Thomas, *Religion and the Decline of Magic* (London, 1971), p. 164.

35. J. W. Hebel, *The Works of Michael Drayton* (Oxford, 1961), Vol. 4, pp. 529–30: *Poly-Olbion*, XXVI, 311–44. This poem was first published in 1622.

36. *Ibid.*, lines 354–6.

37. Underdown, *op. cit.*, p. 101. For the prevalence of charivari in wood–pasture regions, see also the same author's essay, 'The taming of the scold: The enforcement of patriarchal authority in early modern England', in Fletcher and Stevenson, *op. cit.*, pp. 126–132.
38. Pettit, *op. cit.*, pp. 172–3. For 'Captain Dorothy' and 'her' consort, 'Captain Pouch', see D. G. C. Allan, 'The rising in the West, 1628–31', *The Economic History Review*, 2nd Series, 5 (1952), pp. 76–85, esp. pp. 76–7 and n. 6.
39. Lambarde, quoted in J. Walter, 'Grain riots and popular attitudes to the law: Maldon and the crisis of 1629', in J. Brewer and J. Styles (eds), *An Ungovernable People: The English and their law in the seventeenth and eighteenth centuries* (New Brunswick, 1980), pp. 47–84, esp. p. 63.
40. M. Ingram, 'Ridings, rough music and mocking rhymes in early modern England', in B. Reay (ed.), *Popular Culture in Seventeenth-Century England* (London, 1988), pp. 166–97, esp. p. 177.
41. N. Zemon Davies, '"Women on Top": Symbolic sexual inversion and political disorder in early modern Europe', in B. B. Babcock (ed.), *The Reversible World* (Ithaca, N.Y., 1978), pp. 147–90; G. Rudé, *The Crowd in History, 1730–1848* (London, 1981), pp. 84–5; D. J. V. Jones, *Rebecca's Children* (Oxford, 1990), *passim*.
42. P. Stallybrass, '"Drunk with the cup of liberty": Robin Hood, the carnivalesque, and the rhetoric of violence', in N. Armstrong and L. Tennenhouse (eds), *The Violence of Representation: Literature and the history of violence* (London, 1989), pp. 45–76.
43. R. B. Dobson and J. Taylor, *Rhymes of Robin Hood: An introduction to the English outlaw* (London, 1989), p. 4; R. Axton, 'Folk play in Tudor interludes', in M. Axton and R. Williams (eds), *English Drama: Forms and development* (Cambridge, 1977), pp. 1–23, esp., p. 3; Edmund Spenser, *A View of the Present State of Ireland*, ed. W. L. Renwick (Oxford, 1970), p. 144.
44. B. Reay, 'Popular culture in early modern England', in Reay, *op. cit.* (1988), pp. 1–31, esp. p. 17; R. Kevelson, *Inlaws/Outlaws: A semiotics of systematic interaction: Robin Hood and the king's law* (Studies in Semiotics 9) (Bloomington, Ind., 1977), p. 67. For the myth of Shakespeare as deerslayer, see S. Schoenbaum, *William Shakespeare: A documentary life* (Oxford, 1975), pp. 78–87.
45. E. P. Thompson, *Whigs and Hunters: The origin of the black act* (Harmondsworth, 1977), p. 64.
46. Quoted in Trench, *op. cit.*, p. 100.
47. *Ibid.*, p. 106; Thompson, *op. cit.*, pp. 55–6.
48. R. Weimann, *Shakespeare and the Popular Tradition in the Theater* (Baltimore, Md., 1978), pp. 25–30; 'The last instructions to a painter', ll. 387–88, S. S. Donno (ed.), *Andrew Marvell: The complete poems* (Harmondsworth, 1976), p. 167.
49. Marvell, ll. 377–8; Underdown, *op. cit.*, pp. 100–11; B. Sharp, *In Contempt of All Authority: Rural artisans and riot in the west of England, 1586–1660* (Berkeley, Calif., 1980), p. 104.

50. Underdown, *op. cit.*, pp. 106–45; for the social and economic background to skimmingtons, see Ingram, *op. cit.*, pp. 166–97.
51. See, for example, the New Arden edition, ed. A. Latham (London, 1975), p. 54, where the term is contrasted. with 'outlandish' as a usage, but without commentary on the precise Elizabethan connotations and in defiance of the *OED*, which cites Shakespeare's line under definition 2, 'Interior of the country, parts remote from sea or frontiers.'
52. Caesar, *Gallic Wars*, Bk. v, 12. Quoted from the Loeb edition, trans. H. J. Edwards (London, 1917); T. Browne, *Sir Thomas Browne's Pseudodoxia Epidemica*, ed. R. Robbins (Oxford, 1981), Vol. 1, p. 441.
53. *OED*, quoting from the *State Papers of Henry VIII* (1546), Vol. xi, p. 75.
54. A. Hughes, *Politics, Society and Civil War in Warwickshire, 1620–1660* (Cambridge, 1987), p. 107.
55. Sharp, *op. cit.*, pp. 18–21.
56. V. H. T. Skipp, 'Economic and social change in the Forest of Arden, 1530–1649', *Agricultural History Review*, 18 (1970), pp. 84–111; Drayton, *Poly-Olbion*, xiii, 20–38, cited. in n. 35, above, Vol. 4, pp. 275–6.
57. Quoted in P. Stallybrass, '"Wee feaste in our defense": Patrician carnival in early modern England and Robert Herrick's *Hesperides*', *English Literary Renaissance*, 16, (Winter 1986), pp. 234–52, esp., pp. 237 and 239.
58. Quoted in C. Whitfield (ed.), *Robert Dover and the Cotswold Games: Annalia Dubrensia* (Evesham, 1962), pp. 18 and 134.
59. D. Brailsford, *Sport and Society: Elizabeth to Anne* (London, 1969), pp. 103–16.
60. Whitfield, *op. cit.*, p. 150.
61. *Ibid.*, p. 2.
62. R. Manning, *Village Revolts: Social protest and popular disturbances in England, 1509–1640* (Cambridge, 1988), p. 15.
63. M. Foucault, 'The order of discourse' (1971), trans. I. McLeod, in R. Young (ed.), *Untying the Text* (London, 1981), p. 52.
64. J. A. Yelling, *Common Field and Enclosure in England, 1450–1850* (London, 1977), pp. 175, 186–90; see also Skipp, *op. cit.* (1970), cited in n. 31, above, p. 91.
65. For Warwickshire, see Walter, *op. cit.*, p. 117.
66. *Ibid.*, 125.
67. Thomas Fuller quoted. in Underdown, *op. cit.* (1985), cited n. 8 above, p. 19; Edmund Gibson, *Camden's Britannia, Newly Translated into English: With large additions and improvements* (London, 1695), p. 510; Gibson, also quoted in Skipp, *op. cit.*, cited in n. 56 above, pp. 91 and 94. For local resistance to Fulke Greville's activities in Arden, see Skipp, p. 95.
68. E. Hall, *Hall's Chronicle* (1547, repr. London, 1809), p. 582.
69. S. Schoenbaum, *op. cit.*, cited. in n. 44 above, p. 126.
70. Sharp, *op. cit.*, cited in n. 49 above, pp. 102–4.
71. J. Walter and K. Wrightson, 'Dearth and the social order in early modern

England', *Past and Present*, 71 (1976), pp. 22–42, esp. p. 42.

72. Sharp, *op. cit.*, pp. 86–9, 100–4; Thompson, *op. cit.*, cited in n. 45 above, p. 271.

Against the grain: Representing the market in *Coriolanus*

1. The documents relating to the case of Shakespeare and the maltsters are reproduced in E. K. Chambers, *William Shakespeare: A study of facts and problems*, (Oxford, 1930), Vol. I, 99–106; and discussed in M. Eccles, *Shakespeare in Warwickshire*, (Madison, Wis. 1961), pp. 96–9; and S. Schoenbaum, *William Shakespeare: A documentary life* (Oxford, 1975), pp. 178–81. For Richard Quiney, see E. I. Fripp, *Master Richard Quyny, Bailiff of Stratford-upon-Avon and Friend of William Shakespeare* (Oxford, 1924). For corn regulation during the dearth of 1597–8, see P. L. Hughes and J. F. Larkin, *Tudor Royal Proclamations* (New Haven, Conn., 1969), Vol. III, pp. 781, 784, 789, 795.

2. G. W. Prothero (ed.), *Select Statutes and other Constitutional Documents of the Reigns of Elizabeth and James I* (Oxford, 1913), pp. 93–4: 39 and 40 Eliz. Cap. I, 'An Act against the decaying of towns and houses of husbandry'; Chambers, *op. cit.*, pp. 102–3; E. P. Cheyney, *A History of England from the Defeat of the Armada to the Death of Elizabeth* (London, 1926), Vol. II, pp. 259–71; J. M. Keynes, *The Applied Theory of Money*, in *The Collected Writings of John Maynard Keynes* (London, 1971), Vol. VI, pp. 137–41.

3. Hughes and Larkin, *op. cit.*, pp. 793–4: Order 'Enforcing former Statutes, Proclamations and Orders against forestalling Grain', p. 795: 23 August 1598; Keynes, *op. cit.*, 140–1.

4. Fripp, *op. cit.*, p. 126; R. A. Rebholz, *The Life of Fulke Greville, First Lord Brooke* (Oxford, 1971), pp. 92–3; G. A. Wilkes (ed.), *Fulke Greville, Lord Brooke: The Remains: Being poems of monarchy and religion* (Oxford, 1965), 'A treatise of monarchy', p. 139. All page references of Greville's poetry are from this edition.

5. W. H. McNeill, *The Pursuit of Power: Technology, armed force and society since 1000* (Oxford, 1983), pp. 120–1. For Greville's suppression of the Ostend mutiny by promising and then withholding the troops' pay, see Rebholz, *op. cit.*, pp. 80–1.

6. T. Hobbes, *Leviathan*, ed. C. B. Macpherson (Harmondsworth, 1968), p. 161.

7. T. Eagleton, *William Shakespeare* (Oxford, 1986), p. 73.

8. *Victoria County History*, *Warwickshire*, Vol. III, p. 239; Chambers, *op. cit.*, p. 101.

9. For the economic background to the 1598 crisis, see especially J. M. Martin, 'A Warwickshire market town in adversity: Stratford-upon-Avon in the sixteenth and seventeenth centuries', *Midland History*, VII, (1982), pp. 26–41; and V. Skipp, *Crisis and Development: An ecological case study of the Forest of Arden, 1570–1674* (Cambridge, 1978). See also J. Thirsk, 'Enclosing and engrossing', in J. Thirsk (ed.), *The Agrarian*

History of England and Wales, IV: 1500–1640, (Cambridge, 1967), pp. 228–38. J. E. Martin, *Feudalism to Capitalism: Peasant and landlord in English agrarian development* (London, 1983), provides a detailed analysis of the economic causes of the 1607 Midland Revolt.

10. E. P. Thompson, 'The moral economy of the English crowd in the eighteenth century', *Past and Present*, 50 (1971), pp. 76–136. See also J. Walter and K. Wrightson, 'Dearth and the social order in early modern England', *Past and Present*, 71 (1976) pp. 22–42; R. B. Outhwaite, 'Dearth and government intervention in English grain markets, 1590–1700', *Economic History Review*, 2nd series, 34 (1981), pp. 389–410; A. Charlesworth and A. J. Randall, 'Morals, markets and the English crowd', *Past and Present*, 114 (1987), pp. 200–13.

11. A. Hughes, *Politics, Society and Civil War in Warwickshire, 1620–1660* (Cambridge, 1987), p. 18. See *Victoria County History*, *Warwickshire*, Vol. III, p. 237.

12. P. Sidney, *A Defence of Poetry*, ed. J. Van Dorsten (Oxford, 1966) pp. 41–2.

13. J.-C. Agnew, *Worlds Apart: The market and the theater in Anglo-American thought, 1550–1750*, (Cambridge, 1986), p. 50.

14. M. Foucault, *The Order of Things: An archaeology of the human sciences* (London, 1970), p. 179.

15. J. Baudrillard, 'Symbolic exchange and death', in *Jean Baudrillard: Selected Writings*, ed. M. Poster (London, 1988), p. 125 and *passim*.

16. *Ibid.*, 120.

17. M. Bakhtin, *Rabelais and his World*, trans. H. Iswolsky (Bloomington, Ind., 1984), pp. 281–2.

18. C. Whitfield (ed.), *Robert Dover and the Cotswold Games: Annalia Dubrensia*, (Evesham, 1962). See P. Stallybrass, ' "Wee feaste in our Defense": Patrician carnival in early modern England and Robert Herrick's *Hesperides*', *English Literary Renaissance* (Winter 1986), pp. 234–52; D. Brailsford, *Sport and Society, Elizabeth to Anne* (London, 1969), pp. 103–16; D. Underdown, *Revel, Riot and Rebellion: Politics and culture in England, 1603–1660* (Oxford, 1985), p. 64.

19. Bakhtin, *op. cit.*, 282.

20. Fripp, *op. cit.*, p. 129; *Acts of the Privy Council*, 32, ed. J. R. Dasent (London, 1907), *PRO*, pp. 314–16. For criticism of the Poor Law by merchants and farmers, see S. Macfarlane, 'Social policy and the poor in the later seventeenth century', in L. Beier and R. Finlay (eds), *London, 1500–1700: The making of the metropolis* (London, 1986), pp. 252–4.

21. Cheyney, *op. cit.*, 263; J. E. Neale, *Elizabeth I and her Parliaments* (London, 1957), pp. 335–51; 366.

22. For the Statute of Apprentices as an attempt to restrain the market, see G. Unwin, *Industrial Organisation in the Sixteenth and Seventeenth Centuries* (Oxford, 1904), pp. 138–40. For details of Stuart hiring fairs, see H. Best, *Rural Economy in Yorkshire in 1641, being the Farming and Account Books of Henry Best* (Surtees Society, XXXIII), (London, 1857), pp. 132–6; Lord Ernle, *English Farming, Past and Present*, 6th edn

(London, 1961), pp. 87–9; and W. Hasbach, *A History of the English Agricultural Labourer*, revised edn (London, 1966), pp. 84–5. For Stratford's Mop Fair, see C. Hole, *English Custom and Usage* (London, 1942), pp. 94–5.

23. B. Bushaway, *By Rite: Custom, ceremony and community in England, 1700–1880* (London, 1982), p. 118; M. Bristol, 'Lenten butchery: legitimation in *Coriolanus*', in J. E. Howard and M. F. O'Connor, *Shakespeare Reproduced: The text in history and ideology* (London, 1987), pp. 207–24.

24. Baudrillard, *op. cit.*, pp. 124–8.

25. D. J. Gordon, 'Name and fame: Shakespeare's *Coriolanus*', in S. Orgel (ed.), *The Renaissance Imagination: Essays and lectures by D. J. Gordon*, (Berkeley, Calif., 1975), 203–19.

26. J. Dollimore, *Radical Tragedy: Religion, ideology and power in the dramas of Shakespeare and his contemporaries* (Brighton, 1984), pp. 78–81.

27. Hobbes, *op. cit.*, pp. 218–21; M. Kishlansky, *Parliamentary Selection: Social and political choice in early modern England* (Cambridge, 1986), pp. 3–9. See also D. Hirst, *The Representative of the People? Voters and voting in England under the early Stuarts* (Cambridge, 1975).

28. J. Rees, *Fulke Greville, Lord Brooke, 1554–1628: A critical biography* (London, 1971), p. 20.

29. J. Aubrey, *Brief Lives*, ed. A. Clark (London, 1898), Vol. I, p. 67; Rebholz, *op. cit.*, pp. 188–90.

30. Rebholz, *ibid.*, p. 92; M. Prestwich, *Cranfield: Politics and profits under the early Stuarts: The career of Lionel Cranfield, Earl of Middlesex* (Oxford, 1966), p. 181.

31. Rebholz, *ibid.*, p. 92; Fripp, *op. cit.*, p. 190; Hughes, *op. cit.*, p. 88.

32. J. E. Neale, *The Elizabethan House of Commons* (Harmondsworth, 1963), pp. 241–4.

33. T. Kemp (ed.), *The Black Book of Warwick* (Warwick, 1898), pp. 409–11; M. Jannson and W. Bidwell (eds), *Proceedings in Parliament: 1625* (New Haven, Conn., 1987), p. 703.

34. The most important work on the 'county community' as a 'semi-independent' polity is A. Everitt, *The Community of Kent and the Great Rebellion* (Leicester, 1966).

35. Kishlansky, *op. cit.*, pp. 25–31; R. Cust, 'Politics and the electorate in the 1620s', in R. Cust and A. Hughes (eds), *Conflict in Early Stuart England: Studies in religion and politics, 1603–1642* (London, 1989), pp. 138–9.

36. Cust, *ibid.*, pp. 145–7. Speaking for the JPs, Benjamin Lovell recalled that 'whilst I lived in Warwickshire we were wont to advise together about the knights of the shire': Kishlansky, *op. cit.*, p. 27.

37. Neale, *op. cit.*, (1963), pp. 48–9.

38. For newsletters and parliamentary reports in the Shakespearean period, see R. Cust, 'News and politics in seventeenth century England', *Past and Present*, 112 (1986), pp. 75–9. For Livian constitutionalism as an oligarchic discourse see J. E. Farnell, 'The social and intellectual basis of

London's role in the English Civil Wars', *Journal of Modern History*, 49 (1977), pp. 646–52. Farnell sees Fulke Greville's heir, Robert, 2nd Lord Brooke, as the most radical of the parliamentary leaders to use the Livian discourse, but one who also typically argued that 'the *faece* of the people should not meddle in the sphere of the well born', a view that echoes his uncle's repudiation of the people's 'Tribunes' (p. 650).

39. *Acts of the Privy Council*, 32: pp. 247–8. Expected since August, 3,000 Spanish troops landed at Kinsale on 21 September.
40. Kishlansky, *op. cit.*, p. 191.
41. *Acts of the Privy Council*, 32: p. 248.
42. Eccles, *op. cit.*, pp. 97–8; Fripp, *op. cit.*, pp. 167–73, 176–84.
43. *Ibid.*, pp. 173–5, 182–5. For the relationship between the 'greater bench' of assize judges and the local JPs, see C. Holmes, 'The county community in Stuart historiography', *Journal of British Studies*, 19 (1980), pp. 62–4.
44. Kishlansky, *op. cit.*, p. 17.
45. Hirst, *op. cit.*, p. 160.
46. See, for example, A. Gurr, '*Coriolanus* and the body politic', *Shakespeare Survey*, 28 (1975), pp. 63–9; and W. Gordon Zeeveld, '*Coriolanus* and Jacobean Politics', *Modern Language Review*, 57, 3 (1962), pp. 321–34.
47. S. Schama, *The Embarrassment of Riches: An interpretation of Dutch culture in the golden age* (London, 1987), p. 341.
48. Hirst, *op. cit.*, p. 41.
49. P. Stallybrass and A. White, *The Politics and Poetics of Transgression* (London, 1986), pp. 27–31.
50. G. Wither, *Opobalsamum Anglicanum* (1646), quoted in C. V. Wedgwood, *Poetry and Politics under the Stuarts* (Cambridge, 1960), pp. 90–1.
51. Neale, *op. cit.*, 1963, p. 241.
52. M. Weber, *The Protestant Ethic and the Spirit of Capitalism*, trans. T. Parsons (London, 1930), p. 104.
53. *Ibid.*, p. 115.
54. T. J. B. Spencer (ed.), *Shakespeare's Plutarch* (Harmondsworth, 1964), p. 321.
55. Eccles, *op. cit.*, p. 98; Fripp, *op. cit.*, p. 147.
56. *Acts of the Privy Council*, 32: pp. 222–5, 239–42, 251, 273–84.
57. Fripp, *op. cit.*, pp. 185, 190–2; Eccles, *op. cit.*, p. 99.
58. The list is reproduced as an appendix to P. Williams, 'Court and polity under Elizabeth I', *John Rylands University Library Bulletin*, 65 (1983), pp. 280–6.
59. The literature on the Buckinghamshire election is very extensive and provides a conspectus of the ongoing debate about Stuart elections. See in particular S. R. Gardiner, *History of England from the accession of James I to the Outbreak of the Civil War* (London, 1983), Vol. I, pp. 167–70; G. R. Elton, *The Tudor Constitution* (Cambridge, 1960), pp. 259–60; J. P. Kenyon, *The Stuart Constitution* (Cambridge, 1966), p. 27; D. Hirst, 'Elections and the privileges of the House of Commons in the early

seventeenth century: Confrontation or compromise?', *The Historical Journal*, 18, 4 (1975), pp. 851–62; R. C. Munden, 'The defeat of Sir John Fortescue: Court *versus* country at the hustings?', *English Historical Review*, 93 (1978), pp. 811–16; J. H. Hexter, 'Power struggle Parliament and liberty in early Stuart England', *Journal of Modern History*, 50 (1978), p. 36; L. L. Peck, 'Goodwin *v*. Fortescue: The local context of parliamentary controversy', *Parliamentary History*, 3 (1984), pp. 33–56.

60. *Acts of the Privy Council*, 32: p. 248; Fripp, *op. cit.*, pp. 187; 189–90.
61. Hobbes, *op. cit.*, p. 217.
62. J. Hall, *The Advancement of Learning*, ed. A. K. Croston (Liverpool, 1953), pp. 36–8. See Agnew, *op. cit.*, pp. 96–100, and J. Barish, *The Antitheatrical Prejudice* (Berkeley, Calif., 1981), pp. 82–3, 94–7.
63. F. Greville, 'A dedication to Sir Philip Sidney', in *The Prose Works of Fulke Greville*, ed. J. Gouws (Oxford, 1986), pp. 134–5.
64. E. Spenser, 'An epitaph upon the right honourable Sir Philip Sidney', in *The Poetical Works of Edmund Spenser*, ed. J. C. Smith and E. De Selincourt (Oxford, 1912), p. 559.
65. S. Gosson, *Plays Confuted*, quoted in Agnew, *op. cit.*, *128*.
66. F. Greville, *op. cit.*, (1986), pp. 103, 112–13.
67. Agnew, *op. cit.*, p. 126.
68. *Ibid.*, p. 50.
69. *Select Statutes of the Reigns of Elizabeth and James I*, 101, pp. 39 and 40 Eliz. Cap. IV, 'An Act for punishment of rogues, vagabonds and sturdy beggars'.
70. Baudrillard, *op. cit.*, p. 136.
71. W. Perkins, *A Treatise of Vocations, or, Callings of Men* (Cambridge, 1603), quoted in Barish, *op. cit.*, p. 105.
72. M. Walzer, *The Revolution of the Saints: A study in the origins of radical politics* (London, 1966), pp. 210–19.
73. W. Raleigh, 'On the life of man', in *The Poems of Sir Walter Raleigh*, ed. A. Latham (London, 1951), p. 55.
74. Cited by T. Davidson, 'Plough rituals in England and Scotland', *The Agricultural History Review*, VII, (1959), pp. 27–37. See also Bushaway, *op. cit.*, pp. 168–70.
75. *Ibid.*, pp. 116–17.
76. Foucault, *op. cit.*, pp. 195–9. See also J. L. Amariglio, 'The body, economic discourse, and power: An economist's introduction to Foucault', *History of Political Economy*, xx, (1988), pp. 583–613 for a valuable commentary.
77. Quoted in Keynes, *op. cit.*, p. 141.
78. Eccles, *op. cit.*, p. 99.
79. Prestwich, *op. cit.*, p. 70. For the description of Greville's anger on losing his seat and office, see M. Young, *Servility and Service: The life and work of Sir John Coke* (London, 1986), p. 36; and for his death, Rebholz, *op. cit.*, pp. 314–16. For the quarrel over Fulke Greville's estate, see Hughes, *op. cit.*, pp. 24–5.
80. A. Patterson, *Censorship and Interpretation* (Madison, Wis., 1984), p.

63. For the evolution of a 'Country' mentality, see especially P. Zagorin, *The Court and the Country* (London, 1969), pp. 32–9.
81. Young, *op. cit.*, p. 34.
82. Charlesworth and Randall, *op. cit.*, p. 212.
83. For the 1615 enclosure, see Schoenbaum, *op. cit.*, pp. 233–4. The remark about Shakespeare was attributed to Fulke Greville by David Lloyd in *Statesmen and Favourites of England since the Reformation* (London, 1665), p. 504: cited in S. Schoenbaum, *Shakespeare's Lives* (Oxford, 1970), p. 118.

The quality of mercy: discipline and punishment in Shakespearean comedy

1. W. M. Wallace, *Sir Walter Raleigh* (Princeton, N.J., 1959); R. Lacey, *Sir Walter Raleigh* (London, 1973); M. Foucault, *Discipline and Punish: The birth of the prison* (Harmondsworth, 1979), pp. 32–69.
2. M. Lee (ed.), *Dudley Carleton to John Chamberlain: 1603–1624: Jacobean letters* (New Brunswick, 1972), pp. 38–52.
3. A. Latham (ed.), *The Poems of Sir Walter Raleigh* (London, 1951), p. 50.
4. For Prince Henry's remark, see Wallace *op. cit.*, p. 237. Burghley quoted in S. Shepherd, *Marlowe and the Politics of the Elizabethan Theatre* (Brighton, 1986), p. 37. Elizabeth's speech to the 1586 parliament quoted in J. E. Neale, *Elizabeth 1 and her Parliaments, 1584–1601* (London, 1957, p. 119. Foucault, *op. cit.*, pp. 49, 58.
5. C. Belsey, *The Subject of Tragedy: Identity and difference in Renaissance drama* (London, 1985), p. 190. For the execution speech as a set-piece acted before 'thousands of sorrowful spectators', see J. A. Sharpe, '"Last dying speeches": Religion, ideology and public execution in seventeenth century England', *Past and Present*, 107 (May 1985), pp. 144–67.
6. Latham, *op. cit.*, p. 51.
7. D. J. Gordon, 'Rubens and the Whitehall ceiling', in S. Orgel (ed.), *The Renaissance Imagination: Essays and lectures by D. J. Gordon* (Berkeley, Calif., 1975), pp. 35–44.
8. Lee, *op. cit.*, p. 52.
9. N. Machiavelli, *The Prince*, trans. G. Bull (Harmondsworth, 1961), pp. 95–6.
10. C. H. McIlwain (ed.), *The Political Works of James 1*, (New York, 1965), p. 10.
11. Machiavelli, *op. cit.*, p. 98; Foucault, *op. cit.*, (1979), p. 82.
12. P. Spierenburg, *The Spectacle of Suffering: Executions and the evolution of repression: from a preindustrial metropolis to the European experience* (Cambridge, 1984), pp. 202–5.
13. L. Beier, *Masterless Men: The vagrancy problem in England, 1560–1640* (London, 1985), pp. 164–9.
14. S. Schama, *The Embarrassment of Riches: An interpretation of Dutch culture in the golden age* (London, 1987), p. 17.
15. *The True Narration of the Entertainment of His Royal Majestie, from the Departure from Edinburgh; till his Receiving at London* (London, 1603),

quoted in G. P. V. Akrigg, *Jacobean Pageant: The Court of King James I* (London, 1962), p. 18.

16. F. Moretti, 'The great eclipse: Tragic form as the deconsecration of sovereignty', in *Signs Taken For Wonders: Essays in the sociology of literary forms* (London, 1983), pp. 42–82.

17. S. Greenblatt, 'Invisible bullets: Renaissance authority and its subversion, *Henry IV* and *Henry V*', in J. Dollimore and A. Sinfield (eds), *Political Shakespeare: New essays in Cultural Materialism* (Manchester, 1985), p. 44; McIlwain, *op. cit.*, pp. 5 and 43.

18. J. Dollimore, 'Transgression and surveillance in *Measure for Measure*', in Dollimore and Sinfield, *op. cit.*, (1985), pp. 72–87.

19. Lee, *op. cit.*, p. 48.

20. Foucault, *The History of Sexuality*, Vol. 1: *Introduction*, (Harmondsworth 1981), pp. 137–41.

21. *Ibid.*

22. Belsey, *op. cit.*, p. 101.

23. R. Strong, *Portraits of Queen Elizabeth I*, (Oxford, 1963), p. 10.

24. E. Spenser, *The Faerie Queene*, ed. A. C. Hamilton (London, 1977), v, ix, 33. Whether or not 'Mercie, be of Iustice part. . . . She . . . pour'd down on men, by influence of grace', in Spenser's judicial allegory (v, x, 1). See F. Kermode, '*The Faerie Queene*, I and v', in *Renaissance Essays* (London, 1973), pp. 56–8: 'In Mercilla's presence we are in the prerogative courts of England', where 'the people seek the true justice denied them by the common law.'

25. See M. E. Andrews, *Law versus Equity in 'The Merchant of Venice'* (Boulder, Colo., 1965); W. N. Knight, 'Equity, *The Merchant of Venice* and William Lambarde', *Shakespeare Survey*, 27 (1974), pp. 93–104. See also W. J. Jones, *The Elizabethan Court of Chancery* (Oxford, 1967), *passim*.

26. W. R. Prest, *The Inns of Court under Elizabeth I and the Early Stuarts, 1590–1640* (Oxford, 1972), p. 135; *The Rise of the Barristers: A social history of the English bar, 1590–1640* (Oxford, 1986), p. 201.

27. *Ibid.*, p. 186.

28. J.-P. Vernant, *Tragedy and Myth in Ancient Greece*, trans. J. Lloyd (Brighton, 1981), pp. 8–10.

29. See J. H. Baker, *An Introduction to English Legal History* (London, 1979), pp. 92–3.

30. C. Hill, *The Intellectual Origins of the English Revolution* (Oxford, 1965), Chap. 5.

31. B. Shapiro, 'Sir Francis Bacon and the mid-seventeenth century movement for law reform', *The American Journal of Legal History*, xxiv (1980). See also A. K. R. Kiralfy (ed.), *Potter's Historical Introduction to English Law* (London, 1958), pp. 158–60.

32. See, for example, T. Eagleton, *Shakespeare* (London, 1985), p. 37: 'Shylock is triumphantly vindicated even though he loses the case.'

33. Moretti, *op. cit.*, pp. 56–61.

34. P. Anderson, *Lineages of the Absolutist State* (London, 1974), pp. 40–1.

35. *Ibid.*, pp. 35–6.
36. T. Hobbes, *Leviathan*, ed. C. B. Macpherson (Harmondsworth, 1968), II, 30, p. 388; Moretti, *op. cit.*, p. 45.
37. M. Foucault, 'The political technology of individuals', in L. H. Martin, H. Gutman and P. H. Hutton (eds), *Technologies of the Self: A seminar with Michel Foucault* (London, 1988), p. 150.
38. S. Johnson, *The Plays of William Shakespeare* (London, 1765), Vol. I, pp. xix-xx.
39. Beccaria, quoted by L. Radzinowicz, *A History of the English Criminal Law* (London, 1948), Vol. I, pp. 127–8. T. Hobbes, *A Dialogue Between a Philosopher and a Student of the Common Laws of England*, ed. J. Cropsey (Chicago, Ill., 1971), pp. 152–3; *Leviathan*, I, 14, p. 199. See M. A. Cattaneo, 'Hobbes's theory of punishment', in K. C. Brown (ed.), *Hobbes Studies*, (Oxford, 1965), pp. 279–83.
40. Foucault, *op. cit.*, (1988), p. 152.
41. See C. C. Weston and J. R. Greenberg, *Subjects and Sovereigns: The grand controversy over legal sovereignty in England* (Cambridge, 1981), pp. 13 and 23.
42. *Ibid.*, pp. 12–13.
43. F. Jameson, *The Political Unconscious: Narrative as a socially symbolic act* (London, 1981), *passim*. For a characteristic literal and Christianising interpretation of the religiosity of Shakespearean comic form, see R. G. Hunter, *Shakespeare and the Comedy of Forgiveness* (New York, 1965).
44. Moretti, *op. cit.*, 'The soul and the harpy: Reflections on the aims and methods of literary historiography', pp. 19–20.
45. Sir John Holland, quoted in V. Morgan, 'Whose prerogative in late sixteenth and early seventeenth century England?', *The Journal of Legal History*, v, 3 (1984), p. 38. See also R. W. K. Hinton, 'The decline of parliamentary government under Elizabeth I and the early Stuarts', *Cambridge Historical Journal*, XIII, 2 (1957), pp. 116–132, for a detailed analysis of the partial eclipse of statute by 'unparliamentary law-making' such as letters patent. Hinton shows that administrative government was legitimated as 'what is good and necessary for the common wealth' (p. 125).
46. Morgan, *op. cit.*, p. 39.
47. Hobbes, *op. cit.* (1968), II, 30, p. 388; Foucault, *op. cit.* (1979), pp. 220–1.
48. Foucault, *Ibid.* (1979), p. 113.
49. T. W. Baldwin, *William Shakespeare Adapts a Hanging* (Princeton, N.J., 1931). Baldwin sees an allusion to the execution of William Hartley, a seminary priest, on 5 October 1588 in Finsbury Fields beside the Theatre and the Curtain playhouses.
50. Foucault, *op. cit.* (1979), pp. 25–6.
51. Anderson, *op. cit.* (1974), p. 113.
52. Hobbes, *op. cit.* (1968), II, 17, pp. 227–8.
53. The records of Jonson's indictment and branding are reproduced in *Middlesex County Records (Old Series)*, ed. J. C. Jeaffreson (London,

1886), pp. xxxviii-xlii.
54. *The Byble in Englyshe* (the Bishop's Bible) (London, 1572).
55. All quotations from Jonson's plays, *Ben Jonson*, ed. C. H. Herford, P. Simpson and E. Simpson, 11 Vols (Oxford, 1925–52). A. Barton, *Ben Jonson: Dramatist* (Cambridge, 1984), p. 79.
56. *Ibid.*, p. 117.
57. Foucault, *op. cit.* (1979), p. 25.
58. J. S. Cockburn, 'Trial by the book? Fact and theory in the criminal process, 1558–1640', in J. H. Baker (ed.), *Legal Records and the Historian* (London, 1978), pp. 75–9. Cockburn traces the 'mini-revolution' of the 1590s, when clemency began to replace clergy as the courts assumed increasingly discretionary powers, with a wealth of detailed evidence of remissions.
59. C. B. Herrup, *The Common Peace: Participation and the criminal law in seventeenth-century England* (Cambridge, 1987), p. 63. Herrup's study of crime and sentencing in Sussex is an exhaustive confirmation of Cockburn's theory of a legal revolution in the 1590s (n. 58). For clergy and branding, see, pp. 48–50.
60. J. A. Sharpe, *Crime in Seventeenth-Century England: A county study* (Cambridge, 1983), p. 148.
61. D. Hay, 'Property, authority and the criminal law', in D. Hay *et al.* *Albion's Fatal Tree: Crime and society in eighteenth-century England* (Harmondsworth, 1977), pp. 40–9.
62. *Ibid.*, p. 41.
63. N. Zemon Davis, *Fiction in the Archives: Pardon tales and their tellers in sixteenth-century France* (Cambridge, 1988); Hobbes, *op. cit.*, (1968), II, 28, p. 353; I, 15, p. 210.
64. Foucault, *The Order of Things: An archaeology of the human sciences* (London, 1970), p. 16.
65. G. P. V. Akrigg (ed.), *Letters of King James VI and I*, (Berkeley, Calif., 1984), p. 218.
66. E. Thompson, *Sir Walter Raleigh* (London, 1935), p. 211.
67. Hobbes, *op. cit.*, (1968), II, 17, pp. 227–8.
68. Lee, *op. cit.*, p. 51.
69. Foucault, *op. cit.*, (1979), p. 29.
70. *Ibid.*, pp. 65–9, 112.
71. *Ibid.*, p. 110.
72. C. Ribton-Turner, *History of Vagrants and Vagrancy* (London, 1887), p. 133; A. E. Smith, *Colonists in Bondage: White servitude and convict labor in America, 1607–1776*, (Williamsburg, 1947), pp. 90–100, 136–41. James evidently viewed transportation as a social panacea. On 21 November 1617 he signed an Order in Council for the deportation of all 'the most lewde persons' and 'notorious ill livers' in 'Northumberland, Cumberland, etc.'; and on 13 January 1618 he ordered the shipment to Virginia of 'divers idle young people . . . to clear the court from them' (*Acts of the Privy Council*, 35, p. 381; Ribton-Turner, p. 143).
73. Lee, *op. cit.*, p. 52.

74. Moretti, *op. cit.*, p. 61.
75. Hobbes, *op. cit.* (1968), i, 15, p. 210.
76. Foucault, *op. cit.*, (1979), pp. 195–9.
77. *Ibid.*, pp. 200–9.
78. *Ibid.*, pp. 213–14.
79. *Ibid.*, p. 216.
80. *Ibid.*, p. 217.
81. For Lady Pembroke's boast, see S. Schoenbaum, *William Shakespeare: A documentary life* (Oxford, 1975), p. 126. On Pepys, see F. Barker, *The Tremulous Private Body: Essays in subjection* (London, 1984); Marvell, 'An Horatian ode upon Cromwell's return from Ireland', in *Andrew Marvell: The complete poems*, ed. E. S. Donno (Harmondsworth, 1985), p. 56; for Raleigh's comment on the mercy of James i, see Thompson, *op. cit.*, (1935), p. 221; Latham, *op. cit.*, (1951), p. 51.

Observations on English bodies: Licensing maternity in Shakespeare's late plays

1. John Hall, *Select Observations on English Bodies or Cures both Empirical and Historical performed upon Eminent Persons in Desperate Diseases* (London, 1657), To the Judicious Reader, p. 4. This text is published. as an appendix to Harriet Joseph, *Shakespeare's Son-in-Law: John Hall, man and physician* (Hamden, Conn., 1964).
2. Quoted in Joseph, *op. cit.*, p. 12.
3. M. Foucault, *The Birth of the Clinic: An archaeology of medical perception*, trans. A. Sheridan (London, 1976), p. 107.
4. Hall, *op. cit.*, 1st Century, Observation xix, p. 24; To The Judicious Reader, pp. 10–11.
5. F. Bacon, *The Advancement of Learning*, ed. W. Wright (Oxford, 1900), Bk ii, x, 2:, p. 137.
6. J. Derrida, 'Plato's pharmacy', in *Dissemination*, trans. B. Johnson (London, 1981), p. 167.
7. Hall, *op. cit.*, 2nd Century, Observation xxxiii, pp. 176–9.
8. *Ibid.*, lst Century, Observation xxxvi, pp. 47–51.
9. *Ibid.*, Testimony, p. 8.
10. Foucault, *op. cit.* (1976), p. 166.
11. Quoted *ibid.*
12. See F. J. Cole, *Early Theories of Sexual Generation* (Oxford, 1930), and J. Needham, *A History of Embryology* (New York, 1959).
13. Foucault, *op. cit.* (1976), p. 166.
14. G. Herbert, 'Vanity', in *The Works of George Herbert*, ed. F. E. Hutchinson (Oxford, 1941), p. 85.
15. P. Willughby, *Observations in Midwifery*, ed. H. Blenkinsop (1863), reprint ed. J. L. Thornton (Wakefield, 1972), p. 254.
16. W. Harvey, *The Works of William Harvey*, ed. R. Willis (London, 1847), (repr. New York, 1965), pp. 364, 480–81.
17. Willughby *op. cit.*, p. 65. For the 'ceremony of childbirth' as a process of

enclosure and confinement, see especially A. Wilson, 'Participant or patient? Seventeenth century childbirth from the mother's point of view', in R. Porter (ed.), *Patients and Practitioners: Lay perceptions of medicine in pre-industrial England* (Cambridge, 1989), pp. 133–41. For male exclusion from the birth chamber, see also A. Rich, *Of Woman Born: Motherhood as experience and institution* (New York, 1976), p. 134: 'Misogyny attached itself to the birth-process so that males were forbidden to attend at births' because the church 'saw woman – and especially her reproductive organs – as evil incarnate'; and H. Smith, 'Gynecology and ideology in seventeenth century England', in B. Carroll (ed.), *Liberating Woman's History: Theoretical and critical essays* (Chicago, 1976), pp. 97–114.

18. Quoted in J. B. Donegan, *Women and Men Midwives: Medicine, morality and misogyny in early America* (Westport, Conn., 1978), p. 23.
19. Quoted in M. George, *Women in the First Capitalist Society: Experiences in seventeenth-century England* (Brighton, 1988), p. 207.
20. Hall *op. cit.*, 2nd Century, Observation LVII, pp. 221–2.
21. *Ibid.*, 2nd Century, Observation LVIII, p. 223.
22. *Ibid.*, 2nd Century, Observation LII, pp. 213–15.
23. Willughby *op. cit.*, p. 233.
24. *Ibid.*
25. Foucault, *op. cit.*, (1976), pp. 34–5. For the place of midwifery and female healing in the medical marketplace, see especially L. McGray Beier, *Sufferers and Healers: The experience of illness in seventeenth-century England* (London, 1987), pp. 15–19, 42–50, 211–17.
26. L. Montrose, '*A Midsummer Night's Dream* and the shaping fantasies of Elizabethan culture: Gender, power, form', in S. Greenblatt (ed.), *Representing the English Renaissance* (Berkeley, Calif., 1988), pp. 42–3.
27. Quoted *ibid.*, p. 43.
28. Hall, *op. cit.*, To the Friendly Reader, p. 4. For Montpellier as a centre of humanist surgery, see V. Nutton, 'Humanist surgery', in A. Wear, R. French and I. Lowie, *The Medical Renaissance of the Sixteenth Century* (Cambridge, 1985), p. 81.
29. N. Zemon Davis, 'Proverbial wisdom and popular errors', in *Society and Culture in Early Modern France*, (Stanford, Calif., 1975), , p. 261.
30. Quoted *ibid.*
31. Quoted in K. Thomas, *Religion and the Decline of Magic: Studies in popular beliefs in sixteenth- and seventeenth-century England* (Harmondsworth, 1978), pp. 16–17.
32. R. Burton, *The Anatomy of Melancholy* (London, 1932), Vol. II, p. 210; Thomas, *op. cit.*, (1978), p. 17. The connection between *All's Well That Ends Well* and Harveian medicine was sketched. in C. J. Sisson, 'Shakespeare's Helena and Dr. William Harvey', *Essays and Studies* (London, 1960), pp. 1–20.
33. F. Nietzsche, *The Gay Science*, trans. W. Kaufmann (New York, 1974), p. 38. Quoted (with translation from Greek) by G. C. Spivak in his Preface to *Of Grammatology* by J. Derrida (Baltimore, 1976), p. xxxvi.

34. T. R. Forbes, *The Midwife and the Witch* (New Haven, Conn., 1966), pp. 117, 127–8. See also J. Gibson, *Hanged. for Witchcraft: Elizabeth Lowys and her successors* (Canberra, 1988), pp. 96–106; and J. Towler and J. Bramall, *Midwives in History and Society* (London, 1986), pp. 31–9.

35. M. Nelson, 'Why witches were women', in J. Freeman (ed.) *Women: A Feminist Perspective* (Palo Alto, Calif., 1975), p. 339.

36. Towler and Bramall, *op. cit.*, (1986), pp. 126–9.

37. J. Adelman, 'Fantasies of maternal power in *Macbeth*', in M. Garber (ed.), *Cannibals, Witches, and Divorce: Estranging the Renaissance* (Baltimore, Md., 1987), p. 91.

38. For death from Caesarian surgery, see B. K. Rothman, *In Labor: Women and power in the birthplace* (New York, 1982), pp. 51–3. For the death of Jane Seymour, see R. L. DeMolen, 'The birth of Edward VI and the death of Queen Jane: The arguments for and against Caesarian section', *Renaissance Studies*, IV, 4, 1991, pp. 359–91.

39. T. Eagleton, *William Shakespeare* (Oxford, 1986), pp. 92–3.

40. Towler and Bramall (1986), *op. cit.*, p. 56. Midwives were instructed. to question the mother about paternity 'when the pains of labour are greatest' so that her resistance would be overcome: see M. Wiesner, 'Nuns, wives, mothers', in S. Marshall (ed.), *Women in Reformation and Counter-Reformation Europe* (Bloomington, Ill., 1989), pp. 24–5. For details of such interrogations, see also M. Ingram, *Church Courts, Sex and Marriage in England, 1570–1640* (Cambridge, 1990), pp. 262–3.

41. P. Erikson, 'Patriarchal structures in *The Winter's Tale*', *PMLA*, 97 (1982), p. 827.

42. Quoted in A. Wilson, 'The ceremony of childbirth and its interpretation', in V. Fildes (ed.), *Women as Mothers in Pre-Industrial England* (London, 1990), p. 82.

43. See R. M. Warnicke, *The Rise and Fall of Anne Boleyn* (Cambridge, 1989), p. 203: Anne 'was charged with inciting, in witchlike fashion, five men to have sexual relations with her by the use of touches and kisses that involved thrusting her tongue into their mouths and theirs in hers (called pigeon kisses). The kisses, touches, and caresses were minutely described.'

44. For the Stuart rites of *accouchement* see W. F. Bynum, 'Medicine at the English Court', in V. Nutton (ed.), *Medicine at the Courts of Europe, 1500–1837* (London and New York, 1990), p. 265. For the legend of the baby in the warming-pan, see H. van der Zee and B. van der Zee, *1688: Revolution in the family* (Harmondsworth, 1988), pp. 73–7.

45. Quoted. in D. E. Underdown, 'The taming of the scold', in A. Fletcher and J. Stevenson (eds), *Order and Disorder in Early Modern England* (Cambridge, 1987), p. 119. See also Ingram, *op. cit.*, (1990), 292–319.

46. J.-F. Lyotard, *The Postmodern Condition: A report on knowledge*, trans. G. Bennington and B. Massumi (Manchester, 1986), pp. 18–41.

47. Davis, *op. cit.*, (1987), pp. 252–3. For Perrault and Louis XIV, see also D. Malland, *Culture and Society in Seventeenth-Century France* (London, 1970), pp. 244–51, 274–5; and L. Marin, *Portrait of the King* (London,

1989), *passim*.
48. S. L. Chapin, 'Science in the reign of Louis XIV', in P. Sonnino (ed.), *The Reign of Louis XIV: Essays in celebration of Andrew Lossky* (London, 1990), p. 185.
49. R. Darnton, 'Peasants tell tales', in *The Great Cat Massacre and Other Episodes in French Cultural History* (Harmondsworth, 1985), p. 69.
50. S. Macintyre and A. Sooman, 'Non-paternity and prenatal screening', *The Lancet*, 338, 8771, (5 October 1991), p. 869.
51. J. Donnison, *Midwives and Medical Men: A history of inter-professional rivalries and women's rights* (London, 1977), pp. 13–15; Towler and Bramall, *op. cit.*, (1986), pp. 77–81; P. Elmer, 'Medicine, religion and the puritan revolution', in French and Wear, *op. cit.*, (1989), pp. 21–2. The official interpretation of the Chamberlen's petition as a document 'in the history of feminism' is offered. in G. Clark, *The Royal College of Physicians of London* (London, 1964), p. 236.
52. S. Shahar, *Childhood in the Middle Ages* (London, 1990), p. 35. See also D. McLaren, 'Fertility, infant mortality and breast feeding in the seventeenth century', *Medical History, 22* (1978), pp. 380–1.
53. C. Hill, *Society and Puritanism in Pre-Revolutionary England* (Harmondsworth, 1986), Chap. XIII; Hall, *op. cit.*, (1657), 'To the Judicious Reader', p. 7.
54. E. Jones, *The Life and Work of Sigmund Freud* (Harmondsworth, 1964), pp. 173–4; Donegan. *op. cit.*, (1978), p. 29.
55. Hall, *op. cit.*, (1657), 2nd Century, Observation LIV, pp. 216–18.
56. K. D. Keele, *William Harvey* (London, 1965), pp. 82–3; I. Veith, *Hysteria: The history of a disease* (Chicago, 1965), pp. 130–1.
57. Wilson, *op. cit.*, (1989), p. 38.
58. *Ibid.*, pp. 38–9.
59. Quoted in Thomas,*op. cit.*, (1978), p. 68.
60. Quoted *ibid.*
61. R. Herrick, *The Poems of Robert Herrick*, ed. L. C. Martin (Oxford, 1965), p. 286.
62. Seventeenth-century Welsh superstition cited. in Thomas, *op. cit.*, (1978), p. 43.
63. Quoted *ibid.*, p. 68.
64. E. S. Haldane, *Descartes: His life and times* (New York edn, 1966), pp. 376–7.
65. Harvey, *op. cit.*, (1847), p. 367.
66. Quoted in Haldane, *op. cit.*, (1966), p. 281. For Descartes's mechanistic theory of conception, see especially D. Fouke, 'Mechanical and "organical" models in seventeenth-century explanations of biological reproduction', *Science in Context*, III, 2 (Autumn 1989), pp. 366–88.
67. J. MacVicar, *Man-Midwife* (Leicester, 1975), p. 6.
68. Harvey, *op. cit.*, (1847), pp. 480–1.
69. Aubrey, *op. cit.*, (1972), p. 287; see also L. Chauvois, *William Harvey: His life and times; his discoveries; his methods* (London, 1957), pp. 142–5.
70. For Henrietta Maria as guest of Susanna Hall and the dispersal of Hall's

library, see S. Schoenbaum, *William Shakespeare: A documentary life* (Oxford, 1975), p. 249; and *Shakespeare's Lives* (Oxford, 1970), pp. 125–6.

A constant will to publish: Shakespeare's dead hand

1. E. M. Thompson, 'Handwriting', in W. Raleigh (ed.), *Shakespeare's England* (Oxford, 1916), p. 304. The Quiney case was first examined by H. A. Hanley, 'Shakespeare's family in Stratford records', *Times Literary Supplement*, 21 May 1964, p. 441; and was discussed in E. R. C. Brinkworth, *Shakespeare and the Bawdy Court of Stratford* (Chichester, 1972), p. 80. For an early but still useful account of Shakespeare and property law, see W. L. Rushton, *Shakespeare's Testamentary Language* (London, 1869). I am particularly grateful to Dr Susan Brock of the Shakespeare Institute, Stratford-upon-Avon, for her assistance in the research of this essay.
2. S. Schoenbaum, *William Shakespeare: A documentary life* (Oxford, 1975), p. 246.
3. BL, Lansdowne MS, 721, fo. 2. Quoted *ibid*.
4. M. Arnold, 'Shakespeare', in *The Poetry of Matthew Arnold*, ed. K. Allott (London, 1965), pp. 48–9.
5. B. R. Lewis, *The Shakespeare Documents* (Stanford, Calif., 1940), Vol. 2, p. 471.
6. E. A. J. Honigmann, 'The second-best bed', *New York Review of Books*, 38, 18 (7 November 1991), pp. 27–30.
7. G. E. Bentley, *Shakespeare: A biographical handbook* (New Haven, Conn., 1961), p. 61.
8. Honigmann, *op. cit.*, p. 30.
9. Schoenbaum, *op. cit.*, p. 246.
10. T. Eagleton, *William Shakespeare* (Oxford, 1986), p. 1.
11. Lewis, *op. cit.*, Vol. 2, p. 489.
12. E. P. Thompson, 'The grid of inheritance', in J. Goody, J. Thirsk and E. P. Thompson (eds), *Family and Inheritance: Rural society in Western Europe, 1200–1800* (Cambridge, 1976), pp. 328–50; J. Goody, 'Inheritance, property and women: Some considerations', *ibid.*, p. 15.
13. The classic Marxist thesis that there was a tenurial revolution in England during the sixteenth century, when economic activity was uprooted from communal forms by modern individualistic property law, has been challenged, notably by Alan Macfarlane who finds economic individualism already well established in the late medieval period. His argument that 'the majority of ordinary people in England from at least the thirteenth century were already rampant individualists, highly mobile both geographically and socially; economically "rational"; market-oriented and acquisitive; ego-centred in kinship and social life', is contradicted, however, by J. P. Cooper, J. Thirsk, E. P. Thompson and others. They find that the most important instruments for the individual control of land – freedom of testation, universality of primogeniture and

the abolition of local manorial customs, such as partible inheritance, widow's freebench, and communal use-rights - were only effective from the Shakespearean period. See A. Macfarlane, *The Origins of English Individualism: The family, property and social transition* (Cambridge, 1978); and Goody *et al.*, *op. cit.*, *passim*. And for the persistence of customary inheritance, see n. 107 below.

14. Thompson, *op. cit.*, p. 337.
15. M. K. Ashby, *The Changing English Village: A history of Bledington* (Kineton, 1974), pp. 162–4, 194–5.
16. L. Stone, *Family, Sex and Marriage in England, 1500–1800* (London, 1977), esp. pp. 4–9, 652–8.
17. R. T. Vann, 'Wills and the family in an English town: Banbury, 1550–1800', *Journal of Family History*, 4 (Winter 1979), pp. 346–67. Vann argues that:

> Most of the changes [in family formation] Stone discusses in the squirearchy and aristocracy can be shown to have occurred in the lower social strata in Banbury, close to the time he has argued that they occurred in the upper classes. The change is most marked at the top of the status pyramid in Banbury. After the Civil War prestigious families, in particular, recognise fewer friends and remote kin, close to or even below the degree of extension found in landed families.
>
> (p. 366).

He concludes that in market towns like Banbury it is Stone's thesis, not Macfarlane's, which applies, since in the half century between 1560 and 1610 'we enter a world with different emotional coloration' in the West Midlands, as care for distant relatives gives way to distrust and coolness towards even close ones, such as sons-in-law (pp. 357–8).

18. E. Cheyfitz, *The Poetics of Imperialism: Translation and colonization from 'The Tempest' to 'Tarzan'* (Oxford, 1991), p. 50.
19. Honigmann, *op. cit.*, p. 27.
20. Thompson, *op. cit.*, p. 337.
21. P. S. Clarkson and C. T. Warren, *The Law of Property in Shakespeare and the Elizabethan Drama* (Baltimore, Md., 1942), p. 218.
22. Cited in L. Stone, *The Crisis of the Aristocracy, 1559–1641* (Oxford, 1965), p. 168.
23. Thompson, *op. cit.*, pp. 349–50; and J. Goody, 'Inheritance, property and women: Some comparative considerations', *ibid.*, pp. 10–36; and see L. Holcombe, *Wives and Property* (Toronto, 1983), pp. 20–3. See also B. Todd, 'Freebench and free enterprise: Widows and their property in two Berkshire villages', and M. Prior, 'Wives and wills, 1558–1700', both in J. Chartres and D. Hey (eds), *English Rural Society, 1500–1800: Essays in honour of Joan Thirsk* (Cambridge, 1990), pp. 175–200; 201–25. For a brisk discussion of the position of the heiress in Renaissance literature, see L. Jardine, *Still Harping on Daughters: Women and drama in the age of Shakespeare* (Hemel Hempstead, 1983), Chap. 3.
24. Stone, *op. cit.* (1965), p. 171.

25. A. J. Fletcher, *A County Community in Peace and War: Sussex 1600–1660* (London, 1975), p. 39.
26. N. Davis (ed.), *Paston Letters and Papers of the Fifteenth Century* (Oxford, 1975), Vol. 2, p. 413.
27. Stone, *op. cit.*, (1965), p. 647. For an account of the dowry system as it is represented in the plays, see M. L. Ranald, ' "As marriage binds, and blood breaks": English marriage and Shakespeare', *Shakespeare Quarterly*, 30 (1979), 30, pp. 68–81.
28. Stone, *op. cit.* (1965), pp. 638–40.
29. For instances of such a dynastic calamity, see especially M. E. James, 'Two Tudor funerals', in *Society, Politics and Culture: Studies in Early Modern England* (Cambridge, 1986).
30. Stone, *op. cit.* (1965), p. 632.
31. K. E. Mauss, 'Transfer of title in *Love's Labour's Lost*: Language, individualism, gender', in I. Kamps (ed.), *Shakespeare Left and Right* (London, 1991), p. 211.
32. Stone, *op. cit.* (1965), pp. 172 and 175.
33. A. Macfarlane, *Marriage and Love in England: Modes of reproduction, 1300–1840* (Oxford, 1986), p. 264.
34. Vann, *op. cit.*, p. 362.
35. For Ward's report, see Schoenbaum, *op. cit.*, p. 155. Chambers, *op. cit.*, Vol. 2, pp. 52–71; S. Lee, *A Life of William Shakespeare*, revised edn (Oxford, 1925), p. 315. For the average dowry for a merchant's daughter in London between 1550 and 1600, see J. P. Cooper, 'Patterns of inheritance and settlement by great landowners from the fifteenth to the eighteenth centuries', in Goody *et al.*, *op. cit.*, pp. 307–11.
36. Mauss, *op. cit.*, p. 211.
37. *Ibid.*, p. 220.
38. *Ibid.*, p. 215.
39. L. Tennenhouse, *Power on Display: The politics of Shakespeare's genres* (London, 1986), p. 174.
40. *Ibid.*, p. 169.
41. B. Jonson, *Epicoene or The Silent Woman*, ed. R. V. Holdsworth (London, 1979).
42. E. Wilson, 'Morose Ben Jonson', in *The Triple Thinkers* (Harmondsworth, 1962), p. 244; John Dennis, letter to Congreve, June 1695, in *William Congreve: Letters and Documents*, ed. J. C. Hodges (London, 1964), p. 175; see Holdsworth's edition of *Epicoene*, p. xxix.
43. Lucian, *Dialogues of the Dead*, v, trans. H. Williams; reproduced in B. Jonson, *Volpone*, ed. P. Brockbank (London, 1968), p. 158.
44. Thompson, *op. cit.*, p. 357.
45. Stone, *op. cit.* (1965), p. 595.
46. *Ibid.*, p. 178.
47. L. Stone, *An Elizabethan: Sir Horatio Palavicino* (Oxford, 1956), p. 305.
48. *Ibid.*, p. 304.
49. *Ibid.*, p. 320.
50. For the shift from 'propriety' to 'property', see C. B. Macpherson, 'A

political theory of property', in *Democratic Theory: Essays in Retrieval* (Oxford, 1973), pp. 127–8.

51. K. Duncan-Jones, *Sir Philip Sidney: Courtier poet* (London, 1991), p. 301.

52. B. Jonson, 'To Penshurst', 59–60, in *Ben Jonson: Poems*, ed. I. Donaldson (Oxford, 1975), p. 90; D. E. Wayne, *Penshurst: The semiotics of place and the poetics of history* (London, 1984), pp. 120–3; R. Williams, *The Country and the City* (London, 1973), pp. 40–1.

53. Duncan-Jones, *op. cit.*, p. 299.

54. *Ibid.*, p. 300.

55. *Ibid.*, p. 304.

56. *Ibid.*, p. 299.

57. H. Swinburne, *A Brief Treatise of Testaments* (London, 1590), p. 162. See Clarkson and Warren, *op. cit.*, p. 189 for the origin of this dictum in the law of property in animals. Since the paternity of swans, supposedly monogamous, was never in question, the law quaintly made an exception of this species and divided its offspring equally between the owners of cock and hen.

58. Norse law quoted in E. Le Roy Ladurie, 'Family and inheritance in sixteenth-century France', Goody *et al.*, *op. cit.*, p. 67; and Saxon saying of 'fire and pyre' quoted in Howell, 'Peasant inheritance', *ibid.*, p. 126. For the custom of equal shares for bastards, *ibid.*, pp. 194 (Ireland), pp. 235–8 (Castile), and p. 302 (France). Stone, *op. cit.* (1977), p. 30.

59. Tennenhouse, *op. cit.*, p. 174; C. H. McIlwain (ed.), *The Political Works of James I* (Cambridge, 1918), p. 307.

60. P. Rackin, *Stages of History: Shakespeare's English chronicles* (London, 1991)., pp. 188–9.

61. Howell, *op. cit.*, p. 154.

62. Cheyfitz, *op. cit.*, p. 50.

63. Quoted in J. H. Baker, *An Introduction to English Legal History* (London, 1990), p. 293.

64. S. Greenblatt, *Renaissance Self-Fashioning: From More to Shakespeare* (Chicago, 1980), p. 1.

65. S. Greenblatt, 'Psychoanalysis and Renaissance culture', in P. Parker and D. Quint (eds), *Literary Theory / Renaissance Texts* (Baltimore, Md., 1986), p. 220.

66. For the legal construction of the concept of intention as a function of property ownership, see J. H. Baker and S. F. Milsom, *Sources of English Legal History: Private law to 1750* (London, 1986), pp. 106–7. For Dacre's case and its ramifications for the legal rights of the individual, see J. M. Bean, *The Decline of English Feudalism, 1215–1540* (Manchester, 1968), pp. 275–83.

67. For the evolution of the entail in Elizabethan inheritance strategy, see J. P. Cooper, 'Patterns of inheritance', in Goody *et al.*, *op. cit.*, pp. 199–206.

68. P. Ariès, *The Hour of our Death*, trans. H. Weaver (Harmondsworth, 1981), p. 27.

69. *Ibid.*, p. 19.
70. J. Donne, 'A valediction forbidding mourning', 1–2, in *John Donne: The complete English poems*, ed. A. J. Smith (Harmondsworth, 1973), p. 84.
71. Ariès, *op. cit.*, p. 28.
72. For the law relating to heirlooms and its occurrence in Elizabethan drama, see Clarkson and Warren, *op. cit.*, p. 240.
73. Ariès, *op. cit.*, p. 40.
74. F. Moretti, 'The great eclipse: Tragic form as the deconsecration of sovereignty', *Signs Taken For Wonders: Essays in the sociology of literary forms* (London, 1983), p. 45.
75. P. Anderson, *Lineages of the Absolutist State* (London, 1974), p. 140, n. 37. For the debate about capitalist tendencies under Richard II, see n. 13 above and Macfarlane, *op. cit.* (1978), pp. 103–6.
76. J. H. Hexter, 'Property, monopoly and Shakespeare's *Richard II*', in P. Zagorin (ed.), *Culture and Politics from Puritanism to the Enlightenment* (Berkeley, Calif., 1980), pp. 1–24.
77. J. Hurstfield, *The Queen's Wards: Wardship and marriage under Elizabeth I* (London, 1973), pp. 168–9, 174–7, 344–5.
78. C. Howell, 'Peasant inheritance customs in the Midlands, 1280–1700', in Goody *et al.*, *op. cit.*, pp, 113–14.
79. W. Harrison, *The Description of England* (London, 1587; repr. Ithaca, N.Y., 1968), pp. 133, 202, 204, 217, 257–8.
80. J. M. Keynes, *The Applied Theory of Money*, in *The Collected Writings of John Maynard Keynes* (London, 1971), Vol. 6, p. 137.
81. Greenblatt, *op. cit.*, (1986), p. 220.
82. B. R. Lewis, *op. cit.*, Vol. 2, p. 489.
83. *Ibid.*, pp. 498–9.
84. A. Lewis, 'The law of dower', *The Times Literary Supplement*, 15 February 1991, p. 11.
85. B. Todd, 'Freebench', in Chartres and Hey, *op. cit.*, pp. 175–80.
86. M. Spufford, *Contrasting Communities: English villagers in the sixteenth and seventeenth centuries* (Cambridge, 1974), p. 112; Honigmann, *op. cit.*, p. 30.
87. For the custom of the City which 'had long made the widows of wealthy Londoners even more attractive matches than their daughters', see Cooper, *op. cit.*, p. 225. For the complicated conveyance of the Blackfriars Gatehouse of 10 March 1613, the practical effect of which 'would be to deprive Shakespeare's widow of her dower right to a third share for life in this part of the estate', see Schoenbaum, *op. cit.*, p. 223.
88. Chambers, *op. cit.*, p. 176.
89. A. Lewis, *op. cit.*, p. 11.
90. B. R. Lewis, *op. cit.*, Vol. 2, p. 489.
91. Chambers, *op. cit.*, pp. 170–9.
92. Quoted in R. Houlbrooke, *The English Family, 1450–1700* (London, 1984), p. 230.
93. L. Montrose, '"The place of brother" in *As You Like It*: Social process and comic form', *Shakespeare Quarterly*, 32, 1 (Spring 1981), pp. 28–54.

94. J. Thirsk, 'The European debate on customs of inheritance, 1500–1700', in Goody *et al.*, *op. cit.*, p. 186.
95. A. Macfarlane, *The Culture of Capitalism* (Oxford, 1987), pp. 16–17.
96. A. Macfarlane, *The Family Life of Ralph Josselin, a Seventeenth-Century Clergyman: An essay in historical anthropology* (Cambridge, 1970), pp. 120–3.
97. S. Amussen, *An Ordered Society: Gender and class in early modern England* (Oxford, 1988), p. 90.
98. Houlbrooke, *op. cit.*, p. 232.
99. K. Wrightson, *English Society, 1580–1680* (London, 1982), p. 74.
100. Stone, *op. cit.* (1965), p. 595.
101. For the literary fascination with the *patria potestas* as an expression of 'Elizabethan authoritarianism', from which Shakespeare significantly diverges in *Romeo and Juliet*, see L. Salingar, *Shakespeare and the Traditions of Comedy* (Cambridge, 1974), pp. 313–14.
102. L. Boose, 'The father and the bride in Shakespeare', *(PMLA, 97 (May 1982)*, p. 331.
103. Tennenhouse, *op. cit.*, p. 173.
104. C. Leventen, 'Patrimony and patriarchy in *The Merchant of Venice*', in V. Wayne (ed.), *The Matter of Difference: Materialist feminist criticism of Shakespeare* (London, 1991), p. 72.
105. J. Goody, *op. cit.*, p. 3.
106. Quoted in Stone, *op. cit.* (1965), p. 598.
107. *Ibid.*
108. Leventen, *op. cit.*, p. 72.
109. Stone, *op. cit.* (1965), p. 597.
110. See Thirsk, *op. cit.*, p. 186.
111. Thompson, *op. cit.*, p. 342.
112. Leventen, *op. cit.*, pp. 70–1.
113. W. Lambarde, *A Perambulation of Kent* (London, 1576; repr. Bath, 1970), p. 20; 'It is commonly taken that the custom of Gavelkind is general, and spreadeth itself throughout the whole Shire' (p. 485). The Kent Customal, which lists the rules of gavelkind, first printed in Tottel's edition of the Magna Carta (1556), was reproduced by Lambarde, pp. 513–22. The standard account is C. I. Elton, *The Tenures of Kent* (London, 1867), pp. 391–406. For a discussion of the legal ramifications of gavelkind, see N. Neilson, 'Custom and the common law in Kent', *Harvard Law Review*, 38, 1928, pp. 482–98.
114. P. Clark, *English Provincial Society: Religion, politics and society in Kent, 1500–1640* (Hassocks, 1977), p. 121; Harrison, *op. cit.* (1587; 1968), p. 172; J. Selden, *Opera Omnia*, ed. D. Wilkins (London, 1725), Vol. 2, part 1; and see also Swinburne, *op. cit.* (1590), p. 78. For a discussion of the origin of partible inheritance in pre-Conquest law, see Goody, *op. cit.*, p. 31. For Kent as the bastion of customary inheritance, see also A. Everitt, *Continuity and Colonization: The evolution of Kentish settlement* (Leicester, 1986), p. 179; and C. W. Chalklin, *Seventeenth-Century Kent: A social and economic history* (Rochester,

1965), pp. 55–7.

115. For the disgavelling acts of the Tudor era, see Clark, *op. cit.*, p. 7; Chalklin, *op. cit.*, p. 55. Because these acts did not schedule the lands affected, these tended to revert in time to gavelkind, especially as the legal presumption was always in favour of the application of the custom: see W. S. Holdsworth, *A History of the English Law*, 3rd revised edn (London, 1923), Vol. 3, p. 262.

116. J. Thirsk, 'The common fields', *Past and Present*, 29 (1964), pp. 12–13; M. Campbell, *The English Yeoman Under Elizabeth and the Early Stuarts* (New Haven, Conn., 1942), pp. 146–7.

117. Annesley's will, which itemises his licence 'for the only bringing in of all manner of steel from the parts beyond the seas', is in the Public Record Office, 68 Harte, Prob. 11/104. For the receivership of fines he shared with Francis Harvey, see *HMC: Salisbury Papers*, Vol. 4, p. 257; for his fur monopoly, presumably a benefit of the Mastership of the Queen's Harriers, see *Acts of the Privy Council*, Vol. 27: *1595–1597*, p. 554, December 1597; for his property in west Kent, *ibid.*, p. 308, 25 November 1596; E. Hasted, *The History of Kent* (Canterbury, 1778), Vol. 1, p. 40; E. H. Hart, *History of Lee* (London, 1882), pp. 4–5; L. L. Duncan, *History of the Borough of Lewisham* (London, 1908), pp. 116–17; and for the Mastership of the Harriers itself, *APC Domestic, James I*, p. 190, 30 January 1605 (the grant to his successor). I am grateful to Richard Martin and Jean Wait of the Lee Manor Library and Local History Centre, Lewisham, for their kind assistance in this research.

118. See C. C. Stopes, *The Third Earl of Southampton* (London, 1922), p. 274; G. M. Young, 'Shakespeare and the Termers', British Academy Lecture, 1947, in *Today and Yesterday* (London, 1948), pp. 300–1; G. Bullough, '*King Lear* and the Annesley Case', in E. Kolb (ed.), *Festschrift Rudolf Stamm* (Berne, 1969), pp. 43–9. For the name of the youngest daughter, generally spelt Cordell, but Cordelia in both her marriage licence and burial register, see G. Isham, 'The prototypes of King Lear and his daughters', *Notes and Queries*, 149 (1954), pp. 150–1.

119. J. Dollimore, *Radical Tragedy: Religion, ideology and power in the drama of Shakespeare and his contemporaries*, 2nd edn, (Hemel Hempstead, 1989), p. 197.

120. G. Bullough, *Narrative and Dramatic Sources of Shakespeare* (London, 1973), Vol. VII, pp. 270–1, 309–11.

121. For Annesley's profits from the Wardenship, see BM. Lansdowne MSS. Plut. 75 D. ; A. Harris, *The Oeconomy of the Fleet* (London, 1621: Camden Society repr. 1879), p. 171; J. Ashton, *The Fleet: Its river, prison and marriages* (London, 1888), p. 261. For comments on Annesley's reputation as a cruel governor prone to use 'irons and stocks', and on the murder of Cawlton, his deputy, see Harris, *op. cit.*, p. 9.

122. *APC*, Vol. 28, 1597–8, pp. 415, 432. For Annesley's graduated. charges, first instituted by him in 1593, see J. Southerden Burn, *The History of the Fleet Marriages with Some Account of the Wardens*

(London, 1846), p. 39. His own imprisonment is recorded. in *APC*, 22, p. 397, 26 April 1592. (But see his detention of Recorder Fleetwood, *APC*, 9, p. 233, 19 November 1576.) For Annesley as friend and legatee of Hawkins: see R. Gregory, *The Story of Lee* (London, 1923), p. 125.

123. *Historical Manuscripts Commission* (*HMC*), Salisbury MSS, Vol. 15, 1930, p. 262; reproduced. in Bullough, *op. cit.* (1973), p. 309, document A. For pre-mortem transmission and the medieval tradition of the sojourner, see Goody, *op. cit.*, pp. 28–9; Howell, *op. cit.*, p. 116; and Spufford, 'Inheritance and land in Cambridgeshire', in Goody *et al.*, *op. cit.*, pp. 173–5.

124. *HMC*, Salisbury MSS, Vol. 15, p. 262, repr. in Bullough, *op. cit.* (1973), p. 309, document A.

125. N. Llewellyn, *The Art of Death: Visual culture in the English death ritual, 1500–1800* (London,1991), pp. 13–18.

126. *Ibid.*, p. 18.

127. Spufford, *op. cit.*, p. 175.

128. Llewellyn, *op. cit.*, p. 38.

129. For the non-ambulatory nature of wills prior to 1837, see Clarkson and Warren, *op. cit.*, p. 250.

130. See K. Muir (ed.), *King Lear*, The Arden Shakespeare (London, 1972), pp. xxxix and 80.

131. For Sandys's participation in the 1601 rebellion, which Essex claimed was that of the ringleader, see G. B. Harrison, *The Life and Death of Robert Devereux Earl of Essex* (London, 1937), pp. 285, 292, 297 and 303.

132. Muir, *op. cit.* (1972), p. xxxix, n. 2.

133. *HMC*, Salisbury MSS, Vol. 15, p. 265; repr. in Bullough, *op. cit.* (1973), pp. 309–10.

134. *HMC, Cecil Papers*, Vol. 187, p. 119; repr. in Bullough, *ibid.*, p. 310.

135. Bullough, *op. cit.* (1969), p. 47.

136. Holdsworth, *op cit.*, (3rd revised. edn, London, 1923), Vol. 3, pp. 555. Holdsworth wonders whether the prerogative court of Canterbury 'ever attempted. to exercise an effective jurisdiction . . . to safeguard the rights of children, settle their shares, and look after their interests' in the teeth of testation (p. 556). Its sentence (verdict) in the Annesley case suggests not, at least in the seventeenth century: *PRO* 93 Harte.

137. J. W. Hales, *Notes and Essays on Shakespeare* (London, 1884), p. 310.

138. A. Everitt, *The Community of Kent and the Great Rebellion, 1640–1660* (Leicester, 1966), p. 47.

139. Lambarde, *op. cit.*, pp. 20–1. The episode of the moving wood, which was supposed to have taken place at Swanscombe (or 'Swains-camp'), is first reported by a thirteenth-century monk, Thomas Sprott, whose history of the Augustinians at Canterbury was edited as *T. Sprotti Chronica* by T. Hearne in 1719.

140. Everitt, *op. cit.* (1966), p. 47.

141. P. Laslett (ed.), *Patriarcha and other Political Works of Sir Robert Filmer* (Oxford, 1949), pp. 63 and 24.

142. Everitt, *op. cit.* (1966), pp. 47–8.
143. J. G. A. Pocock, *The Ancient Constitution and the Feudal Law: A study of English historical thought in the seventeenth century* (Cambridge, 1957), p. 197. For the Kentish antiquaries and the influence of gavelkind on their constitutionalist ideas, see also Holdsworth, *op. cit.*, (London, 1924), Vol. 5, pp. 402–4; Everitt, *op. cit.* (1966), pp. 46–7; and Chalklin, *op. cit.*, pp. 206–8.
144. W. Camden, *Britannia: Kent*, ed. G. J. Copley (London, 1977), p. 7; J. Evans, *A History of the Society of Antiquaries* (London, 1956), p. 13; C. Hill, *The Intellectual Origins of the English Revolution* (Oxford, 1965), p. 177.
145. Lambarde, *op. cit.*, pp. 7, 511 and 514.
146. Everitt, *op. cit.* (1966), p. 46; W. Somner, *A Treatise of Gavelkind, both Name and Thing* (London, 1660). For a commentary, see W. Urry (ed.), *William Somner's 'The Antiquities of Canterbury'* (Ilkley, 1977), p. xiii.
147. Lambarde, *op. cit.*, p. 7. For resistance to serfdom in the sixteenth century, see D. MacCulloch, 'Bondmen under the Tudors', in C. Cross (ed.), *Law and Government under the Tudors: Essays presented to Sir Geoffrey Elton* (Cambridge, 1988), pp. 98–100.
148. For the myth of Anglo-Saxon liberty, see especially C. Hill, 'The Norman yoke', in *Puritanism and Revolution: Studies in interpretation of the English Revolution of the seventeenth century* (London, 1968), pp. 64–87; and J. P. Sommerville, *Politics and Ideology in England, 1603–1640* (London, 1986), pp. 89–92.
149. E. Hasted, *The History of Kent* (Canterbury, 1778), Vol. 1, Introduction, p. cxxxvi.
150. Chalklin, *op. cit.*, pp. 232–3.
151. Lambarde, *op. cit.*, p. 507.
152. Marshall McLuhan is (uncharacteristically) representative, when he opens *The Gutenberg Galaxy* with the remark that 'When King Lear proposes "our darker purpose" as the subdivision of his kingdom, he is expressing a politically daring and *avant garde* intent for the early seventeenth century' ((Toronto, 1962), p. 11).
153. L. Jardine, *op. cit.*, p. 78.
154. Lambarde, *op. cit.*, p. 476. Strict partibility also survived as the local custom in isolated, less populated pastoral areas of Wales and of the north, such as Furness, Rossendale, the Cheviots and the Yorkshire Dales; while the common-law rules continued to obtain throughout the ecclesiastical province of York (until 1692), in Wales (1696), in the city of York (1704) and in London itself (1724), in which places they operated in cases of intestacy until 1856. In Kent, gavelkind was only abolished in 1926. See Holdsworth, *op. cit.*, (1923), Vol. 3, pp. 551–4; Thirsk, *op. cit.* (1964), p. 13.
155. Goody, *op. cit.*, p. 32.
156. Howell, *op. cit.*, p. 116.
157. Clark, *op. cit.*, pp. 123, 256; W. K. Jordan, *Archaeologia Cantiana,*

Vol. 75: *The Social Institutions of Kent, 1480–1660* (Ashford, 1961), pp. 16–17, 142–5.
158. R. Halpern, *The Poetics of Primitive Accumulation: English Renaissance culture and the genealogy of capital* (Ithaca, N.Y., 1991), p. 223.
159. Tennenhouse, *op. cit.*, p. 75.
160. For the Mountjoy case, which was heard in the Court of Requests on 11 May 1612, when Shakespeare deposed that he could not now remember the precise sum of the promised settlement, see Schoenbaum, *op. cit.*, pp. 208–13.
161. Thompson, *op. cit.*, pp. 359–60.
162. For Elizabethan common law as historical amalgamation, see Somerville, *op. cit.*, pp. 90–1; and for the influence of Kentish lawyers as the 'custodians of custom', see Clark, *op. cit.*, pp. 289–90. Goody, *op. cit.*, p. 31; Le Roy Ladurie, *op. cit.*, p. 41.
163. Le Roy Ladurie, *op. cit.*, pp. 37–41.
164. W. Empson, 'Bastards and barstards', *Essays in Criticism*, 17 (1967), pp. 407–10.
165. D. Levine and K. Wrightson, 'The social context of illegitimacy in early modern England', in P. Laslett, K. Oosterveer and R. M. Smith (eds), *Bastardy and its Comparative History* (Cambridge, Mass., 1980), p. 158. See also M. Ingram, *Church Courts, Sex and Marriage in England, 1570–1640* (Cambridge, 1987), p. 166; see also, pp. 160–3, 371–2; and Wrightson, *op. cit.*, pp. 84–6.
166. Swinburne, *op. cit.*, p. 200.
167. Quoted. in H. Morley (ed.), *Ireland under Elizabeth and James I* (London, 1890), p. 379. For the partible customs of the Celtic fringe, see H. L. Gray, *English Field Systems* (London, 1915), pp. 268, 303–4.
168. Cooper, *op. cit.*, p. 302.
169. For Sandys's £5,000 fine, see *APC*, 31, 1600–1, p. 348, 11 May 1601. His property had been seized in the immediate aftermath of the rising (p. 149), and he was confined in the Tower from 14 February (p. 159) to 5 August (32, 1601–4, p. 143), when his fine was presumably paid. His wife was under house arrest, though pregnant, from 18 February (31, p. 166), and her husband's political eclipse was confirmed. when he was ordered not to stand for Parliament in September 1601 (32, p. 218).
170. Thirsk, *op. cit.*, p. 181.
171. Stone, *op. cit.* (1977), p. 95.
172. *Ibid.*, p. 94.
173. *Ibid.*, p. 166.
174. Swinburne, *op. cit.*, Preface.
175. Holdsworth, *op. cit.*, Vol. III, pp. 555–6; Ingram, *op. cit.*, p. 37; C. Kitching, 'The prerogative court of Canterbury from Warham to Whitgift', in R. O'Day and F. Heal (eds), *Continuity and Change: Personnel and administration of the Church in England, 1500–1642* (Leicester, 1976), p. 208.
176. That is the inference to be drawn from the absence of any record of a fee for representation paid by the Halls in the PCC accounts, which are

complete from 1600. See Kitching, *op. cit.*, p. 206; and S. Lee, *A Life of William Shakespeare* (revised edn London, 1915), p. 493. For a brief discussion of the unequal division of the Shakespeare estate, see also W. N. Knight, 'Patrimony and Shakespeare's daughters', *Hartford Studies in Literature*, 19 (1977), pp. 175–86.

177. Kitchling, *op. cit.*, pp. 207–8.
178. Chambers, *op. cit.*, p. 179.
179. A. J. Cook, *Making A Match: Courtship in Shakespeare and his society* (Princeton, N.J., 1991), pp. 261–3.
180. *Ibid.*, p. 4.
181. Brinkworth, *op. cit.*, p. 84; Schoenbaum, *op. cit.*, pp. 240–1.
182. K. Wrightson, 'The nadir of English illegitimacy in the seventeenth century', in P. Laslett *et al.*, *op. cit.*, p. 179. For the moral panic over illegitimacy, see also Levine and Wrightson, 'The social context of illegitimacy', *ibid.*, pp. 158–75; Ingram, *op. cit.*, pp. 153–5, 259–81; and S. Amussen, 'Gender, family and the social order', in A. Fletcher and J. Stevenson (eds), *Order and Disorder in Early Modern England* (Cambridge, 1985), p. 207.
183. Schoenbaum, *op. cit.*, pp. 236–7.
184. For John Hall's support of the Puritan campaign waged against the Stratford brewing interests by the zealous vicar, Thomas Wilson of Evesham, see E. Fripp, *Shakespeare: Man and artist* (London, 1938), Vol. II, pp. 885–91.
185. B. R. Lewis, *op. cit.*, p. 506.
186. Chambers, *op. cit.*, p. 180; Lee, *op. cit.*, p. 515, n.1. There was also a bizarre redundant legacy for one Thomas Welles, a remote Arden 'cousin' of Carlton, Bedfordshire, who according to Chambers was a parson who had died aged 'about 100' some twenty years earlier (*op. cit.*, Vol. 2, p. 180).
187. Thompson, *op. cit.*, p. 360.
188. Yorkshire saying, quoted *ibid.*
189. *Ibid.*, p. 348.
190. J. Derrida, 'Signature, event, context', in *Margins of Philosophy*, trans. A. Bass (Chicago, 1982), p. 328. For a discussion, see C. Norris, *Deconstruction: Theory and practice* (London, 1982), pp. 109–13.
191. Derrida, *op. cit.*, p. 316, M. Foucault, 'What is an author?', in P. Rabinow (ed.), *The Foucault Reader* (Harmondsworth, 1984), p. 102.
192. See Greenblatt, *op. cit.* (1980), *passim*; J. Finemann, *Shakespeare's Perjured Eye: The invention of poetic subjectivity in the Sonnets* (Berkeley, Calif., 1988), *passim*; M. Garber, *Shakespeare's Ghost Writers: Literature as uncanny causality* (New York and London, 1987), p. 21. See also T. Docherty, *John Donne Undone* (London, 1986), pp. 124–44.
193. P. Kamuf, *Signature Pieces: On the institution of authorship* (Ithaca N.Y., and London, 1988), pp. 59–67.
194. P. de Man, 'Autobiography as de-facement', in *The Rhetoric of Romanticism* (New York, 1984), pp. 68–78; Kamuf, *op. cit.*, pp. 60–1. J.

Milton, 'On Shakespeare', in *Milton: Poetical works*, ed. D. Bush (Oxford, 1966), p. 82.

195. T. Docherty, *On Modern Authority: The theory and condition of writing: 1500 to the present day* (Brighton, 1987), pp. 130–1 and 249.

196. Foucault, *op. cit.*, pp. 101–5.

197. For theories concerning the dedicatees of the *Sonnets*, see Schoenbaum, *op. cit.*, p. 219.

198. Finemann, *op. cit.*, pp. 268; 290–6.

199. M. de Montaigne, *Essays*, trans. J. M. Cohen (Harmondsworth, 1958), p. 57.

200. D. Quint, 'Introduction', in P. Parker and D. Quint (eds), *Literary Theory / Renaissance Texts* (Baltimore, Md., and London, 1986), p. 3.

201. C. Norris, 'Post-structuralist Shakespeare: Text and ideology', in J. Drakakis (ed.), *Alternative Shakespeares* (London, 1985), p. 50.

202. A. Burgess, *Shakespeare* (Harmondsworth, 1972), p. 17.

203. Chambers, *op. cit.*, Vol. 2, pp. 371–5.

204. Foucault, *op. cit.*, pp. 118–19. Shakespeare's defence of authors' rights is discussed in Schoenbaum, *op. cit.*, pp. 219–20.

205. Foucault, *op. cit.*, pp. 108 and 118.

206. Ariès, *op. cit.*, p. 201.

207. J. Donne, *op. cit.*, pp. 85 and 91. For a scintillating reading, see Docherty, *op. cit.* (1986), pp. 72–7, 106–10.

208. S. Greenblatt, *Shakespearean Negotiations: The circulation of social energy in Renaissance England* (Oxford, 1988), pp. 1–6.

Index

Lyotard, Jean-François, 173

Macfarlane, Alan, 191, 211
Machiavelli, Nicolo, favours
    arbitrary power, 121, 137
Machyn, Henry, chronicler, 36
Manning, Brian, 17, 25
Manning, Roger, 17
Manwood, John, jurist, 64
Marcus, Leah, 16–19
Markham, Griffin, trial of, 119, 151
Marlowe, Christopher, 142
    The Massacre at Paris, 42
Marvell, Andrew, 12, 75
Mary I, jeered by crowd, 25
Mary, Queen of Scots, alleged
    adultery, 172
    disinherited, 223
Mayerne, Theodore de, physician,
    166
Maynard, Lord, parliamentary
    candidate, 100–1
Marston, John, 194
Marx, Eleanor, 11
Marx, Karl, 11–13, 113
Mauss, Katherine, 192
medicine, 158–66, 175–8
The Merry Milkmaids (anonymous),
    62
mercantilism, 135–44
Middleton, John, 194
    Women Beware Women, 198
Midland Rising (1607), 67, 73, 81,
    117
midwives and wise women, 162–83
Milton, John, paid £5 for *Paradise
    Lost*, 12
    ridicules churching, 179
    on Shakespeare, 234
modernism, retrograde influence on
    Shakespeare studies, 4–8, 10,
    25–7, 29–30, 40
Montaigne, Michel de, 235
Montrose, Louis, 9, 64, 164–5, 211
Moore, Giles, squarson, 191
More, Thomas, 169
Moretti, Franco, 12, 125, 135, 137,

140, 152, 206
Mountjoy, Christopher,
    Shakespeare's landlord, 223
Muir, Kenneth, 217–18
Mullaney, Stephen, 41, 50–1
Munday, Anthony, *Earl of
    Huntington*, 71

Nash, Thomas (husband of
    Elizabeth Hall), 229, 231
Nashe, Thomas, *Pierce Penniless*,
    42–3, 47, 50
National Theatre, 22–3
Neale, J. E., 101, 107
New Right, 8
Nietzsche, Friedrich, 13, 167
Norden, John, sabbatarian, 71
Norris, Lord, encloser, 63–6, 80
Norris, Christopher, 17
Northampton, Countess of, patient,
    158
Olivier, Laurence, 23, 43
Orwell, George, 33
Owen, David, 23

Palavicino, Horatio, financier, 197–8
Parsons, William, Stratford burgess,
    110
Paston, Bridget, 191
Paston, John, 189
Patterson, Annabel, 17
Peele, George, *Descensus Astraea*,
    40
Pepys, Samuel, 157
Perkins, William, puritan polemicist,
    95, 114
Perrault, brothers, Charles and
    Claude, *Contes de ma mère
    l'oye*, 173
pharmakon, 50, 160–1, 165, 174
Philip, Prince, 43
Platter, Thomas, Swiss tourist, 45,
    48
poaching, 72–6, 82
Poe, Edgar Allan, 26
Pope, Alexander, 209
Pound, Ezra, 6